boogaloo

boogaloo

The Quintessence
of American Popular Music

ARTHUR KEMPTON

THE UNIVERSITY OF MICHIGAN PRESS

Ann Arbor

To JR (because without you there would be no me)

Published by the University of Michigan Press 2005
Published by arrangement with Pantheon
Books, a division of Random House Inc.
First published by Pantheon Books 2003
Copyright © 2003 by Arthur Kempton
All rights reserved
Published in the United States of America by
The University of Michigan Press
Manufactured in the United States of America
⊗ Printed on acid-free paper

2008   2007   2006   2005   4   3   2   1

Permissions Acknowledgments begin on page 467.

A CIP catalog record for this book is available from the British Library.

Library of Congress Cataloging-in-Publication Data applied for
ISBN 0-472-03087-6

CONTENTS

ACKNOWLEDGMENTS

Since I am my book's only original source, I am indebted to those tillers of unbroken ground whose harvests I plundered: Michael Harris and Daniel Wolff, biographers of Thomas A. Dorsey and Sam Cooke respectively; Anthony Heilbut, author of what remains, more than thirty years after he wrote it, my favorite of all books about music; Peter Guralnick; Rob Bowman, a meticulous documentarian of the life cycle of Stax Records; Nelson George, still the most efficient teller of the Motown tale; and Ronin Ro, chronicler of Death Row.

My unretired debts extend across decades, for the tutelage of the many accidental schoolmasters of my youth, particularly Melvin Best II (alias Timmy Yates), and Robert Wheeler, Jr. (a.k.a. Bebop), who could sing stars out of the sky. I owe my title, and more, to K. Rashid Nuri who, nearly forty year ago, was the first of my acquaintance to refer categorically to what was then called "soul music" as boogaloo.

And my thanks to Erroll McDonald, who saw the way clear, and to Robin Reardon, who made easier the slog.

PREFACE

One Saturday afternoon in June 1965, deep into the Apollo Theater's three o'clock show, a fat man with a wooden stool ambled onstage, shouldering the bolero jacket of a burnt-orange suit. Six piled inches of his greasy curls glistened under the spotlight. So did moisture caught in creases between folds of neck, disclosed by the open high-rolled collar of his satin shirt. As he moved, narrow silk-and-mohair pants rode up the crack of his wide behind. Front rows of unsparing high school girls cackled at the sight.

Piped in from the wings, the disembodied voices of two Manhattans and a Pip had filled the room with a high-fidelity reproduction of his current record's opening refrain. He detached the microphone from its stand and sat on the stool, apparently grateful for being relieved of his bulk. Just before the impromptu harmonizers broke off their last blended note, he cocked back his head with a sideways tilt and bit into "Sitting in the Park"'s first mincing lines. The murk was pierced by female shrieks of recognition.

I'd come upon Billy Stewart before the crowd lately gathered. The punch line from the first record of his I bought had been rapidly absorbed into my interior life, providing the coda for scores of daydreamed revisits to emotional crime scenes. Stewart's proverbial "Itzalikeitzalike thegood book se-e-ezz . . . youlafata reap just whatta you sow . . . I knowIknowIknowIknow . . . whattayou sow . . . nownownow . . . little girl" was the tabernacled scrap of holy writ in a mind ablaze with the profane.

Six months before, I'd lain in darkness listening to Jocko's nightly shift on WADO, transmitted from New York via Dixie cup and string otherwise used to communicate in Spanish. Douglas "Jocko" Henderson, the suave, university-educated son of Baltimore's superintendent of Negro schools, was dean of the "you talk more shit than the radio" academy of black broadcasting and the justifiably self-proclaimed father of modern rap poetics. By his grace such antique coinage as "from the rooter to the tooter it's a bad motor scooter" sounded fresh-minted to newly sixteen-year-old ears.

I felt washed over by a mesmerizing stream: of rhymed patter . . . "My Girl" . . . "the Temptations on the nation's sensation station" . . . "you get a nickel and I'll get a dime"—an old Nitecaps record's muted blare underneath a homespun commercial for Golden Spur, "the wine that won the West" . . . "Shotgun" . . . more syncopated chatter "about this and thatter and things that matter" . . . "A Change Is Gonna Come" . . . a jewelry-store spot with a live tag delivered in rhyming couplets . . . "How Sweet It Is (To Be Loved By You)." Radio fare was sumptuous those days.

By the time Jocko talked over half the climax of "You've Lost That Lovin' Feeling" straight through a furniture-store pitch, I was as dulled and dreamy as a dog getting its full belly rubbed. "Hickory dickory dock"—an ear pricked up at the sound of a master's voice—"here comes the Jock"—who was beating out rhythmic accompaniment on a tabletop—"and I'm back on the scene with the record machine, correct time now, eleven fifteen."

About twenty seconds into the song he next played—new from

Billy Stewart—wonder's sudden grip jerked me upright in my bed. At first encounter "I Do Love You" seemed a glimpse of God's face.

This day at the Apollo, Stewart's turn came again to sing that song, as it would three times more before the job was finished, at about half past midnight on Sunday morning. The languid guitar chords that proclaimed "I Do Love You" kicked up a gale of salutatory high-pitched squalling. Last Valentine's Day this song struck a common chord on young black America's heartstrings, and it had been the lubricant of choice for the boogaloo nation's dance-floor couplings until "Ooh Baby, Baby" came in the spring.

The house band lurched into a tempo expedient to accompanists-in-passing of itinerant balladeers. A pace too quick by half required less precision of hands grown indifferent to distinctions among objects of the same common type. It was also the natural cruising speed of a rhythm singer of slow songs whose freaked-off style synthesized church, King Pleasure, Harry Belafonte, and certain D.C. street corners of the mid-1950s.

Billy Stewart could skate across the top of a ballad taken at this clip, darting in and out of its tight places, skirting hard vocal passages to avoid wear and tear. With the record so fresh in memory, he had only to evoke it for an audience to fill in the blanks in a perfunctory performance. After a brisk run-through three choruses long, the band receded, leaving its rhythm section to softly mark time while the "fat cat who knows where it's at" worked his show.

Stewart mopped his face with a handkerchief he'd brandished in hand with the microphone since midway through "Sitting in the Park." He stepped toward the thicket of upraised arms rustling in the front rows right of center stage, to engage the massed humanity stirring unseen beyond the spotlight's blinding edge. With a sly, shy smile he asked all the young ladies in the house to rise when called upon, place their right hands over their hearts, and join in singing back to him what he sang to them.

Offstage voices then began to croon, "I do love yoooou . . ." in crystalline three-part harmony. Stewart overlaid a perfectly fitted conjoining note that he kept stored in the rafters of his upper register and had to stretch for to reach. Unbidden, an answering chorus of "I do love yooooou . . ." welled in the throats of a ragged female choir.

The band stopped playing altogether, to let the crowd marinate in the sound of its own voice. I looked around to scan rows of girls standing like soldiers under command, hands on hearts, raptly singing their pledged allegiance to this object of their recent scorn. Alternately sweet and shrill, the chorusing grew louder and stronger in each of three successive waves, which broke upon Stewart's interjected "I luvaya love you so right now," dispersed into tumult over an ensuing crescendo of scatbursts, and re-formed as the approving roar at his back that swept him grandly from the stage. Right then I would have forsaken the rest of my life's promised possibilities for mere moments in possession of his gift.

PART I

Sightseers in Beulah:

Original Soul—Thomas A. Dorsey, Sam Cooke, and the Classic Age of Boogaloo

1. Rock in a Weary Land

Two days before his first inauguration Bill Clinton's rounds brought him to Howard University for an appearance at a program celebrating Martin Luther King's birthday. Pictures on the news that night framed the next president's face behind the blue-satined torso of a young woman singing "Take My Hand, Precious Lord." She sang it stiffly, in the old-fashioned Tuskegee Institute Choir style, as though it were not the grittiest of Christian blues but belonged instead to the tradition of composed Negro spirituals that is official America's idea of black religious music mannerly enough to be presentable.

A song of the soil, "Precious Lord" had been run through a wash, rinse, and spin cycle until all the shout was out. Sixty years ago, when he started peddling songs to congregants of Negro churches, its author had forsworn as commercially unpromising the high-toned gloss imparted to their presentation by the conservatory-trained. But when appearances counted, black America was always ready to put on long white gloves in the middle of the morning. Public sacrifice of the private self is one of the endlessly undone chores of a despised tribe.

While Clinton was listening to the gentled echo of Thomas A. Dorsey's cry, the old man was somewhere alive but already lost to the ravages of Alzheimer's disease. If a nursing-home attendant had wheeled him into the dayroom to watch television reports of his dish being set before a king, Dorsey can be imagined failing to recognize in them anything of a former self. Instead, he may have had in mind hoof-beats of wild horses clattering through great halls crowded with starchy church women in "home-laundered" white uniforms fanning away the waves of heat escaping from an unbuttoned choir, or with off-duty laborers made sweaty and shrill by the transporting spectacle of a lady from home in "glittering gown" and breastplate made of golden coins, "bellowing" across the footlights, "If I . . . could fly like Noah's dove, I'd heist my wings and fly," back to where the air tasted of fish scent to "chitlin' stomp" girls cavorting on floors slick with snuff juice and spilled gin, and "belly-rubbing" rent-partyers called out to him, "Play 'em daddy, if it's all night long."[1] Anytime Dorsey could peer through murk of church light or theatrical haze into the crowded room beyond his piano and tell himself "the house is hot," he truly felt alive.[2]

Before he became the "Father of Gospel Music," Thomas A. Dorsey was a "king of the night." There is a photograph of him taken then that has suggested to more than one caption writer the word *unsaved*. He is wearing an oversize knit applejack cap, and the collar of his topcoat is rakishly upturned. His face is half-shadowed but for his large and arresting eyes that seem glazed as if from drink. His lips are parted to admit a cigarette, which he is poised to light with a match held aflame in the elongated fingers of his right hand, as nimbly curled as the forelegs of a mantis. It is the portrait of Georgia Tom, a sloe-eyed "sportsman," redolent of "tired sweat, bootleg booze, Piedmont ciga-rettes and Hoyttes Cologne,"[3] not long before he made the profane respectable in Afro-Christendom's highest churches. The man who said, "[My] ivories speak a language that everyone can understand."[4]

Aframericans are a tribe marked once by bondage and again by the lie of their freedom, which for most of those unleashed meant only con-scription into an indefinite term of volunteer slavery. The American South is their old country now. The salve of a selective remembrance of ancestral hard places in bad times has unscarred the tissue layered over wounds that once seemed too raw to heal. Any visceral memory of the old country's depredations has been outlived by the romance of "all-day preaching, dinner on the ground, green grass far as you could see"—a bygone burnished by the rub of contemporary disenchantments into a version of the official American mythic past, when families were closer and food was tastier, where streets were cleaner and houses, yards, and children better kept. Every summer across the South there are reunions of graduates of defunct black high schools that become occasions of attendees' rueful reflections on how much was lost to children in their communities when desegregation "washed away our schools." At least then the socially conservative traditions of Aframerican life were intact enough to produce people who withstood the worst assaults of outsiders.

Most black Americans still live among elders whose own elders were bred and born "down home," when many places there were as bitter and backward as Mississippi. But none other stood more for the biblical Egypt of the Jews' captivity. In tribal consciousness Mississippi is mythopoetic territory where people drank tears for water and suffered in the heart of a darkness that time has since softened into a pervading twilight in which no place seems as different from any other as it used to. This place that once seemed pernicious to those who fled it has become an object of nostalgia.

It was hard to be black in Mississippi and stay out of the way of the plantation's long shadow, even for the slender subset of postslave generations who were the young males some white people called "masterless men."[5] They sized up workaday black life in Mississippi as a sucker's play and so became outlaws or were otherwise enlisted into the backstreet demimondes of Jackson, or Greenville, or Clarksdale. In the 1890s, when farm economics went bad all over the South, cities and towns began filling up with enough unruly black young to constitute an official new class—America's first—of "bad Negroes."

Thirty years after Emancipation this new breed was noticeable enough to provoke anxiety and reaction in propertied white people and loud loathing in the others, as well as embarrassment and consternation among the settled classes of black folks, ever mindful of needing to tiptoe through hair-trigger times. The "leading" Negro citizens believed that the lives even the lowest of their kind lived were admissible as evidence before the hostile court of opinion they were petitioning to grant them provisional membership in the society of white Americans. They were afraid this "reverse element" created enough stench to fill white nostrils with an odor that would confirm the old race calumny about black people smelling bad. So this earliest iteration of what modern social science calls a black underclass was said to give "the whole race an evil reputation."

Among the most blatant of these unseemlies were the stars in the Delta's dim firmament—the traveling singers who made livings circuit-riding the countryside and playing sawdust-on-the-floor joints in town, and who never hit a lick for any white man. By 1920 or so the best and brightest of these was Charlie Patton. Born around 1890, raised on Dockery's plantation in the northern Delta, Charlie Patton was playing and singing for money as a teenager. It was already evident that he "hated work like God hates sin."[6]

He told neighbors he was too smart to labor hard. His father once had to bullwhip him. His mother said she never could do "nothing with him . . . he was just called to pick that guitar." On it Patton became a refinement of the region's distinctive style. Long after he was gone, history considered the legend of Robert Johnson and still anointed Charlie Patton "King of the Delta Blues."

His niece later described him as a "free man" who "didn't make no crops" and "just left when he got ready." When Patton was grown, he got put off Dockery's plantation for being a bad influence on its working women, keeping too many too regularly up too late. He roved, caroused, got high, fought in bars, went to jail.

He played his guitar between his legs and behind his back and beat it like a drum sometimes. He was like a troubadour in another country's feudal times and, since there were thrice as many black Delta residents as white, in a way the region's most listened-to social commentator. Charlie Patton was the Snoop Dogg of his day and place, and by 1930 he was a certified recording star.

Mississippi did its best to break "bad Negroes" whose conscientious objections to the way of things turned trangressive, by making the price for getting caught at it payable in the currency of the cotton fields—chopping and picking—on the acreage of the state penitentiary at Parchman. Parchman was the last plantation. Its workforce was undisturbed by the mechanical cotton-picker, which had displaced so many who remained on the land after World War II that local powers-that-be were chortling out loud that now they could finish shipping their "Negro problem" north. For those come lately from the fields, the Industrial Revolution would last less than half a generation.

The father of the "Father of Gospel Music," Thomas Madison Dorsey, a freedman's child, grew into one of those "highly trainable young black men" the succoring agencies of church and state hoped to find when they were outstretched to the formerly enslaved after the Civil War. Whether they were earnest bearers of "Christian civilization" or bureaucrats administering the former assets of the ruined South, these instruments of black uplift were mostly white Americans educated to British precedents. They were naturally inclined toward the imperial British model of looking after the populations they conquered and then felt obliged to improve. This meant raising up among the subjugated an educated elite to help acculturate and control others of their kind.

As soon as the war ended, missionaries from several of the big Protestant denominations fanned out across the former slave territories, setting up schools. Church schools proved the handiest method of sorting out the most assimilable Negroes. Thirty years after the war there were more "universities" for Negroes in the South than there were in England and France, though fewer than half taught any college-level courses. In 1894 Thomas Madison Dorsey graduated from one of the schools missionaries made—the Augusta Baptist Institute, which became Morehouse College—and was ordained a "competent, consecrated Christian leader for the uplift of his race."[7]

Many of America's first slaves had been dispersed among the South Atlantic colonies, where they were halfheartedly proselytized by Anglicans. They were generally as unwarmed by this version of religion, which seemed to them to come out of books, as they were unwelcomed by its adherents. But there were unseemlier Christians around on the margins of early American life willing to admit into their fellowship outcasts and even slaves.

Baptists and Methodists had entered the colonies as a trickle of rogue sectarians. In the middle of the eighteenth century they caught the upswells of religious revival known as the Great Awakenings and broke in hard waves over the backs of the high church establishment. Their early appeal was strongest among the ill lettered, the landless, and the scorned. Baptists believed, as West Africans did, in adult rebirth and spirit possession. When the descendants of Africa encountered these others trembling "in the spirit," writhing on the floor, jabbering indicipherably, they saw for the first time manifestations in white people of something they could identify as genuine religious expression. "You must be born again" was an appeal to which they were predisposed to be susceptible, and many came when called.

By 1860 nearly all of this country's 4.5 million black residents were already second-, third-, and fourth-generation Americans.[8] They found their common voice in a language they fashioned from what they heard here and from what they remembered from Africa. They made a faith of their own out of the religion they were taught here and the habits of belief that lingered with them after the memory of their original African places was gone.

Afro-Christianity fused these fragments of West Africa into an American tribe. For a long time their churches were the only institutions black people made and owned for themselves. For these reasons the church was central to Aframerican life. Their churches have been like force fields in which social and cultural currents pulsated and surged, crackling when they crossed.

After his ordination in 1894, Thomas Madison Dorsey confounded the expectations of his sponsors—the American Baptist Home Mission Society—by forgoing a settled pastorate. He became instead an itinerant preacher. His travels brought him thirty miles west of Atlanta to a hamlet called Villa Rica, a whistle-stop along the Southern Railroad

line that ran through to Birmingham. There he met and married Etta
Plant Spencer, the widow of a railroad worker who had shown her
something of the world. Etta was so much a striver after what promises
her era disclosed to children of freed slaves that she stretched far
enough out of the deep country poverty into which she was born to
acquire some land, some education, and an organ.

Organs were inordinately prized in those days among the black and
country bred. Booker T. Washington wrote reprovingly of a household
he visited in backwoods Tennessee that was adorned by an organ while
four of its members shared a single fork. A farm-laboring family of
twelve in turn-of-the-century Georgia was found by researchers from
Atlanta University to have dedicated seventy-five of its annually earned
$819 to purchasing an organ.

Her properties and his profession certified the Dorseys as what
passed for elite Negroes in Carroll County, Georgia. But in a society
whose overlords believed that educating a Negro just ruined a good
field hand, these were not enough to spare the head of the house from
needing to sharecrop, pastor two churches, and teach school the three
months a year black children could go, to keep his growing family
afloat. A hard year shy of the new century Thomas A. Dorsey—their
eldest son—was born.

His early childhood left behind in the junior Thomas a habit of
associating music and ministry with status and approbation. But he also
learned that his mother's refinement and his father's education put
together couldn't support their family. The Dorseys became casualties
of the agrarian depression that had settled over the South late in the
nineteenth century.

In 1908 they moved off their land into Atlanta, where Thomas M.
Dorsey tended white people's grounds and gardens and never preached
again. He ceased to belong to the huge majority of black Georgians
who labored on the land and became part of the third of them who
worked at serving white people in their homes and businesses. His son's
young life came unmoored in the city. When he entered school there, he
was put back into the first grade. He was acutely conscious of being on
the wrong end of color-struck, stratified Atlanta Negro society and felt

"looked upon as . . . common . . . dark-skinned, poor, shabbily-dressed and homely."[9]

From the direct account he left of his first forty or so years—pieced together by a biographer from interviews, an unpublished auto-biography, speeches, and other scatterings—Dorsey's everyday world seemed nearly uninhabited by white people. He was conscious of them as he would be of weather or Wall Street or world wars: he knew white people only by their effects. His family had arrived only two years after thousands of the city's white citizens burned and looted much of black Atlanta in four days and nights of vicious marauding that left twenty-five Negroes dead and a couple hundred badly hurt.

The mob had wreaked its cruelties pointedly upon the homes and businesses of successful black Atlantans. This rampage was intended to intimidate and demoralize the social betters of penurious outlanders like Thomas Dorsey. It did both, but the city's black strivers were resilient. Many soon returned who fled Atlanta's mobs howling tearily in pain and fury at having fulfilled their side of the bargain they thought they'd made with white people, only to have been wantonly violated by them anyway.

They were charier than ever of white society but undeterred in their commitment to make themselves acceptable to its better classes. The elite of black Atlanta regrouped around their inviolate sense of who they were when hostile Others weren't around. By the time the Dorseys came to town, they had resumed upholding the standards of their community, which partly meant exercising their license to "run those browns down."

An unstinting influx of young black men from the countryside and its disturbing effect on the protocols of transracial engagement were seen as particularly inciting of the mobsters' savagery. Their conspicuous increase attracted the unhealthy notice of white people, who complained of their "impudence" and made the "Decatur Street dives" where they congregated notorious as nests of criminality and vice.

The boy Dorsey was drawn to the liveliness of Atlanta's black downtown and started hanging around music and vaudeville houses on Decatur Street. He got a job in a theater selling soft drinks and candy.

When he finished fourth grade, he was thirteen years old. He left school and made the theaters his classrooms. He studied the piano players and set about learning to play. He taught himself to read and write music from books. He had extraordinary facility, the kind of ear and memory that enabled him to hear something once, then reproduce it exactly.

Dorsey was dedicated to the piano with the fierce focus of a teenage boy who discovers how to overcome his social infirmities and make himself attractive to girls he figured would always be beyond his reach. It was no empty boast for Thomas A. Dorsey later to say that he made himself an accomplished musician when he was fourteen.

In those days piano players were functional equivalents of juke-boxes or record players. They were hired for all types of social gatherings and were commercial necessities for bars, dance halls, trick houses, and rent parties. Dorsey played wherever he could and before long found favor around town, as much for his quiet touch as for his precocious idiomatic command of blues songs and popular standards.

When he was fifteen, he began to think of himself as a working musician, albeit one whose services could be had for pocket change, "all the food [he] could eat, all the liquor [he] could drink, and a good-looking woman to fan [him]."[10] But his ideals of professionalism were embodied in the theater musicians he admired. It seemed what separated them from him and others he considered peers was their ability to read music. Dorsey took a few uncomfortable lessons from a lady at Morehouse but learned sight-reading and notation from self-study books. He already considered himself a star in the dim little firmament of Atlanta's rent-party piano players and felt he had exhausted all local possibilities.

In 1916 Dorsey got a job at a Philadelphia shipyard by answering one of the advertisements posted in those days on billboards above street corners in Atlanta, enticing thousands to leave the South in this earliest of several cycles of black migration. He set out for Philadelphia by way of Chicago, where his uncle lived and which was then bustling with upsouth traffic. Before the waves of migrants came, about sixty thousand black people lived in Chicago.

The year Dorsey went to look around, thirty thousand others came to stay. Within ten years the black population more than doubled and its living space stayed the same size. The already-there were aghast at these hordes of just-arrived, who "didn't know how to act" and "spoiled things."

In 1919—the year Dorsey settled permanently in Chicago—the animus of some of its white residents toward the Negroes piling up in their midst exploded into another of those massacres that got called a race riot: 38 were killed, 537 injured, and more than 1,000 left homeless. Dorsey was unfazed; Chicago was where he could "move up higher," and once he landed there, he never left it willingly for long.

It was the city of steadiest importance in the development of black popular music for much of this century's first sixty years: even then it was New York's only rival as a center for the "commercial exploitation and mass diffusion of music." Near the turn of the century it had been a nursery for the black vaudeville business and in the next decade a capital of the ragtime trade. After that Chicago was where new music from New Orleans called "jass" passed through on its way to all over.

Many of the musicians thrown out of work when New Orleans shut down its tenderloin district in 1916 made their way to Chicago. By then it was crowded with émigrés from southern and midwestern cradles of prophetic musical styles. Scott Joplin, King Oliver, Louis Armstrong, Jelly Roll Morton, and W. C. Handy had all sojourned there.

The industrial bulk-up for World War I, and the concomitant freeze on European immigration, meant there were jobs in northern cities even for Americans usually served last when there was anything on the menu but a hard way to go. Between 1916 and 1919 half a million black southerners headed north. Once they began arriving in trainloads, old settlers shuddered.

Even by 1914 an editorialist in the *Chicago Defender* suggested that "n[egro]" was a term "rightfully" applied to "the handkerchief heads that are coming to this city from many of the southwestern states." Another member of Chicago's Negro press, writing in 1920, just a year after the city's nasty race riot, decried the degradation of community life by unacculturated migrants who hung out of tenement windows or sat "half naked" on littered stoops hollering to passersby across the street and chattered disturbingly in movie theaters. He complained of soiled dandies in loud clothing who sprawled across the seats of street-cars and accosted even white women.[11]

Behavior on streetcars was a touchy subject to the black middle class, as these were the principal venues in northern cities for race mixing at close quarters and so frequently made respectable Negroes vulnerable to racial embarrassment. The strictures of residential segregation meant middle-class blacks were cut off from higher ground as a downpour of the just-arrived inundated their quarters with people they considered the least of their least. Nearly a million more followed in the 1920s. The worst job in Chicago then paid four times as much as every-day black people made in Clarksdale.

Dorsey played gutbucket piano, a style considered homely in Chicago. It would have required equal parts of arrogance and naïveté for a half-schooled kid like him to think he could find a place there as a working musician. But at eighteen he already valued his identity as a piano player too much to give it up because he wasn't altogether sure it could produce a regular income.

He was insulated when he came from Atlanta by an inflated sense of who he had become there. He still bore the flush of self-esteem natural in someone who had felt himself scorned when he was young and then had succeeded well enough in plain view of the once-disdainful that he could leave his hometown entitled to think all his accounts there were settled.

In Dorsey's memories of his early trials, there often seems about him the aspect of a young man wellborn who, though forced to make his way mistaken for one of the "common class," always knew he was meant for better and in the end would have it. As it happened, a job he took in a steel mill to avoid the draft in 1917 was the last he ever had outside of music.

Dorsey chipped away at every performance opportunity until he made a niche in Chicago's after-hours "buffet flats." These rooms were redolent of migrants' "tired sweat, bootleg booze, Piedmont cigarettes and Hoyettes cologne," where "lights were so low you couldn't recognize a person ten feet away and the smoke was so thick you could put a handful of it in your pocket."[12] As in Atlanta, the relative subtleties of his style had the practical advantage of not annoying the neighbors enough to provoke them into calling the police. He became known around these establishments as the "whispering piano player."

His small successes reinforced his confidence. He recognized that his ability to elaborate on "popular numbers and drag them out" could be the basis of a commercial style. He wasn't interested in jazz because it "took too much energy to play, you couldn't last an evening."[13] But the way he construed the blues was merchandise he could sell.

Dorsey was a student of his game even before it had rules. He discovered that many more musicians in Chicago could read music than write it. The best-paying jobs were in structured settings like bands and theaters, where players needed written parts, and he saw opportunities for someone who could prepare and arrange their music. That was "where the money was." In 1920 he enrolled at the Chicago School of Composition and Arranging, right on time for the start of a business in recording black performers making music intended for black consumers.

The mounting influence of jazz and blues on American popular music after the war upraised a constellation of black songwriting stars in New York who wrote hit songs and successful shows. Many formed publishing companies so they might profit exclusively from authorship of their work.

Since the late nineteenth century commerce in popular song had been controlled by music publishers. The most substantial of these were arrayed along a two-block stretch of Twenty-eighth Street in New York City popularly known as Tin Pan Alley. Their business was built on the sale of sheet music for home entertainment. Around 1900 it was enlarged by the demands of the nascent recording industry.

Publishing houses were tunesmitheries employing assembly lines of composers and lyricists accustomed to expropriating anything they found useful in the black music they heard. The vitality of black vaudeville assured them of having a regular supply to refurbish and resell. By the middle of the first decade of the new century vaudeville began supplanting minstrel shows as entertainment for the Negro masses. It evolved by adapting the traditions of minstrelsy to the more sophisticated environment of cities.

This made the dominant strain of black popular music more con-genial than ever to mainstream white tastes. Thus it became a source for Tin Pan Alley of a choicer grade of swag. After the publishers' mill-workers blanched out of these songs any native flavors they thought too pungent for the palates they had to please, the "upgraded" material was given to white performers to set before prospective record-buyers.

Even at that, in 1901 the American Federation of Musicians wanted ragtime banned—along with all other manifestations of the "negro school"—on grounds that it degraded public taste and morality. These men wanted their customers protected from a class of products they were unable to make; in the music business, like most others, the Negro was never considered so pernicious as when he was a threat to white employment.

In those days only Bert Williams, the black star of white vaudeville, and a couple of groups of "colored" singers of sacred songs had recording careers at all, and they were sold by Victor as novelty items. For more than twenty years after it began, Columbia Records didn't record any black performers at all. Nevertheless both major labels com-peted to keep their market "up-to-date" with "comic songs in Negro dialect."[14]

In 1909 Congress enacted the first copyright law, which meant that record companies were required to pay royalties to writers and publish-ers of songs. Within five years a trade organization called the American Society of Composers, Authors and Publishers was formed to adminis-ter this windfall. ASCAP monitored the commercial performances of its client members' songs, collected royalty fees, and disbursed them among composers, lyricists, and publishers according to the entitlements they held. ASCAP was established to serve and protect the industrial elite headquartered in New York, and few outsiders belonged.

In 1920—when ASCAP fattened the publishers' end of royalty splits and widened the field of payers for play to encompass movies and radio—only ten blacks were members. The record companies contin-ued to exclude them altogether, preferring not to break their custom of selling knockoffs of Negro-made originals. The two biggest records of 1917 were Sophie Tucker's version of Handy's "St. Louis Blues" and the first release of the Original Dixieland Jazz Band, five white boys from New Orleans who played in the black style. Each sold more than a million copies.

Perry Bradford was the first of his contemporary class of black show-business entrepreneurs to talk a label into recording a black singer backed by black musicians performing something akin to black music. He was growing up in Atlanta when Dorsey arrived there and, like Handy, was a translator of the musical vernacular of southern black people into popular songs white Americans would buy.

Bradford was persuaded that "fourteen [sic] million Negroes will buy records if recorded by one of their own."[15] He was rebuffed by both Columbia and Victor, but in 1920 he convinced a smaller label to let him make "Crazy Blues" with Mamie Smith. Within a month of its release on Okeh Records 75,000 copies were sold.

This alerted the white men making up their new business as they went along to the rightness of Bradford's premise that Negroes had something in their pockets worth reaching in to take, the first of their recurrent discoveries that black Americans are manic consumers of their own popular culture. This newly disclosed market was like found money to the flagging record business. Inside of a year more than a dozen small companies were started, including four upstart black-owned labels: one in Los Angeles, one in Kansas City, and two in Chicago—one belonging to W. C. Handy and a partner, the other to J. Mayo "Ink" Williams.

Mamie Smith was a vaudeville singer; and her accompanists were New York musicians too sophisticated to be easy with the commanding chords and propulsive rhythms of genuine blues. Bradford had to scour Harlem's least fashionable nightspots to assemble Mamie Smith's Jazz Hounds. All the same, far as it was from the authentic style of everyday black Americans, "Crazy Blues" was a huge success among them and confirmed the hunger they had to participate in a cultural commerce of their own.

According to Bradford, who composed the song and oversaw its recording, "Crazy Blues" was at least blues enough to afford Mamie Smith a setting in which "[she] could for a releasing moment rejoin the part of ourselves we have sacrificed for civilization." It sold more than 200,000 copies and made its composer $53,000.[16]

Suddenly Dorsey saw blues singers "sweeping the country," and songwriters "popping up like popcorn." In 1920 he copyrighted his first song, "If You Don't Believe I'm Leaving, You Can Count the Days I'm Gone." Then for a while he was gone, back to Atlanta in nervous exhaustion, leaning and depending on his mother's care, convalescing from too much Chicago.

Thomas Dorsey's development was episodically stimulated by fertile crises, of which this case of "nervous exhaustion" was his first. Some months later, having recovered, he returned to Chicago. When the National Baptist Convention of 1921 came to town, his uncle the druggist invited Dorsey to stop by on its last day. The convention was a trade show lively with commerce and entertainment. It was as though the sales force of a company with a 60 percent share of its market had gathered to socialize, talk business, and size up new product lines.

There, sitting in the back of a large auditorium, Thomas A. Dorsey was unexpectedly borne to Jesus by Reverend A. W. Nix, a singing evangelist who was performing a song called "I Do, Don't You" to promote a new hymnal black Baptists were offering for sale. Nix was using the rhythm-bending, melody-slurring, and hard song–selling that Dorsey knew as tools of his secular trade to make congregants who were trained to decorum in their churches jump and shout. The force of a revelation struck him like a falling tree: "My heart was [then] inspired to become a great singer and worker in the Kingdom of the Lord—and impress people just as this great singer did that Sunday morning."[17]

Within a year he had written and registered several religious songs and become director of music at a small migrant Baptist church. But his new vocation couldn't withstand the alternative prospect of a steady income of forty dollars a week; the first time God tugged at Dorsey, his landlord pulled him back hard. After it beheld the revelation of Mamie Smith, the record industry's blush was enough to send most of

Chicago's best musicians scampering to New York. Dorsey was still around and looking for work. He was hired into a band called the Whispering Syncopators. Dorsey specialized in playing soft dance music—whispering syncopation—and the band was popular around Chicago. But right before they left on a road trip to California, its other members threw him over for a better-known piano player.

Three labels—Okeh, Columbia, and Paramount—emerged into early prominence as merchandisers of black music. But even as this new market opened wide, the advent of commercial radio was badly hurting record companies of all sizes. Nearly all the fledglings succumbed to the intractable problems they had trying to promote and distribute their records. All the black start-up labels folded within a year or two. Columbia filed for bankruptcy in 1923; sales that had produced a $7 million annual profit fell off so quickly that two years later the company faced a $4.5 million loss. Victor's revenues were halved between 1921 and 1925.[18]

These straitened times made especially critical the fresh money that Negroes were bringing to market. Okeh found and worked its viable niche by the maneuverings of Ralph Peer, who was in charge of the company's profitable line of "race" recordings. "Race" quickly became the commercial appellation used for music made by and intended for Negroes.

It was a coinage attributed to Peer, though he likely lifted the term from the pages of the *Chicago Defender* and—hoping for an advantage with the customers he aimed for—applied it to advertising his inventory; he sought to appropriate its prideful and progressive connotation for his employer's brand. By 1923 Okeh had issued forty records by black performers: six jazz instrumentals, eleven of sermons and sacred songs, and twenty-three designated as blues.

Then Columbia released Bessie Smith's first record. The industry had considered her too country to sell. She was shopped around and passed over by several labels; finally Frank Walker, Columbia's deputy for the colored, agreed to use her. The result was a shocking demonstration of the raw appeal of southern music to black consumers; "Downhearted Blues" sold three-quarters of a million copies—about a fifth of all the "race" records bought that year—at a time when selling more than five thousand of any record made it profitable.[19]

Walker shrewdly organized a southern tour to spike sales where Smith's appeal was strongest. Ralph Peer snapped to attention and led a field expedition into Atlanta to find and record talent thereabouts. But for six months after "Downhearted Blues" came out, Bessie Smith was all a market hungry for southern blues could buy to satisfy its appetite, and Columbia had the only supply. The "Empress of the Blues" had saved an empire.

She had been brought to Walker by Clarence Williams, who'd been hired to find and furnish black singers for Columbia to record. Williams was from New Orleans by way of Chicago. He was an owner of record stores there and publishing companies in two other cities. He was once a performer who had become a successful songwriter. Lately he'd started using what he knew from years of dealing with record companies to manage acts who were getting their first chances.

The deal he brokered for Smith at Columbia paid her $125 for each of the eleven songs she recorded plus a percentage of royalties. These went to Williams, and he took half her fees as well. Once Smith realized how much of her profits Williams kept for himself, she negotiated her next contract directly with Walker. By dealing Williams out, she got to keep all of her recording fees.

But in return for a thousand-dollar yearly guarantee, Smith traded every other advantage her fast-rising stardom should have afforded. She agreed to sell her piecework at the same price and allowed Columbia to avoid paying her any more royalties. By 1925 Bessie Smith had made Columbia prosperous enough to buy valuable new patents and the next year to absorb Okeh Records, a major competitor. Bessie Smith made a million dollars for Columbia Records in ten years. For this she was paid $28,575.[20]

Walker's deal with Smith enabled him to divide the copyrights of her songs between Columbia and one or another of his own publishing companies. Peer had the same hookup at Okeh, using his publishing arm to get into his own hands as much as he could take of the cash value in other people's songs. He never recorded anyone who didn't write his own material and worked out an approach to paying them that became the industry's standard: all rights to their original material were assigned to the label in exchange for a recording fee of twenty-five dollars a side and a royalty rate that paid a dime to the artist for every thousand copies a record sold.

Peer moved on to Victor and by 1928 would control more than a third of all the nonclassical music recorded there. He received 75 percent of the royalties they generated—$250,000 in a single quarter of 1927. Peer's profits from publishing grew large enough to be unseemly in a record label's employee; to keep from arousing Victor's retaliatory ire, he turned over to them one of the companies—Southern Music— he'd built on proceeds from race and hillbilly music.

Their employers were going to steal the copyrights anyway, so Walker and Peer merely found a way of extracting a sort of finder's fee. But if Bessie Smith and other new tricks in the trade weren't yet mindful enough of copyright laws to keep from getting pimped by those who were, an obscure piano player and aspiring songwriter in Chicago knew better.

In 1923 Thomas A. Dorsey copyrighted seven songs of an assortment that suggested he was setting out his traps across as wide a range of commercial possibilities as he could see. These included a sentimental ballad in the contemporary popular style, several composed "blues," and others with titles like "Don't Shimmee No More." Three of them were recorded—one, "Riverside Blues," by the famous King Oliver—and another was sold to a major publishing house. Dorsey had his first bona fide—albeit modest—success at writing songs and improved his standing among habitués of the House of Jazz. This record shop had belonged to Clarence Williams before he moved to New York and was still a hangout, hiring hall, and rehearsal space for Chicago's black musicians and "showfolks." One such was "Ink" Williams, by then a finder of blues singers for Paramount and slickest of all the black show-business hustlers in Chicago, which by now had superseded New York as a manufacturer of race records. Since so much of the market for black music was in the South, record labels were leaning heavily on releases of country blues and sermons that outsold even Bessie Smith.

Dorsey was smart to interpret the boom in southern singing as the doom of old-school "composed" blues. Gutbucket was now in high style, and Dorsey's particular abilities were suited to fashion's latest demands. The southerners being recorded didn't sing much that was written down; the publishing business was unused to documenting casual creation. But rules of commerce are generally made flexible to accommodate the unconventional as long as established interests are served.

Procedures were revised so that ownership of songs never sung the same way twice could more readily be assigned to people other than their creators. Property rights could now be secured in shorthand, by registering "lead sheets." These were transcriptions of song fragments, usually no more than a melody line and a verse or two of lyrics.

Dorsey's fluency in the gutbucket vernacular and facility for formal notation suited him to the vital function of translating what these singers could speak but not write into language recognizable to accompanying musicians. While accomplishing this feat, he also recast their songs into a form suitable for copyrighting. He switched from being a composer to being an arranger. To prosper, arrangers needed regular access to singers who were preparing to make records. Dorsey assured his through an association with "Ink" Williams.

Williams was said to have gotten his nickname in recognition of his talent for signing talent. He had figured out how to shortstop some of the money that flowed from makers of music in a steady stream toward the men who ran record companies. His singers came packaged with ready-made repertoires comprised of songs owned by his Chicago Music Publishing Company. Over the years he profited in this way from such of his best-selling "discoveries" as Ida Cox and the country bluesmen Blind Lemon Jefferson and Blind Blake.

Dorsey's job was to write the arrangements, copyright the music, and train the performers: "A guy'd come in with a song and he'd sing it. He had nobody to arrange it, put it on paper. So I put it on paper. . . . I would take them, feel the words out and then feel the music out and accent them in a way that it will grasp the public."[21] Unsettled by the general slackening of their sales, record companies scrambled to find Bessie Smiths of their own. By 1924 Paramount had opened its branch office in Chicago and hired Williams, who delivered the services of Gertrude "Ma" Rainey. Rainey recorded ninety-three songs for Paramount in the 1920s—a third of which she was credited with writing— and never received royalties. "Ink" Williams owned the publishing rights to every one of them.[22]

Rainey was the original show-business blues singer, originator of elements of style and manner that came to be called classic in those who followed. She came young out of Columbus, Georgia, when the century had newly turned, a teenager singing and dancing in minstrel shows with her husband. She began featuring blues songs in her act in 1905, and they became her trademark. Ten years later the Raineys were known across the black belts as "Assinators of the Blues."

By 1917 she was on her own and blossoming in black vaudeville houses along a circuit run by the Theater Owners Booking Association (TOBA), a cartel that fixed the wages of show-business labor in every decent-paying workplace available to black entertainers in the South. As a teenager in Atlanta, Dorsey saw her perform at the Eighty-One Theater when Bessie Smith was a kid—fresh from Tennessee and scuffling—who sang there whenever she could for ten dollars a week.

TOBA became known as the "chitlin' circuit" and eventually expanded into the Midwest and cities along the eastern seaboard. By the mid-1920s it was a confederation of fifty theaters employing hundreds of black entertainers who most weeks drew roughly thirty thousand ticket-buyers. Few of these franchises were ever in black hands, though the syndicate was codirected by Charles Turpin (a Negro theater owner in St. Louis) during its primest of times. Ma Rainey was one of TOBA's biggest attractions when she signed with Paramount, but she'd never made a record and after twenty years on the road hadn't worked anywhere north of Baltimore.

Not long after Paramount began releasing her records, Rainey was short a piano player. "Ink" Williams recommended Dorsey. She hired him as her accompanist and to organize and direct her Wild Cats Jazz Band. Dorsey describes opening with Rainey at the Grand Theater in the Chicago spring of 1924 as one of the highlights of his life:

> The room is filled with a haze of smoke, she walks into the spot-light, face decorated with Stein's Reddish Make-Up Powder. She's not a young symmetrical stream-lined type, her face seems to have discarded no less than fifty-some years. [Rainey was thirty-eight.] She stands out high in front with a glorious bust squeezed tightly in the middle . . . She opens her mouth and starts singing: "It's storming on the ocean, it's storming on the sea, My man left me this morning, and it's storming down on me."[23]

Dorsey was drawn to the intoxications of performance like other men are to romance or whiskey. His enthrallment with transporting moments onstage—and child-hearted wonder at their creation—infuses his tender evocation of the showtime of Ma Rainey with awe:

> When she started singing, the gold in her teeth would sparkle. . . . She possessed her listeners; they swayed, they rocked, they moaned. A woman swooned who had lost her man. Men groaned who had given their week's pay to some woman who couldn't be found at the appointed time. By this time she was just about at the end of her song. . . . The bass drum rolled like thunder and the stage lights flickered like forked lightning: "I see the lightning flashing, I see the waves a dashing, I got to spread the news . . . I got the stormy sea blues."[24]

If Rainey showed Dorsey that a theater could be like a church, she taught him too that show was the business on any stage:

> The curtain rose slowly and these soft lights played on the band. . . . Ma was hidden in a big box-like affair built like a Vic-

trola. . . . A girl came out and put a big record on it. The band picked up "Moonshine Blues"; Ma sang a few bars inside the big Victrola, then she opened the door and stepped out into the spotlight with her glittering gown weighing twenty pounds, wearing a necklace of five and ten dollar gold pieces. The house went wild. . . . Ma had the audience in the palm of her hand. Her diamonds flashed like sparks of fire falling from her fingers.[25]

Dorsey wrote, arranged, directed, and played all Rainey's music. Stage-named Georgia Tom, he made himself an embellishment to her act. Dorsey claimed he was first to arise from a piano stool in calculated abandon, kick it to the side, and play standing up"—quite a novelty back then."[26] It would seem as novel to kids thirty years later when, by getting up and pounding away, Jerry Lee Lewis solved the kinetics problem presented to someone stuck behind a piano who had to meet an early rock-and-roll star's showmanly obligation to make young girls wiggle and squeal.

Given Dorsey's appreciation of the art and science of stopping a show, he might have felt as rewarded by Lewis's unacknowledged indebtedness to him as he was enriched by Elvis Presley's use of one of his songs. He never sounded so proud as when he boasted of his stage-craft.

Dorsey stayed with Rainey two years. "She was one of the loveliest people I ever worked for or . . . would know," he later wrote. While in her employ, his life was never more regular. He traveled, made some money, and met and married a young woman from home named Nettie Harper who lived at his uncle's house. Ma Rainey's career never came out the other side of the Depression. She went back to Georgia, where she died in 1939 at the age of fifty-four.

Dorsey's interlude of relative prosperity was ended in 1926 by a wasting illness that nearly killed him and eluded diagnosis for most of two years. He was too debilitated to work. His depression slid through despondency into despair. But then one Sunday morning in his sister-in-law's church, the minister spoke to him directly.

He admonished Dorsey to have more faith and told him he would not die with his apportioned work undone. Then, according to Dorsey, "a live serpent" was pulled from his throat. He was so moved by the sudden and complete remittal of his suffering he had another epiphany—a reconversion—and vowed to "consecrate [himself] fully to God."[27]

Dorsey "took on new faith" that he would "attract the attention of the world and grow strong." In the aftermath of this drama, he was prompted by the death of a friend to write "If You See My Savior," his first "gospel blues": "I was standing by the bedside of a neighbor, who was just about to cross the swelling tide."

"I began to write songs," he recalled. "Not the blues and double meaning songs that we played for the Saturday night parties, but songs of hope and faith. . . . This was the turning point of my life."[28] But Dorsey's turnings often twisted; his bent toward spiritual commitment never went unresisted by a nature solicitous of worldly acclaim or by the want of enough money. He printed up a thousand copies each of two of his titles and peddled them door-to-door.

When he could, he demonstrated them to ministers and choir directors. "I got thrown out of some of the best churches in them days," Dorsey used to say, long after it should have ceased to matter, hinting at the depth of old resentments: "If they'd been good ministerial men they would have helped me."[29] He spent all the money he had and borrowed some more to send promotional copies to a thousand far-flung churches listed in a directory compiled by the National Baptist Convention. For nearly two years he didn't get an "answer, order or reply of any kind."

Not much of his experience in the music trade was helpful in selling these songs. Copyrighting them may have assured him of the prerogatives of ownership, but it didn't address the problem of getting somebody to pay him for their use. Church songs were mostly sung by congregations or in live performances by evangelists and choirs. So sheet music was still the way to reach most consumers. But in the business he knew, sheet music was a sales medium of waning importance. Songs circulated widest—and made the most money—when they were promoted and sold as records.

2. Got to Know How to Work Your Show

In 1926 the record industry's revenues peaked at $128 million—the near equivalent of $1.5 billion in today's dollars—a figure unsurpassed until after World War II.[1] A couple of years later five hundred race records were released; a fifth of even late-coming Victor's output was meant for black consumption. While white Americans were buying less of what was increasingly available on radio, blacks spent feverishly for what they couldn't otherwise hear. By then the three major companies alone were selling about six million records a year to Aframericans.

During one year of the 1920s, eleven million black Americans accounted for sales of ten million records. At the time a phonograph record cost seventy-five cents, and the average family income among black southerners was three hundred dollars a year. Since church music was entertainment without frivolity, it made the extravagance of purchasing phonographs and records justifiable for grassroots Aframericans who wanted so badly to be entertained but as observant Afro-Christians, would have felt constrained from enjoying anything disreputable. Religious material was a big part of the diet that nourished the black music business through its early years.

The first records by black quartets singing spirituals in the prevailing jubilee style came out in 1921. Quartet singing was a socially approved pastime for young black men in southern communities in the first decade of the twentieth century. It moved into cities when they did.

Beginning in the 1930s the music of Dorsey and other modernists would constitute a new repertoire for gospel quartets to sing. The conventions of quartet singing were thereby opened up to inventions of form and style that were the basis of much of the best of what would come when church and state later merged in the popular music of black America.

Three years after they recorded on Okeh as the Norfolk Jazz Singers, the Norfolk Jubilee Quartet—singing different words the same way—was Paramount's most popular male group in 1924. The Birmingham Jubilee Singers sold thirteen thousand copies of their second record on Columbia in 1926, and the following year seventy quartet records were made. Around 1926 the music of itinerant evangelists began showing up on records.

These singers were of the broad community of country-sanctified churches. Most who recorded were like Blind Joe Taggart and Blind Willie Johnson, singers and guitar players in the style of contemporary country bluesmen. But there was also the pianist Arizona Dranes, who traveled under flag of the Church of God in Christ. Her way of playing turned ragtime into boogie-woogie. And in 1927 a dulceola player from Memphis named Washington Phillips used as ingredients in a song he called "Denomination Blues" the gentle mockery that versifying "saints" of the Holiness Church made of the vain strivings of the upwardly mobile: "You can go to college, you can go to school, but if you haven't got religion youse an educated fool." Eleven years later Sister Rosetta Tharpe, whose stardom was the apotheosis of this tradition, recorded the song with Lucky Millinder's big band.

Preaching records were first brought to market in 1925. These were three-minute sermonettes punctuated by singing. Most recorded sermons had the structure of songs; the preaching served as verses, the intervals of singing were like choruses. They were usually flavored by the calls and responses of small bands of congregants who were in the studio as accompanists. The simulated congregations made these records sound like "good church."

Seven hundred and five recorded sermons were released between 1925 and 1928, most after one by Reverend J. C. Burnett sold eighty thousand copies in 1926—four times as many as a typical Bessie Smith record—for a little black-owned label out of Los Angeles. Between the fall of that year and late spring of the next, sixty sermon records were made, forty by the most celebrated of the genre preachers, the Reverend J. M. Gates of Atlanta.

Gates set a precedent in 1926 by making his sermons lively with singing and shouting. His first record sold thirty-five thousand copies within six months of being released. Gates somehow avoided being bound over to his "discoverers" from Columbia, and his subsequent output fell like a steady rain over at least six labels. On the recorded evidence his voice was not impressive nor his tongue agile, but Gates was nevertheless so much in demand that once in three weeks' time he was called upon to make forty-two sermons for sale.

When 1926 ended, he and Burnett were among six preachers making records; the next year there were thirty. If Gates is the best remembered of these and all who followed, the most memorable was that original instrument of Dorsey's spiritual awakening, Reverend A. W. Nix. A record of his—"The Black Diamond Express to Hell"—was the most famous sermon of the decade.

In general, it wouldn't be fair to say that black music rescued the record business in the 1920s because the Depression would kill most of it off anyway until after the war. But the race market certainly saved Columbia Records, which then grew rapidly into the world's biggest merchandiser of sound and air. It also proved it could make rich whoever controlled sources of the products it wanted to buy. But though Dorsey was in the right place—and skilled in the right ways at the right time—to capitalize, he had the wrong disposition. He chose Ma Rainey over "Ink" Williams.

At twenty-seven Dorsey would find irresistible the belated fulfillment of the dreamy teenage longing he'd had in Atlanta to be on stage at the Eighty-One Theater. He needed most the gratifications serially induced by short-acting doses of intense public acclaim, and so chose show over business. Like us all, he was prone to a residual attachment to the idea of some romance he should have outgrown. Dorsey set aside his pursuit of property, just as the valuation of songs like those he was likely to copyright was leavening in the overheated market for race recordings.

Four years later and in the throes of another of his lurches toward rectitude, Dorsey was reminded that while property could remove some taint of his chronic disreputability, propriety was conferred only by certifying social institutions. So for Dorsey, desperate again for money after two years' sick leave, a franchise in church music had obvious appeal. But though the trade in records aimed at Afro-Christians was thriving, most who made them used arrangements of traditional songs beyond the reach of copyright laws. No function had yet evolved in their production process comparable to the one Dorsey served when he worked for "Ink" Williams.

Although publishers of black religious songs had once been the biggest part of their business in Chicago, by 1928 none were still around. With that option foreclosed and most recording of black church music being done elsewhere, no buyer of Dorsey's songs in Chicago could have gotten them recorded, even if he had been discouraged enough to sell them off too cheaply. It would be three years yet before the Blue Jay Quartet of Alabama made the first recording of one of his songs.

If nothing else, his unrewarded efforts at direct sales of sheet music were reaffirming his presumption that songs sold best when customers bought them under the influence of a performance. What was put to paper didn't express much of how different Dorsey's sounded from other contemporary religious music; his work had to be heard to make its truest appeal.

He decided from then on to use live performers to present his inventory: he would bring singers with him into churches to give recitals of his songs and afterward sell sheet music to the audiences they entertained. The first he hired was a young woman sweet-voiced and conservatory-trained, to help slip him past the watchful acculturators in

Chicago's established black churches who guarded temple gates against the coarseness outside trying to push its way in. But however socially acceptable, her cultured voice singing in the approved style couldn't sell his songs.

By 1928 he was broke and going nowhere, so he took a job as staff arranger at Brunswick Records, one of six companies that mattered in the black music business. Soon after, Dorsey recalled, a friend named Hudson Whitaker "came to my home":

> He had some words written down and wanted me to write the music and arrange a melody to his words. . . . I looked it over carefully and told him I do not do that kind of music anymore. I was now giving all of [my] time to gospel songs. . . . I looked around at our poor furnishings and our limited wearing apparel. "Come on, once more won't matter," he said quietly with a smile.[2]

Whitaker was a born Georgian raised in Florida who had come to Chicago in the mid-1920s. As Tampa Red and Georgia Tom, he and Dorsey recorded the song for Vocalion Records the next day. "It's Tight Like That" was a phenomenon from its inception. It was released within days of being recorded; the public "went wild" and made it the era's best-known party song.

Before any record sold in the race market even had benefit of airplay on radio to draw the attention of its intended audience, "It's Tight Like That" was an event in the popular culture of black Americans. Its fashion was so protracted that Whitaker and Dorsey reprised the song in four more versions. It was still so much in the air in 1930 that hitmaker A. W. Nix put out a sermon record that year called "It Was Tight Like That." His partner's talent for double entendre gave Dorsey the unexpected gift of a recording career.

Of course, before their collaboration Whitaker had worked only sporadically in neighborhood joints and sung on streets for spare change. As a result of it, he became one of Chicago's earliest blues stars. He arrived in town as a slide guitar player trained on his native ground to a lighter touch than transplanted Mississippians brought from theirs. Once Tampa Red got Chicago's attention, the city came to know him as the "Guitar Wizard."

Dorsey and Whitaker's pairing of piano and guitar was innovative, and the ribaldry of their songs seemed in step with the unbuttoning times. It amounted to the invention of a fresh commercial style that was trademarked "hokum." The "hokum sound" was light, quick, and danceable. As much as the Illinois Central Railroad did, it took the country to the city, and for a couple of years it was nearly as popular as preaching records.

Lester Melrose—Vocalion's white man in charge of black recording—made it into a sort of brand and kept Dorsey and Whitaker producing until the market for it fell off. Their success exalted Melrose, who soon became the most important publisher, producer, and profiteer in the business of blues recording. He claimed to have been responsible for 90 percent of the black-oriented popular music that came out under the various imprints of RCA Victor and Columbia between 1934 and 1951.

Melrose was a prewar prototype of the postwar white merchandiser of black popular music. He refined the "Ink" Williams approach of bundling talent with songs he owned and selling the package to record companies. Melrose was a kind of general contractor. He hired the talent, recorded them himself, and sold the labels finished goods; he bought the song and the singer, and he paid the band.

Melrose was criticized for making records that sounded too much alike. It has been called the "Bluebird beat," after the RCA Victor specialty label that profited from so many of them. Melrose was thirty years ahead of his time, anticipating the production shops of the late 1950s and 1960s, known for making records that shared characteristics that made them identifiable as coming from the same manufacturer. What he conceived in Chicago during the 1930s and 1940s spawned the Chess brothers and their like. Tampa Red and Georgia Tom—the Famous Hokum Boys—was the original franchise Melrose parlayed into his chain of many others.

Dorsey's knowledge of the game paid off: his first royalty check came promptly, in the amount of $2,400. But inasmuch as Georgia

Tom made about sixty more records over the next several years and never again got as near to prosperity, Melrose had much the better part of his commercial arrangements with Dorsey and Whitaker. The nature of their business was that anyone called "talent" always had to pay too dearly for every chance he was given to be exploited.

Though his attitudes about race were said to be liberal—he drank whiskey from the same bottle as the musicians he took advantage of— Melrose was intolerant of performers' claims against any money he made from the resale of their intellectual property. In 1955, four years into Melrose's retirement, a former subcontractor he'd often employed named Arthur "Big Boy" Crudup wrote him from Mississippi, upon hearing Elvis Presley's version of one of his songs on the radio, inquiring after royalties he thought he might have coming. He got back a letter from Melrose promising to look into it. Over the years Crudup's old songs were persistently remade by stars of rock music, but until a court intervened in 1971, all the royalties accruing from his having written and published them were paid to Melrose or his heirs.[3]

Dorsey wouldn't have expected any different treatment. If their positions were reversed, he would probably have done as Melrose had. He knew the real value in songs derived not from recording them or even writing them but from owning their copyrights. The rules of commerce were made to favor—and respectability adhered to—legal holders of property.

Dorsey recognized that overseers of the music business thought of performers as panderers would think of their whores. So he never regarded being a Famous Hokum Boy as a path of social advancement. It ceased being a source of much economic benefit soon after the stock market crashed.

Dorsey lost all the money he made from "It's Tight Like That" when the bank he kept it in "went broke and closed." His wife understood this as a clear message that he could no longer trifle with promises made to God. "That is right, dear," he says he replied, "and I shall from this day dedicate my life to gospel songs only." But for several more years few of the records he made seemed intended for religious audiences, since most had titles like "Pat That Bread," "It's All Wore Out," and "Somebody's Been Using That Thing." He says he was fearful all the while of imperiling his soul, but in his music the sacred and profane were mingling indiscriminately.

In 1932 Dorsey sandwiched two popular recordings in February and April around one in March he made with Whitaker of "If You See My Savior." For a time he might give up writing one or the other, but never repudiate either. Whitaker recalled that when they last went to New York to fabricate more hokum, once the recording was done Dorsey spent the rest of his time there calling on ministers and choir directors with a briefcase full of sheet music.[4] He was always prepared to work both sides of his straddle; Dorsey's convictions were strongest in those days about getting paid.

Nineteen thirty was a pretty good year for Dorsey, but the Depression would ruin the record business. In the aftermath of such an unforeseen financial disaster as befell late in 1929, any enterprise that lived by exerting a claim on the spending money of everyday Americans was in trouble from having already produced much more than it could any longer sell. Record sales fell by 60 percent in a single year and declined another 40 percent during the one that followed. Many millions of broke Americans forsook buying phonograph records for listening to the radio. Within only a couple of years the industry shrank to a quarter the size it had been in the summer of 1930, when the National Baptist Convention was held again in Chicago.

A young woman there from St. Louis sang "If You See My Savior" and upset the whole house. People were "in the aisles . . . jumping, singing and humming." Dorsey hadn't known until a friend came to him breathless with the news that fifteen thousand delegates were "singing and humming" his tune. Since "the gig at that time was to grab what you could while you could, for if it went away you never saw it anymore," he hurried down to the convention hall, where he was ushered onto the floor in triumph. He was invited to set up a stall and sold four thousand copies of his sheet music to the assembled Baptists, "and I been in the music business ever since."[5]

There Dorsey also met Theodore Frye, a singing preacher from Mississippi in whom he saw an image of A. W. Nix, still his model of how he wanted his songs presented. Frye had a developed sense of church as theater and an identifying stage technique—"strutting"— that Dorsey refined into a polished act:

> We teamed and traveled through the South, East, and Midwest making the national meetings and winning the acclaim of every audience. . . . They got to the place if Frye didn't walk, they'd holler . . . "Walk, Frye, walk!" Then Frye'd start struttin'. He would walk and sing: I would stand up at the piano and pound the beat out. . . . Frye could get over anywhere with anything.[6]

But Dorsey still hadn't breached Chicago, the Vatican City of Afro-Christendom. That he would accomplish guerrilla style, by training "gospel choruses" made up of immigrants from the South too unsophisticated to sing the European masterworks typically undertaken by choirs in Chicago's established black churches. The largest of these was Olivet, the mother church of Chicago's black Baptistry.

Its congregation originated in 1853, and what had splintered off it since 1882 built nine other churches. By 1928, when Dorsey started trying to peddle his religious songs, Olivet claimed fifteen thousand members and called itself "the largest Protestant church in the world." Ever since 1816, when free men in Philadelphia who had been treated shabbily by white congregations renounced old affiliations and started the African Methodist Episcopal Church, the Afro-Christian establishment had taken as its sacred cause civilizing their benighted own.

By the middle of the nineteenth century Daniel Payne—an AME bishop—was railing against the backwardness of the "folk" church, ensnarer of the ignorant in religious practices that were barriers to their social progress. He disparaged the singing of "cornfield ditties" that provoked emotion in the "thoughtless" and was disgusted by such unexpurgated Africanisms as "bush meetings" and ring shouts.

The remedy prescribed by "progressive" Negroes like Payne required purging black churches of indigenous music, and the associated vulgarities of congregational singing, hand-clapping, foot-patting, and—worst of all—shouting. To the acculturators who held sway in institutional Afro-Christendom throughout its first century, music was a cultural ministry. This was the conviction of churchmen in Chicago who brought into their worship services the choral study groups they had sponsored to "create a desire for better music among [the city's] Negroes."

These choirs were often directed by gifted and otherwise unemployable conservatory-trained musicians of the breed that took the shout out of slave songs when they "composed" them into spirituals. In the early 1920s choirs of all the big churches were giving monthly concerts of European music on Sunday afternoons; the first opera performed by Aframericans in Chicago was sung in 1921 at Bethel AME Church.

Dorsey was awed by these spectacles of refinement, though he didn't care too much for the music. He ardently admired the men who produced them, and whenever one shook his hand, he was as gratified as he was when the local bandleader Erskine Tate greeted him by name at the Original House of Jazz. The city's black ministers were struck by the correlation between the sizes of their congregations and the reputations of their choirs. They started competing for the best choir directors, who were then sought after by the impresarios in their small world as if they were directors of Broadway shows.

One of these, J. C. Mundy, was four times enticed away from an employer by a richer rival offer. In 1918 Olivet Baptist went to Massachusetts for Edward Boatner, a protégé of the famous black concertizer Roland Hayes with fancy Boston credentials. Eight years later the new pastor of Pilgrim Baptist lured him over from Olivet with a doubled salary and a twenty-seven-piece orchestra to play behind his choir. The Reverend J. C. Austin was bent on suppressing any sparks from the embers of fires that had burned in the old country. "We are intelligent folks here," he admonished his congregants, "and we don't do a lot of hollering and carrying on."[7]

During the First World War the city's black population grew by nearly half. Beginning in 1920, Chicago's black churches were made crowded by the just-arrived. Most came as Baptists or Methodists, and they gravitated first toward the old-line churches. Between 1916 and 1921 membership at Olivet Baptist increased by eleven thousand, mostly people whom the old settlers felt they needed to improve.

The migrants usually came hopeful, preferring to believe that in their new place social acceptance was a promise social acceptability would guarantee, and so were attracted to the culture of optimism they found in the churches strivers had made. Newcomers would expect their sheltering institutions to help them learn how to become worthier of the society of their betters. The bigger churches served as settlement houses; by 1920 Olivet maintained a staff of sixteen to run a labor bureau, a kindergarten, a nursery, and a welfare department. Pilgrim Baptist got together with other churches to bankroll a fund to help "reliable" immigrants buy houses.

But many expatriated southerners couldn't help being taken aback by the old settlers' mania for appropriating white people's ways, and found the tone of proceedings inside their churches less than congenial. Worshippers were restricted to singing out of their standard-issue Baptist hymnals in "prayer" and "testimonial" services conducted by deacons before the minister's Sunday showcase. Then they went to a service at which any who comported themselves too demonstrably would be reproved. In the afternoon they came back and stood in line to hear music they neither enjoyed nor understood.

By the early 1930s the incoming tide of relocated southerners had turned men in the business of saving black souls in Chicago toward thinking about how best to accommodate these new customers without alienating the better class of their clientele. The shrewdest found it prudent to allow enough of what they could never completely suppress, to appease the many in their congregations who longed to hear at least an echo of the hoofbeats of wild horses they remembered from former places. J. C. Austin described this approach:

> To satisfy middle-class members, an astute pastor of a mixed-type church will present a "prepared message" with moral and ethical exhortations and intelligent allusions to current affairs;

but he will also allow his lower-class members to shout a little. Such shouting is usually rigidly controlled, however, so that it does not dominate the service.[8]

Gospel choruses were a larger concession to preponderating "lower class" southerners in the congregations of Chicago's black churches. The city's first was organized by Dorsey at the behest of a minister just come from Alabama to take over a small Baptist church. He wanted to enliven the dispirited congregation he had inherited and was dismayed at how unhelpful its choir was in producing the desired effect.

Under Dorsey's direction the gospel chorus at Ebenezer Baptist was novel and crowd-pleasing and was soon sought after for performances at other churches. Invited to Austin's, the choristers so stirred his crowd that after they were finished, he reassumed his pulpit, complimented what he'd heard, and pointed at Dorsey, who had presided over them and Professor Frye's antic routine with practiced theatrical flourish. "Tell me this," he asked rhetorically, ". . . where did you get that little black man?" The next day Austin engaged Dorsey to put together a gospel chorus at Pilgrim Baptist.[9]

Edward Boatner—who had long made evident in its senior choir the refinements of the conservatory and the ideals of the "progressive" church establishment—resigned in protest. He said he never knew what a gospel chorus was but understood what was happening as soon as he heard Dorsey playing the piano: "it was nothing but jazz." The sanctuary was being polluted by "that alley junk." Indeed, the piano player Dorsey engaged to accompany his singers at Pilgrim was a dance-hall musician who played the same way on Sunday morning as she did on Saturday night: "Other than the words of the music, there was no difference, none at all."[10]

If Boatner's attitude suggested Dorsey had an uphill climb to social acceptability of the sort he wanted so badly, Austin's was the commercial endorsement that started him on his way. By 1932 Dorsey and his partner Frye had trained a succession of gospel choruses popular enough to force even the most resistant black high church ecclesiastics in Chicago to make a practical business decision: they either had to "get together one of them things [Dorsey] had" or lag behind in the com-petition for souls.

Even at that choruses still were relegated to performing in the off-hours, well away from the Sunday service. But while it hadn't occurred to Dorsey when he was writing his songs that they might be sung by choirs, he knew he'd stumbled onto a way of selling them to the masses.

He would apply some of what he learned in a laboratory of upsouth cultural dynamics—Chicago's black recording and entertain-ment businesses—to selling his sheet music in urban churches: "I get up there and hold the whole church in the hollow of my hand. If some-body don't shout, I'll give you ten dollars. . . . Got to know how to work on the people."[11] Dorsey saw people worked on from stages and from pulpits and saw no distinction. Dorsey understood church as theater and employed the same techniques in both. "Everything's a show," he said, "but you got to know how to work your show."

Just as his affairs were brightening again, Dorsey met the darkest crisis of his life. His wife didn't survive her delivery of an apparently robust baby boy. He'd been in St. Louis when he got the call about Nettie. Dorsey's mind clung to the image of their newborn as a symbol of regenerated hope through the torment of his first night of bereave-ment. When he got home that morning, he was told his son, too, had died.

This time bitterness fortified Dorsey against the despondency that had broken him down twice in earlier episodes of soul shaking distress. But it took an act of creation as unexpected as his misfortune to pierce his gloom. He had gone to ground with his grief for a week before the evening Frye persuaded him out of the house. They walked without particular purpose to a school in the neighborhood.

There was a piano in one of the open rooms, and Dorsey began "browsing over the keyboard," "fumbling" with an "old tune":

I called Mr. Frye. I said, "Come on Frye. Listen to this . . . I got
this tune and I'm trying to put words with it . . ." I played [it] for

[Frye.] . . . He said, "No man, no. Call Him 'precious Lord.' Don't call him 'blessed Lord'; call him 'precious Lord.'" And that . . . hit me . . . I said . . . "That's it!" . . . And that hooked right in there. The words dropped like water . . . from the crevice of a rock.[12]

Precious is a tender form of address meant for an intimate. It affirms its object as a being who comes with love rather than authority. Dorsey had struck a chord perfectly pitched to the sensibilities of Afro-Christians, whose tradition encourages in its adherents a personal relationship with Jesus and a collective identification with Old Testament Jews. Jesus is the maker of domestic miracles, the personal intervenor, healer of the sick, a "mother to the motherless," the lonely woman's "company keeper"; but the state of tribal affairs is allegorized in the story of Job, and its affairs of state in the bondage of the Israelites and their deliverance out of Egypt.

Before "Precious Lord" most songs of the black church were stories from scripture, or about salvation when they were joyful, or holding out till tribulation's end when they meant to be consoling. Dorsey's table-setter was Reverend Charles Tindley of Philadelphia, who early in the twentieth century wrote the classic hymns of the modern black church by addressing them particularly to Afro-Christians in verse descended from the King James Bible: "When the storms of life are raging, stand by me / . . . When the world is tossing me / Like a ship out on the sea, / Thou who rulest wind and water, stand by me."

Tindley implored at a proper distance; Dorsey pleaded with a familiar: "Precious Lord, take my hand / Lead me on, let me stand / I am tired, I am weak, I am worn. . . . Hear my cry, hear my call / Hold my hand lest I fall / Take my hand, precious Lord, lead me home." Dorsey's great accomplishment was to make "precious Lord, take my hand" feel the same as "baby, please don't go." This equation purely expressed his idea of gospel blues.

When Dorsey and Frye introduced "Take My Hand, Precious Lord" in church the next week, "the folk went wild. They went wild. They broke up the church."[13] Dorsey's account of its creation is an anecdote that could serve as well any songwriter ever asked how he wrote his biggest hit. This for him "Precious Lord" surely became, although its pandemic appeal was beyond anything Dorsey could yet imagine. "It's Tight Like That" had flared hot and quickly; "Precious Lord" was a ballad, which generally have to smolder awhile before they catch fire. But once they do, their glow seems fadeless, so ballad hits are songwriters' answered prayers.

In 1935 Dorsey's was the song most often heard at the National Baptist Convention in New York. It was sung by soloists from three states and a choir from Chicago. This was remarkable for having happened without a record; "Precious Lord" wasn't recorded until 1937, the year the National Baptist Convention installed Dorsey as director of the mass gospel choir established at its annual meeting in Los Angeles.

Barely five years removed from "Grandpa Joe got Grandma told, said her jelly was a little too old," Dorsey had an identity certified as respectable. His song would become the most famous modern anthem in the black church—the one that calls folks home—and so ingrained in the South that on his deathbed Frank Clement, a former governor of Tennessee, asked that it be played at his funeral. "Precious Lord" became Dorsey's "White Christmas." It paid him off for life, like an annuity, as though to compensate for the pain of its conception.

Much of the momentum for Dorsey's music now gathered without direct impetus from him. He had begun working with choral groups as a means of securing his foothold in churches, but of the several things he'd ever considered himself or wanted to be, a choirmaster wasn't one of them. Nevertheless, Dorsey tells us, "gospel choirs . . . began to spread like wildfire and in twelve months almost every church throughout the country had . . . or wanted one."

Choruses were "invading . . . every Baptist, Sanctified, and Church of God in Christ" congregation in "entire Negro districts of Chicago."[14] Some of Dorsey's associates were making their ends meet by training choral groups. They founded a local association to promote their work, grandly proclaimed it a National Convention of Gospel Choirs and Choruses, and elected Dorsey its president, an honor he received with indifference and a function he at first ignored. Having acquired much of his inventory of craft working in a branch of show business whose biggest stars were individual performers, Dorsey remained predisposed to using soloists to present his music.

He was inclined to mold their performance styles after the show-business blues singers, of whom Ma Rainey was his image. Black vaudeville was his conservatory as much as Boston and the Longley School of Music had been Edward Boatner's. No less than Boatner, Dorsey felt that music in black churches was improved by its every brush with a hand as mastering as his was of the exactitudes of a higher craft: "I got a lot of my gospel training out of show business . . . Made it help gospel where the gospel didn't have much to help itself."[15]

At the triumphal first meeting of the National Convention of Gospel Choirs and Choruses, he delivered the inaugural remarks, presided, and led the six hundred voices of the combined choruses of Chicago through a program rendered in "true choral style." J. Wesley Jones—the dean of Chicago's old-school choir directors—was there and made a benediction of his "profuse . . . congratulations." Dorsey was pleased to hear himself characterized by colleagues as "the Race's greatest gospel songwriter" and to see the label "eminent" next to his name in the *Chicago Defender.*

Two strands of practice had emerged in the performance of Dorsey's sacred repertoire: one in choral settings, the other applied by soloists. They started to converge in 1928 when he walked into a music class at a church and happened upon a woman there giving a dramatic reading. A "holy roller," she'd come to this Baptist church because she'd heard a song of Dorsey's called "How About You" and wanted to buy a copy. A country-bred Georgian, she'd made her way through Atlanta to Chicago after a stopover in Cleveland with a rounder husband she soon discarded and a young son. Improbably, four years later she would be instrumental in making Thomas A. Dorsey a going concern. Sallie Martin was another of the unsought opportunities on which his career seemed to turn.

Her spirit filled in the Fire Baptized Holiness Church, Martin was determined to become an evangelist. She had equal parts of iron and grit in her voice and character, some musicality, and a fiercely convincing stage presence that served her well enough in performance for forty years to overcome her undependability at carrying a tune. "Sallie Martin can't sing a lick," Dorsey once said, "but she can get over anywhere."[16] When he first heard her, he told her—she thought, condescendingly—"I think you have a wonderful opportunity if you can get with somebody who can transpose for you." Not that Dorsey, scarcely impressed with her raspy "low contralto," was interested.

As a singer, Martin conformed to few of the specifications of Dorsey's prototype, and he ignored her for a year while she languished in the back rows of his choir at Ebenezer Baptist. But she lay in watchful waiting and finally pounced on him in Danville, Illinois, where she wheedled him into trying her out on a solo. He featured her as his vocalist for the next eight years, and together they made his way. Martin was an evangelist looking for a conveyance; he meant his songs to be like sermons and thought of them as evangelical. Dorsey's work mostly eschewed the allegorical for the personal—she was altogether a "testimony" singer.

Sallie Martin was also gifted at managing and organizing; she turned Dorsey's songs into a publishing enterprise. Dorsey had sound instincts for marketing but little aptitude and less appetite for doing business. He was selling sheet music out of his uncle's house, using a bureau drawer as cash register and file cabinet. Martin appraised his operation and remarked with characteristic bluntness, "[Y]ou've got something here but you don't know what to do with it."[17] Dorsey was borne up by strong women all his life and was used to paying their carrying charges, though his friends were rankled by her imperiousness. But whatever the terms of their bargain, it was a fair exchange.

When they parted in 1939, she left him with "a five-room studio with a private office, reception room, shipping department and five people on the payroll."[18] She then followed him into music publishing, making a partner of Kenneth Morris, a younger writer of church songs in Chicago. She did better in business without Dorsey than he did without her; Martin ended up prosperous from publishing and a woman of much property.

Sallie Martin was crusty and commanding enough to field-marshal a gospel blues movement. From Chicago she set out to colonize new territories, sometimes on her own, mostly with Dorsey. They traveled together, giving shows, training singers, and selling sheet music. Within five years of starting out they had flourishing outposts in St. Louis, New York, Washington, Baltimore, Pittsburgh, Philadelphia, and other cities in twenty-four states. Overcoming the resistance of local church establishments sometimes required the missionary's obdurate zeal that was Sallie Martin's battle-ax. After she started singing and organizing in Cincinnati, a group of ministers sent for her to meet with them. She airily refused to be run off or shaken down; Martin told them "she was doing Kingdom work and got her authority from God."[19]

In 1936 she took her group out to Los Angeles, where they worked with Aimee Semple McPherson. Martin admired McPherson, not just for being the prime female attraction in the soul saving business and a woman in charge, but because at her revivals church was integrated. Other Dorsey acolytes like Willie Mae Ford of St. Louis—as great as Bessie Smith, they said—helped Martin make his Convention of Gospel Choirs a training institute for consumers of his songs. Thanks to them, gospel blues became the black church's mainstream music. Meanwhile, Dorsey had come upon the singer who would be its brightest star.

Dorsey spotted Mahalia Jackson in Chicago when she was seventeen, just arrived from New Orleans and working storefronts and small migrant churches. She was singing with what she has claimed was "the first organized gospel group to circulate the city." The Johnson Singers, Dorsey recalled, "were really rocking them everywhere they went. Mahalia was . . . killing them off, I mean she was laying them out."[20] When she got in the spirit, she hiked up her skirts and did the "holy dance" she had learned as a child from the Holiness church next to her Baptist household. Mahalia's "snake-hipping" exuberance caused enough scandal and excess shouting among "high society Negroes" in Chicago's better churches to get her thrown out of nearly as many as Dorsey had. In those days Jackson sang like an unbroken colt running loose over pasture, and to the come-lately she seemed "a fresh breeze from . . . down home."[21]

Dorsey recognized early indications of other attributes that distinguish a star entertainer from a great performer: "She was a good mixer . . . and . . . at least she acted like she loved everybody. She called everybody 'baby, honey, darling.' . . . [She] made a wonderful [impression]."[22]

According to Dorsey, she asked him to teach her his songs and become her coach. Dorsey saw what she had, but a decade in town had changed him from a backward newcomer into an old settler disdainful of backward newcomers. He thought of her first as "one of those coon-shoutin' singers." Still, Dorsey schooled Jackson in all that Ma Rainey had taught him, just as he had Paramount's blues singers, working on technique, repertoire, and stagecraft:

She had [talent] naturally. But you have a lot of things naturally [and] don't know how to use it. [I wanted her] to get them trills and the turns and the moans and expressions. . . . I wanted to train her how to do my numbers . . . with the beat—shake at the right time; shout at the right time.[23]

Dorsey says he "took two months out to train her." He "taught her a number of slow, gentle, sentimental songs so her full program would not all be of the fast, shouting types." He tried to get her "to breathe correctly . . . to use her voice with ease . . . to smooth the roughness out of her singing."[24] But "she wouldn't listen. She said I was trying to make a stereotyped singer out of her . . . [and] she may have been right."[25] Dorsey couldn't all the way shape Mahalia Jackson any more than he could unbend Sallie Martin.

Dorsey found for Mahalia the same employment he had for Martin and Theodore Frye, and she made it the platform from which her career was launched. For five years she was featured in "Evenings With Dorsey," the vehicle he used for more than a decade to extract from members of his widening public the price of an admission paid in pennies and dimes and to sell his sheet music for five cents a copy. Dorothy Love Coates, a gospel star of the next generation, recalled seeing them in Alabama: "Mr. Dorsey would just keep handing Mahalia these ballads and she would stand there reading the words while she sang. She'd do fifteen, twenty songs a night like that."[26] Though her job was demonstrating the products in Dorsey's showroom as if she were a juke-box into which he dropped coins, such an appearance of unprepared-ness would chafe Dorsey, who insisted that his choirs never perform while holding sheets of music, since "it looks so much better if we mem-orize."

Mahalia was never less than respectful in her public references to the man even Sallie Martin called "Mr. Dorsey." She would later explain him to television audiences as "our Irving Berlin." But all the accounts of Dorsey's long labors at buffing her surfaces are his. Mahalia never credited his influence, or any other, on the development of her style. Natural gifts as prodigious as hers can seem to their pos-sessors less requiring of cultivation than upkeep; like Sallie Martin's view of her ministry, Mahalia thought the authority her voice carried came from God. She rather gloried in her defiance of strictures that acquiring too formal a sense of tempo, breath control, or text would have imposed.

She paid attention to technique only after she had become middle-aged and ailing, as the basketball player Julius Erving would at the stage of his athletic life when he reined in his gift of improvisatory flight to save aching knees and preserve a lucrative career. Mahalia likely absorbed all she wanted of Dorsey's instruction and threw away her consciousness of where she got it along with everything else she wasn't going to use.

Dorsey may have disagreed with Jackson about a professional's obligations to her craft, but not about her entitlement to an artist's exemption from most of the rules he vainly invoked. She so moved him that he arose spontaneously after a performance of hers in 1939 to pro-claim Mahalia Jackson "Empress of Gospel Singers." The honorific he chose suggested her presence had grown large enough to fill space emp-tied by the departed giantess Bessie Smith.

Once Dorsey started Mahalia off, she set her trajectory and flew it for herself. During the 1930s she became a fixture in black Chicago's church circles and civic life. She sang at rallies and meetings for South

Side politicians, notably William Dawson, a machine Democrat who ran the city's black wards, and won with her help in 1942 the congressional seat he kept nearly thirty years. The mantle of propriety that the National Baptist Convention wrapped around Dorsey covered her, too; in 1937 she gained official standing as a "national evangelist."

This endorsement was a marketing coup, since it put her on the organization's short list of freelance faith-propagators whose services it commended to those who ministered to millions of black Baptists. But Mahalia never considered Dorsey her teacher nor herself his devotee; they were business associates, and when a better deal was available somewhere else, she made it. When she recorded four songs for Decca that year, none of them were his. She wouldn't record again for nine years.

In 1938, though, Rosetta Tharpe made one of the decade's biggest gospel hits of Dorsey's "Hide me in thy bosom till the storm of life is over, Rock me in the cradle of thy love." Dorsey was less characteristically a hit-maker than a writer of songs that circulated long and widely enough to become part of standard hymnals.

He couldn't help but think of churches as just another theatrical workplace, where he catered for a particular clientele the menu they'd chosen from his varied bill of fare. Though his artistic nature was imbued with the aesthetics of gutbucket, his professional disposition inclined more toward working in the optimistic vein of traditional American popular song. Before he semiretired into eminent personhood in the small world big enough to suit him, Dorsey was by long habit a workaday tunesmith whose living was made by finding the emotional triggers to his public's response. He was as ready to pluck on heartstrings as "prick" hearts. For either job he came handily equipped with a sentimentality as versatile as Irving Berlin's or Harold Arlen's.

Church was still black America's most important social instution, no less to the hundreds of thousands who had chased an idea of doing better into northern cities. The migrations made crucibles of urban churches, where just-arrived rubbed against already-there until sparks flew. These people ignited Dorsey's movement, which in spreading overcame the dampening effects of the die-hard acculturators who were the arbiters of approved church culture.

Ironically, by subverting the cultural ministry of the Afro-Christian establishment in the 1930s and 1940s, Dorsey helped preserve the relevance of its institutions in the emotional lives of the congregants it thought should learn to repress their inbred proclivities for emotional excess. Dorsey's unbidden mediation in the 1930s was a reason the mainline black churches still had ample reserves of influence left when they were needed later in waging high-stakes battles over integrating American society. This campaign was the historical mission to which generations of its leadership had pledged their allegiance.

Once they permitted urban settlers to hear inflections of an old tongue in their new lands, established black churches could serve well enough in socializing another quarter-century of migrants. But a church of the rejected also prospered in the cities, where so many who came were often disappointed. Once they concluded that moving had changed nothing much in their lives but place, they fortified themselves against despair in churches whose natures were as unreconstituted as their own. Since slavery settings like these had sustained survivals of the "folk" religion that had been strong enough to sustain slaves.

Outcaste churches grew many and large but never became established. In 1928 one academic surveyor characterized 60 percent of the 278 black churches in Chicago as preserves of "rural religious practices" located in storefronts, rooms, or people's houses.[27] These were the spiritual franchises of the unassimilable.

Some were disreputable enough to have been called "cults." They served no purpose useful to formal institutions; their influence was cultural. In them music was an exalted form of religious expression, and the only form of sanctioned entertainment. Churches like these deplored standard hymnals; only the spontaneous was considered authentic:

Some people get happy, they run
Others speak in an unknown tongue

Some cry out in a spiritual trance
When I get happy, I do the holy dance

They were gospel blues's purest context. They provided gospel music with its permanent audience.

The established and outcaste churches of black America had Dorsey in common. With a comfortable place now secured in their circumscribed world, Dorsey never again ventured away. He stopped touring in 1944 and nestled into the thick of black Chicago's polite company.

He stayed above the fraying temperaments and bitten backs that marked affairs of court in the church-music matriarchy that dominated the capital city of gospel's golden age. He bestrode his expanding Convention of Gospel Choirs and Choruses, Inc., from its national headquarters on Oakwood Avenue. "Professor" Dorsey made speeches and received the overwrought courtesies accorded meritocrats in the black church world, while others carried out the organization's work. This made for him a perch in the warm shade on which to prosper quietly and grow venerable.

Though the era's faith-propagators sowed and reaped on one side of the color line or the other, the undiscriminating currents of their business carried Dorsey's music far afield, and he became a favorite of white southerners. His side of this affinity began in boyhood one "colored night" at a Billy Sunday revival. Dorsey was impressed by the preacher's showmanship—the loosened collar to stir the crowd, the jacket shed to make it boil.

White evangelists had been among Dorsey's first customers, and by 1939 his tunes were being packaged and sold by Stamps-Baxter, the leading publisher of white church music and hillbilly songs. Once Red Foley and Elvis Presley had each sold a million copies of "Peace in the Valley," Dorsey was invited to join the whites-only National Gospel Singers Convention. After "Precious Lord" this was Dorsey's biggest hit, owing to its popularity in the country-and-western market. He kept writing in the style of the sentimental ballads that had been staples of his youth; in the late 1940s Guy Lombardo popularized one called "It's My Desire."

Dorsey and his disciples had already mapped and paved the "gospel highway" for Mahalia Jackson and truckloads of other itinerant "church wreckers," men and women capable every day of moving people to unconsciousness, sometimes even to death. Their stopping-off places were churches, high school auditoriums, Masonic halls, and civic arenas where the stars of this road show—less often the divas who occasionally got famous than the male singing groups who never did—worked the crowds they drew for the price of a ticket to get to the next stop.

Like their audiences, gospel singers were mostly the working poor. Those of the highest rank could aspire only to owning a house and changing cars every year, unless they were one of a handful that entertained white people in nightclubs and concert halls. Nevertheless, in its heyday, traffic was thick on the gospel highway, and rowdier than was seemly.

By that time Dorsey had so outdistanced his former disreputability that he was scolding others who lived by professions of the sacred for their overindulgence in the profane: "I can't go to church, shout all day Sunday, go out and get drunk and raise hell on a Monday, I've got to live the life I sing about in my song." In the whole of his life Dorsey would never disavow Georgia Tom. But once tenured as Professor in the college of respectable Negroes, his station no longer permitted him the companionship of Ma Rainey's piano player or Tampa Red's partner, except as subjects of colorful reminiscences.

After the war Mahalia Jackson began recording again, on Apollo Records, one of the many independent labels of the period sprung up to cater music to the urbanizing Negro public. The outgrowth of a record shop in Harlem, Apollo was run by Bess Berman—the notoriously difficult wife of one of its principals—with whom Mahalia sharply contested royalty statements throughout the eight years of their stormy association. Berman knew her business well enough to have contracted with Roberta Martin, a presence in commercial black church music at least as large as Mahalia's, and with Dinah Washington—who started out as Sallie Martin's piano player—while Washington was "Queen of the Blues."

In 1947, when there were roughly 3.5 million black American households and her records were for sale only where white people rarely went, Mahalia's recording of "Move On Up a Little Higher" sold a million copies. She was then on the verge of being noticed by people who mistook for a discovery something they had overlooked.

By the time Studs Terkel introduced her to white audiences on radio in Chicago in the late 1940s, Mahalia Jackson had already turned a profit at gospel singing, the stoop labor of American show business. She had acquired along the way an unbending resolve in matters of money. She demanded every dollar due in cash before each of her performances, and she stayed faithful to the lessons of scarcity's classrooms by using her brassiere as a bank vault and her pocketbook as a checking account.[28]

Even after she was managed by the William Morris Agency, Jackson never was reconciled to being paid indirectly by means of a check from which 10 percent had been extracted. Such an arrangement violated instincts sharpened by a lifetime of becoming property of herself. Her implacable enterprise lifted her out of penury in the early 1930s, when she parlayed her first mother-in-law's hair and skin care preparations into a string of beauty parlors around Chicago; it was stirring still in the relative abundance of her later life, when she became a partner in a fried-chicken business bearing her name.

Though they would acknowledge Mahalia as queen, many of her old road partners were jealous of her ascension. They thought she did too little for them with the attention white people gave her. For her part, Mahalia resented being resented by "jealous-hearted singers" just because she knew so well, as Dorsey put it, how to "work her show." "I just tell them I got out here on my own," she said. Her Carnegie Hall breakthrough in 1951 was self-promoted—"I worked my ass off"—and certified a triumph by Whitney Balliett, the jazz critic of *The New Yorker.* This served as her letter of introduction to other arbiters of approved culture.

Shortly afterward, when Columbia Records began to press its courtship of Jackson, John Hammond advised her that Columbia might make her rich but would surely break her heart. Hammond was an honorable man in a sleazy business who nevertheless made his living delivering products of black culture to white markets. He had carried enough performers like Mahalia in the back of his truck to know what awaited at the end of the ride.

Hammond could well anticipate that taking Columbia's money would compel a steady blanching of her art to make it palatable to a general audience. Of course, he was right; the company put her with Percy Faith's orchestra, gave her spirituals and pop "inspirationals" to sing, set her against Mormonesque choirs, and even paired her with Harpo Marx. Mitch Miller, who supervised Columbia's output of popular recordings, assigned Jackson to George Avakian, his most sympathetic producer.

Avakian had once seen Mahalia in her natural setting ten years before, working a church in San Francisco, an event he said made him "tremble with excitement." But later he dismissed with faintest praise when he wrote, "[C]alling Mahalia Jackson the world's greatest gospel singer is like calling Babe Ruth a fair base runner."[29] The community of gospel singers from which Avakian set her apart would roll its eyes at this assessment, resigned as it was to warm condescension from friendly strangers. But they regretted for Mahalia, maybe more than she did, some of what they knew she had to do to hold her high office.

Once she signed with Columbia in 1954, Mahalia Jackson was as much as standing at the threshold of America's living room waiting for permission to enter. Later she said that there was more of her "original" self in the one album she made before Columbia than in the whole of what she recorded while she was there. This was the price she was ready to pay for being sold under the imprimatur of an empire of sound and air. Soon after she pocketed Paley's shilling, Mahalia would be broadcast so often into so many living rooms, she became like an ambassador to suburban America from its kitchen help.

Jackson was on television enough to seem a presence when not much else her color was that had any purpose but easing older viewers into a new habit of leisure by serving them up comic stereotypes handed down from movies and radio, or selling fresh music to the consumer class being made of America's young. Jackson's marketers aimed her at middle-class, middle-aged white Americans whose country still reverberated with echoes of its old colonizers. These had equated primitive with childlike and thus ascribed to the darker-skinned peoples whom they disparaged as primitive the same capacity for pure and simple faith they idealized in children. Americans who thought Negroes had a gift for spirituality were also used to thinking of that gift as the constructive expression of an otherwise disreputable propensity for emotional abandon.

So Mahalia's album covers and publicity photos were images of beatitude. She was usually dressed in baptismal white and set against a woodland backdrop, her hands clasped before her expansive bosom, her eyes uplifted or closed as if in prayer or song, her countenance radiating serene conviction. Contrived as these still lifes were, they captured an aspect of her that was real. Mahalia was crafty enough onstage to calibrate the heat of her performance to the temperature of any audience, but she wasn't actress enough to simulate the quality of authentic belief that convinced her audiences of the spirit-filled all those years she was still being paid to make wherever she worked into a church.

She was packaged by Columbia for display to a public that conceived of Mahalia Jackson as it wanted her to be and granted her some provisional acceptance as long as she never appeared to be anything else. It responded to what in her it thought it saw of qualities that it often sentimentalized in the household retainer whom they cherished as "one of the family." Being black and female meant that Mahalia was allowed some public display of the strength that upholds a cheerful forbearance of the routine indignities to which servants should strive to become inured. Two embodiments of the Hollywood maid—Ethel Waters and Hattie McDaniel—were models for her career. Both began as singers of black popular music, as she then was, and both finished as movie actors, which for them was like starting as field hands and working their way inside the house.

The only employment movies ever had for the "World's Greatest Gospel Singer" was the small but memorable part of herself in *Imitation of Life* when it was remade in 1959 for Lana Turner. She sang "Soon I Will Be Done with the Troubles of the World" at the funeral of the character Louise Beavers originated in 1934—the devoted, self-sacrificing servant and mother. Even more compelling than the $10,000 a week she received was the irresistible opportunity to certify herself as a star to the purveyors of low white culture.

Columbia Records and *Imitation of Life* propelled Mahalia onto the TV variety-show circuit in the late 1950s and early 1960s, making her in a small way part of middle-American domestic life. She was already a familiar face on television when talk shows were invented, at about the same time race troubles flared up in the South. With her occasional commentaries on daytime television about the social revolution unfolding on the evening news, Mahalia softened white audiences by bringing into their living rooms the moral and political perspective of the black church. By the middle of the century, when Mahalia Jackson's star was hung, most Aframericans were living in cities. For more than thirty years serial migrations had made these into places where successive generations of "new Negroes" were produced.

The mainline urban black churches accommodated this process well enough to preserve their institutional preeminence in tribal life. When the population shifted into cities, a new political base was formed. The educated clergy there were already the resident leadership class and so they became the biggest part of the black political establishment; this was what the missionary founders of the colleges they went to had intended for them.

Partly because she was a Baptist by birth and custom and was Sanctified in her leanings, both the established and outcaste churches of Aframerica had Mahalia Jackson in common. Before her concert career began, she had been, as Dorsey was, a one-size-fits-all supplier of her services to the soul saving industry. Because she was good for their business, she was useful to the men of the black religious establishment, and from half her lifetime on the road she knew them all. Becoming a Negro celebrity made her respectable. Television made her important. When television mixed in the politics of social change early in the 1960s, Mahalia made herself useful.

In Mahalia's time the civil rights movement unfolded on television in serial snippets at the dinner hour. Nightly news shows were the national stage for repertory companies of real people performing a scene a day from several simultaneous productions. Some players and some plays came and went quickly, while others stayed on and on. The campaign against racial segregation in the South made good television for ten years. It had arresting visuals, a simple, uplifting story line, dramatic conflict, a big climax, and a happy ending.

Southern Negroes were the heroes of this story. Many men of the church, and women of the sort Mahalia symbolized, were its backbone. Hampered though she often was by faulty health, and as preoccupied with being Mahalia, Jackson still showed up regularly for the work of her times.

She would become an agent, a friend, and a patron to Martin Luther King, but her idol was a Holiness star of the 1930s. Elder Lucy Smith was charismatic enough to build a large church in Chicago with franchises in many other places, and theatrical enough to stipulate that when she died, her body would be drawn behind six white horses to the site of her grave. She was young Mahalia's first idea of a woman doing good and doing well in a business men controlled.

For twenty of her later years Mahalia collected money from people to build her own "temple." She never built and never stopped preparing to build. It seemed she needed this dream running like a thread through her life, connecting where it had taken her back to an earlier self.

The audience Columbia Records brought Mahalia Jackson were parents of the white kids who bought Sam Cooke's records and Motown's. It would not have been as large unless it understood her simply. She represented its idea of the sunny side of her people's nature: soulful, openhearted, and absolving. From 1954 on Mahalia made most of her living singing to white people. She spent the currency this gave her with them in the cause of her tribe.

She was a race woman of the old school, working behind the scenes across the wide circles that her acquaintanceships configured to help when she could. In 1964, when church leaders in Chicago quailed at the

threat of Mayor Richard Daley's disapproval, Mahalia brokered
Martin Luther King into the city to campaign for fair housing.[30] That
it worked out badly was no less a demonstration of the combined forces
of her influence and her will.

In those days television made obvious the dignity and strength in the
comportment of Negroes in the South who resisted malicious assaults
with unyielding passivity. In a fairer world James Bevel and other strate-
gists of the civil rights movement would be revered as industrial
pioneers. Nonviolence eliminated moral ambiguities that might have
clouded their message. It was a strategy conceived by people who understood that America only made black heroes who were also its victims.

To victims obtained some moral authority—the least insistent
kind—and once in a while a little of that could be wrapped inoffen-
sively, packaged as a triumph of the human spirit, and sold to white
consumers without unsettling any of their assumptions or seeming to
indict. The civil rights movement allowed Americans to feel affirmed
by the character that their society had produced in its least by doing its
worst.

Years of media focus on the South made it easy for the general public to mistake the southern Negro for the whole of his tribe. For four
decades by then Aframericans had abandoned the South for cities
north and west. Now the world had eyes only for those who stayed
behind. With the Voting Rights Act passed and war on poverty
declared, the televiewing public had its happy ending and switched
channels.

Dr. King spent the last years of his life trying to sell a sequel, but on
the whole white Americans weren't that interested in this story anymore. They would resent having their attention recalled to it by anything untidy or unresolved in its aftermath. By 1964 black Americans
living in cities had started to attract notice by setting fire to their neighborhoods. This gave the story line on television a sour and complexify-
ing twist.

Asked to watch another installment of a teleplay they thought
already well concluded, most of the audience turned away, being
unable to understand what more these people wanted. The long cru-

sade for equal rights was over and had been declared victorious, yet its most immediate effect was the stoking of white hostility into a social phenomenon nasty enough to be called a "backlash." This repudiation served to remind Aframericans of everything about their history that suggested they were holding a check written against insufficient funds.

The three years after Martin Luther King's death saw the onrush of Mahalia Jackson's unpeaceable decline. She lived as much of them as her health permitted on international concert stages, like an older opera star who is no longer fit for the rigors of giving a full performance and so finishes up as a touring singer of famous arias. The audiences she played to by then were customarily 90 percent white. By the time she'd reached her late fifties, Mahalia's outlook had for so long been conditioned by consciousness of the specter of her early wants that the distortions in it were permanent and could sometimes seem grotesque.

Though her career was lucrative and she became a woman of considerable property, Mahalia persisted in thinking of herself as one missed payday away from being broke. She became notorious for clutching a dollar so hard, the eagle screamed. Her instinct presumed that anyone else who handled her money would cheat her and that the recipients of her kindnesses would eventually mistake them for weakness. So at the end, when her affairs supported lawyers enough for a small firm, she moved them into her house, the better to manage her managers.

Whoever was around Mahalia for long was sooner or later treated as an employee in her domestic service. She fired husbands, lawyers, agents, and friends. Mahalia was a woman in charge of herself, whose version of the storybook life she felt entitled by hard-won prerogative to author included the idea of a man who could, whenever she felt permitting, take charge of her. This made her susceptible to never feeling more womanly than when she was choosing unsuitable men or living with the consequences.

Among the memoirists of her later years, John Sellers, a "godson and protégé" whom she took very young into her household, depicted darkly the life around a woman he thought had been ruined by money and too much of the corrupting attention of white people. Sellers was a gospel and folk singer whose career as a junior-varsity edition of Josh White wouldn't have happened but for Mahalia's intercession, and he unbridled his resentments after she was gone to punish the memory of her long-ago good deed. He describes a woman who took back at the cruelest possible moment whatever she bestowed and so was mostly alone near the end, in her eleven rooms, blistering her face with skin bleaches, a diva hardening into a gargoyle.[31]

Sellers is barely present at all in other accounts of those years, which suggest a woman beset by failing health and without energy for much beyond her preoccupation with the wearisome demands and duties of being Mahalia Jackson. This preoccupation encompassed the court intrigues attending her reign as queen of a realm from whose day-to-day existence she had mostly been absent for years. But as long as Chicago was the seat of a throne, Mahalia was "gonna rule the roost."

She couldn't keep herself from deprecating even those of her fancied pretenders she was actually fond of, by reminding them in public that she was Mahalia Jackson and they weren't. Deloris Barrett Campbell, last of the great female gospel soloists of the old Chicago school and by then a mother of grown children, rolled her eyes when she told Anthony Heilbut thirty years ago, "The other night Mahalia introduced me, 'And here's our little Deloris . . . we just love to hear our little Deloris.' And there I was, looking like Big Maybelle." Alex Bradford, a gospel star in his own right, left Chicago when he was coming into his own because he could no longer stand being Mahalia Jackson's and Roberta Martin's perpetual "little Alec."[32]

For as long as it seemed she had been around, Mahalia Jackson was only sixty years old when her afflicted heart wore out in January 1972. Her death announcement appeared on the cover of black America's national tabloid, *Jet* magazine. It read, "World's Greatest Gospel Singer Dies Alone."

Before she died, Mahalia had decided she finally had enough money to buy the vacated synagogue that would be converted into her Temple for All Peoples. But she took the dream that had been a lifelong companion with her to the grave. Mahalia left life as she had taken it, with a death grip on her pocketbook.

She was a personage grand enough for two funerals. At the first, in Chicago, she was mourned by ten thousand people. The service was booked into the Aerie Crown Theater and befitted a dignitary. Many notables spoke. Mayor Daley, flanked by bodyguards, muttered condolences. Sammy Davis Jr. conveyed Richard Nixon's hope that "our country press forward in achieving the true meaning of brotherhood to which she gave such . . . poignant voice."[33]

The big room was thick with gospel luminaries, though none were invited to sing. Only Dorsey and Sallie Martin were asked to represent Mahalia's community of origin, and only then with brief remarks. In *The Gospel Sound* Anthony Heilbut reports that Dorsey, "as always, was equable and unruffled. He recited a brief poem, 'just a piece of doggerel I composed this morning,' and returned to his seat."[34]

The star of this occasion was Aretha Franklin, then at the zenith of her reign as "Queen of Soul." Her coronation was held four years earlier, in this city, when she stood spotlighted in her silver-sequined gown on the stage of the Regal Theater, smiling a bit bashfully as Pervis Spann placed a crown on her head, while E. Rodney Jones was becoming the first to publicly proclaim the title that official America would soon confer from the cover of *Time* magazine. Now Aretha was back to mark by her tribute the passing of a fallen queen of her former country, whose head she made uneasier in the months before its uncrowning by telephoning Mahalia to extend a blunt invitation to stay out of her business.

Some of Aretha's early biographers placed Mahalia Jackson often in the Franklin household when Aretha was growing up. Mahalia was purportedly a friend of Mrs. Franklin's, who was banished when her children were young and died when Aretha was ten. Years later, Jackson was quoted by an interviewer as saying, "After [Aretha's] mama died, the whole house lacked for love."

Aretha would find such an assertion nearly unforgivable in any maker. She leaves Jackson unmentioned in her own accounts of early life, but that when she was later approached to play Mahalia on Broadway, she was less daunted by this prospect than she might have been if she hadn't seen and heard so much of the real woman in her daddy's living room. Mahalia might have been her mother's friend, but Aretha was ever her father's child.

The Reverend Franklin was a celebrity preacher in Detroit whose recorded sermons sold millions. He was the epitome of a "whooper" and thus a textbook master of America's greatest homegrown oratorical tradition. "Whooping" is the overdrive black preachers in the old-country style shift into when they've finished engaging a congregation's head and are bearing down on its heart hard enough to wring out every bit of what is expressible of its joy and pain.

It is a kind of rhythm singing—half speech, half melody. Jessie Jackson, who became the C. L. Franklin of the early 1970s, labeled it "soul preaching." When applied by Franklin late in the 1950s to a text from Deutoronomy, the result was a sermon record called "The Eagle Stirreth Her Nest," which made him "the man with the million dollar voice" and as big an attraction on the gospel highway as any singer. On the road he was known to ask customers, "What y'all want to hear?" and then perform whichever of his sermonic greatest hits had been most loudly requested.

C. L. Franklin was a sharecropper's son from Sunflower County in the Mississippi Delta who pastored his way from the cotton patch to Memphis, then on to Buffalo, and finally to Detroit. There, in the pocket of black America's most prosperous industrial laborers, "when the eagle stirred its nest," as Jessie Jackson later put it, "a flower bloomed."

By the late 1950s, when Aretha was a teenager, she was living in a "showplace . . . on a half-acre of floodlit landscaping . . . built in the early years of the century by European craftsmen."[35] Franklin's "gracious" home on the city's west side was a salon where Art Tatum played the piano whenever he stopped by, Clara Ward or Nat "King" Cole or Dinah Washington might be singing in the parlor, and all the stars of the black church world came to pay their respects.

After 1957 Franklin had the conveyance of silver Eldorado Cadillacs and the look of Sugar Ray Robinson, a paragon of ghetto style: sharkskin-sleek, alligator-shod, bejeweled indiscreetly, hair slicked and sculpted in the manner of outlaws and entertainers but rarely sported by dues-payers to the National Baptist Convention. C. L. Franklin was among the money-getting elite of the small army of freelancers in the business of saving black souls. Some among his 4,500 tithers called him the "Black Prince." He was known to others around Detroit as the "jitter-bug preacher." Back in the day, old heads used to say, all the best pimps and preachers were men of the South.

Aretha took her earliest inspiration and every bit of her early style from Clara Ward, her father's friend and Mahalia's rival. Aretha's first recordings were made in her father's church, and she was set out on the gospel highway when still a girl.

The first singing job she went out alone for was in Chicago. Mahalia promoted her, plied her with *baby*s and *darling*s—and then reneged on a promised fee. Jackson sent Aretha home "heartbroken" and empty-handed but for regards to her daddy.[36] She picked up such "road savvy" as this, until Sam Cooke's example shone so bright in her father's eyes that he sent her to New York to make her way in show business.

The Franklins knew Cooke, of course, and Aretha had a schoolgirl crush on him that lasted as long as he lived. She and her sister Erma were driving, on a dark night in the deep South trying to catch up to their father, who had flown ahead to the next job, when "You Send Me" came on the radio. Hearing it for the first time, they became so agitated they had to pull the car over to the side of the highway until their squirming and squealing subsided.[37]

At sixteen she kept up with Cooke from afar, on the road, where the itinerant sisterhood reverberated with news of each reported sighting, of how Sam had married his high school sweetheart, how cute she was, how they had a little girl from before, and how he'd bought such a beautiful house in California. At seventeen Aretha "switched cigarette brands . . . because Sam smoked Kents." At eighteen she thought, "If Sam could make it, perhaps I can too."[38]

The gospel world Mahalia knew was unforgiving of any of its own who left and succeeded with what they took along. Among what was left of that world to gather at her funeral service in Chicago were members of the last generation to uphold distinctions that no longer mattered anywhere else:

> [The service] ended with Aretha Franklin, simply dressed and beautiful, singing, "Precious Lord." . . . When Aretha's name was announced, people began applauding, not a customary funeral response. Sallie Martin was beside herself. "Worst thing I ever heard . . . a night-club singer at a gospel singer's funeral."[39]

3. A Handsome Negro Lad

Near the end of his performance at C. L. Franklin's gala Easter show in 1957, Sam Cooke mingled with the crowd's clamor a "holy laugh" to emphasize his pleasure in that moment—then took off his jacket, descended the stage, and walked out the center aisle of the State Fair Coliseum singing all the way, like Frank Sinatra with his coat slung over his shoulder, as if stepping off an album cover into the mists.

Less than a year after the Reverend C. L. Franklin's spirited introduction cued the Soul Stirrers onto a stage in Detroit that Julius Cheeks had just vacated, Cooke was preparing to open for a Jewish comic at the Copacabana. He would be trying out for legitimate show business before a better-decorated version of the summer Saturday-night crowd in the Catskills; this would be like auditioning for Sammy Davis Jr.'s job. Cooke's manager had as little direct experience at this as he did, but Bumps Blackwell knew what a nightclub act looked like and that his boy didn't have one.

He hired a choreographer to teach Cooke a little of Bob Hope's soft-shoe. He selected material like "Begin the Beguine" from the classic repertory of American popular song. From cookie-cut pieces of others' work, Blackwell spliced together a lounge act. Somehow he didn't remember to have arrangements written for a full-dress orchestra like the Copa's.

They went to Tony Bennett's show there on a reconnoitering mission. Blackwell reports that a feeling passed between them akin to the bystanding viewer's at the naked emperor's procession: Bennett sang a whole song out of tune, and the audience at the Copa didn't know any better.[1] Though Cooke could only have seen as many white people together in so confined a space if he'd mistakenly opened the door on a faculty meeting at his old high school, swelled with the quartet gun-slinger's assurance that he had survived worse and beaten better in the many shoot-outs he'd walked into and out of in the highway towns of his recent past, he thought himself prepared to stand their inspection.

Cooke had earned his share of the dogged arrogance of the older elite of gospel singers who knew that however little known and unre-warded they felt, they had established their places of esteem when the best voices in black America sang from their songbook. It wouldn't have occurred to Cooke that Tony Bennett might be as good in his workshop at using a deficit to enrich his craft as he was in his. He didn't know how much Bennett's craft differed from his own; Sam Cooke wasn't near ready for the Copa.

We may wonder across these forty years why a singer as warmed by the heat of young America's crush needed so badly to be approved of by its parents; but in 1958 Sam Cooke wanted only what he was told he needed to have if he were to have a career in real show business. He tried to soften the ground he had to plow by telling interviewers his influences were Frank Sinatra, Billie Holiday, Harry Belafonte, and Johnny Mathis. But when he got to the Copa, Cooke met audiences he could not charm, though it is true that none there saw him except in the disguise of other, older entertainers' misfitted hand-me-downs.

What they did see was so awkward in its effects that when Cooke, cold-sweating from the frosty blast of his first audience's indifference, resorted to habits of his former working life—clapping his hands and exhorting from the stage—the club's overseer, Jules Podell, told him he'd be fired if he ever coon-shined like that again. One imagines Cooke mor-tified and confused, then angry over having been badly prepared. He limped through his three-week engagement, adjusting this and that to make things better but never getting it right. "Among the savvy Copa clientele," sniffed the reviewer from *Variety*—the bible of the entertainment business—"there was a feeling he had overstayed his welcome," though he allowed Cooke was indeed a "handsome Negro lad."[2]

The Mississippi Delta, where numberless years of the great river's seasonal overflowings spread loam rich as cream across an area fifty miles wide and two hundred miles long, was the best cotton-farming land in the country. Much as it became the enduring symbol of the old feudal South, Delta society wasn't fully organized until after the Civil War. Clarksdale, near its northern end, wasn't incorporated until 1880. Its streets were unpaved until after the First World War, when it was already known as a regional hub of high commerce and low culture.

Once tamed, the Delta became America's cotton patch. Near the turn of the century W. C. Handy, whose band was working out of Clarksdale when it was awash in cotton money, playing tea dances and cotillions for white people up and down the Delta, was so struck by the region's lushness he called it "a green Eden." He also suggested that it was a place where "everyone prospered,"[3] which was untrue of its black majority.

In those days funeral parlors were Clarksdale's only substantial black businesses. The Delta was created in the image of a colonial outpost and, like the countries those became, was debilitated by the permanent imbalance in its money flow: those who profited from exporting its resources spent where they sold.

But Handy can be forgiven some sentimental excess, since it was in the Delta, waiting uneasily in the Tutwiler train station at two o'clock one morning on his way back to Clarksdale, where he shared the platform with a git-fiddling vagrant who sang of an absconded lover gone "where the Southern cross the Yellow Dog,"[4] a location at the confluence of two rail lines as specifically identifiable as it would be on a road map. It was as good a line as he ever stole, and it awakened Handy to fresh and fertile commercial possibilities. Thereafter he began to apply the refinements of his conservatory training to the musical vernacular of everyday black southern folk and ultimately became official America's "Father of the Blues," famous enough to be played by Nat "King" Cole in the movie of his life and to get his face on a postage stamp.

Handy, a minister's son from Alabama, was as much a stranger to the indigenous music of the Mississippi Delta as the Lomaxes were when they first ventured into the "field" for the Library of Congress with tape recorders strapped to their backs. He encountered the blues from nearly the same distance as Irving Berlin and others of his generation of eastern European immigrants who appropriated from them whatever they could usefully apply to making a better brand of popular music. When Handy moved on to Memphis a couple of years later, he left Mississippi as an exploiter of the only natural resource besides hard labor its black citizens had to sell.

The Delta's soil and climate were congenial to the production of a commodity that became a controlling influence on the architecture of society wherever it was grown. The invention of the cotton gin in 1795 made the American cotton industry possible; previously restricted to coastal areas, the cultivation of cotton now moved into the southern interior. Since it was so lucrative, eventually more than a million of America's slaves were dedicated to producing cotton. For more than a hundred years, wherever the cotton business thrived, it depended on the availability of a lot of unskilled labor without recourse to other kinds of jobs. After Eli Whitney cotton farming was essentially untouched by the Industrial Revolution until the near middle of the twentieth century.

When the Civil War ended, without the wherewithal to go far freed slaves mostly collected where they had been pooled by cotton growers. This determined the whereabouts of most black Americans for more than seventy-five years after Emancipation. The slaveholding South was divested of some property and prerogatives when it fell, but chastisement didn't improve its character.

It replaced slavery with sharecropping—transforming most of the region's black population from chattel into debt servitude—which pervaded the South for as long as most livings there were made on the land and landless peasants were plentiful. The Delta, nearly all of it contiguous cotton plantations lightly freckled with towns, was sharecropping's longest-standing bastion. As late as 1930 three-quarters of the people living there were black and mostly lived and worked on farmland that belonged to somebody else.

This arrangement served the interests of property even better than slavery, which had required proprietors to feed, clothe, and house their workers; sharecropping permitted them access to labor on nearly the same terms as before and even a way to get paid for what they had once been obliged to provide. It was a system with a structural skew toward the landowners, who generally compounded its disadvantages to their tenants by rigging the accounts that were the running scores of these individual commercial relationships. Sharecroppers were usually bound to the land by Sisyphean indebtedness, or else they were escaping it on one plantation by moving to another, albeit without expectation that next year's outcome would be any different. Across the "black belts" of the South and Southwest, generations toiled into obsolescence on other people's land.

It was an economic institution so essential to the well-being of the South that government became its handservant. Official suppression of the region's black population—by means of disenfranchisement, segregation, state-sanctioned terrorism, and schooling withheld—helped assure that an adequate supply of cheap, landlocked, and stupefied labor was on hand for as long as it was needed. Between Reconstruction and the First World War, regional boosters were sloganeering about a New South where cheap land and labor would attract capital investments to kindle its conversion to an industrial economy.

But for most of the South industrialization never amounted to more than textiles, which purchased its license to exploit white women and children by promising not to hire blacks to work alongside them. Even after a quarter-century of flight, in 1940 more than three-quarters of all black Americans still lived in the South, nearly half in the countryside. There were more living in a single Delta county than in seven western states combined. This abundance served white Mississippi so well that for a better part of a century even its schoolteachers could afford cooks and maids.

Charles Cook, father of "the man who invented soul," grew up in Jackson, Mississippi, a son of sharecroppers who had been slaves and had graduated to a more genteel impoverishment in town. He went out into the Delta to find work when he was young—cotton prices had never been higher than they were in 1918, and farm wages were up by nearly 30 percent. After he married a girl from the country, he was forced back into the business of both their families, "making crops" for a couple of years on a plantation fifteen miles outside Clarksdale. Charles had one uncomfortable foot in the fields and his other on the rock of another of black Mississippi's native institutions: the Holiness Church, wherein his parents were among the original followers of the founding reverend, C. P. Jones.

The Holiness movement was started after the Civil War by rogue Methodists, but it was fallen-away black Baptists who picked it up and spread it broadly across the hardest of modern times for Aframerica, the period from the 1890s to the aftermath of the First World War. They hadn't intended to break away but rather to reform the church that they felt was growing embourgeoised and pale-faithed. The Baptists cast them out for being fanatics, and C. P. Jones reluctantly started a new denomination.

The rebuked were proud to be the "Lord's despised few." They believed that "sanctification" was a requirement of salvation and that prerequisite to its appropriation was surrender to God. The individual strove to perfect his developed spirit: as the song puts it, "I'm running Lord, trying to make a hundred—ninety-nine and a half won't do."

In this view the Christian vocation is not to make the world better but to build impenetrable fortifications of faith against its immutable evils. Wickedness will not be transformed, or human society perfected, until the Apocalypse comes. The object of life on earth is to endure it to the end.

Jones hooked up with C. H. Mason—already run out of Arkansas by riled Baptists—and preached Holiness revivals in Mississippi, which in 1896 got both drummed out of the state Baptist Association for promulgating renegade doctrine. The partners fell out over misgivings Jones had about Mason's unequivocal doctrinal assertion that the only true affirmation of Holy Ghost–possession was speaking in unknown tongues. In 1907 Mason spent five weeks in Los Angeles at the Azusa

Street revival meetings conducted by William J. Seymour, a black Holiness preacher out there setting fire to the "tongues movement," as Pentecostalism was then called. Seymour preached the necessity of a "third work of grace"—a baptism in the Holy Ghost—authentically manifested in tongue-talking. Mason reported being moved upon by the Spirit at his moment of his conversion, and "when I opened my mouth . . . a flame touched my tongue . . . my language changed and no word could I speak in my own tongue."[5]

In his three years at Azusa Street William Seymour became the Johnny Appleseed of what almost ever since has been the world's fastest-growing Christian persuasion. Seymour turned out an entire generation of white Pentecostal leaders who militantly prosecuted their faith across America and then spread it over the underdeveloped world. The movement Seymour seeded has grown into the trunk of America's contemporary Religious Right. In its early days the Pentecostal community was integrated, but in 1914 growing public intolerance for race mixing caused it to form into distinct and separate black and white church organizations.

Mason shrewdly headquartered his reformed Holiness Church in Memphis. His branch, the Church of God in Christ (COGIC), bloomed into the largest of all the descendant varieties of black Pentecostals. It is thought now to have more than 3.5 million members. Ironically, because COGIC was the only existing incorporated Pentecostal church between 1907 and 1914, it was the sole ecclesiastical authority for the ordination of independent Pentecostal ministers.

The white men who founded the Assemblies of God, which has grown to become the predominant church within the world's largest Protestant denomination, were mostly ordained by C. H. Mason. But by 1924 they were already excluding Mason's church and all the black others from Pentecostal fellowship organizations, which were like denominational trade associations. The FBI began a protracted surveillance of Mason, its attention drawn by the subversive race mixing that his work was thought to promote. Mason slipped his evangelists into the migrant streams flowing north and west, so that over the years his would become a mostly urban church.

In the early twentieth century in Mississippi Holiness congregations sprouted up faster than they could be ministered to; by 1937 there were more than eighty black churches in and around Clarksdale, most with fewer than eighty members. Saved since he was eight, subsequently sanctified, filled up, and called by the Holy Spirit, Charles Cook, in whom conviction and enterprise were unembarrassed bedfellows, was sure he could do better by doing good. He wanted to preach. "If you do right," he later said, "God will bless you . . . money ain't never been no question with me. 'Cause if it could be made, I'd go out there and make it."[6]

If he caught on preaching like he thought he could, it would not only release him from his sentence of two-years-to-life at hardscrabble labor in the cotton patch but also confer on him the respectability attaching to the only occupation in Mississippi at which an undereducated black man could make money with clean hands. Where black doctors were regarded by white society as less useful than black menials, the only social distinctions among black people that mattered were those they made among themselves. These mattered so much that black clergymen would commonly be addressed as "doctor" and choir directors were often called "professor."

Charles Cook's elevation to the ministry was in the casual style that upwardly mobile Negroes took as a measure of the social infirmity of their tribe's low classes. Booker T. Washington expressed his contempt for black country preachers by telling a story about a field hand who in the middle of July put down his plow and looked to the sky and said, "O Lord, de work is so hard, de cotton is so grassy, and de sun am so hot, I bleave dis darkey am called to preach." One hot day when he was twenty-one years old, Charles Cook walked into a church revival in Greenville and did so well preaching, the minister offered to split the take with him whenever he came back.

By the time his fourth child, Sam, came along in 1931, Charles Cook was simultaneously pastoring three churches and working in the household of a Clarksdale cotton baron who lived accordingly until plunging prices at the onset of the Depression suddenly offset what three generations of his family had extracted from its five thousand acres. The ruined master of the House of Mullens no longer needed houseboys, so Charles Cook became another of his family's men to be turned off a white man's land. Now he was jobless in Mississippi with the Depression on and a gang of kids to feed, and neither God nor the generosity of his small dirt-poor congregations could provide enough sustenance.

Sam Cook was five years old when his father left for Chicago, hitch-hiking with thirty-five cents in his pocket. Doing bad in one place is enough like doing bad in another to make Chicago seem less a promised land to Charles Cook than it had to the many thousands of other black southerners—mostly from Mississippi—who had moved there already in the first wave of what became the largest internal migration in the nation's history. For the first time ever Mississippi's black population was declining. But the Depression reduced the tide to a comparative trickle. In Chicago the black population had more than doubled in the 1920s and increased sevenfold between 1910 and 1930. During the 1930s it grew by less than 20 percent.[7]

In 1936, when Charles Cook headed north, black southerners had just started to stir again after hunkering down to ride out times that weren't any better where they wanted to go than where they were. He had the advantage of his family's church connections. The Holiness churches were borne by migrants into northern cities like a message from home, and black Chicago was honeycombed with them. He was given an assistant pastorate as soon as he got there. Then he found work in the stockyards and retrieved his family, which now had five children, with another on its way.

The Cooks arrived in what was becoming the capital of Aframer-ica and encamped near the heart of the nation's largest and densest black settlement: a quarter-million people shoehorned into contiguous neighborhoods in an area eight miles long and a mile and half wide—dubbed "Bronzeville" by the local press—at the northern end of Chicago's South Side. Where the Cooks lived, on Cottage Grove Avenue, had changed over from working-class white to entry-level black in less than ten years, and the neighborhood was said to have "decayed." Forty percent of its residents were on public assistance. That his children never were was owing to Charles Cook's enterprise and hard-rock Mississippi commitment to toil. Charles and Hattie

Cook sent their kids to school and kept them churched, clothed, well fed, and mostly clear of big-city snares.

Within five years Charles had his own church, and it was booming. He had a union job at a metals plant and a job in the union. He had his children performing together in church; they were already semiprofessional, they looked good, and they all could sing. The Singing Children got a manager and started doing programs for money. As family lore has it, Sam was simply God-gifted with a clear, sweet voice, and he exercised it freely as soon as he could toddle.

When he was ten, he was making extracurricular coinage singing "I'm in the Mood for Love" and "South of the Border" from a tub he mounted during the afternoon rush hour on the corner of Cottage Grove and Thirty-fifth, or table to table in the bar up the street. One suspects that even then Sam Cook loved the street, maybe learned to love it then. When that happens, the feeling never goes away. But much as he liked the hustle and profited from its bustle, Sam had already acquired the habit well-brought-up boys in cities have of never bringing the street home.

He was "saved" when he was eleven, in his father's church—the first step for most on the Holiness path of spiritual progress. Oddly, for someone who spent his boyhood in church all day every Sunday and would spend the next fifteen years entertaining in churches or in other rooms he was paid to make seem like churches, this event more or less concluded his formal religious life.

Holiness worship is sweaty, immediate, and unrestrained, and Sam Cook was too cool by nature to get too near anything that felt like "fire shut up in [his] bones." Later, even when he was a gospel star whose business was overheating houses of worship, he was never a "hot" performer; he worked hard at simulating immediacy to overcome his natural inclination to address himself to an audience somewhere out in the middle rows.

In 1943 the Reverend Charles Cook took over a church in Cleveland, which led him into a career as a roving evangelist. His family stayed in Chicago while he freelanced coast to coast. Summers were peak revival season, and when they weren't in school, the Singing Children were part of their daddy's package, added value in a business that was nakedly entrepreneurial, where cash flow ran through the collection plate and daily revenues were a percentage of daily receipts. Revivals were cheap entertainment before there was television, and the circuit— white preachers called theirs the "sawdust trail"—was dog-eat-dog.

With or without his children, Reverend Cook made money on the road, and he liked being out there. Sam liked it, too; these trips were his earliest classrooms in the ecology of the gospel highway. His older siblings didn't let him sing lead, so he studied harmonies and bided his time, still unconscious of how much gift he had and thus lacking for it specific ambitions.

When Sam was a sophomore in high school, the Singing Children were broken up by a brother's military induction and a sister's marriage. Unmoored from his family's enterprise, he ran with a "social club" called the Junior Destroyers and sang Inkspots tunes with neighbors on street corners. One of them was Johnny Carter, who would later be part of the best of two generations of Chicago's singing groups, the Flamingoes and the Dells.[8]

In the late mid-1940s black vocal groups singing popular songs for the pop market were a backwater off the mainstream of black popular music. The Inkspots, the Mills Brothers, and the Golden Gate Quartet gave religious music pop inflections in a sweetly sung older style called jubilee, characterized by skin-tight, four-part a cappella harmonizing largely unobtruded by lead singers untrained in vocal theatrics; it bridged the nineteenth-century barbershops of the South and the harder-edged postwar gospel groups.

Church music was the cradle of black vocal group singing. After the war, as gospel's high season as a lively branch of black popular music was beginning, it was aflower with male singing groups. These were called quartets, even though by then most had five members, because they were still predicated on four-part harmony.

The urban doo-wop pioneers—straddlers of the Golden Gates and the street singers of the mid-1950s—mostly brought together and trained in church music settings, were still collecting themselves in places like Baltimore, New York, and Virginia, recasting pop songs for an audience that wasn't quite there yet. So for a young man who wanted to sing for money in the late 1940s, gospel was the logical career option, particularly in Chicago, the capital of black religious music. Sam Cook fell in with four like-minded teenage boys who decided to call themselves the Highway QCs, after a Baptist church in their neighborhood.

At the end of the 1940s the black population of Chicago was nearly half a million, up 77 percent in a decade. By then nearly a third of Illinois's black residents were born in Mississippi.[9] The war was just over, work in the factories and foundries hadn't slowed down much, farms were mechanizing fast, and black Mississippi was on the move again.

Among them were the last generation of Delta bluesmen who moved into Chicago to serve as the talent base that launched the city's independent record labels, which specialized in selling brand-name "Chicago blues" to hundreds of thousands of the just-transplanted. In 1937 McKinley Morganfield came into Clarksdale from an outlying plantation and got his mojo working in crowded rooms with sawdusted floors along Issaqueena Street. During the war he moved on to Chicago, and from there became the last carrier of the Delta's old ways. These made him internationally famous as Muddy Waters.

But even in its citified adaptations, nothing of Charlie Patton's musical tradition would never again be in style with the children of a migrant generation, who were as disassociated from country blues as they wanted to be from their families' country origins. Postwar adolescents like Sam Cook were only indifferent to the blues singers who dominated the soundtrack of black Chicago's street life; the next cohort coming along would hold them in contempt.

"You see, everybody hated the blues," one of the teenage doo-woppers of the early 1950s later recalled. "We used to laugh at the blues . . . thought it was funny . . . we were going to school every day and these blues singers hadn't even gone to grammar school. That . . . stuff was . . . old music."[10]

But one plantation folkway, older even than the blues, survived the youth of Chicago's postwar flight to modernity. "Hambone" was a living artifact of slavery, when it had been called "patting juba" and it was a method of percussively slapping hands, chest, knees, and thighs to create a danceable beat. "If you're good," recalled a man who had been young in Chicago during the 1940s, "the mouth was added to the rhythm pattern." A rhyme went along with the hambone beat.

Hambone had become an obscure pastime among the city's children, until three of them polished a routine that one had been taught in the schoolyard by another kid just up from Mississippi, and made a record of it. "Hambone," by the Hambone Kids, was released early in 1952, sold a couple hundred thousand copies, and was Number 20 on the pop charts for a week. This recording, which transposed unaltered a play ritual ingrained so lastingly in the domestic culture of black Americans that it links eighteenth-century Africa with the late-twentieth-century Bronx, became such a novelty hit that predatory major labels released their own versions by Jo Stafford and Frankie Laine. Although these required special effects to approximate the sound of the real thing, they quashed sales of the original.

In the late 1940s Chicago was headquarters for Thomas Dorsey, Sallie Martin, and Roberta Martin, who between them dominated the black side of the gospel publishing business. Both Miss Martins kept vocal groups in their service stocked with performers who were among the greatest soloists of their generation, abetted by the young James Cleveland, who would one day be hailed as crown prince to Mahalia's queen. Mahalia presided over all, and in her shadow other comparable talents were obscured.

Chicago was also where the Soul Stirrers, top drawer among the touring gospel quartets, came off the road. Their leader, Rebert Harris, was the dean of quartet singers, a man of such rectitude and know-how that he was nicknamed "Pop" before he was forty. He established the National Quartets Union—after the model Sallie Martin brought Dorsey for cross-country organizing of choirs and soloists—and located it in a storefront on the South Side. It was a combination clubhouse, rehearsal hall, and home office, the site of an annual convention, and a battleground rutted by aspiring young locals who sang against one another for respect and reputation.

The Highway QCs, with Sam Cook singing lead, did well enough in their encounters at the Quartets Union, and on the junior-varsity performance circuit around town, to attract the attention of older heads and a following of younger girls. Quartet singing was a rigorous discipline, and groups in their formative stages who were serious about it knew they needed training. In some cities there were men, usually associated with local schools or churches, who specialized in training gospel quartets; qualifying to run on group singing's fastest track meant years of standing around broomstick "microphones" honing craft. A member of the Soul Stirrers, R. B. Robinson, drawn by his sense of Cook's potential, agreed to train the Highway QCs. He told Sam to study Rebert Harris and did his best to make the QCs into junior Soul Stirrers.

When Sam Cook entered Wendell Phillips High School, it was already so overrun with migrant children that it had to hold two sessions of classes a day to accommodate them all. It was like a lot of city schools now: run by white women who started out teaching kids who looked like them, then got buried in avalanches started by sudden demographic shifts, but never stopped pining for the children they used to teach.

By the mid-1940s Phillips was all black and so had the reputation of being the worst high school in Chicago. In their glancing four-year acquaintance with the adolescent Sam Cook, its staff discerned in him only an aptitude for mechanical drawing.

One service biographer Daniel Wolff has rendered was to unearth Cook's high school yearbook. The space below his picture is barren of the honors and affiliations that are distinguishing features of a high school student's identity of record. Passing through, he seems to have left barely a faint footprint on the memory of any of the school's adults. But by the time he graduated in 1948, most of the students at Phillips would have known of Sam Cook; his minor-league singing successes made him at least as much of a high school celebrity as an all-city basketball player would be.

Singing's value on the teenage status market was higher even than sports, particularly to females, who clamored loudest and spread reputations quickest. And Cook was fine, funny, and cool besides: a little shyness veiling the quiet arrogance that is the inner grace of the truly gifted, flickers of temperament suggestive of restless depths, and a mama's boy's good manners made him catnip to high school girls. He was the sort of attractive adolescent who is rarely overlooked by adults in the business of being interested in young people.

Even considering his schoolmasters' predisposition to see only the most apparent of their students' qualities, it seems unlikely that Cook's distinctions could have gone so unnoticed unless he concealed them himself. He would always be wary of the parts of life that couldn't be lived out of the way of white people.

The month he graduated from high school Sam Cook, at seventeen, was sent to jail for thirty days because some dirty pictures he'd been sharing with his girlfriend came into the possession of her tender-aged sister. It wasn't the last time he overpaid for failing to suppress the appetite he sometimes had for raunch. When his "little bit of trouble" was over, he rejoined the Highway QCs, not so much chastened as painfully aware that some of his tastes were too indelicate for polite company and—lest they be seen to belie the generally good opinion it held of him—must be kept well out of its sight.

The QCs got a break when they were engaged as the opening act on a Soul Stirrers program in Detroit, and used it to prove they were good enough to enter traffic on the gospel highway. They were seen there by a man who became their manager and got them their first job out of town. Reverend C. L. Franklin—not yet the million-selling recorded sermonizer and celebrity father he would become but even then a shrewd calculator of the value of show in his business—caught their act and gave the QCs a regular spot in his services at New Bethel Church. Then they got a call from Memphis about coming down to do live radio broadcasts on the "Mother Station of the Negro."

WDIA was considered the nation's first black radio station, even though it was owned and operated by white people. They at least had sense enough to save a failing business by selling their air to advertisers chasing the hundred million dollars a year or so that black Memphians

were spending by 1950. A regular spot singing on radio in a market like
that was a career move for any gospel group—a big one for the Highway QCs, because it would afford them more exposure sooner than
they ever figured to get.

Memphis was Chicago's old-country first cousin. It might have
been in Tennessee, but it was more the capital of Mississippi. It was rife
with young, sharp quartets and no place for beginners. Philadelphia
was close, but Memphis was gospel music's second city because W. H.
Brewster was there.

Brewster wrote million-sellers for Mahalia Jackson and Clara Ward
and gospel operettas for the pageant plays he staged in church. He was
also a working pastor, a political activist, and a "biblical scholar." As
Dorsey had Mahalia for a while to introduce his songs, Brewster had
the great unsung singer Queen C. Anderson doing the same. A community of talent gathered around him in Memphis and served as his
instrument, like Duke Ellington's band.

The QCs stayed in Memphis a couple of months, half stranded
and scuffling. The radio exposure they had gone there to get amounted
at first to steady underemployment. Mostly they sang in churches for
freewill offerings, which didn't always cover expenses. Brewster said
Sam Cook came around in those days to "study composition" and
learn to sing "How Far Am I From Canaan" from the man who
wrote it.

By accounts, Cook was studying a self-made craft curriculum—
conditioning his voice, developing technique, learning repertoire, writing songs, rehearsing the group relentlessly. The QCs were able to
break out of Memphis into Indianapolis, Milwaukee, Cincinnati, and
St. Louis. But they couldn't get a record deal. There already was a Soul
Stirrers, and the Highway QCs were thought to be too much in their
mold.

Sam Cook and his road partners were away from home a year and a
half before Rebert Harris shocked the 2,300 souls assembled in the
auditorium of a Chicago high school by announcing from its stage his
retirement from the Soul Stirrers. It was said that Harris's disaffection

with the road started when he first felt like a stranger to his children and had hardened into a resolve to leave it when what he thought of as a kind of ministry began to seem too much like an entertainment business. He was offended by the wantonness of the women who approached him after performances.

There were new-breed swashbucklers now on the set who were brandishing their showmanship at audiences like male peacocks trying to mate. "I can't stand to hear folks sing a lie," he said. But what Harris disparaged as "clowning" was going to make it harder for even a great standstill croonmaster like him to hold a stage.

Harris was an artful singer without artifice. Both cerebral and passionate, he could invoke or evoke deep emotion without melodrama. Colleagues and competitors found it remarkable that the many parts of his craft added up to an incandescent sincerity that was purely beyond crafting. This quality was so palpable in his singing that Dorothy Love Coates said Harris once sang her out of a sickbed where she had lain ill and depressed for months. Now he was sincerely dismayed by the complicity of so many of his fellow travelers on the gospel highway in its moral pollution.

"It was the middle 1940s," recalled another of the Soul Stirrers, "when . . . the congregation would be filled with these eager women to take the men out to dinner and, say, entertain them. It happened when records began to make it."[11] It would; records bring command performances into many thousands of intimate spaces and make a performer endlessly available for any use the imagination of anyone in his audience can devise.

Only the very best performers can create the illusion—for as many individuals in a crowd as make themselves available to the experience—of speaking to each directly, personally, exclusively. Records accomplish as much anytime anyone who listens is alone. It is what they are intended for. If it touches us, the performance becomes part of the soundtrack of our interior lives. The performer is objectified, a character among others in the repertory company playing in the imagined scenarios that rerun inside our heads.

The "sharp . . . and clean" photographed images of the quartet singers prowled the imaginations of women who hadn't yet seen their real faces. It isn't surprising that gifted performers consigned to laboring for low wages in the outlands of show business should be susceptible to the allures of sex on the road—a minor occupational prerequisite of pop singers made larger to these men by being the most regular confirmation most ever got of their status as professional entertainers.

"Pop" Harris was forty-eight years old when he left the Soul Stirrers, and by then he had already created, endowed, and adorned the modern gospel-quartet tradition. His draftsman's hand drew the line that ran straight through time from places like Birmingham and Bessemer to places like Detroit, from Blue Jays through Kings of Harmony and the Fairfield Four all the way to the Temptations in their prime as the most highly evolved species in a lineage of Alabama quartets that went back to the day of shaped-note singing. He redesigned the architecture of singing groups.

Harris "brought the lead singer out front," added a second lead—the fifth voice—and exploited the contrapuntal possibilities. He changed their structural dynamics by using the harmonized voices in the background to convey meaning—by accentuating key words or phrases in the song's lyric—so that a sort of conversation ensues in which the lead singer discourses and other voices in unison periodically remind him of the main points he's trying to make.

Harris cleared away and replaced old tempos and modernized the song repertoire; before him Chicago's arbiters of tasteful worship style "didn't think a quartet should sing [gospel] songs." He made falsetto, ad-libbing, and melismatic phrasing part of the quartet singer's standard tool kit. "All of my singing career is original to me," he claimed; after him no other's could ever be free of his influence.[12]

Turnover was commonplace in even the most stable gospel groups, but the loss of Harris left the Soul Stirrers headless and short of a star. S. R. "Roy" Crain, the tenor, was still around to handle their business, and the road upcoming was thick with bookings. Paul Foster, one of gospel quartet's hardest-singing second leads, was accustomed to the heaviest lifting but not all of it. He got migraine headaches from straining under the extra weight of Harris's workload.

They needed somebody to replace Harris, and R. B. Robinson suggested his boy could do the man's job. "That little fellow," Crain called him then, wasn't Rebert Harris and might never be, but when Sam Cook sang for them the song Brewster had taught him in Memphis, four middle-aged men agreed to put their livelihoods in twenty-year-old hands. Cook's conscience spasmed over leaving the QCs lurched by the side of the road, but the prospect of being instantly transported across all the miles of struggle he faced with them to get where the Soul Stirrers already were was irresistible.

His father was unsentimental about anything but doing better: Sam "is making a living. He ain't singing to save souls." His son was well-advised that there was no better or steadier living available to a quartet singer than the one the Soul Stirrers made on the road.

They rehearsed Sam once, then dress-rehearsed him in front of a preview audience at his old high school, then carried him to Pine Bluff, Arkansas, where they were booked on a program with the Fairfield Four, the Pilgrim Travelers, and the Five Blind Boys of Mississippi: all, in the lexicon of their trade, certified "house-wreckers." One reason some of the best singers of twentieth-century America ended up driving vegetable trucks and school buses or working as janitors and doormen was that the fast lane on the gospel highway ran through too many places like Pine Bluff.

The performances these men gave that illuminated these dim venues are preserved only in the legends they inspired, but back in their day, whenever more than one of them were in the same town at the same time, they battled over who would "take the show," who could carve his fresh notch into a reputation that might outrank his own in the hierarchy of peers. The Soul Stirrers were delivering their callow lead singer into a nest of gunslingers.

In his book *The Gospel Sound* Tony Heilbut describes Sam McCrary of the Fairfield Four as "a bluesy Caruso." The Pilgrim Travelers' Kylo Turner "would hoist his leg, shake his skinny hip and holler . . . the people couldn't stand it."[13] And most formidable of all was Archie Brownlee of the Blind Boys, early in his prime then as the "baddest man on the road." S. R. Crain once characterized Brownlee as the "out-singingest blind boy in the world," meaning that he sang with such scarifying intensity, he seemed to come all out of his body. Another veteran ruefully acknowledged, "Nobody out there broke my style until Archie Brownlee came along."

Brownlee's style was seminal; his voice and Julius Cheeks's—his true rival showstopper—launched a thousand soul singers. He is one recognized premise of Ray Charles's mature style, but the original James Brown—before he turned his voice into a rhythm instrument—is even more derivative. Brownlee punctuated his hard, edgy, blues-inflected crooning with piercing shrieks that seemed to come out irrepressibly, as if he had inside him an ungovernable, dark, and agonized spirit that just broke loose.

The effect was both lacerating and eminently musical. "Archie started that scream you hear all the soul singers do," the great Ira Tucker of the Dixie Hummingbirds observed. "Now plenty of us used to scream, but Archie really brought it out."[14]

Because of Brownlee the Blind Boys were the biggest draw of all the groups, and because of his maniacal intensity as a performer they had to post peace bonds in some cities they played. He seemed possessed: diving off stages into crowds; running blindly down church aisles; once, in St. Louis, throwing himself from the balcony of an auditorium. In 1959, when Brownlee's health was decimated by road rigors and alcohol, the Blind Boys hooked up in New Orleans with Julius Cheeks and his Sensational Nightingales, who by then had superseded them as star attractions.

Brownlee got out of a hospital bed to perform. Cheeks recalled that "he was so thin I didn't think he'd be able to sing. But he wailed like he usually do. Then he must have known, cause when they left the stage, he ran back."

Brownlee encored with "I'm Gonna Leave You in the Hands of the Lord," the song that was his calling card. Before he got further than the middle of the first verse, to the line that goes, "Just like the mother told her child on the day before she died, I'm gonna leave you in the hands of the Lord," Cheeks said, for "the first and only time I fell out. . . . I woke up [later] in the dressing room."[15]

There can be no greater compliment from a master of the art and craft of bringing an audience to the edge of hysteria than to have himself been so transported by the performance of another. A few months afterward Brownlee was dead of a perforated ulcer.

Years later, when Sam Cooke was a great star in the wider world, when he was alone and melancholy, sometimes he played Archie Brownlee records because "he's the only one who could move me like that." But back in 1951, in Pine Bluff, Arkansas, with Brownlee and the others to contend with and an audience expecting to see Harris, Cook—fortified only with the two songs he had learned and a pencil-thin mustache to make him look older—stood offstage absentmindedly wringing his hands. This had already become for him a preperformance tic, the only sign of stage jitters anybody ever said they saw in him.

He got through his debut without embarrassing his colleagues or impressing his competitors, who after the show inducted the rookie into the company of his betters with gentle derision. The others had, as Roy Crain put it, "shouted the house unmercifully, all over Sam, Paul [Foster,] and me."

But something remarkable happened during intermission, when the singers went out into the audience to mingle and hawk their photographs and souvenir programs. The crowd was around Cook. He wasn't just a pretty youngboy with grace and perfect pitch. He had a gift for public likability, which spends like cash money in the entertainment business.

At least one other man besides the sharp-eyed Crain had taken notice. J. W. Alexander, baritone and majordomo of the Pilgrim Travelers, caught the fresh scent of possibility and followed it into an acquaintance with its source. Alexander, who would become Cook's closest associate, gave him a tidbit of trainer science about what he had to do to be able to run the same track with all those experienced mud-kickers: "if you can't sing loud enough just make sure they understand what you say."[16]

Cook brought a different set of tools and so had to figure out a different way of doing the job. From then on the highway was his school house, wherein the bell rang for class five or six days a week, ten months a year. The young man loved being on the road. "I had a wonderful time . . . a wonderful life [then]," he said. "I was doing [what] I liked best and getting paid. . . . The fifty dollars a week I got in the beginning seemed like a fortune." He was like a well-funded graduate student on a traveling fellowship.

Even in its high season gospel music was below the sightlines of any mass media except the big-city Negro press. So some news took months to circulate, and during Cook's first time around a circuit that ran from coast to coast and border to border, people still came to see the Soul Stirrers expecting Harris. Crain knew that to shake off being ghost-trailed, Cook needed to get away from Harris's songs and tailored arrangements.

The group had to re-form its identity around him. They needed new repertoire and a new record. Once they got both in 1952, for four years they were bigger than ever.

The Soul Stirrers recorded for Specialty Records, which was owned and operated in Los Angeles by Art Rupe, one of the smartest of the white men who were mining urban migrant niches in the black music business after the war. Deserters from the army of black-belt poor who originated in Texas, Arkansas, Oklahoma, and Louisiana tended to move west, and Los Angeles was their main destination. The music they brought from their old country was lighter, cleaner, and jazzier than Mississippi's; in effect, more contemporary, and in Rupe's hands it found wide favor.

The Soul Stirrers were from Texas, and others in their business thought they discerned cowboy influences in the group's nondescript harmonies. "The Soul Stirrers were always a western group," sniffed Ira Tucker, himself a crafty master of his trade. "They never did care too much about harmony nohow."[17] While that wasn't entirely true, the Soul Stirrers' harmonic approach allowed for neither a tenor who over-laid filigree on top of their basic blend nor a conspicuous bass who undergirded it with rhythmic support. They just coalesced around four parts of a tone and sang it tight and clean. By comparison with other groups more ambitious in their approach to harmony, the Soul Stirrers' sound had an aspect like pop music, which made them just the right family for Sam Cook to grow up in.

Art Rupe, whose entry into the record business was planned and market-researched in an MBA program at UCLA, assembled the glossiest roster of gospel acts any label had in the early 1950s, on the sound theory that while their records might not sell a lot by the standards of other marketplaces, they never stopped selling. Among these properties were the Pilgrim Travelers. J. W. Alexander had become Rupe's informal adviser about gospel artists and repertoire.

While Rupe's instincts were better and his approach to record-making more intentionally plotted and pursued than those of nearly all his contemporaries among white proprietors of the new race music, he shared their problem of mistaking what they knew for everything they needed to know. He became as conservative as any purveyor comfortably adapted to customers whose tastes he thought predictable.

So when the Soul Stirrers showed up to record and didn't have Harris with them, Rupe balked at S. R. Crain's assertion that the new kid would suffice. He was a little placated by Alexander's reassurances and felt pressed by his need for a new release from the group enough to suspend his disbelief. Even then it took him months to overcome his queasiness and issue the record. Ironically, when he did, Cook's maiden voyage with the Soul Stirrers, taken over a Lucie Campbell number out of the black Baptist songbook called "Jesus Gave Me Water"—made with lilting tempo in the old a cappella style—became the best-selling gospel record Art Rupe or Sam Cook ever had.

Over the years it sold about sixty thousand copies; no record of Harris's had ever sold half as many. It's hard to know why this should be so, except that the song's rendering was light, pleasant, and ingratiating—all reliable qualities of commercial popular music. Cook's voice sounded utterly original, so distinctive and appealing it became insistently memorable.

Yet none who ranked high in the hierarchy of quartet singers when Cook came along ever thought him great. Not even his mentor Crain believed Cook ever sized up to Harris. Of course, in the family lore of many black American sports and entertainment heroes is a big brother back home who, if he hadn't gotten mixed up with drugs or the wrong crowd or had to marry that girl and take a job at UPS, would have been just as good. Or a father or uncle who would have done at least as well with the same chance. These elders didn't begrudge Cook; they recognized in him a distinction that set him apart, but thought it had more to do with his package—"youth, education and presentation"—than his singing.

Most of them were underschooled older men from the country, to whom the smooth, clean-dictioned, recently Chicago high school–graduated Sam Cook was one of those "new Negroes." But they loved him as they would a little brother who goes out into the world at large and succeeds in it beyond their limit of imagined possibility, and came back whenever he could as easy in their company as he would have been if he'd never left.

For half a decade he was more in the society of these men than any other, and though a half-decade removed from it, he was still respectful of an authority whose limits he'd outgrown. Six years after he left church music, with "Having a Party" climbing to the top of the pop charts fast behind "Twistin' the Night Away," he told a journalist, "Real gospel music has got to make a comeback."[18]

Their general opinion credited Cook with being a "great thinker," but to the old heads who'd brought him up in church singing, great work meant going to unreasonable lengths to transport people to a place beyond reason. The thinking, to them, was about how best to apply their resources to storming the gates of an audience's reserve. That the assault would be made was beyond question.

In a profession wherein earnings were never a reliable measure of worth, they assessed their own in the currency of people "slayed" and churches "wrecked." Their art required aggression and fearlessness in amounts Cook's nature didn't permit him to spend: "Sam wouldn't tackle any song the least bit too high," said Crain. "[He] used his head. Harris would tackle any note." Cook found his trademark yodel by accident one night trying to compensate for his unwillingness to stretch too far for a note he knew he couldn't reach.

Cook was immersed for all his childhood in the emotional flamboyance of the Holiness Church, but something about it made him uncomfortable enough to withhold from it his whole self. He would then have been naturally indisposed to releasing himself onstage to the self-abandonment required to release an audience. Julius Cheeks sojourned with the Soul Stirrers for about a year in the early 1950s and became so frustrated by Cook's unyielding collectedness that he pushed him off a stage in San Francisco, admonishing through clenched teeth, to "move, man." "People thought he got happy," Cheeks recalled. "I gave him his first shout. . . . I was the one caused Sam Cook to sing hard."

This impatience with a young boy who thought he could cheat his profession and be a professional is understandable in a man who could sing Archie Brownlee to a standstill and shredded his voice night in, night out for the price of Sam Cook's tip money. But Cheeks had love for him, like most of the rest of the old heads did. Of the many singers in Cheeks's debt, "Sam's the only one treated me right . . . gave me the first five-hundred-dollar bill I ever saw."[19] And the only one who left and never knew how to keep from looking back.

Cook learned to "sing hard," but never could without debasing his style. Of course, his undistorted vocal qualities were so fine that only their coarsened version was accessible to imitation, and from this a strand was spun off into a thread that runs through Bobby Womack into Rod Stewart. Singing hard was hard, too, on other sweet singers, like Claude Jeter of the elegant Swan Silvertones.

Jeter is the root of falsetto soul singing in all its modern forms; in the continuum of classic soul singers he is to Al Green what Cheeks is to Wilson Pickett. But even Jeter was prepared to offer up dignity on the altar of his duty to "shout" a crowd. Meeting the demands of his workplace often meant he had to so distress his voice that he once allowed that when people wanted to make fun, they compared it to a screeching cat. To listen to Jeter singing that way is to hear a man pushing himself as close as he can get to the edge he knows he might fall from. When Cook was called upon to rise to such occasions, he skirted the brink.

There is a live recording of the Soul Stirrers in 1955 that describes Cook's limits as a workaday gospel singer. The group was headlining a Specialty all-star package playing the Shrine Auditorium in Los Angeles, and Cook was their star. This meant they were closing the show, so their audience had been heated and reheated and was waiting to boil.

The Soul Stirrers had already been onstage for thirteen minutes and two songs, and Cook was halfway through an extended version of "Nearer to Thee," gospel music's biggest hit du jour, yet still fighting for his audience inch by stony inch. He was deep enough into it to have used up all the verses on the record, so he was ad-libbing out of his stockpile of song fragments that are pieces of the public property of black churchgoers; he was throwing darts at the audience's heart and hoping one would hit.

"Nearer to Thee" is not the old song itself but a story about the song, and telling stories in song is what Sam Cook was known for. Making sure an audience understood what he was saying was among many things he'd gotten good at. But the congregation was unmoved by Cook's exertions until Paul Foster bestirred it by reminding everybody of what they came there to do with a sound like a long burst of low rolling thunder. Cook still could not have them until he found the right heartstring to pluck, and he couldn't do that without resorting to the cheap device of invoking the trials of motherhood to a roomful of mothers, with a verse that began, "I wonder do you know bad company can make a good child go astray," and ended, "but no matter what the crime, that mother says 'this child is mine.'"

Spurred by the crowd's response, Cook bore down as hard as he could, but to keep its emotional pitch high he still needed Foster's muscle bearing him up. He had to sing himself near ragged to produce less of an effect than, say, Julius Cheeks did at cruising speed. Cheeks was in a small class of "anointed singers," so called because without supernatural inspiration "you wouldn't do what he did over and over and over of yourself."

Cook used his instrument and an adaptive intelligence to avoid having to make the self-immolating commitment he saw in Cheeks and Brownlee, throwing themselves on the pyre to kindle Holy Ghost fires night after night. Singing was his business, not his calling.

Nevertheless, the best of Cook's work as a gospel singer is no less brilliant for having to overcome the mismatch between what it required of him and certain of his truest inclinations. And very little he made after he was done with this work ever overcame its disassociation from the only emotional content he could rely on to give his singing more depth, honesty, and coloration than he could otherwise provide.

In the long view of Jerry Wexler, Sam Cooke was the best popular singer of the last half-century. Wexler, a creator of Atlantic Records, had tastes in black music strong enough to steer a generation of white kids in the 1960s and sharp enough to steadily anticipate which new flavor their black contemporaries would next find appealing. Wexler said his high opinion of Cooke was based entirely on his work as a gospel singer, since nothing he did in popular music approached that standard.

Even the old-school quartet singers of 1956, whose parsimony with expressions of regard for Cook's relative abilities grew flintier as his star got brighter, must have thought his recording of "Jesus Wash Away My Troubles"—his last as a Soul Stirrer—nearly immune to criticism. But in it they would also recognize the call of a different species.

The audience for gospel music had always been drawn from the church's regular constituency of old men, women, and children young enough to have their attendance compelled. Suddenly teenage girls of a new breed, who thought of gospel as their mothers' music, turned out for Sam Cook, squealing "Sing, baby," and cooing "Take your time" from the front rows of churches.

However much his refusal to be one of "those deep, pitiful singers" might have disappointed many women of a certain age, it was an absolute virtue to daughters inclined to think their mothers country and uncool when they got overwrought in church. Whenever the old-school mother-flusterers watched Cook work, they were facing the future from the past, and what they saw in it made them suspect that there wouldn't be much of the past left to them after the present was gone.

Colleagues who saw Cook being swarmed by admirers they felt they'd done more to deserve must have somehow thought him a young man to whom too much was given. Still, he was too likable to resent with a clear conscience, and so to remind each other of his place among theirs, they deprecated him with faint praise. J. J. Farley, a long-standing Soul Stirrer, once said of him, as preamble to a compliment, "Sam started out as a bad imitation of Harris."

Even those who carped that sex appeal was his distinguishing gift credited Cook with knowing how to sell what he had better than anyone else, leaving implicit their judgment that his talent for finesse didn't equip him for their kind of hard work. But the road was a fraternity, and Sam would always be their little brother; he had shared too many cans of Vienna sausages with too many of them in too many cars across too many miles ever to fall out of good standing. He belonged for life to a small fellowship of men who ever called a bologna sandwich "quartet chicken."

Bobby Bland celebrated the credo of all itinerants who trolled for their livings in the backwaters of Negro show business when he sang, "I'm gonna play the high-class joints, I'm gonna play the low-class joints, and baby, I'll even play the honky tonks." Those who made their business singing for Jesus got used to plying the "highways and hedges." Gospel music was in peak season then, and the road seemed to those laboring on it like a long series of widely scattered fields to harvest.

The Soul Stirrers might perform before ten thousand people in Columbus, Georgia, one night and on the next for a couple of hundred at a church in Waycross; they stopped in even the smallest plot to pull out a fee. In 1953 they grossed $78,000—as good as it got in their business—but to earn it they worked about 250 dates, which meant an average wage of around $300 per appearance.

But their road was never more beckoning; by early 1954 even *Billboard* magazine had noticed that the Specialty gospel package, touring under the flag of Art Rupe's Herald Attractions, was doing as much business as Nat "King" Cole. So the Soul Stirrers traveled relentlessly—more than a hundred thousand miles a year—every day, six men in a car, sometimes for more than three months straight. Gospel groups rarely stayed a night and a day anyplace they worked.

The backseat of a car became Cook's living room; he read, napped, wrote songs, and entertained his companions. Finances were pinched and accommodations limited, so eating and sleeping arrangements were often haphazard. Under these circumstances obliging women were more than diversions—they were materially useful. Women and whiskey were the road's worst habits. Cook found its very waywardness releasing.

For many of us, getting from one place to another induces a kind of suspension: our lives are held in abeyance until we get where we're going. For someone like Cook, who traveled for a living, getting to the next job was the backbeat in the road's steady rhythm. This preoccupying quality of life on the road made it seem a sealed compartment out of which the traveler, if he cared to look at all, looked upon the other parts of his life as having been suspended. The road is both a gift and a curse for the chronic traveler prone to avoidance; being away on business for a long time and recuperating from it are two of the best excuses for not taking care of business at home.

Still just into his early twenties, Cook's life already had untidy corners, like the baby in Chicago his girlfriend Barbara from high school had when he first got with the Soul Stirrers, or another born a year later to a woman in Cleveland he'd known since his father had a church there. He supported neither child, and there is no evidence that either woman made an issue of it; Sam was the sort of sweet seducer who could leave a note on the pillow the morning after with some assurance that the abandoned would read it and say thank you. Besides, he wasn't up to child support, since he was then such a wastrel, according to R. B. Robinson—his landlord for a while—that if he owed you twenty-five dollars on his rent and was downtown with the money in his pocket, he'd show up broke because he'd bought a shirt on the way home.[20]

Sam Cook loved being on the road when he was young, and he filled up cracks in the routine of travel and showtime with hard carousing. This included plucking off women as if they were hanging fruit. Cook was trained as a mama's boy to the companionship of women and conditioned to exploit it through his companionship with men.

"The road offers a lot of temptations," a confederate once reflected, "and we yielded. Quite often." If, within weeks of becoming a Soul Stirrer, Cook had been turned into a sexual predator, it was from being remorselessly stalked by prey. The neoplayer got played by a woman in Fresno, California, who within two weeks of seeing Cook onstage in 1953 chose him, pursued him, and captured him.

As she approached him after that show, the innocent who was still much a part of the twenty-two-year-old Sam Cook must first have gazed upon the straight hair, hazel eyes, and striking countenance of twenty-three-year-old Delores Mohawk and deduced that a recess had been declared in heaven. Even those she left uncharmed conceded she "was a whole lot of good-looking woman." The older men around him shrugged, in the way of parents watching their boy eat the piece of candy that's finally going to make him sick: "let him get his head bumped," they said.

Her name was really Milligan, and she came from a town in Texas to a smaller town outside Fresno with the aunt to whom she had early been abandoned by her mother. She got pregnant at seventeen, around the time she changed her name to Mohawk in anticipation of a singing career, married a coworker of her uncle's who was not her Mexican boyfriend, and named the baby after him. After he left, she changed her son's whole name and put him mostly in the care of the woman who raised her, while she worked at elaborating on her checkered past.

Delores Mohawk was slick, quick, and slightly disreputable in a way Cook would have found stimulating; he never was drawn to women life hadn't tainted. She took him home with her, wrapped him up there for several days, and then talked her way out onto the road with him for the rest of the Soul Stirrers' California tour. Two months later they were married.

Cook brought her and the boy back to Chicago and stashed them in a three-room apartment in R. B. Robinson's basement. If he seemed a bit casual to some when he spoke of having gotten married, it might have been because marriage doesn't seem so consequential when you're away from it ten months a year.

By 1955 three and a half years of crisscrossing the country and the concurrent release of nine records had secured Sam Cook's place among gospel music's most popular attractions. At twenty-four he had learned

to make virtues out of perceived deficiencies by mastering the align-
ment of talent to task. When he was fifteen, the singer Jerry Butler—
who also had to overcome the deficit of being too cool when heat was
in season and did it well enough to become celebrated as the "Ice-
man"—watched Cook pick up the debris Archie Brownlee left behind
one night in Chicago: the Blind Boys, he said, "just tear your soul
out . . . I was sitting there thinking . . . 'how do you go onstage when
the Five Blind Boys just got everybody in the place jumping out of their
seats?' . . . [Cook] didn't try to step into the space that the Blind Boys
had. He moved it to the left and up a notch. . . . And it started off and
it swelled, and it swelled and it swelled [until] everybody was in
tears . . . and shouting."[21]

If S. R. Crain was a gentle headmaster of the finishing school where
Cook's skills were polished, life on Art Rupe's plantation taught him
hard realities of the record business. From the beginning Cook wrote the
songs he recorded with the Soul Stirrers; by 1955 he was writing and
often arranging most of their hits. When he was twenty, Cook was
happy to sign Art Rupe's standard writer's contract, which made whatever he wrote the property of Specialty's house publisher, Venice Music.

This meant Rupe had a half-interest in any money the songs made.
For singing on Soul Stirrers records, Rupe paid Cook the unvarying
rate of fifteen dollars a side and a one-fifth share of the group's penny-
and-a-half royalty on every record sold. Accordingly, the most Cook
made for any of his gospel records was about $180.

Crain has called Cook a "genius so far as melody was concerned,"
though it must be said that the traditions of gospel singing have only
slightly more regard for the integrity of a song's melody than for its
tempo. Cook had an uncomplicated talent for several variations on
about three melodic themes, which later served him well as a writer of
music for mass markets, a business that prefers creativity to be reitera-
tive and, being rarely prophetic about what will sell, relies too much on
what is already known to have sold.

Cook based his approach on the premise that the best songs told a
story, and executed it best when he had at his disposal the narrative
material of "the greatest story ever told." Crain has described Cook in

the back of a car on his way to a recording studio, thumbing through a dog-eared Bible until he found something in the Book of Matthew he could turn into the lyrics of "(I Want to) Touch the Hem of His Garment," one of his late, great Soul Stirrer recordings.[22]

In 1955 Cook got a road partner near his own age, the twenty-year-old Leroy Crume, whom he knew from Chicago. Once Crume joined the group, Cook had someone to play with, and from the start they were "running wild." Neither the toll of three grueling years and his ostensible marriage, nor one too many times burning up a thousand miles of highway to get to a canceled program had slowed Cook down, slaked any of his appetites, or changed his habits.

Living as he did, Cook always needed money. After a song he wrote called "Nearer to Thee" became a hit, he beefed with the other Soul Stirrers about their policy of splitting all writers' royalties equally. "I want my money," he told these men who had honored this arrangement for twenty years, "or I'm not going to the [next] program."[23] The group felt violated, but eventually conceded to Cook and Crain the prerogative of signing personal services contracts with Art Rupe.

Cook's frustration was simmering by then. He'd heard Ray Charles make a few word substitutions in the lyrics to a church song and, sounding like Archie Brownlee on sedatives, set jukeboxes playing off the hook. He noticed that a rock-and-roll show headlined by black acts Alan Freed had mounted in New York over Christmas of 1954 did $124,000 of business in a single weekend. He knew there were more teenagers around than ever, and that a lot were white kids buying music made by and intended for black people; some of what they bought were Art Rupe's records. Cook wasn't working hard as he was to be laying up treasure in heaven's savings bank.

4. Feet Strike Zion

In the mid-1950s Art Rupe shrewdly opened a pipeline to New Orleans, where a distinctive rollick in the rhythms native to the city's raucous music culture was calling a generation of white kids to play. Rupe's business quickly got bigger than he could handle alone. The man he hired to help was a self-educated sophisticate, small businessman, and occasional leader of minor local bands from the northwestern outlands named Bumps Blackwell. Blackwell came from the small black enclave in Seattle, so detached from the rest of Aframerica that it was like a gnat in a bowl of grits.

The perspective from there, and thirty-seven years of enforced culture-straddling, made Blackwell the rare black record man in 1955 with habits of mind formed over years of engagement with the problem of how to make an identifiably black product acceptable to white people. This made him particularly suited to puzzling out the highly nuanced problem of how to package black music for the consumption of others.

But Blackwell didn't know much about gospel music when he came aboard, so Rupe, sort of by way of showing him around the premises, took him to see the Specialty road show when it played in Los Angeles. What Blackwell discovered there about Sam Cook was "too much voice to be in such a limited market"; and too much youth appeal to waste on church women, just when teenage girls were starting to buy most records: "Shit, girls were following him around like the pied piper."[1]

He cornered Cook after the show and told him so. Cook was worried about the bridge burning behind him as he crossed; one of the precepts his elders had taught him about the business he was in was that the gospel audience was unforgiving if scorned.

Roy Hamilton and Clyde McPhatter were then on the pop charts—thirteen of the Top Thirty of that moment were black records or white cover versions—and both had begun as singers of sacred music. But they were at best semiprofessional gospel singers, so nobody but the people around them would have noticed when they switched; they didn't even have an audience to lose.

Cook was a star, however circumscribed the firmament he brightened, with a following big enough to call a "market," and gambling his stake of it could mean forfeiting a reliable source of succor if he lost. On the other hand, he was restless: "I wanted to do things for my family, and I wanted nice things of my own. Making a living was good enough, but what's wrong with doing better than that?"

Charles Cook was the rare national evangelist of the Church of Christ (Holiness) who didn't believe that losing your soul was the inevitable price of gaining the world. In his heart Father, Son, and Holy Ghost shared space with the Wizard of Tuskegee. So Reverend Cook advised, "You working for money, boy! That's your living. . . . Don't let nobody tell you nothing about no church song."[2]

Blackwell kept prodding, Cook was listening, and Art Rupe's assumptions were blinding; it wouldn't occur to him that any property of his would be on the road pointing at Harry Belafonte's picture in a magazine and saying, "I want to be just like him." Even if it had, given what he thought he knew, he would have believed Sam Cook deluded.

As if he were trying out his mind in another place, Cook sweetened a coy little ballad, written, oddly, by Theodore Frye, Dorsey's old tour guide through the gutbucket church circuit. "Wonderful" was so bent toward where he was inclining that it hardly sounded like gospel music at all. Cook's was the rare artistic personality that changes its chosen medium of expression in the course of adapting to the disciplines required.

What he came upon as the blackest of popular music Cook made into something more conforming to the specifications of his talent. The doing of this confirmed in him a prejudice he'd acquired from the fraternity of quartet singers: that the only difference between gospel and popular song was the words. This axiom was a pillar of their collective self-esteem, since it allowed those in their highest echelon to compare estates with Ray Charles's and be able to say, there but for my higher self go fortune and fame. Once he received this assurance, Cook never challenged it; nor would J. W. Alexander, who was moving in closer to become his mentor, friend, and eventural business partner.

In a way Sam Cook capstoned his gospel career in the summer of 1956 by facing down Rebert Harris on the same stage in a city that loved them both. Atlanta was so much the Soul Stirrers' that their local promoter enjoined them from walking the streets there lest they draw crowds otherwise willing to pay to see them. Harris had put together a group of mostly used-to-be Soul Stirrers called the Christland Singers. They rarely left Chicago, but for a fat Atlanta payday and the itch to reclaim one big stage on one big night.

Harris was lured down for what was being sold as a generational "battle of song." He went first and met all expectations, which for many of the assembled—including his former colleagues—were higher for him than for Cook. Crain swears that during Harris's performance a man was so transfixed he "walk[ed] every bench from the back to the stage and didn't hurt nobody."[3] Whereupon Cook came out and sang "Wonderful," spinning this confection into so sweet a spell that the candlepower of his smile across the room burned up the trail of Harris's ghost.

It was as though an artist had walked into the workshop of artisans and made in their manner, of materials they had on hand, something enough like their product, but so transcendently his own that it illuminated the distinction between art and masterly craft. That he applied himself so studiously to the gospel highway's hard disciplines was a reason no other singer of pop music could ever sound like Sam Cooke. It was also a reason why Cooke never sang any song in the pop music repertory of his times as if it meant anything to him, except a very few he wrote himself; he could renounce the one and never bear to really be gone, embrace the other and never hold it in his heart.

In his way he was as groundbreaking as Rebert Harris was, but he broke into ground outside the conventions of the self-contained tradition he inherited. By doing so, he made that tradition permeable to the mainstream of black popular music, which quickly leached as much out of gospel as needed to for its own refreshment, before long diminishing what was left into a torpid commercial backwater.

At about the same time a letter came to Art Rupe printed in Cook's careful schoolboyish hand, the first letter of every word capitalized as he might have done if he were in the habit of writing to people who didn't read all that well. In a manner both earnest and offhand, Cook informed Rupe that he had been approached by a nameless friend offering to broker him a deal to record "popular ballads" for some major label, that he had agreed to let him try, and now all he needed was Rupe's permission. This was a young man unfamiliar with white people who was making a formal inquiry of his white employer intending to be ambiguous about his own intentions and probative of Rupe's; thus it discloses something of Cook at his most complicated.

The care he was taking not to alienate a more powerful man while telling him something he wasn't going to like resulted in a tone so poised on the joining edge of respectful and casual that it suggested a kid trying to slip out of the house to go to a party, who, upon encountering his father near the door, breezily announces his departure as if it were a matter so routine he only had to notify and not ask permission. Cook already knew he didn't want to work for Rupe anymore. Rupe blundered when he was careless enough to let Cook see that he wouldn't, or couldn't, regard him as anything special. Cook already knew he was special enough to make the Soul Stirrers more profitable for Rupe than ever, and had by then begun to suspect he could be some different kind of special altogether.

Rupe, of course, declined to give permission and counterproposed that if Cook wanted to record "pop material," he could do it for Specialty Records. Rupe said later he was not averse to this idea, but more probably—since it wasn't his idea to begin with—he figured he'd humor Cook by letting him record something and then make his point by letting the record die unpromoted. Rupe came west to get into the movie business and there adapted a Hollywood studio technique for disciplining recalcitrant performers. In this respect he became a pioneer among proprietors of the black music business.

Rarely had any contended with an undocile employee who had a better option than was available to Muddy Waters when he agreed to paint the offices of Chess Records to work off an advance his record sales hadn't redeemed. Fifteen years later Berry Gordy used an aggressive variation of this approach in trying to subdue Marvin Gaye's insurgent campaigning for creative control of himself. It didn't work then only because the record Gordy issued under threat from Gaye and quickly tried to kill turned out to be "What's Going On" which got too big too fast to be choked in its cradle.

It was six months before Rupe arranged for the session at which Sam Cook would first record "pop material," and when a record emanated a month later it turned out to be a tepid secularized version of "Wonderful," credited to one Dale Cook. "Lovable" sold less than Cook's last four Soul Stirrers records, and he was unsurprised but chagrined that Rupe didn't promote it. Nobody but Cook's gospel audience—for whom it was at least a curiosity—could have heard it much; the name change was such a transparent ploy that they couldn't have mistaken whose it was, and they likely constituted most of the buyers of the fifteen thousand copies sold. The Soul Stirrers, who had to regard a dollar spent on a Dale Cook record as a dollar unavailable for buying one of theirs, felt aggrieved and fired off a letter to Rupe asking him to desist from trying to disestablish their franchise.

As the Soul Stirrers went around, Cook was hearing from white men he thought were important, like Bobby Schiffman of the Apollo Theater, that he was bigger than his small life. Though he was still among them in the early months of 1957, the Soul Stirrers already knew they were going to have to find out if it still held true that one monkey don't stop no show. Cook just never told them when: "I didn't know Sam was gone until he was gone," Leroy Crume mused. "There wasn't no big fight. . . . He just didn't show up."[4]

Bumps Blackwell then went to work, with J. W. Alexander as Cook's consultant: Rupe's man for rock and roll on one side, his man for gospel on the other, and in the middle a man who, though temporarily reduced to sleeping on Blackwell's couch, had more ideas of his own than either suspected.

The part of Blackwell for which Cook had the strongest affinity was the falsely self-advertised college graduate who was so good at his pretense, nobody thought they needed to see his résumé to take him at face value.

Blackwell's life among white people disinclined him to overrate them, and his assuredness about being as smart as they were was emboldening to Cook. But Alexander was a custodian of wisdom Cook acquired on the only road yet traveled, a professor of the closest thing he thought he had to professional certainties. On the one hand there was Blackwell, urging him to dare; on the other was Alexander's implicit caution not to dare too much.

Alexander, who had been among the very first to sense the true scale of Cook's possibilities, paused regularly in his attention to the affairs of his Pilgrim Travelers to lift up his head and sniff the air for a prevailing scent. His sensitive nostrils lately flared to the smell of a changing climate; before he was able to reliably predict which way the weather would break, the best he could think to do was send up test balloons in his backyard.

He hired Charles Brown, the blues balladeer, and a tenor saxophone to play on a Travelers record, which so annoyed the church motherhood that served his bread and butter he had to apologize or leave the table. But in Cook he recognized someone with an aptitude for causing people to forget their scruples. He could imagine how useful this gift would be to anyone who hoped to maneuver through a crack in an unbreached social barrier and be invited to stay on the other side without forfeiting his welcome home.

Because home was so fixedly his viewpoint, Alexander's perspective on the territory ahead was narrower than Blackwell's. It was hard for him to conceive of a world so changed that it could open up to any Soul Stirrer a passage into deep white pockets. He was thinking of a more immediate target: "At that particular time the young black girls didn't have anybody [to idolize]. . . . The time was just right." The idea that white girls might get caught in the same net was too unsettling for a middle-aged black man from a part of Texas where even thinking the wrong way about transracial seduction was perilous.

But that was just what Blackwell planned for, and nothing in his recently direct experience of buying and selling in this turbulent marketplace suggested he wasn't cheek by jowl with a large and plausible opportunity, or that his instincts for catching it weren't properly attuned. His vision, however, was occluded by the view he shared with most others in his business who were strip-mining this freshly upheaved lode—by then brand-named rock and roll—without regard to conserving or developing it because they were sure this windfall could never be the sustaining basis of an industry. Trained to the refinement of an older tradition, Blackwell had so little respect for the quality of what was newly popular that, like the others, he would think it disaffirmed the values of the official American popular music they regarded as its permanent tradition and therefore couldn't last.

The first new act Blackwell "handled" for Art Rupe—Little Richard—created an overnight commercial brush fire in 1957 out of music made in a style that seemed a caricature of its black antecedents of the sort white people were always comfortable mistaking for characteristic. So it seemed to men like Blackwell that if they really were beholding some new thing—and "Little Richard" Penniman was at least unprecedented—it would still be subject to familiar cultural assumptions.

For Blackwell, selling any black performer to any white audience of large scale meant having to disassociate him from his implicitly disreputable origins. He wrote Alexander of his plans for recording Cook anew: "We are not interested in blues at the present time . . . in writing the lyrics try to write 'white' for the teen-age purchaser rather than 'race' lyrics. It seems the white girls are buying the records these days."[5]

Blackwell hoped to use children as stepping-stones to their parents, the audience he presumed Cook would need to sustain a career in legitimate show business. He envisioned a "modern Morton Downey" who could appeal to "both teenagers and housewives." He dared not suggest aloud the actual career from which he cut his pattern for Cook's: that of Frank Sinatra, who had been an idol of teenage girls in the early 1940s and had become an institution in the cultural life of middle Americans by the late 1950s.

Blackwell's working premise was audacious, without any incorporated illusions about a comparable status being attainable for any Aframerican, or that any white audience would cleave to a black performer long enough for them to grow old together. Blackwell's use of Morton Downey as a point of reference not only suggests how low the ceiling of high ambition was those days for blacks in his business, but also how bereft they were of any antecedent experience from which could be learned much that was helpful in plotting Cook's course. It also reveals the problem Blackwell shared with most of his industry: confronted with the threats and opportunities presented by unforeseen circumstances that made long-held territories vulnerable and revealed others yet unclaimed, they planned their assaults and defenses as if they were generals fighting the last war.

Cook sent Blackwell a demo tape of seven songs he might record, mostly of his own composition. They included his rendition of "Summertime," which seemed to Blackwell the most promising. He brought in Rene Hall—the rare black technician in New York City's pop music manufactory—as arranger, and Cliff White, who had been guitar player for the Mills Brothers. He hired white background singers and moved the recording session to a more upscale studio than the one Specialty Records customarily used.

He took the precaution of booking it for a time when Art Rupe, an inveterate meddler in his employees' creative affairs, was supposed to be away in Las Vegas. Blackwell was aiming for classy and knew that class was something Rupe wouldn't think a commercially useful property. Cook was much involved in these doings; his sensibilities ever inclined him toward lightening dark tones, including those intimations of the blues in "Summertime" that its composer had intended.

He insisted on starting the song Gershwin wrote in a minor key with a major chord. Then Rupe turned up unexpectedly at the session and was so appalled by what was going on that he fired Blackwell summarily and replaced him in midrant with the first untainted hanger-around familiar to his wild eye, a truck driver named Sonny Bono.

Rupe was no longer comfortable with Blackwell anyway; he hired Negroes to work with and oversee other Negroes, but didn't intend to ever employ any independent Negroes. The session continued after Rupe left, but not before Cook told him he felt so disrespected, he wouldn't work for him anymore. The price of Rupe's divorce from Blackwell was Cook's contract and ownership of the tapes that got him fired. Among them was a song of Cook's they recorded that seemed to the professionals formless and puerile—the same words over and over around a couple of "ice cream changes."[6] It was called "You Send Me."

Rupe had so little regard for anything he heard on those tapes, he thought himself a canny negotiator for having avoided an outlay of cash. Rupe didn't know Blackwell had already been label-shopping for a couple of months. He walked out of Rupe's office into a deal with Keen Records, a little start-up label owned by a manufacturer of airplane parts and run by a former clarinetist in Artie Shaw's band.

With Little Richard's records kicking like a forty-mule team of Rockettes and three more just like them in storage, Blackwell was betting those tapes against about $50,000 in royalties he estimated Art Rupe would have owed him. He was that sure "Summertime" would be a hit record.

The release of "Summertime," with "You Send Me" on the other side, wouldn't happen for three and a half months, and in the interval Cook squatted with Blackwell in Los Angeles with nothing much to do but read the trade papers and watch television, while subsisting on money Crain sent him from the road. He added an "e" to his last name because he thought it classier that way. This cosmetic alteration was for Cooke a token of his being in sure-enough show business now, like the acting class he took.

He vacated a marriage he was habitually distant from anyway, which his wife interpreted as evidence of his indifference so conclusive she cut her wrists. As Roy Crain, who was often detailed to do Cooke's cleaning up, saw it, "Usually when he was with a woman awhile he didn't want her no more."[7]

On a regular foray hunting new music at his local distributor's in St. Louis, a disc jockey named E. Rodney Jones, future dean of mid-1960s black radio in Chicago, recognized Sam Cooke's voice on a label he'd never seen before and thought he heard a hit. Jones took the only copy of the record in town back to his radio station and played the flip side on his show early and often. Whenever he did, a switchboard riot flared, much provoked by the aroused and agitated local fandom of Sam Cooke. Black St. Louis was famously devoted to gospel music and knew him from the Soul Stirrers.

Their unequivocal affirmation of him exposed as a myth the legend gospel singers handed down to their young, about the irrevocable rebuke the black church crowd reserved for any who fell away from it in chasing the illusory satisfactions of money and worldly acclaim. It also certified to Cooke that his grassroots loyalists would follow him over the bridge he had crossed. He would pledge to return their allegiance: "I'm not gonna leave my base. . . . When the whites are through with Sammy Davis Jr. he won't have anywhere to play. I'll always be able to go back to my people because I'll never stop singing for them."[8] Even when it seemed like he mostly had, they never left him.

"You Send Me" broke on the black side in St. Louis, and with the dominoing radio effect knocking over market after market lickety-split, the campaign Blackwell hoped and planned for was suddenly under way. With the beachhead established, he prepared his assault on white radio, guardians at the gates of Blackwell's heard-of city with streets of gold—the so-called general market, his true objective. He put five thousand dollars in his pocket to buy airplay, put Cooke in his car, and set out for the territories on a promotional tour, brokering work for his singer as often as he could along the way.

Casey Kasem, who eventually became as familiar as smog to consumers of Los Angeles air and a star of syndicated radio in the 1980s, spurned Blackwell's entreaties to play "Summertime," which its makers thought they had custom-tailored to fit white fashion, for their throwaway goods on the other side. Kasem saturated his nightly broadcasts with "You Send Me"; within a week the adolescent population of Detroit lay at Sam Cooke's feet. Other important white stations in other big markets snapped to attention.

Within two weeks "You Send Me" was Number 3 on *Billboard*'s pop charts, and the major labels defended their positions in their usual way—by counterattacking. A barrage of cover versions of Cooke's song rained down on Blackwell, aiming to quickly seal off his incursion and then to attrit any profits taken at their expense.

Typically, cover versions by white singers on major labels sold three to four times as many records as the black originals. The careers of such as Teresa Brewer and Pat Boone were entirely made of these covers. Boone's record company reportedly lubricated the marketplace with seventy thousand free copies of each of his records. Most of them were given away to be resold and so were fungibles exchanged for airplay and favorable handling by distributors.

But "You Send Me" blindsided the marketplace with such breath-stopping force, the skirmish was over and the prize already snatched before Blackwell could be outflanked. If they hadn't missed the point of "You Send Me," fewer in the industry would have bothered trying to fool even brand-new consumers of genuine articles with an old-fashioned bait-and-switch. The phenomenon was not about the song but the singer. Record companies had hundreds under contract who could sing "Mary Had a Little Lamb," but none who could sing Sam Cooke's version of it.

So far the big record companies had slept through most of the whirl-wind development of kids into a discrete and self-sustaining market to which radio was already catering so lavishly by 1957 that it was possible for an unknown black act on a tiny label to directly engage, as Sam Cooke had, the buyers of nearly two million records. Cover versions of black records by white singers started as a segregated marketplace's last defense against miscegenating impulses in American popular culture.

By the early 1950s covers had become a profit center for the six major companies—Columbia, RCA, Capitol, Decca, Mercury, and MGM. Their last-ditch function was to try to make music that kids liked palatable to their parents. Even as pop music's reformation inflamed the burning America's young masses had for their own new gospel into a blaze that had begun to consume old show-business dogmas, the industry's establishment still went to church in Las Vegas.

When kids bum-rushed the pop music marketplace in the mid-1950s they rumbled so fast and heavily, they set off a seismic shudder. Kids became a market before the record industry had even considered them a market segment. In their business there had never before been such an unforeseen class of white consumers. When the industry discovered the shadow nation of Aframerica in 1921, it was like found money in the street; this new crowd was inside their emporium knocking over market stalls and display tables in their milling around, displacing old customers in their raucous urgency to be served.

The film *Blackboard Jungle,* which came out in 1955, turned into the firstborn of the kind of youth-culture-event movie that sells its soundtrack by the truckload—in this instance a song called "Rock Around the Clock"—and becomes stuff of which generational identities are formed. Before too long, during the first six months of 1957, a former radio executive in Los Angeles named Lew Chudd would be selling teenagers $3 million worth of Fats Domino and Ricky Nelson records.

The major record companies were caught short with the wrong inventory. The suppliers of their goods were geared to making albums for adults; all of a sudden a third of the whole business was being done in single records—the kind kids and Negroes bought. Since white kids hadn't yet begun to make much music of their own and the big companies didn't have much on hand these new customers wanted to buy, most of what they bought had to come from other sources of supply.

The quickest-reflexed of the small entrepreneurs like Art Rupe who controlled the flow of product to the Negro market began adapting what they made into goods white kids wanted to buy, then delivered what the big companies didn't yet have on hand to sell. In 1953, under the noses of the established music business, $15 million worth of black records were sold. By 1955 black popular music—now designated rhythm and blues—had become a $25-million-a-year business; according to *Variety,* the record industry had gone "R and B crazy."[9]

Once they found these flavors, the new consumers of pop music were disinclined to accept substitutes. So last year's inventory of rip-and-run cover versions became instant artifacts discarded behind a business establishment that was half-dazed and clambering as fast as it could toward light up ahead, trying not to be caught on the wrong side of history. The major labels would still be able to buy their shares of the market; but they would now have to compete with one another more than ever before to buy talent that could deliver sales, or to purchase goods from straitened independent contractors and resell them. A part of their old system was gone.

If phenomenal payoffs from the lightning-struck successes of Fats Domino, Little Richard, Chuck Berry, and now Sam Cooke were changing the rules of engagement in the business of popular music, these still pertained far less to relationships between labor and capital—which were mostly subject to rules of proprietary convenience—than to keeping an orderly coexistence among those who owned the means of production. These ranks now included proliferating upstarts like Rupe who, because they were doing a fifth of their industry's business, had brand-new licenses to be taken seriously.

Those like him were used to playing against one another for relatively small stakes on the fringes of the big game. Once "You Send Me" sold most of 1.7 million copies to white kids, Rupe was prepared to get contentious about what he'd given away in his deal with Blackwell and fiercely protective of what he hadn't. Cooke maneuvered to move his song out of the way of Rupe's half-interest in its publishing rights. Blackwell busied himself hunting for the uncrossed "t" that might break his contract with Keen. The two partners in Keen Records began disputing the terms of their oral agreement. It's a rare windfall that is discovered far from the debris it scattered in its coming. This is another reason good lawyers are free enterprise's only permanent working class.

Catching a moment in the music business like Cooke's in the fall of 1957 is more like holding the winning ticket in one of those telephone-number-sized lottery drawings than it ought to be. However much it is the product of intention, such an event rarely occurs but when circumstances are aligned in a way that produces a happy accident. One difference is that the kind of winning ticket Cooke drew can encourage its holder to believe that his good fortune rather more confirms God's good judgment than His unearned favor. Within a month of its release "You Send Me" was Number 1 on the pop charts, more popular among white people at that moment than "Jailhouse Rock" or "Wake Up Little Susie." Cooke said he felt as if he were one of those "Cinderella singers like Elvis Presley."

But how a fairy tale spun of such trifling stuff as "You Send Me" ever came true is not easy to figure. However wistful and innocent it contrived to be—and sweetly sung—the song itself justified the official culture's disdain for the quality of music being sold to children, and earned the misgivings of the musicians around Cooke who didn't think it worth recording. But these judgments were expressed without reference to the modern school of popular songwriting's insistence that any song's commercial prospects rise or fall on the gripping strength of its "hook."

Cooke fabricated this song out of a single hook—"Darling, you send me"—repeated over and over and over, varying it enough in the performance to keep its sameness from being boring. The resulting effect made it memorable enough to stand out amid radio's aural clutter. He had again proven himself adept at making a virtue of a deficiency that should have been disabling.

It has been said that the best and most commercial of popular songs are instantly engaging. It's easy to imagine the immediate impression the sound of Cooke's voice made on kids who had heard Perry Como and Little Richard but never Rebert Harris. It would have been as vivid as tasting ripe pineapple for the first time. Cooke found that his familiar virtues still applied: what the church audience had identified in his voice as hope and uplift, white adolescents heard as winsome and youthful, and they were drawn, too.

When pictures of black children being jostled and spat upon by venomous crowds on schoolhouse steps in Arkansas had been so lately on everybody's six o'clock news, white kids' instinctive recoil from those images may have provoked in many the first stirrings of an abstracted empathy. Some might even have started thinking then about the possibility of having a black friend. Sam Cooke would have sounded and looked to them—and their parents—like a Negro who was decent, friendly, and safe. And though the whitening agents Blackwell had applied in the production of "You Send Me" were marring, they probably had the effect he intended of reassuring an audience that he expected would be skittish about Negroes and so would prefer to meet one in a familiar setting.

The reaction to "You Send Me" affirmed that Cooke's likability wasn't specific to the public that knew him first; he had disarmed the sons and daughters of Eisenhower's America. In this respect he was distinguishable from other black applicants to play the parts of leading men in entertainments for white girls, like Clyde McPhatter, who beat Cooke onto the pop charts, and Jackie Wilson, who followed fast behind. McPhatter was a nearly great singer—and a heartthrob—but as much as his handlers dressed him as a college boy or junior executive, he couldn't help looking too slick to be harmless, and his voice's inlaid sensuality undermined any appearance of wholesomeness he tried to affect.

Wilson had found his idea of being a star in movie houses, had received his sense of style from the streets of black Detroit, exercised himself in boxing rings, and had an apparent need to arouse women. He was clearly dangerous; in 1958, if a typical white American father looked over his daughter's shoulder while she was watching Jackie Wilson sing "To Be Loved" on *The Dick Clark Show*, his sweat would run cold.

Once Cooke knew that white people liked the abstraction of him that appeared on television, he worked at composing his public surface into an abstraction of the qualities he thought they liked. He was already being chatted up in the antechamber of established white show business—the William Morris Agency—and taking in its administered doses of conventional wisdom: the way to assure his legitimacy—they called it "staying power"—was to get him into the "nonblack market."

The agency baited its offer to represent him with the promise of a spot on *The Ed Sullivan Show;* if that went well, he could have three weeks at the Copacabana, a sort of New York annex of the Las Vegas show-rooms.

In the meantime he had to make a living, and he was finding the show he was part of now not much different from the business he had known before. The money was still to be had on the road, and most of it came one night at a time. Promoters scrambled to capitalize on the raging appetite for rock and roll by sending out as a package as many as a dozen performers of once and future hit records, to wend by bus through itineraries that had them in and out of forty cities in six weeks.

Cooke did the *Sullivan* show in early November, only six months after he kissed the church mothers good-bye in Detroit. He was to go on last—no compliment in those days of live television, because it meant that if the show ran overlong and something had to be cut, his act was presumed to be the most disposable. In fact, the show did run over, and he was abridged in the middle of his first "Darling, yoooouuoooo," which caused consternation among watchdogs of Negro dignity, who were embarrassed for Cooke and denounced Sullivan as disrespectful. This brief public contretemps served to make Cooke better known. As Blackwell put it, "Sam could always step in some shit and come out smelling like a rose."[10]

Nimble-footed as he had gotten along the business climb, Cooke's casualness about discarding women he left behind into his life's untidy corners was making him harder to clean up after. A high school girl in New Orleans turned up pregnant; then, in the afterglow of "You Send Me," another baby of his came to light in Philadelphia, and this aban-doned mother's mother was noisily threatening to extract a retributive share of Cooke's star wages. She had Cooke arrested backstage at the Uptown Theater while he was working there. She cost him $10,000.

It was time finally to dispose of Delores Mohawk Cook; she was bought cheaply, for $10,000, a new car, and a bicycle for her son. Even in today's dollars the price of these settlements makes it evident that in 1957 not many yet believed rock and roll was here to stay. Blackwell, his manager now, did the tidying up and got it done before Cooke was delivered his proceeds from "You Send Me"—$60,000, about as much as the fourth-best-paid player in major league baseball made that year. This meant Sam Cooke and Willie Mays were two of the "n[egro]-richest" twenty-six-year-old lawfully employed black men in the world.

Cooke retook to the road. The big-city stage-show circuit—comprising the Apollo Theater in New York, the Uptown in Philadelphia, the Royal in Baltimore, the Howard in D.C., and the Regal in Chicago—was the top rung in the Negro leagues of the entertainment business. These theaters operated much as they had in the days of black vaudeville. They all had regular shows—the Apollo's changed every week most of the year—featuring five or six acts, four or five times a day, with a movie in between, for four or five days running. Even in 1965 it only cost a dollar and a half to get in and stay all day, sixty-five cents on Saturdays if you came before eleven in the morning.

Until the late mid-1960s, when Motown acts started doing concerts on college campuses, these were still the best paydays available to most workaday black singers, except for the nightclubs in big cities that employed an act at a time on about the same basis as theaters did. In 1958 Cooke was all of a sudden getting $6,000 a week at the Uptown, to the chagrin of Bobby Schiffman of the hard-bitten Apollo management: "I was paying Dinah Washington twenty-five hundred a week . . . Sarah Vaughan twenty-five hundred a week . . . Sam Cooke, six thousand?"[11]

But Dinah Washington and Sarah Vaughan didn't make records that made kids stand shivering outside theaters in lines several blocks long to spend their baby-sitting money to get inside. It wasn't that Schiffman didn't understand this new commercial reality; he was just constitutionally unwilling to accommodate it. Minor men of property, grown accustomed to having their way in the business of other men who had none but their labor, were affronted by the idea of paying Sam Cooke more than they thought anyone like him could ever be worth.

It assaulted a sense of entitlement based on their deeply felt belief that no one like Cooke was ever free of the debt owed to them; after all, if they hadn't been around and willing to underpay him when he had no other prospect of employment, he wouldn't be annoying them now with his unreasonable expectations about getting paid as much as white people in a better grade of show business.

If Art Rupe had ever thought Sam Cooke could amount to this, he would have expected sooner or later to have him poached away by a major label. But the big companies were deep-pocketed and needed to look respectable, and so would have bought his acquiesence. To be slicked out of a windfall by a couple of neophytes and two Negro hirelings was wounding, but at least Rupe could tell himself that nobody else could have seen it coming. Then Cooke added real injury to the insults his dignity had suffered by legally assigning authorship of "You Send Me" to his brother Charles, a ploy meant to capture Rupe's contractual share of the publishing revenues. Rupe went to court.

A federal judge wrinkled his nose at the coarse business practices he found were Rupe's standard and awarded him merely $10,000 and the rights to any of Cooke's work he already had on tape. He was made to relinquish all other claims and release Cooke from the songwriting contract he'd signed when he was twenty. As soon as it ended, both parties to this lawsuit released new Sam Cooke records, and as banal as both were, they sold broadly enough to keep him on television, which led to his new William Morris agent getting him booked into the Copa.

Cooke's debacle at the Copacabana exposed Blackwell's short-comings as much as his own. Cooke was stung—somebody should have known better than to let him overreach, and whoever left his vulnerable hand unprotected in its outstretch bore responsibility when he drew back a nub. He nursed his hurts with reliable ameliorators. He sent for an old friend, Roy Crain, to renew their traveling companionship as Cooke's road manager.

Crain was overwhelmed by an offer of $250 a week, more than he had been accustomed to in twenty years of Soul Stirring. Then Cooke went back on the road, enlisting in a drugstore magnate's "million dollar package," a caravan of nineteen performers of rock and roll trundling from city to city across much of America. At each stop he would engage in another of a series of quick encounters with his new public.

These were shared by so many others that each act did only one or two songs—maybe three, if they had two recent hits and a record out now, which probably meant they were closing the show. Cooke discovered that it would be a long time before he ever again heard someone in an audience express his appreciation of a long-drawn note of unspeakable sweetness, or a phrase bent artfully into an unexpected shape, by exclaiming, "Take your time, son."

These shows had the manic pace of period radio, and it was the uncomplicated objective of their participants to make performances closely conform to the records their audiences had come to attach faces to. There was no use here for the skills admired in the "deep," gut-twisting singers of his former workplaces; these white kids had backward reactions, shrieking through the fast songs and sitting restively during the slow ones.

Much as he knew he needed this work, and appreciative of its higher pay scale, however consoling for him its familiar rhythms, Cooke must still have found being turned again into migrant labor deflating enough to have his mind crossed, on those long bus rides, by the thought that if he had managed his affairs without benefit of anyone else's counsel, he'd have been no worse off. And somewhere early in this retreat from the Copa, Cooke probably decided Blackwell had to go.

Irving Feld's "Biggest Show of Stars" was one of two rock-and-roll packages circulating in the spring of 1958, and when a white girl under Alan Freed's rival auspices jumped up onstage in Boston and by every appearance abandoned her loins to the child-star Frankie Lymon in a simulated two-stroke grind, the reaction from antimiscegenists was immediate, loud, and scathing. Of course, decrying the licentiousness of Negro culture as socially corruptive was hardly original to Eisenhower's America.

Since 1804, when the landfall in New Orleans of French colonials displaced from Haiti by a revolution of their slaves infected mainland America with their exotic strain of racial corruption, white people who lived among Negroes were as worried about keeping the miscegenational impulse from undermining the basis of their social control as they were nervous about slave revolts. Brutal as they often were as enslavers of Negroes, Haiti's Euro-Caribbean exiles were also carriers of a tradition of laxity in keeping the subordinate species at a proper remove from its betters. The miscegenational impulse in Haiti was so irrepressible that after 150 years of administering its island plantation, the government had to certify 128 distinct grades and types of racial alloy to distinguish among its subjects precisely enough to assign each their proper weight and value.

More than a century later an outbreak of "jungle" fever in the popular American culture of the 1920s was suppressed by the hardships of the next decade, and then by the onset of the war, until zoot suits became a ghetto fashion early in the 1940s. So gaudy a display of disreputable style was taken in those austere times as a blatant expression of disdain for the patriotic duty these young men seemed so visibly to be shirking.

The government banned zoot suits in 1942, on the grounds that any garment requiring so much cloth flouted its efforts at conserving resources in a time of war. This had the effect of stimulating an urban cottage industry in bootleg suit-making. Its patrons included many white adolescents who were attracted by the music, dance, language, and pose of which the zoot suit was emblematic. These were the earliest young white imitators of a black street fashion.

In July 1943 it was reported that "zooters and jitterbugs," mostly white, "stormed" the Paramount Theater to get at trumpeter Harry James. That summer off-duty servicemen, suborned by police, riotously attacked black and brown zoot-suit wearers in Los Angeles, Chicago, and Detroit. Criminalizing the zoot suit created America's first official class of delinquent youth and a small auxiliary of middle-class white teenagers whose Negro leanings were implicitly rejectionist. This phenomenon prefigured the larger problem alarmed antimiscegenationists now felt they were contending with in the Negro-tainted youth culture of the late 1950s.

When that decade was still new, Alan Freed had stumbled onto his early discernment of an aborning teen spirit by playing black music on white radio stations in Ohio and finding kids so thirsty for more, they imagined him a hero for supplying it to them. He knew then that he had located among his adolescent listeners an urgent demand for music that their parents wouldn't say grace over.

He sensed before most others did how central radio was to the culture these kids were forming, how fast and far it would spread, and how big the market could be that served its appetites. Freed foresaw in this phenomenon commercial possibilities for himself on the scale of the enterprise that Dick Clark later became. Recognizing that music was the most heavily traded commodity on the youth exchange, Freed used the leverage his radio celebrity gave him over anyone hoping to sell records to the young to prosper, albeit briefly, better than most other freebooters of that roguish era. Starting with no other capital but himself, by 1958 Freed had amassed some power in the fastest-growing part of the music business. But the scandal in Boston stopped him cold and began his quick and irreversible decline.

This nasty skirmish in the generational conflict for which the 1960s became famous was fought in the 1950s, while congressional show trials of offenders against the American way were television fare, and organized Negro assertion was in its early days. As the lawyer for the Songwriters Protective Association read his testimony into the record of Senator John Pastore's Communications Subcommitee in the late spring of 1958, only the senator himself was present to hear its condemnation of a contemporary teen anthem called "Yakety Yak."[12]

Pastore stayed the hand that held the tarring brush to gently aver that his own as-yet-uncorrupted daughter loved that song. This time, in their reflexive eagerness to impugn Negroes, conservators of the official culture had rebuked their own children. Sharing the brunt of polite society's scorn established a point of identification between these two troublesome classes, which would have implications for both the history and the cultural commerce of the next decade.

When Alan Freed's scandal broke, the heat from it was so searing that the other big rock-and-roll show in wide circulation withered, too. Public anxieties about racially mixed young audiences were inflamed, and local politicians and police invoked public safety in suppressing assemblies of large, integrated, mostly teenage crowds. This left the company that Irving Feld had mounted to hobble back in from the road, and

Cooke decamped in Los Angeles to attend to making hit records. He was circumventing the publishing contract he'd signed with Keen, as he had with Rupe, by ascribing to others authorship of the songs he wrote and recorded.

Leroy Crume remembers being importuned by Cooke to lend him his name. He was told that if he agreed, he'd better be reconciled to the arrangement's single immutable condition: "I want my fucking money," Cooke had said. Cooke had already gone once around this block and was resolved never again to countenance another Art Rupe "messing with [his] money." Years after he was ridden off his claim, Rupe's anger was unabated: Cooke was "arrogant, avaricious, and willing to compromise ethical behavior," he told an interviewer.[13]

But while Cooke recognized the commercial necessity of keeping the general good opinion of white people, he was past caring about the opinions of the white men who thought of their proprietary interests in him as a lien on his idea that he, too, could go into the Sam Cooke business. "Arrogant," after all, was just a white man's way of saying "new Negro."

Blackwell had negotiated Cooke's deal with Keen Records. He assured Cooke it entitled him to a share of the profits from publishing his songs, although it hadn't. Now Blackwell was telling Cooke that the owners of Keen Records planned to give him 20 percent of their company, even as he was having trouble of his own getting them to pay royalties he was owed. J. W. Alexander, who had superseded Blackwell's influence in Cooke's affairs, discovered while he was looking over Art Rupe's shoulder that publishing was the closest to permanent wealth in the record business, akin to owning real estate. He had quietly set up his own publishing company, Kags Music. Cooke became his partner early in 1959.

By then Cooke was past needing Blackwell in the recording studio. Blackwell was nominally Cooke's producer, but after he contracted for studio time and hired musicians and background singers, Cooke did most of the work of recording himself. He didn't read or write music, so he had arranger Rene Hall transcribe for him: "all the arrangements we did were Sam's . . . he knew, note for note, exactly what his orchestrations would sound like before he even went into the studio." And then he would direct the musicians to give him what he wanted by word, gesture, and vocalized example. After eight years of feeling his way, Cooke had become an accomplished studio technician.

He encircled himself with a small group of old and newer loyalists: Alexander, his closest adviser and business partner; Crain, his first vocal coach and longest fellow traveler; Cliff White, his accompanist and de facto music director; and Rene Hall, his technical adviser and house arranger. Then he reached back to Chicago for Barbara Campbell and their eight-year-old daughter. Cooke had amicably neglected them for years, but then he often cared most about people once they were part of his past.

When Delores Mohawk Cook killed herself in the car he had settled on her, he was stricken. He left a job in Miami and flew into Fresno to be with her family. He paid for her funeral, overrun though it was by a badgering crowd that came to see him. A couple of months later he and Barbara were married. They honeymooned in Chicago; for him the hometown he so infrequently visited in those days would seem a destination sentimental enough for this occasion.

By the fall of '59, regrouped and fortified, Cooke was moving to cut himself loose from both Blackwell and Keen Records. Outside Cooke's small circle now, Blackwell—the ostensible manager—was increasingly without a function. Cooke told him he'd decided to change horses. "The doors out there are hard to get through," Blackwell remembered him saying. "And you and I [are] gonna have problems getting through them. I can get through those doors if you let me go. And . . . no sooner than I get through them, I'll come back and get you."[14]

This fragment of dialogue is probably a reconstruction from Blackwell's memory of one of those one-way hard conversations that its object only half-hears as his mind leapfrogs the spoken words to begin weighing their consequences. Still, these are lines from a speech delivered by Sam Cooke as the character Sam Cooke in the movie of Sam Cooke's life. They sound rehearsed, perhaps as a pastime on the bus rides he'd lately finished, part of the dialogue in imagined scenarios he played inside his head against the serial backdrops flickering past his window.

But even if Cooke's words to Blackwell were accurately reported only in their meaning, they offer a glimpse of how confident he had become that he could run his course. By mismanaging their affairs at the Copa, Blackwell had forfeited his claim on Cooke's sentiment. This made it easier for Cooke to conclude, in an unsentimental appraisal of his prospects, that he'd be better off having white men around to deal for him with other white men.

His effort to reassure Blackwell was just mannerly punctuation at the end of the blow-off. Bumps Blackwell tipped his hat and walked away, knowing damn well Cooke wouldn't be coming back but to visit. Breaking his contract with Keen proved easy; the label owed Cooke $30,000 it couldn't pay. Cooke brought suit, and an ensuing audit disclosed other stains on Keen's account books. He was unencumbered before Christmas and being romanced by two major labels and Atlantic Records, the most successful of the independents.

5. Both Ends Against the Middle

In 1959, when Sam Cooke and Atlantic Records were sniffing each other, the company just had righted itself after a stumble taken when the marketplace suddenly shifted again underfoot. If Cooke had attached himself to Atlantic then, he would have engaged men there who thought they knew more than anyone about selling black music to white kids. Two sons of the Turkish ambassador, Ahmet and Nesuhi Ertegun, started Atlantic Records in 1949 with Herb Abramson, an experienced young rough-and-tumbler in the race-record business.

They were lucky to stagger quickly to their feet by making shrewd uses of what others brought them. Then they figured out, as Ahmet put it, that "all the white kids could tolerate was watered-down blues." This realization had disclosed a business plan.

Along with Jerry Wexler, the former song-plugger and writer for music-trade papers who soon replaced Abramson as the company's third principal, the Erteguns were enthusiasts of black music who had in younger days forayed into neighborhoods where they didn't belong to buy records their parents thought beneath their attention. Selling black music connected them to creating it to a degree only before possible in their imaginations.

Atlantic's founders proved sound and sensitive practioners of their chosen craft. They were men of reliable instincts about black popular music—and connoisseurs' tastes—who were never wholly reconciled to the small sacrifices of both that were regularly required in producing the hit records their company needed to survive. The Erteguns and Wexler intruded notions of art into a commercial environment like a bazaar in the Baghdad of Ali Baba's forty thieves.

Ahmet once suggested to Art Rupe that he was lucky to have started in Los Angeles and smart to have colonized New Orleans, places where the things he wanted came naturally to musicians, while Atlantic had to use New York jazzmen and make them copy styles indigenous else-where. If Rupe had only to trust in found objects to unfold the authen-tic style for him, Ertegun had first to locate the elements of authenticity he needed for commercial purposes and then re-create them by con-sciously subverting the sophistication native to his own environment.

In 1958, with business slack and its market skittish, Atlantic imported the writing/production team of Jerry Lieber and Mike Stoller from California. Not much older than the kids who bought their records, these men were among the first to locate the pop market's new solid ground at a time when everyone in the rock-and-roll business was trying to find it. After Lieber and Stoller left to work for themselves, Atlantic stayed profitable by its adaptive use of the New York song mills' most skilled hands. By the end of its first decade, Atlantic was at the head of the postwar class of start-up record companies.

The next phase of Atlantic's development—which lasted until Ahmet succeeded in taking the enterprise global—would be dominated by Jerry Wexler, whose reputation as a producer was made with Ray Charles's rise and later brought close to a small legend's size by his asso-ciation with Aretha Franklin. The influences Wexler might have exerted on Cooke's recording career are only worth a moment's con-sideration, for when they had a chance of working together, the singer demurred.

Atlantic's insistence on owning the publishing rights to his songs was too reminiscent of prior restraints not to stoke his smoldering wari-ness of independent record companies. Cooke also noted the hard fall that Clyde McPhatter had taken so soon after making six Top Ten records for Atlantic in three years.

Atlantic may have run its establishment with more gentility than other like-size stakeholders in the record game, but they all played by the same whorehouse rules. Ruth Brown, its first-risen star, had carried the company on her back in the early 1950s and was so ungraced by her success that twenty-five years later she was working as a live-in maid. Ahmet Ertegun, it seems, would have organized a benefit for Ruth Brown before he would volunteer to her an honest accounting of royalties.

She once illuminated the distinction between the proprietors of Atlantic and those of other labels specializing in black music, who brought to their dealings with the creators and consumers of the records they sold an equal measure of contempt. She said that whenever you got involved in business with one of the era's remorseless predators, like Morris Levy of Roulette Records—who suggested that the contractees he routinely violated should all "go to England if [they] want royalties"—you expected to be raped. In effect, her encounter with Ahmet, she had decided, was like a date rape.[1] Sam Cooke presumed as much: "I don't care what the man promises," he told a friend, "he'll steal it back someway."

It's also true that Cooke couldn't conceive of how any record company that concerned itself primarily with black music would fit into his plans. RCA Victor, big and stodgy, bought its sizable slice of the youth market when it purchased Elvis Presley from a Tennessee record man who was too new at his business to suspect that he might have fattened a frog for a snake. Within a year Presley sold ten million single records and 300,000 copies of his first album.

This was important to RCA because it was trying to convert the young into buyers of long-playing albums, as part of its defense against the encroachments of small business. Albums cost $3.98 at a time when single records were selling for close to a dollar; long-playing records cost more to make, sold fewer copies than singles, and had a thinner profit yield on each unit sold. The disparity between the cash return to a manufacturer on individual album and single sales was so slight, it didn't make sense for small labels to bring albums to market.

The sooner major companies like RCA could make selling albums a business everyone in their industry had to get into, the faster they could rid it of all but the handful of independents like Atlantic able to compete on that basis. Moreover, since the grassroots businessmen who made up the ad hoc distribution network that had abetted the independents' rise made more money from sales of single records, they would face the same problem as small labels.

By making this single market adjustment, the major labels could clear away the underbrush—the many local distributors who were obstacles to expanding their control of the business. They calculated that once order was restored to the marketplace, their advantages of scale would keep grinding away at the capacities of the remaining independents until it became more prudent for them to sell out than go on competing. Sales of single records were off by a third in 1959; the glut of wishful youth-market profiteers meant more records than ever were being produced, even though there was scarcely any music around that lots of white kids felt impelled to buy.

A full belly had inclined RCA toward relying too much on plucking the choicest performers at the top of the specialty genres, repackaging them for mass consumption, and using its considerable throw weight in the marketplace to create the mometum to carry sales. The big companies could afford to be less nimble in their maneuvering; in 1956 Capitol Records, which had been Cooke's other unsuccessful suitor, spurred a 33 percent increase in its profits by selling six million copies of only three titles.[2] Eventually complacency would become costlier for the major labels, but throughout the 1950s they were mostly spared the trouble and expense of having to spot and develop talent.

In 1959 RCA had signed Jessie Belvin—the sweet-singing prince of young black Los Angeles and another Rupe alumnus made good—as a pop balladeer, but his life was soon taken in the Cadillac he wrecked five miles south of Hope, Arkansas, straining to make it to his next job on time. Harry Belafonte was the only speckle left on RCA's monochromatic roster of artists.

RCA's overture to Cooke was made by Hugo Peretti and Luigi Creatore, two cousins whom the company had set up with a prototype of the modern independent production deal on the strength of their oversight of a lucrative string of cover records that nearly drove Laverne Baker crazy with bitterness and needlessly prolonged the recording career of Georgia Gibbs; and then, of ten variously sized hits by an ex-hillbilly singer named Jimmie Rodgers. These last were made for Roulette Records, which the cousins started with Morris Levy, whose silent partner was the Genovese crime family of New York.

Nothing Hugo and Luigi had done in the first nine months of their association with RCA justified the company's investment, until in early 1959 they caught a hit single with Della Reese, a lapsed Meditation Singer from Detroit long gone to nightclub singing in cocktail dresses. They dangled their pop credentials in front of Cooke, and $100,000, and signed him before his free agency had aged even a month.

Of course, RCA hadn't made alliances of any use to Cooke on the black side of the business, but he may have regarded its preoccupation with the pop charts as an asset. Cooke assumed he wouldn't need help from a big label to sell records to black people, and would have spotted Hugo and Luigi for dilettantish hustlers who were unstrenuously prospecting for a second act at RCA crowd-pleasing enough to get their contract renewed. So after they did their worst, it seemed likely that languor and creeping desperation would ultimately impel them to relinquish to him their creative command.

Their worst was done immediately: a record called "Teenage Sonata," swirling with strings and laden with banal rococo effects of the sort thought to certify "good music" by these two grade-repeaters in the school that graduated Montovani. Hugo and Luigi were prone to the style of overdecoration whose examples were available in display windows of furniture stores around old urban Italian-American neighborhoods.

Not even Sam Cooke could overcome the weight of such ornate clutter as these hacks could put in his way. His agent was so appalled, he offered to try getting Cooke out of his contract. "No," Cooke countered. ". . . Let [the record] die, and then you go in and say, 'See, you can't produce Sam Cooke.'"[3] As if to confirm his foregone conclusion, RCA released another dire single, sorrier than the first.

Yet again an accidental turn in the right direction intervened along the path of Cooke's career. Keen Records, hoping to recoup what it could, issued one of the songs he'd left behind just in time to redeem his disappointing RCA debut. "Wonderful World" was an unvarnished demo tape that was eased into the marketplace when nobody was around to improve it. It was an unspoiled two minutes and change of the best of Sam Cooke as both a singer and a writer of popular song. Its arrangement and instrumentation were folk-song spare, the cleanest he'd sung since Soul Stirrers days. Its tempo was dead in the pocket of Cooke's groove, a half step slower than "Jesus Gave Me Water."

Cooke then wrote and produced "Chain Gang" for RCA, in which he used background voices to simulate the synchronized grunts of black convict labor slinging nine-pound steel by a Georgia roadside. This catchy device helped make "Chain Gang" into singsong suitable for sing-along—a congenial companion to "setting-up" exercises at a summer camp or a ladies' gym—and thus a commercial triumph. Its success brought a quick end to any misconceptions Hugo and Luigi had, or RCA, about who was going to be in charge of Sam Cooke.

"I want to sing for my people," Cooke told Luigi Creatore, who shrugged in reply, because as a practical matter he didn't know what that meant different from what Cooke was already doing; he and his cousin were disposed to think of as "their people" anyone who bought a record that paid them royalties. Aiming himself at the white youth market, and his longer-range ambitions at legitimate show business, Cooke as much as determined a trajectory that would land him among white kids and black adults. His commitment to making music that white teenagers would buy cost him currency with their black counterparts.

Pervis Spann, a disk jockey in Chicago in the early 1960s who booked shows into the Regal, noted that "if [he] put Sam Cooke on, black kids weren't gonna break down the doors to get to him."[4] While Cooke engaged most black audiences in grown-up venues like theaters and nightclubs, he was packaged and sold to whites as an item in the boys' and junior-miss departments, part of an inventory that also included Bobby Rydell, Dion and the Belmonts, and Duane Eddy.

As race was becoming America's most closely observed social issue and television made a nation of watchers, by the late 1950s most of

Aframerica resettled outside the South was coming to understand the drama being staged there as an unfolding referendum on all their rights of inclusion. From the first, for many of them the campaign against legal segregation in the South became a living chapter in their national epic. For more than a hundred years the assumptions of assimilationists had shaped the way most Aframericans thought about their affairs of state. Now, with their symbolic petition for redress of old-country oppressions in the hands of the established black church, the Afro-Christian themes of deliverance and redemption were air under the wings of grassroots aspirations.

The black press found in Cooke's story another that it could use to venerate white-certified celebrity and "Negro firsts." Middle Aframerica saw, from his wedding pictures in *Sepia* and his house pictures in *Ebony*, that on Cooke the trappings of anointment were suavely worn and carried lightly. These, and appearances on television, confirmed his look of raised-proper, well-churched, southern-bottomed urbanity that seemed to them an embodiment of some part of the best in their truest selves.

From 1959 on Cooke divided his professional self between RCA and the record company called SAR—for Sam, Alex, and Roy—that grew out of his partnership with Alexander. On the available evidence, Cooke believed himself both lucky and smart and was thus emboldened to launch himself into the record business at a precarious time. The pop music business had taken pause; the youth market was in the post-Presley doldrums, it appetites lethargic and unpredictable.

Television was eating away at movie profits, and so film studios were going into the record business. The industry was overproducing single records—a hundred a week were coming out, nearly five thousand a year in the late 1950s, when only between 5 and 10 percent of them ever sold more than 100,000 copies.[5]

This thicket of releases revealed few discernible trends for an industry to follow that was accustomed to being led. When a record was spoken of as being successful in 1959, it was meant that at least 200,000 copies had been sold, a threshold that was a fifth as high as it had been only a couple of years earlier. People in the record industry weren't sure whether they were now permanently in the business of catering to the young and, if they were, of what next to serve.

The established music industry used this lull in the tide pulling toward the young to remind broadcasters that in their energetic pandering to "the pre-shave crowds that make up twelve percent of the country's population and zero percent of its buying power," they disregarded the adults who bought the albums that still comprised 65 percent of their business. At the same time, because more of the youth market than big labels wanted to lose belonged to the small operators who'd beaten them into to it, the industry tried to find alternatives to black music and its white derivatives that kids wanted to buy.

In effect, the industrial oligarchs were tacitly allied with the antimiscegenists who ruined Alan Freed, pressured national advertisers to withdraw from radio stations that played rock and roll, and prodded Congress to investigate "payola," the heretofore legal—and democratic—practice of bribing disk jockeys to play records. Beginning in the late 1950s for several years the major labels concertedly pushed folk music, trying to make a fashion of it among the young. If they could, it would give them more control of the pop market at a time when 60 percent of the records being played on Top Forty radio were independent productions.

The segmented design and high pulse rate of mass-market radio discriminated in favor of playing single records, and by the mid-1950s radio had outstripped jukeboxes to become the popular-music industry's billboard for advertising its sales inventory. In the early 1950s jukebox operators had created most consumer interest in single records; by late in the decade it was radio programmers. The so-called Top Forty radio format emerged in 1949; stations that used it played records chosen from a small pool of those they certified as popular or about to become popular.

Of the records that were played, ten or so aired far more often than others. Within ten years of its introduction the Top Forty format was being used to program the music on a majority of the nation's 4,500 commercial radio stations. Until FM rearranged radio in the early 1970s, all the products intended for the record industry's biggest marketplace were poured over a small funnel that conducted only a trickle of them into the earshot of most consumers. The nationalizing of *American Bandstand* in 1957—teenage dance shows were the primitive form of contemporary video radio—assured that the universe of pop music on television would be smaller even than radio's.

Rather than trying to create a label full-blown, most who were in Cooke's position of finding their way into the record business in 1959 would have become independent producers. This was Berry Gordy's occupation at the time—making finished goods to sell to bigger companies to resell on their own labels. A lusher variant of the same practice, available only to the in-demand, was Lieber and Stoller's, who now comprised a two-man firm of independent contractors for expensive hire by record companies on a project basis. Don Kirschner built up a successful production house in New York, staffed by Brill Building allstars, and sold it to Columbia Records in the early 1960s for several million dollars. Hugo and Luigi had their boutique inside RCA.

These operations were all set up as hedges against a thinly bankrolled record producer getting too near the perilous risks of distribution and sales. But J. W. Alexander had cobbled together a network of thirty-eight small distributors. Operating at first from an office in his briefcase, Alexander and Cooke were audacious to think they could chew as much of the whole hog as they undertook to swallow.

In his approach to the marketplace Cooke's working premise refigured Ahmet Ertegun's older formulation about selling black music in the youth market, into "all the white kids could tolerate was watered-down gospel."[6] This was true as far as it went, and its implications far-reaching. Over the next decade others who sowed by the light of this insight would reap plenty; Cooke's problem was in having both the opportunity and means to follow his idea to its logical conclusion.

For better or worse, the lifetime output of SAR Records, and Derby—the companion label started as a lodgment for his crossover line—would be chiefly of Cooke's design and would bear the singular

impress of his artistic sensibilities. He was the producer of nearly everything his labels made. As a record producer, he was the kind of director
who gives actors line readings.

"Some of the songs he wrote and some he didn't," the singer Bobby
Womack recalled, "but if he was the producer he was definitely going
to tell you how to sing it." In these matters Cooke had the hardest of
heads, being an entrepreneur who thought he had a better idea.[7]

Sam Cooke's first recruits to SAR Records were the Soul Stirrers,
whose contract with Art Rupe had lapsed; Cooke talked them out of a
better deal with Vee-Jay Records by selling them his dream of popular-
izing gospel music, convincing his former colleagues to forgo the cash
inducements others offered and throw in with him. His next recruit was
Kylo Turner of the Pilgrim Travelers. Cooke raised eyebrows and some
ire by circulating among gospel singers, trying to tempt others onto the
path he'd taken.

His example was already making plenty of them twitchy. Clarence
Fountain, lead singer of the Five Blind Boys of Alabama, to whom Sam
once read hours of cowboy novels when they rode together in the Specialty package tours, claimed Cooke had brandished a fat roll of cash at
him and said, "This is my God now." This tale, like others, is probably
apocryphal, as it enacts what Cooke's mere presence bespoke to gospel
singers whose age and disposition disabled their prospects of ever getting into the youth business themselves. But Cooke was also known as
the old school's most generous alumnus; Julius Cheeks said Cooke gave
him "the first five-hundred-dollar bill [he] ever saw."

For years Rebert Harris rehearsed a story about Sam Cooke being
driven from the stage in tears at a Soul Stirrers reunion by an angry
crowd catcalling, "Get that blues singer down." In fact, for as long as he
lived, Cooke periodically revisited gospel audiences in the company of
the Soul Stirrers, and these occasions were triumphal. J. W. Alexander
said Cooke "killed the house" when he made an impromptu appearance with the Soul Stirrers on a Los Angeles stage in the fall of 1960.

On the last night of 1962 Cooke sang with the group as an advertised "special guest" on a gospel program in Newark, and his star turn "took" the show.

The church mothers still loved him as they would a son who had gone away and made them proud, and whenever he came home, he always delighted them by making plain that no matter how high he rose, he would never be above them. But after he was gone, legends arose to cast him to the devout as a cautionary example of the biblical injunction against gaining the world at the expense of their souls.

SAR Records released fifty-eight singles and five albums in five years, an impressive output for an operation run on a shoestring. Of the records Sam Cooke made with his own money on his own time, almost a third were gospel, and three-quarters involved professional singers of sacred song, either active or fallen away. Of the two or three handfuls of these that were good, and the several that were very good, all were gospel records or made with gospel singers lately unfrocked.

In many respects the first SAR release was its best, a record by the Soul Stirrers called "Stand By Me Father," featuring the man who'd replaced Cooke as their lead singer. Johnnie Taylor, from West Memphis—the Arkansas side of the river—had been around Chicago long enough to have also taken Cooke's place in the Highway QCs. He made his way by hiring out to quartets Cooke had just vacated because he was so able an approximator of his predecessor's style.

"Stand By Me Father" is a characteristic Sam Cooke gospel composition, lightly shaded with pop undertones and sung in imitation of Cooke's phrasing by a singer with a grittier voice. It contains a breathtaking moment wherein Taylor flexes his virtuosity in Cooke's own repertoire of stylistic effects by sucking up the phrase "Hebrew-childrenbeeninafire" like a man inhaling a strand of spaghetti. "Stand By Me Father" accomplished what Cooke and Alexander intended in their mingling of the sacred and secular, which made it a prophetic piece of black popular music.

The Soul Stirrers were Cooke's chemistry set. The fifteen records they made on SAR were a laboratory in which he tinkered with combinations of elements, trying to mix them in proportions that would make his formula work. They were recorded lovingly in Chicago and Los Angeles, at upscale facilities with full complements of the best local studio musicians. It is unlikely that gospel songs intended for their regular customers were ever before recorded with strings and flute, or with a calypso beat, or Latin inflections.

Cooke perceived Taylor as a follower in his footsteps and so first ran him over ground that he had himself lately covered; Taylor's early recordings produced by Cooke were of songs Cooke wrote and instructed him how to sing. The most noticeable of these, "Rome (Wasn't Built in a Day)," was a knockoff of "Chain Gang." Toward the end of their five-year association Cooke evidently decided his singer was more suited to the "deep pitiful" songs he hadn't much affinity for, and gave up superimposing his personality on Taylor's style.

Taylor renounced his appropriation of Cooke as soon as he was freed to be himself, roughening up in the manner of Bobby Bland, who'd begun late in the mid-1950s singing the gospel quartet style in a blues context. By 1964 Taylor was writing his own material, and the records he made then began sounding like those that made him a full-fledged star a decade later, when he was known on black radio as the "Memphis wailer." By the mid-1970s Taylor had become as popular in the black South and Southwest as fried food and high school football on Friday nights.

If elements of Cooke's style are imagined as a form of genetic material, the process of Johnnie Taylor's development discloses one pathway taken in their dispersal across the population of singers who emerged in black popular music during the 1960s and 1970s. After Taylor was lifted from the Soul Stirrers, the too-little-remembered Jimmy Outler was chosen to take his place.

Outler's vocal qualities strongly suggested Cooke's, although they were rawer and lacked the original's sinuosity and pure sweetness. Seven years later he was roadkill on the gospel highway—knifed to death over a woman—but in 1960 Jimmy Outler was the prototype of a modern soul singer.

Jerry Wexler thought sweetness a defining element of soul singing and called Sam Cooke "the prophet of the sweet school." On "Listen to the Angels Sing" Outler proved himself the aptest pupil in the master's schoolhouse. Written by Leroy Crume, who had a knack for Cooke's groove, and even though it was a gospel song, "Listen to the Angels" was the best pop record SAR ever made.

It was eerily like another that was written by Curtis Mayfield and recorded by Jerry Butler at about the same time, half a continent away. "He Will Break Your Heart" became a Number 1 record on the rhythm-and-blues charts, superseding "Chain Gang," and a major pop hit. The marketplace may have given "Listen to the Angels" a brief, obscure life and a long interment in memory's graveyard, but Jimmy Outler was the bridge from Cooke to Bobby Womack and uncounted others.

It's hard to know how much Sam Cooke followed the market's fashions and how much he anticipated them; like most others, the chain of cultural influence has circular links. He and Alexander venerated the traditions of gospel music, even as they were prepared to discard those that the company they aspired to keep thought unmodish. But their narrow inclination was to use gospel as the basis of their design and build it out into a form more readily acceptable to consumers who would have thought the original either too alien or too particular to its native context.

Others working on the same premise from the perspective of rootless popularizers saw the treasury of the gospel tradition as just another source of plunder, useful in the creation of whatever music best served to provoke and fulfill common appetites in the broadest possible public. Intimations of the church style in contemporary black music had been discernible for years.

The year after Ray Charles emerged in 1955, James Brown surfaced on record with an incognito gospel performance so strange and stirring, it made an anomalous hit of a formless ballad he'd written called "Please, Please, Please." He'd crossed Brownlee with Louis Jordan and Little Willie John in his singing ever since. In the summer of 1958 Jerry Butler and the Impressions startled an audience that had gone languid in the latter days of doo-wop by home-crafting a solemn ballad that seemed like a church anthem; "For Your Precious Love" sold 150,000 copies in two weeks—900,000 overall—and some observers said they saw the first light of a new day.[8] In 1959, when Berry Gordy was still groping for a handle on the market, he'd patterned "Money" after Ray Charles's profane testimonies and produced his first big hit.

In 1960 the same year wily Ike Turner from Mississippi—a decade removed from having been, at sixteen, a down-south talent scout for the Bihari Brothers of Los Angeles—introduced a female graduate of Tennessee's country church choirs into his tack-hard St. Louis bar band, Bobby Bland—who'd been tutored by Ira Tucker—added several to his string of nine successive Top Ten records by singing a secular strain of gospel blues with a churchy squall that became his signature. By then 40 percent of black Americans no longer lived in the South, though it would have been easy in those days to mistake the remnant for the whole of their tribe.

In the spring of 1961 the Justice Department's first voting rights suit was filed in Alabama, and that summer the most successful of SAR's releases, "Soothe Me" by the Simms Twins—ex–gospel singers from Louisiana whom Cooke had found in Los Angeles—was much a part of the soundtrack of the private lives of people whose civic affairs the Freedom Riders went south to improve. "Soothe Me" had such an archetypal sweet, southern soul groove, it stayed on the airwaves for four months.

After "Soothe Me"'s tide rose so high it spilled over onto the pop charts, Cooke changed the lyrics and lent it to the Soul Stirrers, then remade the song himself. Six years later it was still around for Sam and Dave—whose act was born of the Simms Twins conception—to refresh. By then younger siblings of black kids of the early 1960s who thought Sam Cooke already out of style had become ardent enthusiasts of music descended from his.

By 1961 Jerry Wexler at Atlantic Records had come upon Solomon Burke, a radio preacher in Philadelphia at twelve and a professional gospel singer who crossed over not long after Cooke; Wexler set off Burke's church-inflected voice and delivery with compatible songs and arrangements, and thus began his five-year term as "King of Rock and Soul." Around then the best of New York's pop music makers recognized the melodramatic uses to which they could put gospel singers rough-edged enough, even when smoothened, to cut across the grain of their glossy productions. The earliest conveyors of Burt Bacharach's ingratiating swoops and swirls were Chuck Jackson, an ex–Raspberry Singer, and the like-sounding Lou Johnson, though the songwriter would soon find his chosen instrument in another church singer who had shed from her voice nearly all traces of its former employment.

In late spring of 1962 Philadelphians Don Gardner and Dee Dee Ford used what they borrowed from their hometown's fiery Davis Sisters—the hardest-singing female group in gospel—to climb into the uppermost echelon of the black record charts, alongside "Something's Got a Hold on Me," Etta James's rewarming of Ray Charles and her memories of being in the choir at St. Paul's Baptist Church when she was a girl in Los Angeles. A couple of months before, in Detroit, the former Violinaire Wilson Pickett scorched a song in his closest approximation of Julius Cheeks's fervid style. The hook of "I Found a Love" was a broken-off piece of the black Pentecostal hymn of affirmation called "Yes, Lord." Cooke appropriated Pickett's impassioned yeah-yeaaaaahs for the opening of the most "soulful" of his own compositions, "That's Where It's At," recorded by the Simms Twins later that year.

If, on balance, Cooke seems to have been carried along as much as he was pointing the way, as he moved ahead he did leave behind landmarks that still stand. After "Wonderful World" there was "Sad Mood," in which he proved it possible to sing pop music in darker tones. "Bring It On Home to Me" accomplished in a popular song what Cooke strove for as a writer and producer of gospel music: church feeling without too much flavor of church.

It employed as its hook punctuating snatches of call-and-response between Cooke and Lou Rawls—a veteran of the Pilgrim Travelers and the Chosen Gospel Singers—that were redolent of church. But otherwise this song's sources would seem to come from the deep place where waters mingle from the wellsprings of the distinct musical traditions of white and black southerners. A sensibility originated there that Elvis Presley, who took field trips to Brewster's church in Memphis, shared with Ray Charles, whose lifelong affection for hillbilly singers was owed to the habit he'd made of the Grand Ole Opry when there was nothing else for a backwoods boy of either color to listen to on the radio. In this respect Cooke's "Bring It On Home to Me" defined the feeling if not the form of southern soul music.

Ironically by 1963, while Cooke was festooning the Soul Stirrers with worldly trappings, others made successes following his original blueprint to its exact specifications, transforming gospel hits into popular hits by merely changing a word or two—"God" into "my man," or "Mary" into "baby." The inflow of gospel influences was rippling the mainstream of black popular music. James Brown stopped a show in Cincinnati when he sang a woman out of a balcony while giving his usual performance of "Lost Someone," in which he half-preached and half-crooned and wailed with the abandon of Archie Brownlee.

Applying implements they had learned to use in church to material patterned after styles indigenous there, Wilson Pickett and Garnet Mimms—who sprang from Philadelphia's Norfolk Four and Evening Stars—made hit records of songs about carnal sin and redemption, into which each inserted twenty seconds or so of secularized sermonettes. Pickett's in particular were clothed in church hand-me-downs like "I'll be your leaning post when you're falling down," intoned with a preacherly tremble in his voice.

As skillful as any of the adaptive craftsmen of soul music's formative days was the writer and producer Jerry Ragovoy, who apprenticed in Philadelphia's doo-wop shops in the mid-1950s before graduating to New York. He was of the school of high-drama production then prominent thereabouts. He achieved the effects that were his signature by pounding a hard church piano up under the symphonic sweep of horns and strings, which ebbed and flowed behind used-to-be gospel singers with voices authoritative enough to subdue the orchestral tide. Beginning in 1963, Ragovoy decorated the next four years with some of the era's best records. They featured surpassing performances by undercelebrated singers like Garnet Mimms, Irma Thomas, Lorraine Ellison, Howard Tate, and Freddie Scott.

Early in October the record that replaced Mimms's "Cry Baby" at

Number 1 on the black record charts was "Part Time Love," a gospel-esque blues ballad searingly sung by Little Johnny Taylor, formerly a Mighty Cloud of Joy; the next week his was supplanted by the Impressions' "It's All Right." So for a month and a half in the late fall of 1963, each of the three most popular records in black America was a variety of church-music hybrid.

The historian Taylor Branch has suggested that while "stars of [black popular] music stood with King as examples of the [mysterious] black church . . . they were still ahead of him in crossing over to a mass white audience."[9] While teenagers in Birmingham were beset with dogs and fire hoses and began in April 1963 to fill the local jails in protest, Sam Cooke was on the road, headlining a show that also featured Jerry Butler, Solomon Burke, the Drifters, Dionne Warwick, Esther Phillips, and others, playing to southern audiences that were mostly mixed.

In a period of two and a half months that began in early May, 758 racial demonstrations were reported in 186 American cities and towns. Martin Luther King's appearance in June at a rally in Detroit drew 125,000 people and brought Berry Gordy belly to belly with the spirit of the times. Motown's cohering "sound" was nearly bereft of church, except for tambourines and its lyricists' occasional borrowings from the Afro-Christian vernacular, as when the Four Tops sang, "[Love] feels like fire shut up in my bones." But that summer a song was written for Marvin Gaye that took for its title—and its hook—a preacher's standard aside.

In August television made the March on Washington a national moment. One of its effects, as Branch has noted, was "introduc[ing] King's pulpit rhetoric as a national hymn."[10] "Can I Get a Witness" became a fair-size hit for Gaye in the fall; its season on the radio began a month after four black girls were blown up in a Birmingham church and ended a couple of weeks after Kennedy was shot.

Ten days after the Birmingham church bombing Cooke appeared in New Orleans with Bobby Bland, Little Willie John, and Dion. The local black press reported that "white girls and Negro girls, white boys and Negro boys [were] seated side by side and together whooping it up." A couple of weeks later, trying to register at a white hotel in

Shreveport, Cooke and his traveling party were arrested for disturbing the peace.

The putative offense to good order had been given by a malfunctioning horn on the red Maserati that Charles Cook was driving. His brother Sam had just bought it from Eddie Fisher—a token transfer of wealth from the old show business to the new. The temper of those times assured that the incident would get national press attention and lent Cooke the aura of a sufferer in the cause of his people. For his part, Cooke was chagrined at being thirty-two years old and still exposed to the hazards of the road nine months a year, while Paul Anka was celebrating his twenty-first birthday during a two-week engagement in Las Vegas.

In the spring of 1963, when another road show Cooke was starring in trundled into Philadelphia, he was introduced to an accountant named Allen Klein, who had already acquired his reputation as a finder of lost royalties. He had been employed by a firm routinely retained by music publishers to detect the accounting flimflammeries that record companies were using to shortchange them. It occurred to Klein that if the record industrialists habitually cheated other men of property, they must be true pillagers of their industry's laboring class.

This insight—along with his self-described "ability to think like a thief"—made Klein something of an industrial pioneer.[11] In 1962 he had recovered $100,000 for the singer Bobby Darin from Atlantic Records, then intervened in the contract he'd already signed with another label to get him a better deal. Klein wasn't interested in building an accounting practice, no matter that he had broken ground on a rewarding new specialty. Among men who knew that treasure was buried under their feet but despaired of ever being able to get at it, Klein's talent for extraction seemed like genius.

The accountant ached to be a player in big-league show business. He recognized that the affairs of the youth market's new moneymakers weren't being handled by men who took their clients seriously enough to think their careers could last longer than the day after tomorrow and so might be worth managing as if there were a mutual long-term interest to be served by protecting them from their industry's predations. This left a door unattended through which Klein slipped past the rampart's gate. Once inside he snared Darin by means that became his standard method of seduction.

To open a courtship, he would bring a premature dowry paid in found money. Then he pressed it with tireless charm. He kept sweetening the pitch of his woo with other people's money until he induced a promise of marriage. It was a choreographed bum's rush, staged in three acts.

Allen Klein was one of those permanently hungry young men whose senses were locked into a state of perpetual attunement to the whereabouts of a main chance. The reasons for the midcareer distemper that made Sam Cooke susceptible to him were plain enough. Cooke was road-weary and scarred by its occupational hazards—an almost-life-taking car wreck, his brother's stabbing by an Apollo stagehand, another empty marriage, the public presumption that he was dying of leukemia created by rumors zigzagging across the nation's Negro press and radio—and still he was out there spending eight cents to make every dime. Cooke was feeling his career then as a bigger exercise inside a bigger terrarium than the one he'd outgrown before.

Klein sniffed ripe opportunity in Cooke's discontent. "I want him bad," Klein said of Cooke to the man who introduced them, Douglas "Jocko" Henderson, the greatest disk jockey there ever was and himself a man of more parts than one. Beholding the object of his inflamed desire within range of his touch made Klein's eyes shine and his teeth grit. Cooke, an amateur champion seducer, was about to succumb to a professional gifted enough to one day become notorious.

"When I met Sam," Klein has often said, "he didn't have a dime."[12] Years later Cooke's man at the William Morris Agency shrugged in affirmation of Klein's assertion: "Every artist of his generation was broke . . . except for Presley, everyone was scrambling."[13] Klein bestowed on Cooke 150,000 previously undisclosed dollars that he was owed by RCA and in return was invited to displace Cooke's sitting white manager.

Klein squeezed RCA into sweetening Cooke's standing deal with a fresh $450,000 advanced over four years, then gave it a twist: a corporation was set up to receive the money that RCA paid Cooke. Cooke would accept RCA's payments as a subcontractor of his own company. This was supposed to have tax advantages. The new company was named after the singer's daughter; Tracey Cooke's father was registered as its president.

A ceremonial photograph of Cooke signing his new contract with RCA ran on the cover of the record industry trade paper, *Cash Box*. He managed a smile of the obligatory candlepower. Though he was still raw from the recent death of his toddling son—drowned in the unfenced swimming pool by the driveway crowded with fancy cars along the front of the "plush $100,000 home in Hollywood" and memorialized in his *Ebony* photo spread—the only effects of this injury that others reported were heavier drinking and the onset of a brittler stiffness in his relations with Barbara. But perhaps there was as well a distractedness that was unremarked upon by keepers of his company who are the keepers of his memory now; because as experienced in misuse and as mistrustful of white people as he was, Sam Cooke should have been unplayable, and yet it happened somehow that Tracey Ltd. belonged from the first altogether to Allen Klein. With a check from RCA and a handshake, he'd gotten too deeply into Cooke's pockets to ever be dislodged.

Within six months Klein was in London, blowing up his negotiations with Brian Epstein about using Cooke as an opening act on the Beatles' American tour by suggesting that he should be handling the group's finances. Epstein properly interpreted this comment as Klein's declaration of his intention to poach and concluded their business. Deflected from his main objective, Klein reflexively re-angled his approach toward a secondary target: he acquired the Dave Clark Five on his way out of England. A year and a half later he persuaded the Rolling Stones to cast themselves in the scenario he'd rehearsed with Cooke, using a $1.25 million advance this time to set up a company in their name that was actually owned by Allen Klein.

The Rolling Stones would soon become a franchise valuable enough to make it worthwhile for someone to indemnify the costs incurred in the welter of lawsuits that disentangled them from Klein. In the meantime Klein became the financial helmsman of the "British invasion," further enlisting Herman's Hermits, the Animals, the Yardbirds, the Kinks, and Donovan as clients. He even made off with three of Epstein's Beatles. A relentless climber, Klein stepped from Sam Cooke to the Rolling Stones as surely as they had put their first foot in America on the backs of Bobby Womack and his brother Valentinos, then steadied their purchase by putting the other foot on Don Covay's shoulder.

The youth market that had coalesced in the 1950s was becoming another one altogether within half a generation. For one thing it was much bigger, and by the end of 1964 a third of the records in the pop Top Ten would be British. The fashion being made of English rock and roll installed a fresh pantheon of cultural heroes for the cohort of white kids who knew Elvis Presley best as a counterfeit movie star. For the first time in half a decade there was a vigorous new strain of music conceived by, for, and about white youth.

While the excitement this created could be depended upon to enlarge the record industry's overall take, it was likely to leave fewer white dollars chasing black music, which would no longer have to suffice as a stopgap currency in the cultural commerce of white people. The next real thing had come along.

Their music would become for these kids the dividing edge of a deepening cleavage between their tastes and attitudes and those of their parents. It had become less possible to sell adults and children the same music. If Cooke had the instincts for his business that peers commonly credited him with, he would have known his future in rock and roll had been preempted.

Although his products still sold, Cooke's share of the youth market was inexorably eroding. No longer in style with young black consumers, his core following would never get bigger. Cooke told friends he would use Klein to get him where he had to go. He was selling more records than anybody at RCA except Elvis Presley, and he hadn't played a white nightclub in four years.

6. Star Time at the Regal

In late October 1962 James Brown made a live recording of his stage show at the Apollo Theater. His employers at King Records considered this idea so unpromising a business proposition that Brown had to finance it himself. At a time when most of his contemporaries were like singing jukeboxes that served up songs two minutes and thirty seconds long, one after another, until no more plays were left on the customers' ticket stubs, Brown conceived his act as a whole forty-five-minute show, and put one on every time he took the stage. Brown had hit records—eight in the Top Ten, fifteen on the charts in the first six years of his career—but he no longer needed them to draw crowds.

A half-decade of saturating the market for his live appearances and emitting a steady rat-a-tat-tat of records that kept his name on radio's lips had amounted to an advertising campaign by rolling groundswells of word-of-mouth. He really was, as he proclaimed himself, "the hardest working man in show business," even by the standards of a profession where nobody ever got a paid vacation.

Brown was a cartoon of the small man with an outsize ego, and his had a crust on it made nearly impenetrable by his conviction that every inch of his way up had been bought and paid for by his own unreasonably hard effort. He honed his sense of beleaguerment to a cutting edge and swung it like a scythe and had already overcome the misgivings of many in the beginning who had thought him unlikely to succeed. They once had included the proprietor of King Records, who when he first heard Brown thought the sound strange and awful.

The habit of feeling opposed made him prickly about felt entitlements. So when- and wherever he worked—television aside—he declined to be abridged. He would do his whole show. This meant that in big-city theaters like the Apollo—where each performance segment usually accommodated five or six acts—he forswore costars who weren't in his employ and took as much showtime as he wanted.

In 1962 this approach made him nearly unique among workaday stars of black popular music in being able to record a long-playing performance in a setting that guaranteed its liveliest audience. Brown spliced together the best parts of an October week's work at the Apollo, and the result was astonishing; its "liveness" enthralled.

When Brown's album came out several months later, it went on to sell close to a million copies. So warm an embrace by such a large proportion of Aframerica's nineteen million made it seem a cultural event. Some black stations allotted a program segment every day to playing a whole side of the album—an unprecedented abrogation of the protocols of the wham-bam commercial radio of that era.

Its highlight—six minutes and change of "Lost Someone"—was, in the idiom of the gospel highway, as "deep" a secular performance as had yet been heard on record. It was raw and unprettified, made without any intended appeal but to its own. Even though it was unadvertised, since none of the radio stations popular among them were playing it, white kids began to buy Brown's albums in significant numbers. Several years later the Alvin Ailey Dance Troupe toured with a piece in its repertoire choreographed to the live version of "Lost Someone" and introduced it to householders in the better neighborhoods on four continents.

James Brown's career had several phases, and this one is often forgotten, but before his voice became a part of his band, he was most successfully a singer of ballads. In 1963 he already had a band as hard as a hammer and tight as a fist—the starter edition of juggernauts to come—but in those days he made his way as a sweat-spraying, microphone-cradling, neck vein–bulging crooner. *James Brown Live at the*

Apollo (Vol. I) was nothing less than a masterstroke of an underdog's applied business sense. Brown knew he wasn't the sort of black man white people found appealing.

Having no choice but to be what he was, in the early 1960s it fell to him to instruct his era in what Mamie Smith and Bessie had taught the record business in the 1920s—and what Mahalia Jackson did again in the 1940s, and what Marvin Gaye would do again ten years after Brown, and George Clinton after him, and then the hip-hop boys: that a rich vein of cultural commerce was to be mined in some conversations Aframericans had among themselves when white people weren't listening.

The boxcar loads of albums Brown sold to black people in 1963 confounded one of his industry's regular assumptions about the buying habits of its customers. It also provoked a flurry of live albums of stage-show performances. The inaugural tour of the Motortown Revue, which rolled into the Apollo two months after Brown recorded there, was commemorated in a series of albums that came out over the next couple of years.

With Brown's example before him, Sam Cooke arranged to record himself in the hardcore black milieu of the Harlem Square Club in Miami. Two of Cooke's shows were taped on the same day: a matinee, meant to be kid-heavy, and another in the evening for grown-ups. Cooke was accompanied by a band comprising top-flight studio musicians confederated under the flag of the much-demanded saxophonist King Curtis, himself the author of a rare instrumental best-seller called "Soul Twist."

RCA balked at releasing what it thought were lackluster results and buried the tapes in its vaults. It moldered there for twenty years until unearthed by a rummaging tomb-disturber. An album was assembled of this material and served, garnished with critical acclaim, to an uninterested public.

Rock critics too young to have seen Sam Cooke anywhere but on television decided that they were present now at the unveiling of an antiquity of museum quality that documented as none other had an important artist's authentic style. Herein, they said, was finally disclosed the real Sam Cooke, in joyful and triumphant Negritude, "getting down" with his people. With this discovered recording began the making of a legend of Sam Cooke the performer, by curators of popular culture who were polishing their find.

In truth Cooke's performance in Miami was an ordinary day at the office. Perhaps he had been wearied by too long a deployment among the ranks of jukebox singers; his show seemed stiff and strained, his voice worn, his patter mechanical. For a man of so many obvious parts, he seems oddly ineffectual at inducing the erotic tension this audience would have expected for the price of admission. Like others he had engaged in churches, they would require that his simulation of transforming emotion seem genuine before they submitted to it. But when he tried to make a gospel moment of the climax of "Bring It On Home to Me," he misread the temperament of an audience more disposed to sing along than shout. And so he seems to be working harder at it than he should have to; once when wheels were spinning, he shifted gears to gun his engine by means of a dry-coughed "holy laugh" barren of any resonance or meaning because it had become only a stage mannerism.

His biographer Daniel Wolff has inventoried the cargo carried along with Cooke by the caravans of stars in which he felt too much of his living had to be made. Jackie Wilson twice accompanied Cooke on extended tours. As the 1950s turned into the 1960s, these two were the biggest of black stars, and for a while their careers had similar trajectories. Both were immediately popular with white teenagers, though Wilson for not as long; in sequence, they each took a turn at having a two-year season of frenzied fashionability, and even these looked alike. Just as Cooke had twenty-four releases on *Billboard*'s black record charts between the end of 1957 and the end of 1963—eight consecutively in the Top Five—from the end of 1958 to the end of 1963 Wilson had twenty records on those same charts, nine straight in the Top Ten. But onstage they operated at different temperature settings.

If the urbane Cooke—advertised by RCA as "Mr. Soul"—was an object of the unquiet desires of women of a certain age and of adolescents' dutiful squeals, Wilson—"Mr. Excitement"—brought sexual heat near any female in the way of his flame, and his effect on audiences of black women was incendiary. Thirty-five years after he watched Wilson work a dingy hall in Flint, Michigan, Berry Gordy's astonishment still seemed fresh: Jackie "hit the stage . . . like a lightning bolt. Strutting and dancing with his coat slung over his shoulder . . . spinning and turning, he jumped off one level of the stage to another, landing in a perfect split . . . without stopping he squeezed his legs together and propelled himself up into a standing position just in time to do another twirl, drop to his knees and finish the song. . . . I had never seen women throw panties on stage before."[1]

And after every show Wilson would have his manager line up as many of the devotees who'd slipped backstage as the corridor outside his dressing room would allow. Then he would come out towel-wrapped and go from one to the next, kissing each in turn. An observer of these scenes recalled, "Fat ones, skinny ones, young and old. They'd scream and moan and faint, dropping like a line of dominoes as he passed by." For Wilson, being and staying a star meant you kissed the ugly women, too.

Some who were hangers around Cooke and have since become the tellers of his life story speak of the mano-a-mano encounters these two had on the road. When Cooke was tired or bored, they say, there were nights or weeks or even a whole tour when Wilson "took" the show; then Cooke, nettled to have been outdone, would rouse himself and retake lost territory in the next skirmish, or battle, or war. But in the view of one who witnessed them, Marvin Gaye, this would have been unlikely.

According to Gaye, when he was a kid in Washington, the Howard Theater was his "real high school." There he would study Sam Cooke and afterward go home and shut himself in a room and practice for a day or two, imitating whatever he'd seen Cooke do. The young and introverted Gaye identified with Cooke so much, he even added an "e" to his name in emulation. But after seeing James Brown and Jackie Wilson throw down, Gaye said he knew that while he still thought he could one day be a version of Frank Sinatra, he didn't have the necessities to be a "real entertainer."[2]

From another's viewpoint, Cooke's live recording in Miami need only be considered alongside two others of the period to take his true measure onstage. One, of course, would be Brown's; the other, Gene Chandler's show at the Regal, recorded in 1965.

Chandler was an underrated, quirky singer with a saxophonic style of vocal attack. His voice's inherent quaver made it a natural conductor of hurt and anxiety. In his day he was Curtis Mayfield's favorite mouthpiece. The only artifact of his career left on general display is his least representative work. In the last days of 1961, when he was a member of the Dukays, a record made of a street song they used as a vocal warm-up quite unexpectedly became the nationwide sensation "Duke of Earl." By 1965 two years of six ballad hits—which are the weightiest in a singer's career—made Chandler worthy of his introduction one night in Chicago as "a young man, went out and made a name for himself . . . been on every record-breaking show at the Regal Theater in the last two years."

It is worth remembering that in the mid-1960s 60 percent of record-buyers were female; that was why so many male singers in those days were begging so hard on vinyl. Females would comprise at least that proportion of any house at a typical stage show on the black theater circuit. These audiences liked to see strong and desirable men on their knees as much as others would later take to the sight of unclothed male strippers. Chandler was suave, clean-cut, and collegiate-looking in precisely the Cooke manner. His voice had a plaintive quality anyway, and he was so ardent and dextrous a foreplayer of his audiences' first four rows—guaranteed to be almost uniformly female and densely, aggressively teenage—that he became known as the "woman handler."

On this night his star turn came on the song that kick-started his career in 1963, after it had used up all the mileage allotted to novelty hit-makers. "Rainbow" was an anguished lament in the southern style, an uncharacteristic Mayfield composition without lyric or melody or story line to speak of. Done live, often paced like a dirge by some borrowed band, its words and music served only as a backdrop for Chandler's vivid stage play of seduction. When the recording of it at the Regal was edited down to about three minutes and released early that December, "Rainbow '65" became black America's next-most-favored record by the crack of New Year's dawn, the biggest Chandler ever had after "Duke of Earl."

In their essentials the entertainments staged for both the devout and the impious amounted then to the same show in different theaters. Gene Chandler had no specific training in the hard disciplines of gospel singing, but no one who did ever stoked any fire under an audience more expertly. There are women in church known proverbially to some preachers and singers as "Sister Fluke"; the strategic targets of practiced fire-starters able to intuit which of the congregated they can likely spark first to ignite the kindling that will set off the blaze.

Their counterparts were present at the Regal that night in the women arrayed nearest the stage. For the two-dollar ticket price, each had purchased her license to commentate, and many used it to loudly profane every discernible deficiency of appearance or skill in the six or seven acts that stood their inspection before E. Rodney Jones brought Chandler on.

Audiences like these were famously tough because so many in them grew up being sent on Saturday mornings in the care of sisters and cousins to the Apollo, or the Uptown, or the Regal, since it cost sixty-five cents to get in before eleven o'clock, and the shows kept kids safely occupied until suppertime. They had become astute and experienced detectors of performance fraud.

Whatever else the young women up front came there to do, they brought a conditional willingness to lavish devotion upon an appropriate object of veneration, whenever one appeared. Most were hoping to be transported by a performer who could earn the favor they were prepared to make him of their ritual submission to his ritualized courtship. In those days the obtaining social code had rules of romantic engagement prescribing that whatever a female's natural inclination toward a proposal, only a male who could talk his way into something was considered worthy of getting any.

Chandler was a homegrown attraction, which would have softened a crowd at the Regal into suspending its general predisposition to require proof of the validity of any reputation it hadn't certified itself. On the other hand, this familiarity would naturally have subverted those elements of a performer's authority that thrived best when his air of mystery was intact. Otherwise, why would so many church singers have said for so long that "home folks never pay their own"?

Chandler begins in full and tremulous cry, as if to override the ragged house band, and women are already screaming at his first indications of intent. Hard as he is singing, Chandler takes time at his work. He meanders in and out of the song as soon as he has run once through its bare verse, extracting from it single lines to elaborate into phrases and turning each one over and over like a worry bead in anxious fingers.

Within about seven of these well-worn minutes, Chandler has taken his audience through a series of emotional undulations: episodic tension-risings that break off just before a releasing peak and are allowed briefly to subside, then are reinduced and steadily stoked, then damped again near the brink, and ratcheted back up, and then finally, abruptly dissipated with the last teased crescendo. He assaults the last redoubts of decorum left in this crowd by making a falsetto note of the "please" at the end of four "I'm asking you baby"'s in a row, and wringing it out for fifteen seconds. Such virtuosic preening is calculated to foment an outbreak of upset.

One who has known his work then imagines his gaze locked onto disembodied eyes shining at him through the halo of the footlights' glare, as he leans over the stage apron dangling his line: "You look so good to me baby . . . You look so good to me this evening . . . Sometimes when I look out at 'cha, baby . . . I just want to reach out"—then hooks his catch—"reach out . . . and . . . uh . . . bite . . . 'cha"—and reels it in with a paroxysm of "babybabybabybabybabies" that starts as pleading and ends in a stifled sob. He has buried his face in the breast of his audience—and been taken into its arms.

In these moments Chandler has created for every woman in the house the plausible illusion that he has been making love only to her, and high-pitched shrieks and squeals are popping around him like kernels of popcorn. With the crowd in hand, Chandler adroitly weaves several strands of emotional complexity out of a string of "I just want to ask you one thing"'s—the question given a different shade of urgency each time it is repeated, then broken into parts and reassembled as a bridge to his exiting punch line. In the spaces between his halting entreaties, women are shouting back at him, the last heard exclaiming, "You can have it, you can haaaave it," as he closes up shop.

This was his job, and Chandler's shift was four shows a day, but when he was right, the work he put in was up to the standard of a licensed croonmaster. Although for much of more than a decade—and on and off after than—he made a good living in leading-man roles on the brightest stages of underlit Negro show business, he was still only one of its featured players and never among its paramount attractions. The extent of his forgottenness now is not too far out of proportion to the public's sense of his relative importance then.

Even in 1965—the best year of his career—Chicago would have been the only American big city where Chandler could have headlined a show that packed a house the size of the Regal. The point about Chandler is not just that he was special but that he was also ordinary. His special skills were commonplace compared with Cooke's natural advantages. But Cooke lacked one particular capacity Chandler had available when he needed it to make an audience his.

An important part of anyone capable of giving Chandler's performance in the third show of the third day of the month's third week of engagements never feels more alive than when he is in front of hundreds or thousands of people. In *The Gospel Sound* Tony Heilbut reports an old trouper's reflection that even back in those days many of her colleagues had been "scared to move out that deep. . . . When the spirit got too high, some of us used to run away from it." For Heilbut, "Those who moved on while people screamed and hollered and fainted—and in a few instances died—were simply the most powerful performers of the century."[3]

James Brown was once such a performer, and so was Jackie Wilson, but Cooke never was, even when he was lighting matches in tinderbox churches. A promoter recalled Brown in his early days, giving a show in Macon, Georgia, for which he was paid seventy-five dollars, falling to his knees on a concrete floor again and again, until his pants were riven at the kneecaps and the calluses underneath were bloodied and torn.

Cooke had all of a star's portions of ego and competitiveness, but without the desperation some had to finally possess every audience that made them willing to beg; stooping to conquer was never work for which he felt constitutionally suited. If necessary, Cooke was prepared to sing harder than he liked, but his sense of dignity proscribed public pelvic thrusting—he wasn't any good at that anyway—and he had neither the disposition nor the dramaturgy to simulate sincere abjection. Both are cornerstones of a house-wrecking stage act.

Evidence of the eyes and ears suggests that the assertions of Cooke's old circle that he could stop a show as Brown did, or Jackie Wilson, or even Gene Chandler, debase the community standards applied to entertainment in those days. They are expressions of the same eagerness to embellish his memory that also produced the apocrypha of a brother's account of nine-year-old Sam saying, "I've figured out my life. . . . I'm never gonna have a nine-to-five job [because] all you can do is . . . be broke when payday comes. The system is designed to work like this."[4]

Cooke's figuring since then had been more right than wrong, but when he was thirty-four he could see clearly enough into the game he was in to know that figuring past the day after next was getting harder than Chinese arithmetic.

In 1964 Cooke announced he was coming off the road except for two months a year. "My future lies more in creating music and records," he told *Billboard*. ". . . [I'd] rather be the creative producer in the control room than be a worn-out singer in the bistro light."[5] It sounds like he had begun to notice Berry Gordy. Gordy's successes had become regular by 1962, and within a couple of years their rate and consistency were indications of both an intention and a capacity to mass-produce black music white kids could be relied upon to buy.

Between spring and late fall of 1964 Gordy had three Number 1 records on the pop charts. Cooke would have thought himself at least as shrewd as Gordy about crossing over. After all, Gordy had named his first record label for Tammy, the movie girl he'd had a faraway crush on, and Cooke, so to speak, had taken her to the senior prom.

But the only real capital Cooke had was his career, and in 1964 a popular singer's most reliable prospect for secure employment was presumed to be in legitimate show business. This was then still the old business of movies, Broadway, saloon singers, and vestigial vaudeville, like television variety shows and Jewish stand-up comedy. So running for the cover of Las Vegas was prudent but speculative, since Cooke's appeal to white adults was as yet unproven.

Older white audiences made nervous work for someone like Cooke, but an easier job. Both the stakes and the expectations were different, since the issue was ever acceptance and never love. But even the offices of the William Morris Agency hadn't gotten Cooke in front of such an audience since 1959 and never one in Las Vegas.

Cooke's eyes were on Bobby Darin and Paul Anka, who served very short terms as teen idols before being paroled into legitimate show business and had quickly prospered there as respectable citizens. While it was reasonable for Cooke to think himself like Anka and Darin, he should have been instructed by the experience of Patsy Cline, a crossed-over hillbilly singer who, like Cooke, had suddenly outgrown a disreputable genre.

She was the right color for overnight rehabilitation, and so at the height of her popularity in 1961 Cline was called to Las Vegas, where she found herself working the graveyard shift in a casino lounge—two weeks of four shows a day, beginning each morning at two o'clock. This varied from Cooke's accustomed work only by being done longer and more lucratively in one place. But for him doing it was a prerequisite of the honorary-white-boy status that would assure him of a permanent career.

The fraternity Cooke wanted to pledge still held its rush week at the Copacabana. Klein got him an engagement there in July and announced it with a $10,000 billboard forty-five feet high over Times Square. Klein believed Cooke's earlier stumble at the Copa was a psychological impediment his client had to overcome, and so he threw himself into ensuring that this time Cooke's passage through was safe. His team built another nightclub act much like the last one, predominated by material they thought obligatory but of the type Cooke didn't handle well. As before, they honed it in the Catskills. Cooke was again deeply disquieted. His brother said that in the weeks before Sam opened at the Copa, he drank a fifth of scotch every night.

Important things had changed, however, in the five years since his first, failed assault on this citadel of low white culture. For one, Cooke now bore RCA's imprimatur; he had become a major-label recording star. Moreover, Negroes had become the bourgeois liberal cause of record, and assimilating worthy Negroes an article of official faith. And since all commerce of sufficient scale becomes important, and sooner or later importance confers respectability on any that isn't outlawed, the youth market's old taint was gone.

Bumper crops of Americans born after the war kept ripening into young people whose susceptibility to suggestible consumption made larger and livelier the marketplace in which their appetites were stimulated and satisfied. As mass-marketers began to identify the commodities whose profitability was most affected by the disposition of young people's discretionary incomes—entertainment, soft drinks, beauty and health care products, and cigarettes, to begin with—teenagers became targets of advertising, and images of youth more prevalent. These trends were climatic stirrings that whipped into gusts the fashion of being youthful; which built into the stiff and steady wind has blown hard across America ever since.

Early in the 1960s middle-aged middle Americans picked up one of their children's discarded playthings and found themselves amused by it. A dance called the twist was first given cachet by the transcontinental dolce-vita crowd on its way to becoming the jet set—a small, reputedly stylish leisure class who were pioneers of modern social celebrity—and through the membrane of television and press seeped so far into the official culture over the next couple of years that its protracted fashion among adults was used by kids as evidence to indict their parents for being corny and out of touch.

"Twistin' the Night Away" was Sam Cooke's most popular record, which meant there was at least one of his own songs that he could safely sing at the Copa. The twist was the only dance Cooke could do onstage, and this crowd would be the first he'd ever faced who might be impressed by his performance of it. Apart from a snippet of "You Send

Me" tucked into a medley, it would be the only piece of original material Cooke ventured there. For this audience he greased his skillet with "Twistin'" and "This Little Light of Mine," lit his fire with "Blowin' in the Wind," and then, when it was time to cook, he closed his show with "Tennessee Waltz."

Nevertheless Cooke's return to the Copa was considered a redemptive triumph. *Variety* said he now "[stood] apart from the usual run of rock and roll singers." The reviewer from *Billboard* touted Cooke's act as "a swinging song affair that has appeal for the adult expense account trade."

After the last show Cooke received commemorative Copa cufflinks, bestowed in his dressing room by Jules Podell in the manner of a commanding officer pinning wings on a newly commissioned military pilot. "I'm ready," Sam told the press. "I plan to appear along the club circuit and in concerts. Someday I'd like to do a Broadway play."[6]

The album recorded during this engagement—called *Sam Cooke at the Copa*—stayed popular for more than a year. Its resonance was beyond any it might have accrued on its merits alone. In its moment it seemed symbolic of assimilation's kept promise and the prospect that acceptability, if merited, would eventually be conferred; it was confirming of the striver's ethos. Other singers daring the same dream studied Cooke's album as if it were their Rosetta stone.

The twenty-two-year-old Otis Redding, an erstwhile Little Richard imitator with a style as country as corn bread, must have been sure he would never have to sing "(Won't You Come Home) Bill Bailey." Nevertheless he wore out record grooves studying *Sam Cooke at the Copa*, trying to assimilate as much as he could of that fabled know-how.

Sam and Barbara Cooke had a funeral for their baby boy on the same June day in 1963 that Medgar Evers was buried. Their souring marriage had curdled in the suppressed anguish and silent recriminations of the aftermath. "I know my daddy's a minister," he told a friend. "But . . . if I ever . . . meet that Man, He better have some good reason why this happened to my boy."[7]

Bridling at the obligation of acquiescence to God's will may be a special entitlement of a runaway from the Holiness Church. Like some other chafed Christians he dabbled in Black Muslim studies, but for him it seems to have been a mostly intellectual enthusiasm. The Nation of Islam was then the cutting edge of race consciousness, and Cooke the bootstrap capitalist would have appreciated its exaltation of black enterprise.

By then Cooke was a card-carrier in black America's national church, but he was a Baptist in the way an Italian man his age would be a Catholic. His faith had been too infrequently exercised for him to carry it now without soon reeling under the burden of a child's needless death. His Soul Stirring forebear, Rebert Harris, once stood at the side of a woman who had lain sick, stricken, and aggrieved for a month after the trauma of laboring torturously to deliver a palsied baby, and sang her out of bed and onto her feet. Her means of conveyance was the pure and simple force of Harris's conviction.

But for all his years of making women cry out in affirmation of the tidings he carried across "highways and hedges," Cooke had been a professional singer, who—as much as he loved it—trafficked in church music on his way to someplace else. Nothing he had learned in the process served him in this circumstance but his habit of the road.

His associates said he'd become "a very different person." Given his emotional reticence, they made this assessment from what was observable of his drinking, brooding, and lost affability. While those around him ascribed his darkened aspect to distempering grief, it was also true that after ten years of being called a star, Cooke was chronically money-troubled and felt his career becalmed, his recording enterprise was looking more and more like an expensive hobby, and the mutual discomfitures of his marriage had brought it to a chilly impasse.

Nothing can be so demoralizing to the dreamer as a life untransformed by the dream come true. He was tired of being too much away from home, but when he wasn't, compartments of his life caved in on each other, and then he had to live in the untidiness he had generally avoided by being somewhere else.

When the habituated itinerant is home for long, the street becomes the road's equivalent. Apart from drugs, bad habits are less costly to the man in motion, since parking them too long on the same street inevitably exacts a higher toll. Whenever he was at home in Los Angeles, Cooke circulated among its music-industry hangouts—nightclubs around Hollywood where the city's resident enclave of black show-business workers, and others passing through, intersected with its demi-monde—and grittier spots he favored on the city's dark underside.

Etta James tells a variant of the same story about Cooke that many others also told usually as evidence that though he was naturally a king, he never lost his common touch. She describes Cooke, casually resplendent in layers of silk, ducking into an alley next to the California Club—a regular Wednesday-night stop for both when either was in town and off duty—to engage its huddled denizens, greeting several of them by name, drinking their wine, and spreading money around.[8] He was a familiar to winos and whores. Sam Cooke loved the street. And as often is said by others in its embrace, the street can love you to death.

Because of the movies Los Angeles was the epicenter of low American culture. Music publishing and recording were long-standing adjuncts of the movie business. Once their cross-country commerce could be more conveniently managed from either coast, the music business started following the sun. By the 1950s Los Angeles had become the record industry's second city.

The popularly imagined California became America's conception of an ideal state. The black show-business elite—mostly stars of music and the few who were in movies—was no less susceptible than other Americans to the allure of living well in the sunshine, and since their livelihoods were portable, more than a few settled in Los Angeles.

Before the war the city's black presence had been slight and sleepy; military spending created industries there that drew many thousands of migrants from black belts west of the Mississippi. Although its black population was still less substantial than those of other cities, Los Angeles was a hotbed of all the postwar forms of black popular music. Many stayed who, like Cooke, first came there to make records.

The city's original black celebrities were film actors in the 1930s, the grandest of whom was Lincoln Perry, known as Stepin Fetchit, the first Negro ever to have a contract with a movie studio. Perry—and another who did similar work, Willie Best—lived a double public life. Each of these publics was shown a persona that was an inversion of what the other saw.

Though Stepin Fetchit made his living by pretending to be an illiterate, he was actually a concealed sophisticate. He impersonated servants on film—and employed servants at home. He dressed for work in rags—but was never less than fabulous on Central Avenue, where he displayed himself in off-hours ensconced in a custom-made white Cadillac, with "Fox Contract Player" written along its side.

Stepin Fetchit was paid to appear before white people as a cartoonish embodiment of their contempt for Negro capacities and character—to shuffle and simper, to leer and laze, to cower with lidded eyes suddenly gone wide as teacup saucers, to play the comic malaprop in a whiny singsong drawl—and yet, when Lincoln Perry moved about in the world, he traveled as he thought Jack Johnson would. He was blatantly a "sportsman" who openly consorted with white women and thus was a frequent target of the law.

He lived recklessly enough to squander the million dollars or so he made in movies during the worst years of the Depression. Privately, he feigned the illiteracy he pretended in films whenever it served him in maneuvering around his employers. He insulated himself from the studio's recriminations against his conspicuously miscreant other self by cultivating the friendship and protection of Will Rogers.

After Rogers died, Fox punished Perry with suspensions and ultimately with dismissal. After he could no longer be a minor motion picture star, Stepin Fetchit grew bitter and strange. He lived a long time without ever making his way back and was last seen in the early 1970s in the entourage of Muhammad Ali.

Willie Best got started in pictures because there wasn't enough of Stepin Fetchit to go around. Like Lincoln Perry, Best was a minstrel show on screen and an unregenerate "bad n[egro]" on the street. His reading of the Stepin Fetchit role brought him twenty years of regular employment in movies and television. All the while he exercised his citizenship in Los Angeles's black underworld as a pimp and a dealer of heroin. His career in white show business was over just before Cooke's began.

By the mid-1950s his particular skills were no longer considered socially useful. Before the end came, Best played the television sidekick and comic foil for Stu Erwin in a popular situation comedy about a befuddled middle-American householder. Perry and Best were heroes on Central Avenue, but they were notorious in respectable Negro society, denounced by both race-upholders and the assimilation-minded, and reviled by its striving classes.

The feelings that unassimilable Aframericans had about these men were more complicated. For one thing, they knew it took more than a fool to get paid that much for acting like one, and so they better appreciated the briar-patch ironies in their performances. If Jack Johnson was Stagger Lee come to life, Stepin Fetchit was Brer Rabbit. They could read the subtext of Perry's movie persona. Beneath the coon-shining was the subtler pantomime of a Negro everyman trying to "get over"—that is, to beguile the white man enough, by appearing to honor his presumed authority, to thwart any of his specific intentions to apply it.

"Getting over" originated among sharecroppers, accustomed to being cheated by landowners, as a tactical response to an iniquitous system. It meant getting the crop over with so that the tenant farmer's obligation was met and his family could labor somewhere else for living wages. It became a metaphor for beating a game that is unwinnable if its rules are followed. Many who are prone to thinking that their circumstances make life such a game celebrate the ways and means of subverting its rules and therefore see guile as a heroic quality.

This is a reason pimps were at the top of the black outlaw food chain for forty years, until drugs skewed the pay scale of street crime. Black men selling white men sexual access to women was a sly, sweet reversal of the power relationship that governed the transaction of interracial sex in the briar patch. It could thus be construed as a heroic calling, particularly by the mythologizing hand of the great writer of pulp fiction Robert Beck—known as Iceberg Slim—whose books have been bought by more black Americans than anyone else's but God's and Donald Goines's. The "bad n[egro]" has always been the folkloric property of the unassimilable. In the 1960s and 1970s the heavy circulation of Iceberg Slim's putative memoir, *Pimp,* established the "player" as an outlaw archetype in the popular consciousness of at least one black generation.

Even today, twenty years after midlevel drug-sellers began consuming more conspicuously than pimps, and the crack epidemic oversupplied the market with addicted women who depressed the price of sex on the street, nostalgia for the idea of pimping pervades the imaginations of many young black males. With so little left of its authentic tradition anywhere in sight, pimping's restoration as a subcultural ideal by a generation removed from the presence of many instructive examples of it suggests how durable is the iconography of "getting over" in the psychic makeup of a big segment of Aframerican society. The romance of pimping is as much an article of faith among members of the unassimilable caste as the efficacy of hard work, education, and a correct appearance is for strivers.

It was only natural that Sam Cooke would play his celebrity in a lower key than Lincoln Perry. Cooke was a child of strivers, a preacher's boy who would have grown up hearing "getting over" used in a different metaphorical sense. On the tongues of citizens of his parents' world it was usually shorthand for a victory after long struggle, like that of the soul which departs its hard-used vessel and crosses over the River Jordan and lands in Zion. The flamboyance Cooke had known longest at closest range was in the style of the black church, which—if it came from the same root and could be just a shade or two less florid than the street's—at least upheld the worthier class of aspirations Cooke embodied in the mind's eyes of everyday Aframericans. The cut of celebrity that fit him best was the kind he'd grown up wearing in churches. Where livelihoods are staked on the public appearance of rectitude, concealment of off-color aspects of the private self becomes a professional discipline as basic as getting to the job on time.

If Cooke's double life was quieter than Stepin Fetchit's—and more straightforward—it was nevertheless demanding. He was as much to whites as blacks the symbolic good son of every good Negro mother. But while the coherence of Cooke's cross-cultural appeal spared him from having to maintain more than one public persona, he still had to account for the nuances of difference in how he was seen and understood on either side of the racial divide.

It behooved even an exemplar of the socially acceptable new Negro to make his way among white men by seeming less than he was. So when Cooke signed his contract, he was shown on the cover of *Cash Box* flanked by RCA executives who were smiling like Rotarians presenting a savings bond to the worthiest boy in the graduating class at the colored high school. At the same time, because Cooke seemed to so many of his own to be representative of their best, so evidently marked by God's grace and the luster of his glamorous calling, the news they got of him marked events in a life of heroic scale. The part of it set in the Hollywood Hills, so like minor white celebrity in its appearance, was airbrushed in *Ebony* for strivers thirsty for inspiration and chronicled in *Jet* for vicarious fellow travelers hungry for the details of his journey.

In times crackling with symbolic meanings, meaningful symbols always have uses. In a way the makers and keepers of his tribe's lore cast Cooke as its surrogate voyager: his origins like theirs; his early encounters with official white culture as awkward as their own; his provisional acceptance by it grounds for their optimism; his public assertions of their dignity in refusing to play to segregated audiences or bow to death threats from disturbed crackers; his path-maker cachet, all made him seem, in the words Ossie Davis applied to Malcolm X, their "shining black prince."

Cooke's progress—through the valley of car crashes and old-country sheriffs, Ed Sullivan's slight and Jules Podell's rebuke, over a testing road that led him back to the lair of his nemesis, again to challenge and this time slay the fearsome Copacabana, then on to the *Tonight Show*, and finally to the gates of Las Vegas—was charted in the pages of the Negro press as though it were a kind of pilgrimage.

In February 1964, with a chance to tell the world what he thought it should know in the moments just after he'd so improbably beaten Sonny Liston for the heavyweight championship, Cassius Clay—the next of his tribe's surrogate voyagers—finished his ecstatic postfight rant amid a writhing triumphal throng and kept the televison camera from cutting away until he could commemorate the presence of the man he most wanted to associate with his life's sweetest moment. On the day that followed he would announce his adherence to an unortho-dox Islam; his savior was watching in Chicago that night, his prosely-tizer was close by, and their God had seen him through, just as they'd foretold. But the only name Clay called out from the ring was Sam Cooke's—to which he appended, with the barkering insistence of a man saying something he knows is indisputable to people he expects think otherwise, "the greatest rock and roll singer in the world."

7. B Movie: Souled Out

Between the March on Washington and passage of the Voting Rights Act of 1965, the black church never had wider influence on the general culture or greater visibility within it. This was also true, in a way, of its music; even as gospel began its commercial decline around 1960, its main ingredients were being incorporated into what would soon be labeled "soul music." "Soul" originally refered to a style of singing that was church-inflected and usually southern, but by the mid-1960s it became the brand name under which all black popular music was sold.

In 1963, when Cooke was being advertised as "the man who invented soul," and Berry Gordy copyrighted its use as a trademark, Curtis Mayfield—once a semiprofessional Northern Jubilee Gospel Singer—dug deeply into the storehouse of his cultural inheritance for a song with a line like "That alright, that's alright, long as I know I got a seat in the kingdom, that's alright." He brightened and fattened it with horns and smoothed its gait into an easy-riding lope; "It's All Right" became a Number 1 record on the black side and a big cross-market success. Though it had a spirit-feel akin to church, its provenance was nearly untraceable.

Mayfield's songs frequently assumed—though never required—an audience conversant with idiomatic Afro-Christianity; the language of encoded messages he put into songs that were intended first to serve the coupling of dancers in dark corners of rooms dimly lit and hazy with smoke. At twenty-one he was already the most sophisticated interpreter of the church style in black popular music.

Curtis was always the quickest thinker in Chicago. After hearing Cooke's "Wonderful World," he improved on it twice within eighteen months—first with "He Will Break Your Heart," written for Jerry Butler, and again when he recorded "Gypsy Woman" with the Impressions. In Sam Cooke Mayfield found a musical sensibility so compatible with his own that the influences of "Wonderful World" were plain enough in "Gypsy Woman" to seem like borrowings, down to the stillness in its internal spaces and faint Latin inflections.

The early phase of Mayfield's work was thus shaped and through it so was a distinctive Chicago style in the music's next era—and as well a young Bob Marley, listening nights to a radio station from across water. Where Cooke stood first, a Mayfield could arise, and though his self-invention might have been subsidiary to Cooke's, it was no less prodigious.

He'd written a Number 1 song, a Number 2, and two others in the black Top Ten before he was twenty. An unschooled musician from the Cabrini-Green projects, Mayfield was also the home-taught possessor of a clean, sinuous guitar style that was innovative and idiosyncratic and widely imitated around Chicago.

When he was nineteen, the established strength of Mayfield's credentials as a songwriter and producer induced a big company to sign his Impressions to a recording contract. When he was twenty, he wrote and sang the lines, "I'm a ship, tossed and driven, under thundering clouds above, but one day I'll drop my anchor in the harbor of your love, then we'll go sailing, keep right on sailing, on the breakers of our love."

Here are echoed the hymns of Reverend Tindley, black church music's first modern master, and others Mayfield heard adapted from eighteenth-century Methodists, the curriculum of his ninth-grade English class, and his demonstrated retention of lessons learned therein about metaphor and its proper uses. To have later written "Minstrel and Queen (Queen Majesty)"—"Queen majesty, may I speak to thee"—a space in his imagination must once have been captured by

Lancelot in some classroom or movie theater and held thereafter by the Arthurian romances of Walter Scott.

Cooke tapped a root of teenage disaffection with the workaday ennui of school life by striking a common chord of playful disdain for its uses—"don't know much about history, don't know much biology." Mayfield the lapsed high schooler often located stories for songs in places he must first have imagined in a social studies class: "and man oh man, before you go home, catch a flight on to the wonders of Rome / Italy's beauty may put on a show / to arouse all your love and make your heart grow." Mayfield wrote for an audience he knew was mostly disposed to think education a way of doing better and so were likely to appreciate the evidence in his work that he'd made good use of such as he had.

Mayfield was of the next half-generation of little brothers coming up behind Cooke's: nine years younger, born to the city, touched by television, part of a world made bigger yet more immediate and a decade more complex. Their environment was more variously stimulated and so had imparted a richer vocabulary of the imagination. Cooke reserved his imagination's most strenuous exertions for the leap-takings required in his campaign to become the property of himself.

A rock-and-roll star who advised a colleague in 1962 to think of her record company as a bank that loaned artist/entrepreneurs money to develop their products in return for a license to profit from them, was ten years ahead of his time, living partly in the reality of his business's next era. Cooke was cautious in his art so that he might be daring in the conception of his life.

But Cooke overrated his own songwriting ability—a natural enough tendency in an endorser of royalty checks of the size he cashed. He was smart, read a lot, and wrote songs habitually, but nearly everything worth remembering about the records he made as a pop star are glints of the singer gleaming through the dross of his songs. In his creation of facile ditties like "Cupid, draw back your bow and let your arrow go," Cooke never rose higher than his assessment of what his market would placidly bear; Mayfield's earliest successes were had by enfolding listeners in his transporting fancy.

While Cooke was "Twistin' the Night Away," young Curtis was already a singer of tales who could deftly sketch a scene: (a guitar thrums and castenets chatter) "From nowhere through a caravan, around a campfire light / A lovely woman in motion, with hair as dark as night / Her eyes were like that of a cat in the dark." Mayfield made the quality of wistfulness that he discerned in Cooke a primary color in his own palette. The shadings he gave it were elaborations of a style as ably accommodating of changes in public taste for fifteen years as it was steadfast in its native personality.

Mayfield's body of work over a decade and a half of the 1960s and 1970s established him alongside Smokey Robinson as preeminent song-writers in the black popular music of this classic period. While he lacked Smokey's inveterate cleverness at wordplay and talent for catchy tunes—albeit many of Robinson's best were written with other people's melodies—Mayfield's range was, if anything, broader and deeper. In 1963 he was made staff producer at Columbia's revived subsidiary in Chicago, Okeh Records. Between his work there and for Butler, the Impressions, and assorted others, Mayfield stamped most of the city's music for the next three years.

While Chicago was becoming a reliquary for artifacts of commer-cially spent gospel and blues traditions, Mayfield made its modern "sound" as identifiable in the black popular music of the early and mid-1960s as Detroit's. By 1963 Mayfield knew he had to muscle up to com-pete with Motown, so he enlisted the collaboration of arranger Johnny Pate, who had a talent for punchy horns. That summer, while Cooke recycled "Frankie and Johnny" as prospective lounge-act fodder, they produced with a singer of threadbare voice named Major Lance a wholly original dance record called "Monkey Time." This was the first in a lineage of midtempo songs in the unhurried-but-always-on-time groove of Mayfield's that is ever evocative of the mellowness of early evenings in summertime.

The Impressions had become a three-man group after losing two of their original members. Mayfield's voice stayed dominant, but the others were now regularly featured as contrapuntal foils and in calls and responses adapted from the conventions of quartet singing. Their characteristic harmonies were high and hard, honing an edge to cut his voice's natural sweetness. "I think it was probably original with the Impressions in r & b and contemporary music," Mayfield has said, "but there was nothing original about it if you ever sang gospel."[1] Their success created a new niche that imitators scrambled to cohabit.

In 1964 Mayfield and the Impressions began coming out with his "songs of inspiration." These came in two clusters: the first was coincidental with the flowering of the civil rights movement and the second with the ripening of "black consciousness" in the late 1960s. The first of these, "Keep On Pushing" ("I've got to keep on pushing / Can't stop now / Move up a little higher / Some way, some how") and "People Get Ready" ("People get ready, there's a train a comin' / don't need no ticket, you just get on board / All you need is faith to hear the diesel's hummin' / Don't need no ticket, you just thank the Lord") were bulletins from church addressed to a polity used to hearing clerics apply themselves to social issues on the television news, and delivered in a package whose origins were disguised to promote broad acceptance of its contents. Imbued by their language with the implicit authority of church and yet specific to a social context, these songs accrued political resonances, much like the speeches of Dr. King.

All the while Mayfield was writing the most darkly contemplative adult-relationship songs anywhere in the contemporary literature of black popular song. For Gene Chandler in 1965 there was, "What now, after you've done me like you did? / Already I'm stringing along like an infatuated kid / You're obliged to do me wrong with no explanation / There's never any love nor conversation / And so after holding back my tears and fighting off my fears, what now?" And for the Impressions: "See me, . . . can you see the real me? / Look through me, and you'll see, a sinner my dear."

For Walter Jackson he wrote that year a bittersweet song of reconciliation called "Welcome Home" ("We'll let pride be something we have in our love, and not just in ourselves") and again for the Impressions, more bruised resignation and quiet despair: "day after day, you treat me any old way / I want to go, but my heart says no / You act so strange, but my love still remains / It says keep on trying, son, she's gonna change." Cooke wrote perhaps four memorable ballads in his seven years in popular music; Curtis reaped twice that many in six fertile months in 1964.

Sam Cooke once advised his protégé, Bobby Womack, that "people will buy the news if it's sung with a melody."[2] He was using hyberbole to make a point; it hadn't occurred to him this formulation might literally be true. He was telling Womack to read more, lest he be limited to writing love songs the rest of his life.

Of course, Cooke reportedly read everything from Aristotle to *The New Yorker* magazine yet never wrote popular songs about anything much besides love and having a party. He was speaking here in the familiar tradition of older men giving younger ones sound career advice that they think themselves past being able to follow. "I'm going to Las Vegas," he said but asserted that the moment of the songwriter-singer was at hand and that soon it would matter less how artfully a song was sung than whether its performance seemed "authentic."

When Sam Cooke recorded "A Change Is Gonna Come" near the end of 1963, he told friends he was "scared of it." He was shamed into its conception, he said, by hearing Bob Dylan's "Blowin' in the Wind." But he was uneasy about singing anything in public that sounded so close to personal testimony ("I was born by the river in a little tent / And just like the river I've been running ever since") and nervous about the commercial riskiness of mixing politics into his business with white people. So he held back its release.

But the fever of his times ran in Mayfield's blood, and the rhythm of their social currents regulated his pulse. After a couple of stalled years trying to engage Motown on those terms, Mayfield renewed himself by reverting to social commentary, this time more explicitly, in a series of records: from "We're a Winner" to "This Is My Country" ("Too many have died and protected my pride, for me to go second class / We've survived a hard blow, and I want you to know, you will face us at last") through "Choice of Colors" ("If you had a choice of colors, which one would you choose my brothers? / If there were no day or night, which would prefer to be right?") and "Mighty Mighty

(Spade and Whitey)" ("It really ain't no difference / If you cut, you gonna bleed / And might I get a little deeper, human life's from the semen seed") to "Check Out Your Mind" and "(Don't Worry) If There's a Hell Below, We're All Gonna Go" ("The blacks and the crackers / Police and their backers / They're all political actors / And Nixon talkin' 'bout, 'don't worry'").

The idea of Sam Cooke was as releasing for Curtis Mayfield as it was for all those gospel singers who flooded into popular music once it began selling what they already knew how to sing. Mayfield had his own publishing company a year after Cooke did, in 1960, before he was twenty-one, when he began writing songs for Jerry Butler; he would come into at least a half-interest in six publishers of his work.

Mayfield was doggedly entrepreneurial. He launched two different labels in 1966, and though both made records people liked and bought, both were aborted the next year, casualties of the intractable problems that small companies usually had in getting records distributed and collecting money owed when they tried to survive unprotected by alliances with larger ones. The next year Mayfield's contract with ABC expired in the heated afterglow of "We're a Winner," leaving behind a last lovely ballad of his smoldering in the Top Ten.

While its embers still burned, Mayfield started Curtom Records and took the Impressions with him. Before "I Loved and I Lost" fell off the record charts in the summer of 1968, Curtis made Curtom's maiden release another Impressions ballad that became even more popular, then followed up with "This Is My Country"; next summer came "Choice of Colors," which sold like cold beer in July. Thus established, Curtom made money more or less for ten years, because while Mayfield took inspiration from Cooke, he had observed Berry Gordy. He first recruited as staff arrangers Johnny Pate and Donny Hathaway (a prodigy then, just out of Howard University) and began assembling a cadre of in-house writers and producers and an inventory of mostly proven, if undersung, young talent. He hired a youngish white man who had been a manager of rock acts, taught him the record business, and grew him into a capable superintendent of the company's operations.

For much of Curtom's run, the performer Curtis Mayfield was its featured attraction. He was in high fashion when so-called blaxploitation movies were coming into their own, and this convergence made the jackpot *Superfly* a million-selling soundtrack album, from which were extracted two singles that stayed on radio the whole last half of 1972. During the mid-1970s he wrote other successful movie soundtrack albums for Gladys Knight, the Staple Singers, and Aretha Franklin.

In its best year Curtom sold $10 million worth of records, but after peaking in 1976 the company precipitously declined. By late in the decade disco held the marketplace in a stranglehold. Mayfield's sensibilities were incompatible with making soulless dance music, and in those days any other kind would have been commercially unrewarding. With his creative prime long spent, another self-reinvention was a race he would not run.

He fell into disinterest and torpor, and by 1980 the carcass of Curtom Records was being picked over by higher-ups in the food chain. By then the distinctive musical cultures that had once been particular to Aframerican city-states were nearly extinct. Mayfield packed up Curtom's recording equipment and left Chicago for Atlanta.

Others of Mayfield's generation of singers in Chicago—young and experienced enough to have been instructed by Cooke's example— tried going into business for themselves. Jerry Butler made a few records on his own labels in Memphis and Chicago. Gene Chandler spawned two labels with production deals subsidized by Mercury Records, the company for which he recorded. He had a big hit and a small one but petered out quickly. In accounting for why his venture failed, Chandler could as well have described Cooke's situation at SAR/Derby. "I kept Universal Studios [in Chicago] booked up and just constantly working," he recalled. "But after a while my sound was beginning to repeat itself. If I'd had [a creative partner,] I would have been fine, like Gamble and Huff [the Philadelphia writing and production team who built a successful midsize label in the late 1960s and 1970s]. I had nobody else."[3]

After his son died in 1963, Sam Cooke told his manager to get him back on the road. He stayed out about a month, and when he got back, he'd already gone over to Allen Klein. He didn't record anything for six

months; Cooke was into his endgame with Hugo and Luigi, his nominal producers, waiting for their deal to expire so he could shed them
without pain. He busied himself at SAR, recording mostly friends and
relatives. He engaged a refugee band from New Orleans to play on
these sessions and accompany him onstage. In 1961 its leader—the
horn player Harold Battiste—had taken up the subversive idea that
labor could own the means of record production. He organized local
studio musicians into an artists' collective called AFO (All For One) that
made and sold its own records.

The AFO label was launched with a towering splash—a Number 1
record by an unknown singer on her first cruise—and was quickly
swamped by this unforeseeable triumph. It sank in the backwash. Their
misfortune—shared by many in the business who were more adventur-
ous than capitalized—was to be ruined by cataclysmic prosperity.

With defeat snatched from the jaws of their victory, the insurgents
disbanded, and the Battiste faction migrated to Los Angeles. Cooke
came upon Battiste there, and together they had the idea of setting up
storefront drop-in community audition sites—dubbed "soul stations"—
to draw out the unidentified talent they believed was languishing in Los
Angeles's black neighborhoods. This concept was a forerunner of the
songwriters workshop that Jerry Butler established in 1970 to develop
from young Chicago sources his own steady supply of high-grade material. Cooke subsidized one such unproductive outpost in Watts. Sonny
Bono—who'd worked hard for years at getting discovered—was its only
notable alumnus.

Meanwhile Cooke's affairs were taken in hand by Allen Klein. By
the spring of 1964 he was purging SAR/Derby's artist roster of Cooke's
entourage. Shortly after they affiliated, the business of Cooke's record
and publishing companies was being conducted out of Klein's office in
New York.

Klein believed Cooke's venture had become a self-indulgence, and
being devious by nature didn't make him wrong. But it was then, former associates say, even before Cooke knew quite how deeply Klein's
hand was insinuated into his pocket, that he first expressed misgivings
about having hired his new manager.

Bumps Blackwell has said Cooke approached him about becoming involved at SAR/Derby and confided his thickening suspicions about Klein. Cooke began doing belated due diligence, calling around to his manager's former clients. On the basis of what he learned, Roy Crain reports, Cooke decided to take his money out of New York. He asked the man he'd jilted for Klein to get him the best contract lawyer he could find. By then Cooke knew enough about who he was dealing with to believe that getting himself disentangled would require the services of a practiced snake-handler.

In June SAR put out a record by the unchurched Womack Brothers that did well before it was overwhelmed by an old-fashioned cover version by the Rolling Stones. "It's All Over Now" was their American breakthrough. Cooke was philosophical, as only a holder of publishing rights can be when his small hit is stolen away and turned into a share of a gold mine. "This will be history," he told the enraged Bobby Womack, ". . . this group will change the industry. They ain't like the Beatles. . . . They gonna make it loose for everybody."[4] Cooke was disinclined, however, to steer the course of his own career by the light of this insight. As he spoke, the record he had out was "Tennessee Waltz."

After the Copa he told friends that negotiations were ongoing with Las Vegas, but he was still reporting for work at places like Club Harlem in Atlantic City and the Royal Peacock in Atlanta. RCA had assigned Cooke a staff producer to replace Hugo and Luigi, but the singer called his own tune in the studio now, and it was familiar. Cooke did stretch for a dance hit by trying to make one in the contemporary style: Motown fashion rules of raw energy dressed up in sophisticated orchestration.

By that prevailing standard, "Shake" sounded a bit frazzled, and when it came out, it had the further disability of being considered undanceable by black kids. It was one of those "shake it like a white girl" records the British fancy well enough to believe its type deserves a name and so coined "rave ups" to serve. It took sixteen takes to record the song to its producer's satisfaction, and the results still suggest a Cooke under duress in the alien dimension of rhythm singing.

By the late fall of 1964 Cooke had concluded that Allen Klein was "no fucking good." He had lately learned that some expenses Klein had told him had been paid by RCA were being charged to him. He had trouble understanding the answers he was given to questions he asked about Tracey Ltd. It was now clear to him that he was being misled. By all accounts of those around him, he decided to end his relationship with Allen Klein. He spoke of firing him after Christmas. Cooke never had a chance to act on his premature New Year's resolution.

If he ever had, he would surely have found himself both a plaintiff and a defendant in a long and lacerating exchange of lawsuits. It seems likely that when the judging in this case was done, Cooke's right to himself as property would have proven as illusory as Dred Scott's. Allen Klein never has lost a lawsuit. Later, when Barbara Cooke tried him, Klein's claim on the company her husband had been assured existed solely as his means of owning himself, was found to be absolute and unassailable.

Sam Cooke's life abruptly came upon its lurid end in the early morning of December 11, 1964. The circumstances of his death were officially made plain, but what really happened can never be known. He was killed by the night manager of the Hacienda Motel in South-Central Los Angeles.

Bertha Franklin claimed he had broken down her door looking for a woman he'd checked in with moments before, then viciously attacked her. Confronted by the relentless assault of an enraged man wearing only underwear, a suit jacket, and his shoes, she drew her pistol and shot Cooke in the chest. When that didn't keep him off her, she picked up a stick and beat him senseless. According to the police, she passed a lie detector test. A coroner's jury took fifteen minutes to rule Cooke's death a justifiable homicide. Their findings became the basis of a $30,000 judgment that Franklin later won against Cooke's estate.

He'd left a bar with Lisa Boyer, a twenty-two-year-old unfailingly identified in the contemporary reportage as Eurasian, and driven her to the motel. She said she had been taken there against her will, although Franklin reported seeing no signs of resistance when they registered.

Boyer later swore that once they were in the room, Cooke tore at her clothes, forced her onto the bed, and pinned back her arms. She said she knew then that he was going to rape her. Boyer asked to use the bathroom. When she came out, Cooke had undressed. Then he went into the bathroom, whereupon Boyer grabbed his clothes along with her own and fled. When he came out and discovered her gone, evidently Cooke looked through a window and saw her knocking on the manager's door. He threw on what she'd left of his clothing and went to the office to find her. Boyer hadn't gone inside but hastened into the street, where she found a pay phone and called the police. She was also said by police to have taken and passed a lie detector test.

Cooke's inquest took a couple of hours. Neither Franklin nor Boyer was cross-examined. The inquiries of government into his death were closed, and so they have remained, and will interminably.

If official Los Angeles was finished asking questions about how Cooke died, its black newspaper raised a few. The *Sentinel*, of course, was experienced in the ways of the Los Angeles police department Chief Roy Parker had made and that Mayor Sam Yorty then presided over, and its habits of collusion with city hall, coroners, and district attorneys. So was the street, and as soon as news of Cooke's death was broadcast the next morning, a crowd mostly of young people gathered at the Hacienda Motel and stayed all that day and night. A local newspaper described them as protesting.

Eight months later many of these young citizens, ignited by the spark of another incident with police, would make the nearby streets riotous, as part of the resident horde that famously sacked Watts. These pillagers of supermarkets, appliance-store looters, and sportive arsonists disregarded public pleadings for restored order from the coalition of established interests and Negro strivers and the tactical advice contained in a message from Motown being broadcast on the soundtrack of their daily lives. A week before the riots started, about once an hour on KGFJ the Marvelettes were counseling reckless indulgers of transient passions that "it's vanity, insanity, to play when you can't win."

But much more of the local air had since been commandeered by the swagger and brimstone of Wilson Pickett, newly a star attraction, whose coming to town under the auspices of Magnificent Montague—grandest of Los Angeles's black radio personalities—nearly coincided with the outbreak of rioting. Because his guaranteed money was already in Pickett's pocket, for a week before the show Montague indecently flogged "In the Midnight Hour" with the remorseless urgency of a promoter who needs a big walk-up crowd to get paid and has four hours of free radio advertising available to him every day.

He would cackle, "It's so nice, I gots to play it twice," as he cued up the record for its third consecutive spin, and then would punch a button on the studio's tape cartridge machine to make a different high school girl's voice coo his trademark, "Burn, baby, burn," over those fat Memphis horns, just before Pickett's voice kicked in.

If there had been a commemorative T-shirt with "I survived the Watts Riot of 1965" on its front, "Burn, baby, burn" would have been inscribed across its back. Some said the Vandellas' "Dancing in the Street" had been last summer's early invitation to this summer's riot season, but more abrasive sounds than Motown's were carried those days on the air currents of Los Angeles.

James Brown had taken his irrevocable turn toward what the future called funk, and Otis Redding was churning into a big wind from the flared-up black South. A larger man than his voice, Redding gave a larger-than-literal meaning to his reasonable demand for "a little respect when I come home." If a want of respect brought people into the streets of Los Angeles in August 1965, its lack induced some whom frenzy had addled to ignore their mothers' admonitions not to bring what went on in the street too near home. After its fetid air finally cleared of smoke, a recurrent echo of Cooke's valedictory, "A Change Is Gonna Come," toned in the pall over Watts.

The New York gossip columnist Dorothy Kilgallen, who knew and liked Cooke, was unsatisfied by the story of record concerning his death and hinted darkly at other, sinister possibilities. But she was resigned to the unlikelihood of their ever being pursued, alluding to the local jurisprudential custom of not looking too hard into unseemly celebrity deaths when she predicted Cooke's would become "another of those Los Angeles 'mystery cases.'"[5]

The degree of notice that official America paid to this event was suggested by the *New York Times*'s consignment of its cursory account to page thirty-four. Many who read it there wouldn't have resisted the presumption of guilt being attached to even the fanciest Negro accused of making a half-white woman his sexual victim. But none who knew Cooke believed that was possible.

Replete as it was with unanswered questions that struck anyone who paid even casual attention, this case had undeniable circumstantial elements that were squalid enough to discolor Cooke's reputation and disable such indignation as might have—had it been loud enough or sustained—scalded shapers of general opinion into caring about making someone accountable for the death of a famous man. On the whole, black Americans winced with pain, then shrank in recoil.

As quickly as their shock subsided, the mutterings began about things not being what they seemed, but many were reflexively embarrassed for themselves. Newspapers said—and the Johnson Publications confirmed—that their emblematic best self got caught so wrong, he had to be shot down like a wild dog. And most Americans then, black and white, were still predisposed to believe an official account, or at least any that stood for all they would ever be told.

Besides, an ending as much alike as this one was to some of the familiar denouements of our most-watched movie melodramas would make the star's life appear properly concluded, even if the scenarist had reneged on the outcome he'd seemed to promise. We thought we were watching something in the inspirational genre and were surprised to have it finally twisted into film noir.

The man from *Ebony* rose to the occasion: "He died there, one shoe on, the other a few feet away. Outside, its motor still running, sat his $14,000 tomato-red Ferrari, under a sign advertising the motel's rooms as '$3 and up.'" But even a bad movie ending brings up the house lights.

Since we are now in a time when worldwide commerce in the private lives of public figures dozes but never closes, the media indifference of thirty-five years ago to Cooke's death is almost incomprehensible, especially in the Los Angeles we've seen combed over with nitpicking thoroughness by inspectors of the life and trials of Orenthal Simpson. Cooke died ten years before investigative journalism became an informal branch of the prosecutor's office, at a time when the city that invented tabloid television was without even a tabloid newspaper.

There was a reporter who poked around in the immediate aftermath of the killing, but she wasn't on duty. Before she married Cooke's last nominal producer at RCA, Joan Schmitt worked for a newspaper in the San Fernando Valley. Angry and baffled at the accounts of Cooke's death, Schmitt went down to the police station where Lisa Boyer's telephone call had been received. She said that as far as the desk sergeant she talked to knew or cared, Sam Cooke had been just flotsam washed up from the wreckage of another Saturday night in Watts, another dead Negro. His autopsied body lay all day and half a night in the city's morgue until Roy Crain, who'd flown out from Chicago at Charles Cook's behest, came to retrieve it.[6]

There are two schools of thought about what happened to Sam Cooke, both of which rely on the same insubstantial dossier of evidence to support a few reasonable suppositions. The first—die-hard heroic—holds that Cooke was set up and killed by people in or around the entertainment business who thought him too independent: people he might have been talking to when he was "negotiating with Las Vegas"; or others, perhaps, with an interest in the Italian cousins Cooke had just forsaken; or Allen Klein, with whom he was noisily disenchanted.

Because Cooke was the cornerstone asset in Klein's aborning empire—and one he couldn't yet afford to lose; because Klein ended up owning nearly everything left of Cooke; and because of his reputation as a sharking law-skirter who gutted unwary prey with a smile and a ballpoint pen, he became a natural magnet for the steely suspicions of Cooke's old crew. Klein's public constancy in his avowed love for Sam Cooke hasn't wavered for thirty-five years. Others think he had all the best reasons for wanting Cooke to die.

To this day the idea that Cooke was undone by a conspiracy carried out by some shadowy caucus of industrial powers-that-used-to-be is a conviction among many who were then part of the business Cooke was in, or trying to be, and knew how it worked. They believe this without proof and without reservation. One who does, Etta James, lived down the street from the Hacienda Motel. As a minor celebrity notorious for being a dope fiend, she felt the need to safeguard her security by monitoring police broadcasts.[7]

When she heard Cooke identified by name as a dead perpetrator, she rushed to the scene and stayed closely enough involved as a friend of the family to see his remains at the mortuary before they were prepared for burial. She reports—and Roy Crain tends to confirm—that Cooke's corpse bore evidence of a beating much fiercer than a fifty-two-year-old woman was likely to have inflicted defending herself with a flimsy stick. Some have speculated that he was killed elsewhere, then removed to Bertha Franklin's office, even though his blood was all over its walls.

The available facts more readily permit the inference of a pettier sort of conspiracy: Cooke was probably killed while being robbed. Lisa Boyer lied when she testified that she met Cooke for the first time on the evening he died. They had been seen together for months. A friend once wryly noted that Cooke would "step past a good girl" in pursuit of a whore, and evidently he tarried too long with one too many.

Although the police said she had no prior criminal record, Boyer was a known prostitute who would have used aliases to confound the account-keepers of law enforcement. She was arrested for prostitution a month after Cooke's death. Joan Schmitt's research later revealed that her particular specialty was thieving from customers. Running off with the shorn sheep's clothing was a standard method of discouraging pursuit.

Boyer and Bertha Franklin almost certainly lied when they claimed not to know each other. Franklin was a retiree from the whore stroll, a former trick-house madam who oversaw the front desk during the hours prostitutes mostly used the motel as a work station. While Cooke's white business associates couldn't imagine that he would have been anywhere near such a place as the Hacienda—one insisted Cooke "wouldn't be caught dead in Watts"—he actually knew well both the neighborhood and the establishment. A close-by bar was a watering spot on his regularly prowled nocturnal range. The band he usually used on the road had encamped at the motel when they came to Los Angeles looking for work, after Little Richard, their previous employer, ditched them for Jesus. A former member of the Upsetters said Cooke had often been around the Hacienda during their extended stay.

This makes likely Cooke's familiarity to Franklin as more than just a celebrated face. If all three parties to this incident knew one another, and two tooks pains to hide this acquaintanceship after the other had died at one of their hands, the surviving pair have the appearance of conspirators. The two women never had to answer any pointed questions about their associations, and they never will. Bertha Franklin immediately relocated to Michigan and was dead within eighteen months. Lisa Boyer dropped from view twenty years ago upon entering prison in California for killing a male companion.

Police say Cooke was found with $108 in his pocket and discounted the possibility of robbery because his wife said he left the house that morning with about $150. But she didn't know he had taken $5,000 from a safe-deposit box that afternoon to go "Christmas shopping." Cooke's dinner companions that night say Boyer saw him flash his ample bankroll at the bar. Neither were the wallet and credit cards he carried ever found.

Though the custodians of his legend have edited it out of their public recollections of him, Cooke was reportedly subject to monstrous rages. But it seems altogether improbable that cheated lust could have provoked this one. On the other hand, Cooke's shocked discovery that a small fortune had been stolen by a whore he'd thought tamed and smitten, along with the attendant recognition that she'd been setting him up for months, would have engendered in a hot flash his infuriating realization that this trifling Chinese bitch had the gall to think she could squeeze the whoremaster Sam Cooke like he was some juicy trick she'd caught at the bar of the Beverly Hills Hotel.

Already seething with an indignation that is reflexive in men who have been caught out and know they should have known better but still expect to be immune from consequences, his glimpse of Boyer knocking on the office door would have instantly implicated its occupant as her confederate. This would have sent him off in an avenging rage to settle accounts with whomever he found in Bertha Franklin's office.

Her refusal to admit him would have been taken by Cooke as confirmation that she was Boyer's accomplice. Once inside and stonewalled by Franklin, the "don't you know who I am" response is the inevitable resort of any who are acculturated to being famous when they are denied something they badly want or need. This sense of affronted entitlement iced over his fury with a retributive resolve that assured the ensuing confrontation of its savage result. Franklin may not have intended to kill Cooke, but her complicity in robbing him would have given her reason to do so thorough a job of it.

It took a week and two funerals to bury Sam Cooke. His body was first flown to Chicago in deference to his mother, who was too sick to travel. Before it was placed in a bronze-inlaid casket with a glass cover to enable display without touching, the mortician tried to compose Cooke's face to redress the insult done to its once-disarming beauty. It took thirty-five patrol cars and fifty policemen to fail to control a crowd of six thousand that, in pressing for a view of Cooke preserved and encased like a specimen in a natural history museum, staved in the funeral parlor's plate-glass windows.

That night a crowd nearly twice as large gathered for the funeral in the year's bitterest cold, outside a church that couldn't accommodate a third as many. Chicago's gospel establishment withheld an official delegation, perhaps in disapproval of Cooke's apostasy and the manner of his dying. Dick Gregory and Muhammad Ali showed up, along with some of the local singers, but mostly it was a profusion of ordinary black Chicagoans who congregated so thickly that police had to clear a path to the coffin. Reverend Cook's family needed forty minutes to wend their way to seats up front.[8]

Cooke's body was flown back to Los Angeles, where it played to packed houses in daylong continuous showings before a second funeral was held for a man who was by then eight nights gone. In the rain this time a throng of five thousand or so waited undecorously for the church to open. The traffic jam they caused made the hearse forty-five minutes late. Street vendors hawked photographs taken in Chicago of Cooke in his coffin. Dominating the scene's ambient noises was a cacophanous mélange of Sam Cooke's greatest hits, as residents of the neighborhood around the church blasted his records from open windows.

Barbara Cooke eschewed riding with the rest of the family in favor of the grander transport of her husband's Rolls-Royce. Bobby Womack came with her, wearing the dead man's clothes. Two months later, on the day she was named executrix of Cooke's estate, the widow announced she was going to marry her husband's protégé as soon as he was old enough to do it without needing parental consent. Within several weeks he was, and indeed they married. Four months later Bobby and Barbara Womack were pistol-whipped in Chicago by an outraged Charles Cook Jr. They'd gone there to haggle, with too much indelicate persistence, over who should get which of his late brother's minor effects.[9]

The service in Los Angeles was convoked by Billy Preston playing "Yield Not to Temptation" on organ, and featured hymn-singing by Lou Rawls and Bobby Bland. The slain star was to have been sung to his eternal rest in the three-octave range of the great Bessie Griffin, who even her competitors said "could moan and move a mountain." But Griffin was unable that day to move anyone; she was so overcome by the spirit of the occasion, she couldn't perform.

Her incapacitation proved Ray Charles's opportunity to steal Sam Cooke's last show. He would find irresistible his chance at any room this charged and teeming, or any audience so exquisitely ripe for his taking. He stepped from the back of the church and was led down its center aisle, as the overflow congregation's murmurings at their unexpected first sightings of him became exhortations once his intentions were clear.

He teased them as he would a nightclub crowd, by asking if they wanted him to sing. Then, after a "Sam, baby, this is for you," as though addressing a colleague in the house who'd happened by some Thursday night to watch him work, Charles proceeded to sit at the piano and hold church so deep that even J. W. Alexander, holding the microphone for him and long inured to such theatrics as these, broke down and wept unabashedly.[10]

Barbara Cooke sold her inherited share of her first husband's published works to Hugo and Luigi for $103,000, a paltry sum even in those times. The tax man was circling over Cooke's estate in a slow descending spiral, and she needed money. The cousins soon found partnership with J. W. Alexander more troublesome than worthwhile and quickly sold out to Allen Klein.

Klein waited for Alexander's own tax problems to worsen, then bought him off cheaply. For the next twenty-five years Klein litigiously asserted and protected his property rights, fending off a Barbara Cooke parry and preemptively thrusting at RCA and its corporate parent, BMG, when they came too near to infringing on his felt prerogatives. Rather than its proprietor, Klein thinks of himself as the vigilant steward of Cooke's legacy, whose beneficence toward the family he dispossessed surpasses any reasonable claims that they might exert on his conscience, since owing them nothing, he provides money now and again when they are needy.

"A Change Is Gonna Come" was released a couple of weeks after Cooke died, just as the year of Freedom Summer turned into the year a president of the United States said "We shall overcome" on television. That slogan had entered the official culture through its use as the title of the national anthem of the civil rights movement, itself adapted from one of Reverend Tindley's hymns by the merest alteration of a few words.

"A Change Is Gonna Come" was intended only as the other side of "Shake," but the record flipped over in the spring of the march from Selma to Montgomery, the Woodstock of civil rights. Nineteen sixty-five was also the year a federal voting rights law—Dr. King's political triumph—was enacted, Watts rioted, Motown sold "sunshine on a cloudy day," a hundred thousand more American troops went to Vietnam, and three youngboys out of Chicago used the word "rap" in a song lyric for the first time.

Undressed of its adorning strings and French horns, "A Change Is Gonna Come" is a companion to "Jesus Wash Away My Troubles," arguably Cooke's purest performance. In it he was up to what smart, contemporary songwriters like Mayfield were doing, bending a "gospelism" to broaden its meaning rather than adapting a song by changing its words. The only real reflection of the personal in a song that Cooke posed as autobiographical is its mood. This was his conscious stab at topical relevance, and he intended to tell a symbolic story in the first-person voice.

Eerily, though, in its original sense, the particular borrowing from the church idiom to which Cooke applied his transposing hand refers to the change death brings in a soul's state of being, as it passes from the body and becomes purely a spirit—as in "One day I know my change will come." In the tradition of religious popular music Cooke came from, this phrase is often associated with Job, who near the end of enduring his merciless trials decides he'll "sit down and rest a little while . . . [and] wait for [his] change to come."

The story of Job was appropriated by slaves as a metaphor useful in their construction of an Aframerican myth of tribal origin, and preserved in Afro-Christianity as a parable about transcendence, as the prize at the end of an afflicted history can be had only by living it through. It would seem that some images can act upon cultural memory as an aroma that provokes the twinge of an old feeling in the memory our senses have.

His use of one of these turned Cooke's valediction into a perfect underscoring, at the point it coincided with the narrative flow of Aframerica's unfolding national epic. The song's layered resonances imbued what would have served well enough as a world-weary but hopeful progress report from the tribe's surrogate voyager with a dark poignancy, which assures "A Change Is Gonna Come" of being both timeless and a permanent artifact of its time.

When Berry Gordy heard that Cooke had died, he thought the life just taken would make a good subject for a movie and imagined Marvin Gaye in the leading role. Gaye, ten years younger than Cooke, used to watch him perform at the Howard and then go home and closet himself, "practicing and memorizing every thing I heard [Cooke] do."[11] He had played Sam Cooke before. But though Gordy was still ten years away from making movies, he would quickly have surmised what others later concluded: that as long as recent memory was around to serve, any film about Sam Cooke would have to be a documentary, since no actor was available who would be plausible in its title role.

Gordy settled for commemorating the first black leading man in American show business whose regular job was romancing white girls with a tribute album by the Supremes. In those days Motown's skills at conceiving, assembling, and packaging record albums were relatively undeveloped, and most people thought the association this one made between Sam Cooke and the Supremes was an awkward commercial contrivance. But it would have made instinctive sense to an interpreter of culture as astute as Gordy. Because of the psychosexual fraughtness of the role he undertook, the romantic persona that Cooke felt he could safely adopt in passing through the interior lives of white females had its basis in Cary Grant. And by then Gordy already believed that in Diana Ross he'd found the makings of a black girl whose career could be like Doris Day's.

PART II

First I Look at the Purse:

Motown and Memphis

8. Family Values

When he was called to Korea in 1951, Berry Gordy Jr. went armed with whatever protections a lifetime of his father's homiletics afforded, and the cadences of Rudyard Kipling's "If" beating away in his head. As with other young men on whom school had landed only a glancing blow, the army had an edifying effect on Gordy. He came home with a high school equivalency diploma and the manner of a counterfeit college boy, professing his devotion to jazz as the "only pure music." A few weeks after his discharge he got married, went to work for his father, and tried to settle into being what he had always hated to think he might have to become.[1]

Detroit in the early 1950s was experiencing the first flowering of the arts among the children of its black immigrants; its nightspots were the workshops then of more than a dozen men and women who were preparing to go to New York and become stars of jazz. Berry Gordy Jr., eager to shuck off his father's gentle but insistent yoke, persuaded his brother to become his partner in a record store that sold only jazz in a neighborhood that was buying only rhythm and blues.

He held out, true to the orthodoxies of his own taste and unyielding to his customers' desires, long enough to go broke. This failure was the purchase price of all the practical education he would ever need about the perils of mixing romance with finance. But with two children by 1955 and a foundering marriage, it left him with no alternative to an eighty-six-dollar-a-week job nailing upholstery to car seats in a Ford Motor plant.

Berry Gordy Jr. worked days in a factory and networked by night in Detroit's choicest venue for brand-name black entertainment, the Flame Show Bar, where his sisters were concessionaires. The Flame's proprietor was a man named Al Green, a paint manufacturer who went into the recording business after the war so that he could move more shellac, the primary stuff of which phonograph records were made in those days. Green also managed the careers of Johnny Ray, a white boy with a hearing aid and a freaky style who was Detroit's gaudiest pop singing star in the early 1950s, and the extravagantly talented Jackie Wilson, who was about to supplant Ray and, in the process, change Gordy's life.

Al Green was exemplary of what white people of relatively minor means could accomplish selling black music in an era before more important white people were paying attention. Mom-and-pop store-keepers, rack jobbers, and song peddlers, alive to an unmet market demand in America's cities after the war, began making records to enliven their more permanent commercial interests. Not many of them cared much about the music, or the people who made it, or the people who bought it.

Some were white retailers of black music in black neighborhoods whose disdain for their clientele had been hardened by the regular ease with which they induced people too poor to have discretionary income into making one last purchase with the money they had put aside for carfare home. Most thought their customers would buy anything, as long as it was of a certain type. They were selling a product they never would have brought into their own homes; thus they had no urge to improve it, and so became an unconscious medium of cultural exchange among aliens, undisturbers of a tradition they were willing to buy and sell but never cared to own.

At first this new wildcatting class of record entrepreneurs was beneath the attention of its social betters, the oligarchs of the music-business establishment. The atmosphere around them was overheated by feverish commercial thuggery; among their standard practices were extorting publishing rights as the price of getting a song recorded, and pilfering writers' credits to jack up their take of the royalties on every record sold. Their end of the business was a gambler's game, requiring money, luck, shrewdness, and nerve in roughly the same proportions as playing cards or dice for a living.

Small-label owners were squeezed between suppliers demanding to be paid and distributors disinclined to pay. In such circumstances sudden success could have deadly consequences. Small companies often choked on their first hit records: they were forced to outlay cash to get more and more "product" manufactured and shipped, while their distributors held off paying them for as long as possible, hoping they would fold up and go away, daring them to come up with another record that people had to have before they got paid for the one they had now.

Berry Gordy Jr. was dedicated to his aspirations as a songwriter, and cultivated Al Green and his young mob-wired assistant Nat Tarnapol to get his songs into Jackie Wilson's golden throat. In 1958 and 1959 Gordy cowrote three big pop hits for Wilson that propelled the singer's meteoric burst into sudden renown. This success certified Gordy as a professional and secured him a position near the elbow of a star, but it left him as broke as before.

Even after he received his thousand-dollar royalty check, a year late, for the last and largest of these commercial triumphs—a song called "Lonely Teardrops"—Gordy figured he was making about $27.50 a week at his full-time self-employment in the music business. He shed his first wife and prepared to marry a woman who could make herself useful.[2]

Gordy met Raynoma Giles in 1958, after she and her sister won an amateur contest at a nightspot called the Twenty Grand. Winehead Willie, the emcee there, sent her to Gordy, whom he knew to be recruiting unknown but aspiring local talent. In those days Gordy ran a floating atelier out of his sisters' apartments, unsupported except by their indulgence and his sparse songwriting royalties. Raynoma met him in Loucye's parlor, where he was rehearsing a vocal group that was part of a stable of young singers he kept around him and trained as a full-time job.[3]

He had the idea he could develop acts to record his songs and then, for a licensing fee, furnish the finished productions to record companies to put out on their labels. Raynoma was surprised that the man she and her sister were appointed to see was short and "pug-nosed," conspicuous for "an ugly brown-striped shirt with both elbows worn completely through" and a raggedy hairdo. Black Detroit was serious about its hair, and if he wore one, the condition of a man's process was his Dun and Bradstreet rating. Gordy's bespoke no steady income.

Raynoma's sister was as dismissive of this ragtag as her mother would have wanted her to be, but Raynoma was intrigued by his "foggy voice," with its uncommon rhythms. She knew he had written hit records for Jackie Wilson and was prepared to think him a "n[egro] rich" eccentric. While they auditioned for him, his face was unreadable. After they were finished, he said to Raynoma, unblinkingly, "Well, what else can you do?" His disapproval only drew her closer, since it came in a form that both implied his continuing interest and challenged her to prove worthy of it. She kept pointing out facets of her musical accomplishment until one of his eyebrows finally arched, and then, still unsure of his disposition, she implored: "I do anything."[4]

He gave the impression of knowing important things that she didn't and would want to learn. By now she was detecting about him an air of "mystery . . . a cool freedom, an original flair." Conviction would have radiated from someone like Gordy, who was willing to set off deliberately in the pursuit of an objective before he had the wherewithal to make its attainment seem plausible. Raynoma was becoming "entranced." Now she noticed his "cute behind" and "beautiful teeth."

For his part, Gordy had uses for a girl who could do lead sheets and had perfect pitch. He took her on as an unpaid assistant. She rode home after this encounter "seeing Detroit as I'd never seen it before," and "want[ing] more than anything else in my life to be a part of what he was doing." He had "pulled" her; she was his.

Gordy had a knack for finding the right people at the right time, and Raynoma was a godsend. Skills she'd learned in high school and had since enhanced by dint of a keen aptitude, he "almost regarded as tricks of magic." Thus she quickly made herself indispensable. At her suggestion Berry and his operation moved into her apartment. At night her nerves were nearly shredded by frustration.

She and Berry slept chastely in the same bed for months. One day when he was feeling particularly weighed down by thin money, he disclosed to her that he'd been trying to augment his working capital by pimping whores on John R Street. But it wasn't going well, he said, because his heart wasn't in it. "I can't do what the motherfuckers down there do," she remembers him saying, "They beat the women up. . . . Heartless sons of bitches . . . I can't do that shit. I feel sorry for my girls. . . . I can't make them go out on the street . . . if [they're] sick or can't work. . . . But then on the other hand I've got so much riding on these acts, no money coming in, a ton of expenses and . . ."[5]

Raynoma was deeply stirred by Berry's revelation. She'd known him barely two months, but her commitment was unshakable, even by such jarring evidence of his habit of concealment. "Even though the idea of living my life in love with someone involved in this was terrifying," she decided, "I would live that life if necessary."

The next day, as if entranced, she got on the same bus he would take and rode to the same destination. She "stepped off onto John R Street, like Dorothy awakening in the Land of Oz." She was "fascinated and repelled" by what she saw there: "No wonder poor Berry felt out of his league. These cats were . . . stalking up and down John R in their big tall hats and silk suits. And their Cadillacs. Berry . . . was just a short, little knock-kneed fellow in raggedy clothes."[6]

Gordy would have met and mixed with many such men in his years of haunting local nightspots, particularly at the Flame, which was the Peacock Alley of the black Detroit demimonde and just a couple of blocks off the whore stroll. No doubt he would have frequently observed their work on its surface, even gotten some casual schooling from men for whom his association with Jackie Wilson would have certified him as worth knowing. Such maxims of their trade as "a pimp is really a whore who has reversed the game on whores" would seem useful insights to an auditor who was being pimped by the music business.

Gordy would appraise these men and think himself their match in guile and gamesmanship. This would incline him to believe he could do as they did. But though his natural affinity for the game might have enabled him to catch a stray whore or two, it couldn't compensate for his want of the enabling hatred that sustains a determination to use any means necessary to get money from whores every day. Like the man unprepared to kill over money who nonetheless thinks he can sell drugs for a living, Gordy would have discounted the evidence of his senses and persuaded himself that he could dip and dab in the street-level sex trade without possessing all the necessities for doing the job. His preceptors would have told him, "Green-ass n[egro], you got to be icy. . . . A whore's scratch ain't never longer than a pimp's cold game."[7]

If Gordy was trying to pimp, he would have been sorely disadvantaged by being without a car or clothes. There is no sorrier display of pretense than someone who calls himself a pimp having to take a bus to where the whores stroll to pick up his money. Such a pretender would be disparaged as a "chili pimp." This term, as defined by Iceberg Slim, the seminal recorder of the lore of his profession, refers to the small-timer, the merchant with one store in a business that requires a high volume of sales to become lucrative.

Even as he had when he retailed records, Gordy was failing as a seller of sex. In 1957 "You ain't no pimp" would have been the street's judgment of him, but the street's view is always shortsighted. Gordy had been given the advantage of a longer perspective on women by his exposure to those of his family; it was clear to him that a lot more money could be made pimping their minds than by pimping their sex.

By then it was as if Raynoma were under a spell that made her do whatever she thought she had to do to be Berry Gordy's woman. If a whore were what he needed, she would be one. She called a friend who arranged a trick for her to turn. She put the wages of her sacrifice— seventeen dollars—on the kitchen table that night for Berry when he got home. But it wasn't until Raynoma figured out how to put real money into his pocket that he consummated her desires. ("Be as sweet as the scratch. Don't be no sweeter. Always stick a whore for a bundle before you sex her.")[8] If he lacked the entire cold-bloodedness required to pimp "by the book," Gordy was familiar with its chapters and verses.

The curriculum taught on John R Street was the backbone of his vocational education.

Berry Gordy Sr., the grandson of a slave and her master, was born into about as hard a life as there was for a resident of Georgia, although his family had the relative advantage of owning the 168 acres near Sandersville on which it scratched out its living. These holdings had been accumulated by his slave-born father over the nearly fifty years between his emancipation and his death by lightning bolt. Out of small profits eked from the ground he already had, the original Berry Gordy had pieced together a family farm and secured it against the chicaneries of agents of the state and local white land-grabbers by record-keeping so precise as to be impregnable. In end-of-century Georgia few other Negroes read or wrote, and 90 percent were sharecroppers.[9] His son, Berry Gordy Sr., was one of only nine of his parents' twenty-three children to survive growing up there.

Most of his boyhood was passed in the decade historian Lerone Bennett has described as "the worst . . . for blacks in the history of America." The racial climate in Georgia was particularly volatile and nasty; during the 1890s there were 159 lynchings there. When he was eight, the Supreme Court decided *Plessy v. Ferguson.* The year he turned nine, 123 American Negroes were lynched. When he was seventeen, an African pygmy of the same age who had been a popular attraction at the St. Louis World's Fair was abandoned by his exhibitors after it closed. The man was displayed in a monkey cage at the Bronx Zoo until the outrage expressed by the Negro press and local black citizens caused the mayor to remove him to a Colored Orphanage in Brooklyn.

When his father was struck down in 1913, Berry Gordy Sr., then twenty-five, filled the breach in his family. This meant mastering the pertinent arcana of estate law in order to survive the games of cat and mouse played by the local bar in its deadly toying with Negro property-holders. He skirted the traps of tricky paperwork and undocumented tax payments.

Administering his father's estate overseen by a county court taught Gordy to move among dangerous white people in the disguise of seeming less than who he was, so that he might confound them by being more than they expected. For the rare freestanding black farm family in Georgia, life's direst jeopardies resulted from owing a white man more money than you could pay back, or from paying it back too quickly.

In 1916, when Gordy became one of 34,000 black Georgians conscripted into wartime service, Aframericans were 40 percent of the state's population and owned less than 5 percent of its available land. As a boll-weevil infestation blighted the region's cotton-heavy economy, increased demand for labor in northern cities pulled the first trickle of what would become serial waves of black immigrants from the South. Ten thousand black Georgians left that year; of those who stayed, sixteen died at the hands of white vigilantes. In 1917 fifty thousand more headed north.[10]

A year later, when the army cut him loose, Berry Gordy Sr. came home to Sandersville. He married a country schoolteacher and started his family. His outlook having been broadened in the world beyond Macon, Gordy was thirty years old and unsettled back on the farm. He went into the business of selling beef from a meat wagon and planned to open a market. In Detroit Henry Ford had begun publishing his race-baiting periodical, and for the next several years every purchaser of a Model T received a complimentary subscription to the *Dearborn Independent,* wherein he was kept informed of an "international Jewish conspiracy" and warned about a late-century America to be "inhabited only by Slavs, Negroes, and Jews."

During America's "Red Summer" of 1919 nearly eighty Negroes perished by lynching. American industry's postwar crackdown on labor unions worsened the overall racial climate, particularly among the many whose subsistence depended upon getting on the payrolls of men like Ford. Negroes were generally excluded by unions and so were used by employers to undercut the price of organized labor. In Georgia clashes among sawmill and railroad workers made several cities and towns the sites of violent exchanges between the races. On the first of September white mobs in several Georgia locations burned black schools and churches.

A month later, within three days of each other, four black men were lynched in three different places. One was killed near Sandersville. During the next three years 150,000 blacks left the state, Gordy among them. In 1922 he sold to a sawmill some tree stumps he had pried out of family ground.

About this time, a hundred miles away in Macon, after a murder suspect was lynched and his corpse left naked in the street, every Negro in sight was shot at or assaulted. The most prosperous among them, a local theater owner named Charles Douglass, was given twenty-four hours to leave Macon upon peril of being hung by the same rabble. Under the circumstances Gordy figured he needed to take the proceeds of his sale—a bank draft for $2,600—out of Georgia before someone of Washington County's overlording white minortiy found out he had it. He didn't cash the check until he got to Detroit, then sent for his wife and three children with part of his share.

Whatever illusions a man of Berry Gordy Sr.'s natural optimism might have had about what awaited him at the end of his train ride north would have dissipated quickly once he got to Detroit. In the early 1920s about fourteen thousand black migrants were streaming into the city every year, on top of the thirty thousand who had preceded them over the previous decade and were already contending with an acute housing shortage and jostling with European immigrants—Poles, Greeks, and Italians, mainly—in a savage competition for jobs that were worth, on average, about three dollars a day.

Detroit became a factory town with a laboring class riven by unremitting racial strife. In 1924 the Detroit chapter of the Ku Klux Klan—believed then to number thirty thousand—nearly elected its candidate for mayor. The next year a black doctor who had moved into a white neighborhood shot a man while protecting himself from the mob of outraged neighbors around his house. The integrity of white neighborhoods was maintained by restrictive covenants that were enforced, where necessary, by cross burnings, stonings, and incendiary devices.

With his share of his family's tree-stump profits, Gordy paid too much for a bad house on Detroit's west side, the gentler of the two neighborhoods to which the city's rigidly segregated housing market confined its black residents. Then he commenced his earnest regimen of hard work and relentless thrift, selling ice and coal, firewood, old car parts, watermelons, and Christmas trees to feed a family that by 1929—when Berry Jr. checked in—had grown to nine.

By 1931 he had lost the house and the family was on welfare. But even as the Depression deepened, Gordy was unbroken. He found a small, failing grocery store on the other side of town and took over the rent payments. He renamed it after Booker T. Washington, patron saint of southern black bootstrappers, tended it with his wife Bertha, and made it profitable. Eventually he got a contractor's license and started a plastering business.

By his own account, Berry Jr.'s early life was as regular as a farm-boy's: a Rockwellian tableau of family gathered around the radio every night after dinner, life lessons learned helping on his father's jobs, and enough benign mischief-making to certify his spunk. But he also reports some darker imprints on his memory of being young: protracted bed-wetting, longings for girls he couldn't have, and never learning to read well enough to be any good at school. When he was eight, he discovered his parents had lied about Santa Claus, and he took this felt betrayal so hard that he henceforth "would . . . automatically question everything anybody told [him]."[11]

While the young Berry often thought of himself as a chronic source of his family's disappointment, it was also true that he was disappointed by the circumstances into which they had delivered him. He was already consumed by "a burning desire to be special, to win, to be somebody." For him, these distinctions were conferred only by accla-mation of "the real world—the white world" and were unlikely to result from a life lived on his father's scale or by his rules. He was conditioned to think his father heroic, but radio introduced him to Joe Louis, a hero who "didn't have to labor from sunup to sundown to be great, to be respected, to be loved [as] Pop did." This revelation, he says, "started a conflict between me and the family work ethic."

The Gordys of Detroit were an effective, self-contained unit, the brilliant invention of a doggedly resilient grassroots entrepreneur and a woman who thought of herself as a scholar and took as her vocation transmitting to her children the reverence she felt for self-improvement. His family would be Berry Gordy Jr.'s first and best idea of a business organization. And its fierce insularity kept him away from many of the snares of ordinary black life while he was growing up in Depression-era Detroit, where by 1932 roilings among the migrant throng—swollen by then to more than 120,000—were enough to dispose some of those the city had most disappointed to establish the first outpost of the Nation of Islam.[12]

During the 1930s Detroit's racial attitudes were manifested in the warm nests that its white citizenry made for such homegrown racialists as the radio preacher Father Charles Coughlin, another popular white supremacist named Gerald L. K. Smith, and the pro-Nazi National Workers League. Even before the crash came, the city's upsouth Negroes had found out that a black man's wages of thirty dollars a week bought about the same life in Detroit as twelve dollars a week had in the old country.

As soon as the industrial mobilization for World War II began, Detroit was awash in another immigrant tide: waves of southern whites rolled into town. Beginning in June 1940 Detroit absorbed a half-million incomers. Competition for jobs in the defense industries was stacked in favor of those whom many blacks perceived as "white trash"; about a third of the nearly two hundred defense plants in and around Detroit refused to hire Negroes.

Hudson's, the big department store, didn't have black sales help. A Negro couldn't drive a Checker Cab. Aframericans were routinely refused service at the city's "better" bars and restaurants. Early in 1942 a cross was burned on the grounds of a new federal housing project on the east side as soon as the first black families tried to move in. Twenty-six thousand white factory hands walked out of a Packard plant rather than "work beside a n[egro] on the assembly line."

The black community's dismay at being revisited by people and practices most had come north to leave behind, was hammered into resentment by the police department's unbroken twenty-five-year habit of harassing and abusing black citizens. These combustible elements rubbed each other wrong until one day in June 1943 when a fistfight over a dice game at an amusement park ignited a race riot in which twenty-five blacks were killed, seventeen by police.

Six hundred people were hurt, and $2 million worth of property was stolen or destroyed. Afterward the attorney general of the United States asked the president to consider "limiting, and in some instances putting an end to Negro migrations." "It would seem pretty clear," he noted, "that no more Negroes should move to Detroit."[13]

Berry Gordy Sr. was undeterred by crackers or their business cycles, since he avoided working for white men and knew of honest ways to live independently in lean times. His family had thrived before in an economy reduced to commerce in basic human needs. The Gordys came out on the other side of the Depression's bleakest years doing a little better than making ends meet. By 1941 they'd put enough aside to buy a small commercial building and install therein another family business, a print shop. "Pops" secured the family's stake and preached his dinner-table doctrine of do-for-self, but Bertha was its iron, and her daughters were its early-rising stars.

Along with minding eight children and a grocery store, Mrs. Gordy would manage in time to piece together a business degree from three colleges and start an insurance company. She and her first two daughters, Loucye and Esther, became business, club, and political women of high local influence. If "Pops" mellowed into a benign and avuncular presence—as much the image of ideal fatherhood for those associated with his son as Robert Young was to the audience of *Father Knows Best*—Mother Gordy was known to be selling something every time she came around.

The younger girls, Gwen and Anna, were sort of working-class debutantes with an enterprising edge that they first applied to the cigarette and picture-taking concessions at the Flame Show Bar. Gwen, in fact, would beat her brother at entering into the record business and her sister at marrying into it. Of the Gordy daughters, only Anna found no other function but to adorn. She made a career of family politics, clothes-horsing, striking splay-footed modeling-school poses for every snapping camera, and molding a greenhorn singer into a celebrity husband.

Marvin Gaye, the Gordy in-law whom Anna made, called them

"the tightest family [he]'d ever seen. No one could break into the circle." The patriarchal dogma of loyalty to clan had been catechized into two freeborn Gordy generations. As with most others, the staunchest protectors and tenders of this faith were its adhering females. Many years later, when a kingdom came unexpectedly to the family princeling, they ascended around him in closed rank.

"King Berry didn't have one queen, he really had four," Gaye mused. "His four sisters . . . were fiercely loyal . . . I never saw rivalry between them."[14] One who'd once had business at court, the singer David Ruffin, observed acidly that the "Gordys ma[d]e the Borgias look like the Waltons."[15] His rancor was not untinged by admiration for Berry and his sisters, over whom, in a decade of dealings, he had never had a moment's commercial or psychological advantage.

Becoming a boxer was Berry's first stab at a self-definition that comported with the sense of special purpose he drew from being a third son who was nonetheless a crown prince, having been anointed as bearer of the name his heroic father already shared with his legendary grandfather, a Gordy household saint. At sixteen, short and slight—a featherweight—he quit school to fight for money.

His professional boxing career lasted two years and fifteen fights. He says his better way came to him one day as he stood before a Duke Ellington poster side by side with one for a local boxing card. It struck him then that the busiest fighters worked once a month and took punishment every day in between, while musicians, if they were any good, worked nearly every night; besides, "the fighters were about twenty-three but looked like fifty; [the musicians] were about fifty and looked twenty-three."[16]

So Gordy, who had banged around a bit on his mother's piano as a kid but couldn't play anything but a jukebox and the phonograph, decided to take up songwriting. First he wrote a radio jingle for the family print shop. Then he sent his first song to Doris Day; a few weeks later he got back an autographed picture.

Gordy's life intersected with Jackie Wilson's in the first of several cycles in the singer's long career, the radiant false spring of his early rock-and-roll stardom. Wilson weathered best in older demographic regions; he never really was suitable for the consumption of children. Another former boxer, as physical as a predatory cat, Wilson's sexual swagger was unabashed.

His supple operatic tenor, however casually developed and indifferently maintained, was an instrument routinely capable of making men quiver and women quake: "no one could approach the electric, kinetic excitement that Wilson created on stage. He'd spin around then slide down into a split . . . jump up in the air, drop the mike and grab it just before it hit the stage, climaxing the song as he fell to his knees, begging."[17] Like other black entertainers of his generation, Wilson apprenticed in the old show business, so that certain of his vocal mannerisms suggested Al Jolson, and the version of celebrity he chose was based on Errol Flynn.

Raynoma recalled a visit from Wilson and his entourage: "When Jackie strutted into my house that morning [in 1958,] the place stopped. What a sight: his perfect 'do and his shimmering shirt unbuttoned to the navel. Diamond rings and gold chains. Major flash and personality. . . . I could see that the reports I'd heard were true; Jackie never went anywhere without make up. His was thick pancake foundation with eyeliner and rouge, maybe a touch of lipstick. . . . There was something both ludicrous and then completely appropriate about it, a way to call attention to [himself] as a star."[18] "If only I could be Jackie, just for a night," Gordy says he used to sigh.[19]

Gordy was starstruck, but not enough to keep sharecropping on Nat Tarnopol's plantation. He was being paid off in sporadic advances of petty cash against royalties, for which no accounting was ever disclosed, and the occasional use of a car. Tarnopol kept a cold hand on his whip handle and bluntly dismissed Gordy's quiet importunings for more money.

The whole of Gordy's professional identity was his connection with Wilson, but Tarnopol's contemptuousness forced Gordy to go his own way; Raynoma later claimed she had had to shame him into it. Wilson was indentured for life to Tarnopol, and to Brunswick Records, so he and Gordy would never again work together. But forever afterward Jackie Wilson was for him the "epitome of natural greatness," the standard against which Gordy compared, and always found wanting, the talent of every other male performer he ever saw.

In the manner of his father Gordy would distill into business axioms the lessons his disappointments taught: to make money at music, he had to own the means of producing it; and if talent and performance were inherently unstable variables in the formulation of hit records, he would have to tightly control all the others.

Within four years of his beginning in 1956 as a struggling supplier of songs, the rawest material of the record business, Berry Gordy Jr. would become one of its franchise-holders: first as an independent producer selling records he made on his own to companies with the wherewithal to put them out; then running a start-up label that released records in Detroit and sold to bigger companies the rights to distribute them everywhere else; and finally by presiding over an operation that managed every facet of its own business. All this resulted less from deliberate calculation than from a sequence of one thing leading to another toward an inescapable conclusion: Gordy had to master the music industry to protect himself from it.

Every step up the ladder was an act of self-defense. The irrepressibly ruthless nature of the business he had to be in to do the only thing he thought he had real talent for, conspired at every turn to cheat him out of even the small successes that should have made it easier for him to keep going. He was a songwriter, so producing records seemed the most straightforward means of ensuring that his songs were done the way he wanted and that he would be paid fairly for them; but then he got a $3.19 royalty check for being the producer of a record he'd made and sold to a label in New York. After his lawyer advised him to walk away rather than sue a publisher who was refusing to pay him a thousand dollars he was owed, Gordy knew he had to find the means to become property of himself.

The first toehold of Gordy's climb was secured by Raynoma's invention of the Rayber Music Writing Company. It was the equivalent of a vanity press for aspiring amateurs who were willing to pay a hundred dollars to have demonstration records made of their songs or to record themselves with professional accoutrements. Her idea opened a portal to the unmet desires of black Detroiters, through which quickly streamed enough cash to turn Gordy's salon into a workshop. Rayber was a cottage industry, with Berry and Raynoma working out of their apartment at the center of a small circle of singers and musicians who would be integral to Motown's original corps and who had about them, when they all began, the innocent aspect of teenagers in a Deanna Durbin movie who spruce up the barn and put on a show.

Raynoma, something of a prodigy, had elaborated on her high school training to the extent of being able to score and arrange music to a professional standard. She organized the talent Berry brought in, helped him shape songs and singers, and ran their fledgling business while he was out trying to make deals. She became his "bottom woman," the tender of his stable. Under her doting gaze, Berry proved a "born leader." For those around him, she said, Gordy was an inspirer, "a coach," a scientific motivator, and "a latter day Socrates" who "would spin beautiful, entrancing monologues about trust and sincerity and honor."[20]

Toward the end of 1958 Nat Tarnopol's effrontery finally became too rank and unrelenting to bear. Gordy had a song he would otherwise have given to Wilson that he thought was a hit. He had another mouth-piece lined up—a local singer he'd lately pulled in named Marv Johnson—who he believed could put it across. He thought of producing the record himself and maybe even releasing it on his own label, but he lacked the means. He had no alternative but to go to his family.

The Gordys had started a savings fund into which each member contributed ten dollars a month, to be used in emergencies or as venture capital. Any withdrawal required the family's unanimous consent. The eight hundred dollars that Berry succeeded in borrowing from the Ber-Berry Co-op required him to account to his formidable elder sister Esther for how little his life had amounted to so far and to use his future royalties as collateral. At twenty-nine Berry was undereducated, under-financed, and—by his own estimate of how he stacked up against the

Gordys' tall standards—habitually unsuccessful. Improbably, he took the money Esther ceded him grudgingly and parlayed this dividend from his daddy's old Georgia tree-stump stock into the biggest black enterprise America had ever seen.

Gordy sold the first fruit of his family's investment to United Artists. He got an advance of three thousand dollars, more money than he'd ever made at one time, as much as the stake his father spirited out of Georgia in 1922 when he'd made his way to Detroit. He had the check cashed into small bills, so they made an impressive pile when he came home and ceremoniously dumped them in the middle of Raynoma's bed.

In 1959 a second record of Johnson's that Gordy produced and sold to United Artists called "You Got What It Takes," and then another called "Money" by a stable hand named Strong—released on his sister Gwen's label—became nationwide hits. Gordy's crew beheld this shiny success with wonder, surprised that something of their homely design could find enough favor in the wider world to make them a little famous, at least in Detroit.

Gordy moved his company into a two-family house in a residential neighborhood on the city's west side. He and Raynoma lived upstairs. A sign was mounted across the front, above a large bay window, grandly proclaiming, "Hitsville, U.S.A." The recording studio inside was cobbled together under "Pops" Gordy's supervision from scrounged materials and secondhand equipment.

Gordy incorporated himself as a theoretical one-stop show-business conglomerate. He formed, simultaneously, Jobete Music Publishing, Berry Gordy Jr. Enterprises, Motown Record Corporation, and International Talent Management, a blueprint of the fortifications he intended to build against the predations of the music business.

Detroit by then had become a city with half a million black residents. Drawn by the auto industry's long postwar bloom, its black population doubled during the 1950s; among places to which upsouth migrants had flocked, only New York and Chicago accumulated more. In 1960 nearly a third of the city was black, and a quarter of the whites who used to live there were already lost to the suburbs.

The opening of the Chrysler Freeway that year on the gravesite of the Hastings Street business district completed the dismantling of Paradise Valley by a decade of urban renewal. Ten thousand buildings were demolished, and more than thirty thousand black citizens were relocated, many into housing projects built as catchments for the runoff of displaced poor caused by this deluge of civic improvements.

Though its dependence on car-making made Detroit as much a one-crop town as any in the Delta, the steady amplitude of its factories' harvests had created and sustained a propertied black working class. Compared with other cities, black Detroit was substantially home-owning, mostly because enough money trickled down from the auto industry to water its grassroots, but partly also because none of its constituents would have been sold a house in the city's encircling blue-collar suburbs.

The city's Negro third was teeming then with unharnessed young talent. As Mary Wells, Gordy's first female star, put it, "Before Motown, there were three careers available to a black girl in Detroit . . . babies, the factories, or daywork."[21] ("Detroit was the promised land for pimps all right. The town was [rife] with young fast whores . . . ain't but one real Heaven for a pimp. He's in it when there's a big pool of raggedy, hungry young bitches.")[22] The city had never had much organized recording activity. Gordy knew that if he built it, they would surely come.

Late in 1960 Berry Gordy Jr.'s first label, Tamla Records, released its first million-seller, "Shop Around" by the Miracles, a "gold record" in the industry's term of art. It gave him all the foothold he needed to begin imposing his will on an industry that had tried hard to break it. The record was largely the work of Motown's cornerstone asset—the singer, songwriter, and producer William "Smokey" Robinson—though the polishing Gordy gave it in the studio was crucial to its success.

When Motown was toddling, Gordy lurched along reactively to the marketplace's jerky motions, like a man in the woods firing his gun at anything that rustles leaves. His early talent acquisitions included a lost patrol of gutbucket singers, upsouth churchy wailers, retro doo-

woppers, and forgotten local half-talents. He made old-school rhythm-
and-blues records, twist records, and what were known later as bub-
blegum records, trying to hitch a ride on whatever the market would
bear. "Berry thought like an oil man," Marvin Gaye once suggested.[23]
"Drill as many holes as you can and hope for at least one gusher."

When John Kennedy became president, teenage girls were weighing heaviest in the pop music market, and female singing groups were
faddish. Late in 1961 Gordy caught his first Number 1 record with five
sixteen-year-old girls from the black suburb of Inkster. The several successive hits by the Marvelettes that were compressed into the next year
established the identity of an upstart record label in Detroit.

These were written and produced by combinations of the erstwhile
Rayber crew, among whom Brian Holland had emerged as a star
apprentice and Mickey Stevenson as shop steward. Gordy was so
appreciative of those Marvelettes records, he bought Brian Holland a
Cadillac. But it was Smokey Robinson's work with Mary Wells in 1962
that gave Motown its earliest trademark style.

The two men found each other when Robinson was seventeen and
Gordy was still bobbing along in Jackie Wilson's wake, hustling songs
and scouting talent. Smokey came to audition his group for Gordy and
brought along a schoolboy's spiral-bound notebook filled with the lyrics
of a hundred songs he'd written. Gordy, ever self-serious—Robinson at
first thought him "pompous"—and, comparatively, the seasoned professional, offered criticism that became advice and then turned into
ongoing instruction. Thus began a relationship that was unique among
all the others in Gordy's life.

Robinson was the only person not named Gordy to whom Berry
Gordy Jr. was unwaveringly loyal, the only unrelated Motown
employee spared the stinging back of its chairman's hand. He made
Robinson a vice-president in 1962, and they were bonded in their
shared enterprise for more than a quarter-century. Smokey named his
first child, the son his wife bore after enduring eight miscarriages, Berry,
and his daughter, Tamla.

Gordy had had convictions about songwriting before he was entitled to have anything more than ideas. When all he had was a co-

writing credit on three hit records, he was a didact whose assurance was his credentials, declaiming on the songwriter's craft to an audience of only Raynoma: "What nobody understands is format. Layout is crucial. . . . It [is] essential to tell a clear story with a minimum of words." His teachers had been the radio, the record player, and the musicians he befriended at the Flame Show Bar.

What Gordy knew about music was as circumscribed as his gift was particular: the two-minute-forty-five-second popular song. His métier was "a verse, another verse, a bridge, a chorus, back to the verse, one more chorus and out." Perhaps because he was a musical subliterate, he attached less value to melodic inventiveness than to song structure—"layout"—and lyrical content—"concept."[24]

"The key," he told Raynoma, "is creating tension with the hook; introduce it in the chorus, bring everything back to the verse, distract on the bridge—that's the tension—and then send the tune out with the hook." The hook is an element of pop music tradecraft borrowed from the advertising copywriter's tool kit: a line or phrase ingratiating enough to catch the ear and clinch the sale. With Smokey Robinson, whose manic cleverness and gift for ironic wordplay—"sort of like holding words to a mirror and checking out reverse images"—made writing hooks the strongest part of his package, Gordy worked on other things.

"He'd take a tune of Smokey's," Raynoma observed,

and literally turn it around. "No, man, you should come from this point of view. Start here in the first person voice." Then, when a strong theme was evident, Berry would guide Smokey further. "Yeah, that's good, very visual. . . . This line here, make it more of a picture." Smokey would incorporate the input, and the line would be, "I will build you a castle with a tower so high it reaches the moon."[25]

Here is Gordy in 1960, an editor before he'd ever finished reading a book, shaping the text of a song as if it were a screenplay, making sure it was both literary and visual. This tutorial preceded another by several years at a staff meeting Robinson later described:

The session started at nine o'clock, but you better get there by 8:45, 'cause once they closed those doors they wouldn't open again, even if the Lord himself had a song to sell.

Every week Gordy convened his company's producers and sales-people to decide what to bring to market that they had lately made. These meetings were Gordy's means of quality control, an idea he'd met on the Ford assembly line. In Motown's early days he sometimes brought kids in off the street to participate—the modern focus group before its time. Robinson tells us:

> [Gordy] built the meeting around the artists; anyone with a song for the Supremes, for example, would play it. Then came the critiques. Sometimes we'd all agree on what seemed an obvious hit. But mostly revisions would be suggested, and mostly they'd be heeded.
>
> When we got to [Robinson's group] the Miracles that morning, I proudly played my tape of "The Tracks of My Tears."
>
> "You crazy?" Berry asked when I was through.
>
> "No. Why?"
>
> "You got a hit but you buried your hook. Bring it up at the end, man. Repeat that shit—that 'it's so easy to trace the tracks of my tears' refrain—until you wear it out."[26]

Smokey, already by then as popular a songwriter as any there was, applied the finishing touches Gordy prescribed. He repeated his hook—"So take a good look at my face / You'll see my smile looks out of place / If you look closer it's easy to trace / The tracks of my tears"—four times in two minutes and fifty-three seconds ("wore it out") planting it so deep in the consciousness of one generation of American youth that it is rooted there still in our middle age. When film director Oliver Stone needed an aural artifact of the mid-1960s to evoke a hands-across-the-racial-divide-in-doomed-brotherhood feeling for the foxhole bacchanal scene in his movie *Platoon,* he used "The Tracks of My Tears" to produce the effect.

His own acumen was an object of Gordy's abiding faith. For as long as he cared about making records, his approval was required of each one his company released, and none ever were that he thought he could still improve. From the beginning Gordy had believed that a small record company was better served by releasing fewer records—provided they were successful—than by making and marketing too many, since of these any that were thought to be of dubious consequence wouldn't be promoted anyway. Such a strategy could be conceived only by someone who is confident he can develop a superior industrial process. It presumes to match the performance of bigger but less proficient competitors by selling half as many products twice as well.

In 1961, when Gordy spun off his namesake label, its logo bore the legend "It's what's in the grooves that counts." He relentlessy insisted on rerecording, remixing, and remastering—a dozen or more times, if necessary—until each release met his standards. He was willing to absorb higher recording costs than his competitors thought tolerable. He worked on the premise that if his goods were fine enough, they would save him money by selling themselves. If you consistently made records that a lot of people wanted to buy, you didn't have to pay distributors to carry your line, or rack jobbers to place it in drugstore chains and department stores, or buy as much airplay, or cajole retailers with giveaways and subsidized advertising.

Gordy's ear and skill at song doctoring had pulled his enterprise through its parlous early days. His adroit tweaking of other people's near misses made commercial triumphs of "Shop Around," "Playboy," and "Stubborn Kind of Fellow" when Motown was aborning, and each hit record was an infusion of lifeblood. As he bet his survival in business on being able to rapidly develop a superior line of products, quality control was among the first management processes that Gordy instituted. Motown put six records at the top of the pop charts before its bookkeepers had a systematic way of accounting for all the money it routinely advanced to the singers who made them.

Despite the besetting operational tumults that accompanied too much growth too quickly, Motown's means of record production were kept tuned and humming by Gordy and his straw boss, Mickey Stevenson. Nothing was ad hoc about quality control. The coordination of this function had been assigned its own box on the company's organizational chart since 1961. A girl Gordy had hired away from the student newspaper at Cass Technical High School to write press releases and liner notes for nine dollars a week was appointed to ask herself recurrently whether she'd "buy this record for a dollar or . . . buy a sandwich."[27]

Billie Jean Brown may have prepared his table, but Gordy alone said grace over every dish Motown served. He graded each on its title, lyrics, arrangement, and vocal performances. In time Brown exercised undue influence in Gordy's name, but even the heavy-handed politics of a workplace intolerant of independent thinking never suppressed the free expression of ideas on the shop floors. Criticism was Gordy's tool for sharpening, and he insisted on its liberal use. The weekly meetings at which producers made their pitches were but one of three winnowing stages in the process of getting a record released. In the end, though, no system Gordy devised ever supplanted his conviction that "he'd know it when he heard it."

Three years after Gordy had attested in a family court to making $133 a week from his music business and owing as much as he theoretically owned in the spring of 1960, Motown sold $4.5 million worth of records.[28] His five-thousandths of a share that year of the industry's total sales was enough to make him rich.

In 1963 he bought the Graystone Ballroom, a downtown dance palace built in the 1920s that had been darkened lately except for occasional boxing cards. When it had been Detroit's grandest venue, Negro patronage was allowed only on Monday nights. Gordy's purchase was considered a highly symbolic transfer of property by boosters of the New Detroit, since for the first time a landmark of official civic life had passed into Negro hands. Apart from announcing by its purchase that Motown had seated itself in the city's Chamber of Commerce, the Graystone's only value for Gordy was as a setting for hometown tryouts of the acts his groups were readying for the road.

Berry was now being addressed as BG by those of his employees licensed to call him other than Mr. Gordy. The model in Gordy's head of the record company he wanted to run didn't look like anything he'd seen in a car factory, as is often supposed, but more like an old-fashioned movie studio. As much as L. B. Mayer had, Gordy determined every aspect of his artists' working lives and made careers or let them die. He kept a stable of writers and producers churning out product, and a company of bit players and stars on salary who worked when they were told to and went where they were sent.

But however much Motown would be identified with the names of the performers it put up in lights, producers were the company's real stars. Even as the rest of the pop music business started to incline in the mid-1960s toward acts whose capacities for creating the music they sold were self-contained, the recording studios wherein Gordy's men blocked scenes and browbeat the "talent" into hitting their marks "ran almost twenty-four hours a day, seven days a week."

The producers making records at Motown had much in common with the directors making movies at Metro Goldwyn Mayer. But because most were also songwriters and had creative control over their projects, Motown's producers were true authors of the company's output. "Motown used to put a picture frame together, paint in all the background and . . . take the artist and put him in the picture," Carl Davis, a competitor from Chicago, once suggested. "They would make a complete record, record it in a certain key. Then the singer had to come in and sing the song in the key they had already determined, whether or not it was appropriate for the artist."[29]

This process was handy for agile, high-speed product development, which had obvious competitive advantages. In the summer of 1965, for example, the company needed to ward off Columbia's effort to exploit the monumental popularity of "I Can't Help Myself" by marketing old Four Tops material stashed in its tape files. "We came up with ["It's the Same Old Song"] in a couple of days," Lamont Dozier reminisced, "and the following Monday it was on the radio."

"Berry's way was to . . . strike while the iron was hot," said Clarence

Paul, a writer and producer best known for his work with Stevie Wonder. "That was his genius. . . . Catch that urgency. No matter what the release schedule might be, if you produced a hotter song, it would get out there . . . within days." "Well no," Gordy once responded to a producer who'd asked him for more notice next time. "You work better under pressure. . . . I like to see guys . . . under pressure."[30]

Gordy paired artists with producers on the basis of proven affinities; a hit record guaranteed a producer the next opportunity to work with the artist he'd made it with. These project assignments had the rhythms of a dice game: players stayed in as long as their hands were hot. As soon as they missed, another producer stepped up. The rules applied even to Gordy and his favorite sons.

In 1964, after a couple fruitless years of trying to come up with an establishing hit for the Temptations, Gordy put the job out for competitive bidding. Gordy had an entry he thought quite good enough, but his was trumped by Smokey's, who'd asked him for forty-eight hours so he could come up with something better. In the year after "The Way You Do the Things You Do" Robinson wrote and produced four more hit records for the Temptations, including "My Girl." When the next—"Get Ready"—faltered a bit in the pop market, Smokey lost the Temptations franchise to Norman Whitfield, who kept it for a decade.

The jockeying among producers to get their records out was remorseless. For many, the hardest part of being successful was securing a slot on the company's release schedule. Whitfield, who had to wait more than a year before a record of his that eventually sold four million copies—Marvin Gaye's version of "I Heard It Through the Grapevine"—was thought worthy of release, nevertheless admired Gordy's system. "The whole thing at the company was about competition," he said approvingly, "and competition breeds giants."[31] Gordy fomented competition among people who made money for him as fervently as his mother loved Jesus. ("A stable is sets of teams playing against each other to stuff the pimp's pockets with scratch.")[32]

The living was thinner and even scrappier on the hungry edges of Motown's deepening pool of creative talent. Writers had to lobby and often bribe producers to use their songs. "I would give half my production money and credit and half my songwriting money and credit to the producer to get my songs produced," one would later complain.

From his standpoint, the game's stakes seemed high enough to justify the steep ante that purchased an opportunity to play. The company was only going to release so many records, a miserly number no doubt by the profligate standards of an industry that was then flooding the marketplace with more than ten thousand singles a year. And these chosen few were likely to make money. In 1964, when Gordy's stable kicked into full stride, forty-two of the sixty records Motown brought to market were hits.

The continuities that Gordy's design for record-making meant to assure were sometimes perceivable as sameness. Motown's disparagers allude to this when they call it a "factory." But the process produced the effect of sameness only when its designer's intention was unachieved. Gordy aimed to create a particular identity for each of his major acts. He admonished producers to "get the tune to the artist it fit." He wanted the talent cast in productions deliberately chosen and adapted for their respective vinyl personae.

Martha Reeves's voice, for example, was blatantly sexual by the prissy standards of music being sung by older girls for younger girls— an early 1960s pop fashion that Gordy was following as far as it went. So she played the wench in such vehicles as "Heat Wave," "Quicksand," and "Live Wire," while on another stage the Marvelettes were acting the tough-minded, tenderhearted high school senior bumpily in love with a troublesome boy. Their character would grow into the worldlier big sister advising schoolgirl record-buyers to stay alert for potholes as romance takes its course. Gordy believed customers of the next Marvelettes record should await it with expectations that were as reliably conditioned by the last as those of people who went to see whatever Doris Day movie next came into town.

From early on the company spread its releases across five labels, hoping to disguise their common origin enough to confound the prejudices of radio stations against overloading their air at any given time with too much music from the same source. But by 1962 they all bore audible markings that were certifiers of a Motown provenance. While most were distinguishable as works of particular combinations of producers and singers—and thus were differentiated by their individual properties—"Motown record" became a generic term in the mid-1960s, with specific meaning to users who by then had learned what could confidently be inferred from it about quality and like characteristics. Gordy never understood the business he was in the same way his competitors did. They were just trying to sell records; he was building a brand.

Whenever they weren't being used by producers, Motown's contract laborers were overseen by the house talent handlers. International Talent Management was Esther Gordy's bailiwick. Even before Raynoma's banishment in 1962, Esther was relied upon to get her brother's horses to the track and keep order in his stables. When Berry put them through their daily paces, he made money on nearly every lap they ran.

Gordy's eager recruits enlisted with him while their dreams were still innocent of lawyers. They owed him seven years on the industry's usual terms, which effectively meant that even their sweat belonged to Gordy—and aimed to squeeze a profit from every drop. "Berry . . . pushed us as far as human beings could be pushed," Marvin Gaye recalled. "If we weren't touring we were cutting sides, and if we weren't promoting we were learning our dance steps."[33] ("Whores in a stable are like working chumps in the white man's factory . . . [and] a good pimp is like the slick white boss.")[34]

Though the royalty rates Motown settled on its artists fell within range of the industry's ungenerous standard, Gordy shrank their modest take-home pay by taxing income they earned from recording. From the 3 percent or so that Motown's artists were generally owed out of the 90 percent of the wholesale value of whatever of theirs was sold, he extracted the costs of producing their records and developing their acts. By such a means did Motown take every possible dollar of the half share that remained after retailers and middlemen had their slices of the cash generated by a record's sales. A performer whose record sold a million copies often accrued as little as ten thousand dollars from having made it. As late as 1975 the Jackson 5, still working off their original contract, got sixteen cents out of every six dollars that an album of theirs fetched in record stores.[35]

Singers lived mainly by the wages of performance. The company sold their services and scheduled the providing of them. Whenever a performance fee wasn't sent directly back to Detroit, a representative of Gordy's was on hand to collect it after every show. Once the company had excised its managerial 15 percent, the money the artist earned was held in an escrow account and dispersed as salary, or an allowance, or to fund a large purchase, or to pay taxes.

"Remember, they were children," shrugged Thomas Bowles,[36] the freshman proctor of many future stars who thought the company's dealings with its help were technically honest, if nothing more. Indeed, Gordy could always say he honored his contracts and accounted for every dollar due. He was scrupulous in his compliance with the terms of agreements like the one David Ruffin's lawyers would later submit that reduced their client to "economic peonage."

Because their managers were agents of Motown, there never was any wrangling over priorities when decisions were made about whether to apply an employee's labor to harvesting a crop that yielded the proprietor about 50 percent of its cash value, or to another from which he could garner only 15. "If you had a hit, and people [at the company] thought you needed a quick follow-up," said Otis Williams, the last Temptation, "they pulled you off the road, flew you into Detroit, and had someone waiting at the airport . . . ready to whisk you straight back to the studio."[37]

While keeping in hand every part of their livelihoods, Gordy kept his Motown "family" believing the yoke he had on their necks was an instrument of mutual improvement. They were beguiled by his mystification of "Motown spirit" as the wellspring of blessings seen and foreseen. Their faith was fed by the ever-more-frequent appearance of signs that Gordy really had found the path of their deliverance from Black Bottom into a state of prosperity appropriate to home-owning in the exclusive preserve of Sherwood Forest, Detroit's highest cotton. Their hearts quickened at such manifestations of Gordy's grace as they saw visited upon some of the faithful. They regularly had their spirits braced and loyalties toned in the communal observance of sacramental rituals.

At monthly staff meetings transatlantic celebrities and million-selling producers sang alike with secretaries and janitors the lines of puerile doggerel in "Hitsville, U.S.A.," the pep song that young Smokey had written in the throes of an overwrought enthusiasm, when he was still capable of being both corny and inept. Gordy was an addicted perpetrator of petty cruelties and spared no one around him but blood-family elders. He would have amused himself at Robinson's expense by memorializing his protégé's clumsy attempt to pass off a rhyme as obviously counterfeit as "unity" and "company," then exposing it ceremoniously to the recurrent scorn of resentful colleagues. But since Berry was also a "loving cat," as Marvin Gaye once put it, he would think of Smokey's crude anthem as a sentimental artifact of the "family"'s purest self, like a small child's crayoned scrawl kept taped to the door of his mother's refrigerator through all the years of his growing up.

While Berry worked his young charges even harder than his father had once tried to work him, Esther tackled their grooming in the spirit of her mother's maxim that "good manners will get you into places money never will." The centrifugal pull of the Gordys was the force of their fierce adherence to the ideology of self-improvement. A major aspect of Motown's first idea for Artists Development was embodied in Maxine Powell.

She was hired by Esther to teach the performing sons and daughters of migrant laborers how to carry themselves, eat in public, gesture onstage, and give innocuous interviews. Powell lived by hustling bourgeois refinements to factory hands' women, as a promoter of fashion shows and modeling contests. She gave "charm school" tutorials to girls from families too lately arrived and tenuous in their footing to have been invited into Jack and Jill, the social club wherein the children of old settlers with good jobs learned the ways of polite company.

"I taught them discipline and how to handle people," Powell

allowed, years later, of her curriculum in home training and public display.[38] Powell held classes in etiquette and stage presence for Motown singers of both genders but focused on the females the full bore of her instructions for living. Martha Reeves recorded the following among Powell's introductory remarks to her seminar: "Charm and grace will take you all over the world. When I 'finish' you, you will be able to wine and dine . . . in the presence of kings and queens. We want to do away with rude, loud, and boisterous personalities and become the prettiest ladies that we can be. . . . You will learn poise and finesse. . . . My models, including Anna and Gwen Gordy, and all of my students . . . represent class in all walks of life, the thirty years that I have been teaching."[39]

Berry's young women made rapt pupils. Reeves remembers a session of Powell's at Gwen Gordy's "luxurious home," when the hostess "proceeded to model, pose and demonstrate . . . on stools and in a variety of lounging positions . . . how good we could look if we carried ourselves right." One of the Gordy sisters was inviting them to become as sophisticated and glamorous as she was. This made their parts in her brother's plans seem even more exhilarating.

Powell was preparing them to act a version of women that they had seen on-screen, to make a statement out of their every arrival. Some would incorporate the role that Powell helped them create into reconstructed permanent identities. Diana Ross called her "the woman who taught me everything I know." Martha Reeves still "appl[ies] her teachings in everything I undertake."

Though one rose far and the other fell deep, both were trained to the manner of a star and adopted it respectively in high places and low throughout long careers. Even twenty years past her heyday, Mary Wilson's imperiousness was so ingrained that while waiting for her tardy baggage at an airport in Austin, Texas, she expressed her displeasure to a handler by announcing that "a Supreme must never be kept waiting."

With a franchise in the youth market at stake in the early 1960s, Gordy was careful of proper appearances. Along with running her in-house "charm school," Powell was sent out to chaperone girl groups on the road. Ten years before major record companies copied the idea and called it "tour support," Gordy had packaged his acts as the Motortown Revue and made them a road show, sending them all over the country on grueling bus tours to build a following and sell their records. His troupe's first time around the ninety-four-stop circuit that Esther had arranged for them in the last quarter of 1962 convinced Gordy to invest money in upgrading their skills.

He brought in teachers of voice and designers of stagecraft. Gwen's husband Harvey Fuqua—former Moonglow and noted group harmony technician—was the producer and wishful record entrepreneur who'd brought Marvin Gaye, Junior Walker, and the Spinners to Gordy as a bride payment. He was put in charge of Artists Development. This department became Gordy's means of polishing performers to a satisfactorily high gloss. Maurice King, the music teacher and vocal coach, said its faculty "worked the kids until they became pros. . . . We heated the acts until they cracked."[40]

"Berry was crazy back then," Marvin Gaye opined. "I can dig the Gordy family approach—work keeps you straight—but Berry carried it too far."[41] Gordy slapped Gaye's face one night at the Twenty Grand when the singer, wracked with anxiety about going onstage, dithered too long in his dressing room. ("The show can't stop when a whore bleeds.")[42]

"By late summer of 1964," Gordy could point, like a Ponzi schemer gulling his next investor, to the "shimmering Cadillacs [that] lined West Grand Boulevard in front of our door" as evidence in plain sight of "more and more people's dreams . . . coming true."[43] The life of this illusion depended upon protecting it from outsiders. Gordy "hated . . . outside lawyers and accountants, interviewers [or] hangers on."[44] ("There's no problem I can't solve," Iceberg Slim told a freshly pulled whore. "There's no question I can't answer about this game.")[45] Martha Reeves accounts herself the "first person at Motown to ask where the money was going." Her apostasy, though not actually original, "made me an enemy. Did I find out? Honey, I found my way out the door."[46]

"The more [success] Berry [started to have], the tighter he ran the ship," Marvin Gaye observed. "Soon Motown was like the Gestapo."[47]

Motown even furnished its performers' hangers-on from an in-house entourage of valets and "personal assistants" who also served as informants paid to report back to the company about who was doing what and seeing whom on the road. Gordy was as watchful of his assets as a hawk over his domain of field and sky.

The Hitsville "family" was interlaced by ties formed of matrimony and matings. First there had been Berry and Raynoma, then Smokey and Claudette. Three Gordy sisters married men at the company, and the fourth's husband was on the payroll. Motown seethed covertly with intramural romances. Illicit couplings served Gordy as well as the licensed ones, since both kept his people's focus inside the circle he'd drawn around them.

Gordy particularly discouraged his female talent from conjugating outside the fold; while they were with him, few slept regularly with civilians. A Marvelette married a Miracle. Another one married a Contour. Mary Wells married a Rayber singer turned staff writer. Kim Weston married Mickey Stevenson. Gordy's niece married a producer. A Supreme married her chauffeur. Another consorted with a married Four Top. Diana Ross made her way to Gordy through Smokey Robinson and Brian Holland, whose wife retaliated by physically assaulting her.[48]

Berry didn't care much about unseemliness in these internal affairs, so long as it wasn't seen from outside, but he was vigilant about his females seeing too much of outsiders. When a Vandella fell in love with one of Little Anthony's Imperials, Gordy intervened. "Choose somebody that's in our family," he advised. "There's plenty of good-looking men at Motown."[49] ("Never forget this family is one against the cold, cruel world. We're strong because we love each other.")[50]

9. Tall Cotton

Stax Records was born by accident at the intersection of a particular time and place. Jim Stewart was a farm kid from a hamlet east of Memphis near the Mississippi border, who grew up dreaming of being a country fiddler. When he was eighteen, he came to Memphis to begin his career in music. He ended up working at a bank.

By the time he was twenty-seven, Stewart knew he was never going to be a professional musician. With Elvis Presley and Jerry Lee Lewis impressing the example of Sam Phillips and Sun Records on the minds of Memphians, Stewart thought to substitute recording others for being recorded as the object of his thwarted aspirations to make a living by making music.

Stewart started recording obscure local hillbilly singers in his wife's uncle's garage, and put out stillborn records on a label he financed with two other men whose three-hundred-dollar investments made them his equal partners. Stewart came from a line of tillers of new ground who never had the option of giving up if their first crop failed.

He asked his older sister to remortgage her house so that he could buy better equipment. Estelle Axton, who was restless in midlife, agreed and became her brother's partner in Satellite Records. They relocated his new Ampex recorder, mixers, and microphones to a vacant store next to railroad tracks in a small country town thirty miles outside Memphis. They languished there, but for a record Stewart made in the desperation to make a record that he shared with a black singing group that had been featured for eight years with Ben Branch's band at the Club Tropicana in Memphis without convincing anyone they were worth recording.

When it came out in the summer of 1959, Mercury Records paid Stewart five hundred dollars for the rights to distribute "Fool in Love" by the Veltones, and he and Axton made their first money in the record business. This convinced them they could do better if they weren't so far away from the city, where people were evidently making music Stewart hadn't known about but others wanted to buy. He started looking in Memphis for an unused church building or abandoned movie theater with the right acoustics.

He found the Capitol Theater in South Memphis, gone dark in a neighborhood that was turning black from white. Stewart spent about three hundred dollars and a couple of months after work and on weekends hanging Estelle's handmade acoustical drapes, carpeting some of the floor, building burlap baffles to curb the echo, and sectioning off a part of the stage to make a control room. He erected a partition to divide the cavernous space in half. It retained such characteristics designed for its former use as a sloped floor and a twenty-five-foot ceiling; these quirks of contouring shaped the sound of every record made therein. To create a reliable source of rent money, which would have otherwise consumed nearly half of her brother's monthly salary, Estelle converted the theater's lobby into a record store.

The appearance of these new enterprises on the corner of College and McLemore Streets drew first the surrounding neighborhood and then musical aspirers from all over black Memphis into acquaintanceship with this odd pair, of which Estelle was the more outgoing and prone to ideas, and stolid Jim the dogged and single-minded pursuer of his consuming notion. One who came around was Rufus Thomas, a many-parted show-business veteran, a fixture in the cultural life of local Negroes.

Thomas, a graduate of the Rabbit Foot Minstrels, had since worked as a song-and-dance vaudevillian; a comic and master of ceremonies at all of Memphis's black theaters; a vocalist recorded by four labels in the ten previous years; and a radio personality on WDIA, "the

Voice of the Negro." He was peddling a tape of a song he'd written and sung with his teenage daughter Carla.

"'Cause I Love You" became the original recording made in Stewart's refitted movie house, and the first anyone ever wanted to buy that bore the imprint of Satellite Records. When it came out in the summer of 1960, Stewart's life was permanently altered. "Prior to that I had no knowledge of what black music was about . . . never even . . . an inkling. [I] was like a blind man who suddenly gained his sight."

Once "'Cause I Love You" had sold about ten thousand copies in three southern cities, word of it reached Jerry Wexler at Atlantic Records, whose ear was always cocked for rustlings in the grassroots from Negroes having cultural intercourse. Atlantic, which had risen to preeminence among postwar independent record labels by deftly adapting black "roots" music to popular tastes, was well past having the capacity to produce any under its own roof. By the late 1950s it had succeeded in becoming an established record company and behaved like one, riding the tamer currents in the mainstream.

Even though his company was prospering, Wexler was dispirited by the habitual compromises of taste that were required to keep it that way. "[E]ntropy was setting in in New York," he recalled. "I lost interest in recording with the same arrangers who were out of ideas. Musicians were out of licks [and] the songwriters didn't have any songs."[1]

Atlantic augmented its own inventory of merchandise the same way other occupants of higher-up niches in the industrial food chain did: by making distribution deals with little labels in the hinterlands like Stewart's. These often turned out records of commercial promise and always lacked the wherewithal to put their products on far-flung retailers' shelfs. Atlantic was better at doing this than most of its competitors because Wexler was a bona fide connoisseur of black music who also had sharp and practiced instincts for what of it he could sell and to whom.

He had lookouts posted far and wide to spot records like Rufus and Carla Thomas's. When he heard it, Wexler reacted with the enthusiasm of a hungry man who had long been denied an authentic meal. "I liked everything about it," he later recalled, "that bespoke Memphis."[2]

Over the next five years Jerry Wexler would be instrumental in the transformation of Jim Stewart and Estelle Axton's cottage enterprise into a major brand name in the popular music of its era. He flew to Memphis and shook hands over a deal with Stewart that guaranteed Atlantic's option to distribute whatever it chose of anything Satellite Records made.

Once Stewart consigned to Atlantic a master tape of a record that he had paid to produce, the bigger company would assume all the subsequent costs of manufacturing, distribution, promotion, and sales. In return, Atlantic paid Stewart and Axton a substandard royalty on every record of theirs it sold. This arrangement would turn out to have hidden consequences, but by assuring him a means of getting his goods into the marketplace, it seemed to Stewart to remove in a single stroke the obstacle he found most daunting.

He was exhilarated by such an expression of confidence in the potential of his business by a man like Jerry Wexler. All he had to do now was find proximate sources of creative talent and make more records that Wexler would think he could sell.

Atlantic's intervention sold fifty thousand more copies of "'Cause I Love You." The notice it created brought Stewart and Axton into acquaintance with a California label that owned the name they were using, so they changed Satellite to Stax, a contraction of their surnames.

While Stewart did their company's business and hand-made its products, Estelle fertilized its prodigious growth. The record shop was a magnet that drew young black dream-chasers in Memphis as powerfully as Motown's early digs on West Grand Boulevard had in Detroit. One who became integral to the Stax house band that impressed on the "sound of Memphis" its most distinctive markings—Booker T. Jones—was sixteen when he started coming around the Satellite Record Shop regularly, right from school, often still dressed in his ROTC uniform.

He and others like David Porter, who worked at the grocery store across the street, participated in the informal songwriting seminars that Estelle conducted from behind her converted candy counter; here the best-selling records of the moment were parsed as if they were knotty sentences under the scrutiny of grammarians. The elements of a song's appeal were isolated, then analyzed to determine why and how they worked.

Porter, who was Stax's first salaried songwriter and became one of its most important, learned his craft in a correspondence course he took from the College of Motown under Axton's supervision. "I was a novice," he recalled, ". . . [and] part of what eventually evolved into the magic of [Isaac] Hayes and Porter's writing was my study of the Motown catalogue and what Holland-Dozier-Holland were doing." Porter started the construction of "You Don't Know Like I Know," the first of several of Sam and Dave's hits cowritten with Hayes, by appropriating from an old church song the "hook" he would use as its foundation. The rest was built by strictly applying what he'd deduced of Smokey Robinson's method from studying the text of "Don't Look Back."

Jones and Porter were beneficiaries of the famously rigorous and fertile music programs at Booker T. Washington High School. Like others who joined them in forming Stax's black core, both were produced by a tradition in black Memphis that gave solid basic schooling to the musically inclined among its young, then on-the-job-trained the best of them to a high level in executing its various indigenous styles. The authors of two of the company's three successes—Jones and Carla Thomas—were in college at the time and recorded only when they came home on vacations.

On the other hand, the white boys who comprised the bigger part of Stax's corps of house musicians had coarser musical educations, acquired on their own from the radio or in parking lots of Negro nightclubs, where they could hear the stars of rhythm and blues they weren't allowed inside to see. Most got to Stax through a chain of associations that linked them to a group of kids who, when they were in high school, used to play together in a band they let Estelle's son join because his mother owned a record company.[3]

"We didn't see color," Axton later said, "we saw talent." This would seem an improbable lapse of breeding in two white people brought up in the rural South in the first half of the twentieth century and living and working around Memphis in 1960, when even a racially mixed band was a small act of social subversion. But if only in a particular way, perhaps it really was true of Axton and her brother.

Stewart's fixedness on any path that might carry him beyond life as an eighty-five-dollar-a-week drudge at the First National Bank and lead him toward the glimmer of a long-dreamed-of career in music made him mostly oblivious to the underbrush he had to tramp through along the way. The doggedness of his determination to rise in the record business made him undiscriminating about his means of ascent. If he had happened first to find the building he was looking for in another part of town, he could as well have been recording girls who sang in the style of Connie Francis and longed to be in Nashville.

By 1963 Stax was releasing a couple of single records a month and three or four albums a year. It had six employees, and Stewart still worked at the bank. Estelle had turned the store into a money stream: "Don't ever let a customer show me twenty dollars," she said by way of affirming her acumen for selling, "'cause I'll get nineteen . . . [and] leave him [just enough] money to get home [so I can] sell him more records [when he comes back]."[4]

Their patron in New York was content to leave Stax to its own creative devices, mindful of safeguarding the purity of its output. But as Wexler saw clearer indications of the market for black popular music listing toward the South, he grew impatient to have the company become a more efficient supplier of goods. When he was told that Stax's balky equipment was slowing production, he sent Atlantic's chief engineer to Memphis to retool Stewart's rudimentary studio. By then Wexler was already contemplating his own uses for the apparatus he was helping Jim Stewart build.

Nineteen sixty-five was the year of Stax's breakthrough, which coincided with the emergence of Otis Redding, the renewal of Jerry Wexler's enthusiasm for making records, and the arrival of Al Bell, who was hired to make Stax a national brand and succeeded so well he ended up the tragic hero of a three-act corporate drama that unfolded over a decade.

In the two and a half years since he came to Jim Stewart as an accidental revelation, Otis Redding had established himself, mostly in the

South, by "worrying" three ballads onto the black record charts in a voice marked by a tremulous bleat that so throbbed with heartbreak and pleading that a disk jockey in Memphis called him "Mr. Pitiful." But late in 1964, when he was twenty-three, he took charge of the process of his own creation. His act of self-assertion catalyzed in those around him a burst of collaborative invention that within the year would make them patent-holders on a trademarked "sound of Memphis."

The uses Redding devised for horns became the signature of the Memphis style. He conceived of them as punctuation, or background voices, or as rhythm, comment, or spur. He applied them in hard, clean lines; Redding was an instinctive minimalist.

When Bob Dylan asked him once if he would consider recording "Just Like a Woman," Redding listened to the acetate of it he'd been given and dismissed the song as having "too many fucking words."[5] Once he had marshaled the full capacities of Stax's staff musicians, their robust support enlarged him. From then on he was known on black radio as "Big O."

In the last seven months of 1965 Otis Redding's voice was never off the nation's airwaves; he had back-to-back records perched that long on their roosts in the record charts' uppermost reaches. The first of these, "I've Been Loving You Too Long," was Redding's biggest commercial success, save for the valedictory "(Sittin' on) The Dock of the Bay." In performing this fitful ballad, Redding evoked a storm on the edge of breaking, and behind him horn play struck like thunder and lightning.

The attention that white kids paid Mick Jagger had prepared them to recognize a genuine article from the storehouse he'd been plundering, and so they pricked up their ears. The second of Redding's albums that year, *Otis Blue*, sold a quarter of a million copies.

In 1965, when black consumers were presumed to be ill disposed toward record albums, selling that many signaled Redding's budding appeal to the so-called general market. One way Stax's association with Atlantic paid off was in establishing it as the rare record company of its small size that regularly made and consistently sold albums.

Jerry Wexler's pulse was quickened by the signs of Stax's flowering.

He suggested to Stewart that they formalize their handshake deal by means of a contract. Stewart, who regarded Wexler as a friend and mentor, was conditioned by his upbringing to the word-is-bond ethos of business dealings in the rural South. Moreover, his work had accustomed him to the gentlemen's agreements and mutual back-scratching that were endemic to regional banking practices.

Stewart signed Atlantic's contract without reading it or consulting a lawyer. He was assured that it contained the only stipulation he'd insisted upon: an option to terminate the arrangement if Atlantic was sold or if Wexler was no longer one of its principals.

For his part, Wexler had just signed Wilson Pickett and was anxious to record him in Memphis. The immediate result was "In the Midnight Hour," perhaps the song most emblematic of the whole era of southern soul music. Wexler hastened to send other contract laborers Stewart's way. Among them were Sam and Dave, who belonged to Atlantic but were "loaned" to Stax. The discovery of a homely workshop wherein a small artisanal family crafted by hand all of its distinctive output reinvigorated the jaded mass-producer.

"Coming to Stax literally changed my life," Wexler recalled. "When I went down [there] . . . it was really inspirational. The idea of . . . a place where four guys come to work like cabinetmakers . . . and hang up their coats and start playing music in the morning, and [make] beautifully crafted records . . . That was the way to make records."[6]

But Jim Stewart soon grew chary of giving away "trade secrets" and closed his shop to outsiders, even Wexler's. By then he'd had several months of exposure to Al Bell's broader perspective.

Bell grew up in North Little Rock, Arkansas, and by the time he was seventeen had distinguished himself as one of its leading young citizens: a student council president, National Honor Society member, and though but a senior in high school, a disk jockey with a regular afternoon shift on Little Rock's black radio station. He went to Philander Smith College, from which he graduated with a political science degree, but not before dropping out in 1959, when he was nineteen, to enlist in Dr. King's crusade.

After a yearlong stint training passive resisters in Midway, Georgia,

Bell left the employ of the Southern Christian Leadership Conference for a radio job in Memphis. There the rounds he made of retail record outlets monitoring his audience's patterns of consumption frequently brought him by the Satellite Record Shop. He developed ties to Stewart and Axton and others involved in their fledgling enterprise, and they were sustained after he moved on to Washington, D.C.

Bell became a special friend of Stax Records, emphasizing its products and other sounds of the South in his broadcasts and using his influence in its behalf with colleagues in northeastern cities as yet unwarmed by southerly breezes. Bell did well in Washington: "My southern romanticism integrated into that great music made me one of the top disc jockeys [there]." He began producing records himself, and his became another of Atlantic's small-label pickups.

By the summer of 1965 it had become apparent that Stax needed more capacity to promote its records. Atlantic's two-man promotion staff could never give any but its own affairs more than their secondary attention. Though Stewart begrudged the expense, he hired Al Bell to get Stax records played on radio stations outside the South; Wexler had to subsidize half of Bell's small salary. His hundred-dollar-a-week salary probably exceeded by about 25 percent the going rate for black radio stars in a market like D.C.

When he first came to Stax, Bell recalled, "we had one phone and one desk. Jim sat on one side [and] I sat on the other."[7] He engaged his mission with a radio veteran's store of professional contacts, a gift for marketing, and ministerial zeal. "My attitude," Bell explained, "was to take the middle and force New York and Los Angeles [into the fold]." His approach to marketing Stax's records was "sociological":[8] he believed that Memphis was linked to the cities of the Midwest by a "Mississippi River culture."

Bell concentrated his efforts in Chicago, St. Louis, Kansas City, and even Detroit, where the black populations mostly came from Alabama, Georgia, and the middle South. Once he could establish a record's worthiness in those places—particularly Chicago—the important others would inevitably follow.

The best radio announcers are able to create the illusion that they are speaking directly to each of their listeners. In this respect they are like the gifted politician who makes each of the individuals he serially engages feel as though, in the moment of their encounter, nobody exists for him but them. Al Bell's personality had outsize quotients of conviction, empathy, and command that could as well have served him in becoming a television evangelist or a successful candidate for public office.

These qualities were combined with the skill at organizing and attentiveness to detail typical of a political campaigner's advance man. In Bell energy and ingenuity abounded. He would wheedle from his contacts at Motown premature knowledge of that company's release dates, so that he might set about coaxing the managers and counter help of key stores in major cities to press customers drawn in by the allure of a new Temptations record to buy what Stax was also selling. Before he'd been there a year, the tactical acumen Bell evinced in his guerrilla campaigning would be employed in the pursuit of imperial designs.

Nineteen sixty-six marked the Stax uprising: three of its records that year became the most popular in black America, three others were in the Top Five, and four others in the Top Ten. Eighteen months after the Voting Rights Act the southern Negro's voice resounded, and white southerners were abetting its expression.

Looking back, those who were involved are uniformly convinced this wouldn't have happened without Al Bell. "He put Stax on the map," according to guitarist Steve Cropper, who was himself integral to the architecture of the "sound of Memphis."[9] Just as Bell was now the public face of Stax's management, he was increasingly looked upon inside the company as the man who really ran things.

To his credit, Jim Stewart didn't seem to mind. He, no less than others, attributed the heavier flow of his company's blessings to the intercessions of Al Bell: "Al could pick up the phone and get your record played."

In March 1967 Otis Redding's manager Phil Walden arranged three weeks of bookings in Britain and Paris for Stax's five major acts. He was angling Redding's rise in the American youth market as a ricochet off the place where so much in recent fashion was certified.

Though it mostly played to adulatory British audiences, the package was billed as a European tour of the Stax Revue.

Walden would build the platform for the transracial stage of Redding's career by bringing him home as the "toast of Europe." Before this trip the outlook from Memphis had occluded his view of much in the world beyond it. Little more than a year earlier, when Redding was asked to make a cover version of "Satisfaction," he was unfamiliar with the Rolling Stones' monumental rock-and-roll hit, which by then was six months old.

"Why would they want us to come over there?" Booker T. Jones had wondered. "I was shocked . . . I couldn't believe . . . people knew my songs in Scotland and France." Steve Cropper was "aghast":[10] "They treated us like we were the Beatles or something." This triumph confirmed for all of them, even the nearsighted Stewart, the plausibility of what Al Bell envisioned.

Their return home was heralded by "Sweet Soul Music," a record by a heretofore unknown member of Otis Redding's entourage that Redding produced from his adaptation of a Sam Cooke song. That spring it became the Number 1 record on the pop charts, even more popular among whites than blacks. On its heels came the southern Negro national anthem, "Soul Man," biggest in the sequence of hit records written and produced for Sam and Dave by Hayes and Porter. For Stax, the summer of 1967 was hot as fish grease.

Monterey was the first of the era's rock festivals and a major event in the annals of modern youth culture, since so much of it then centered on the music about which America's young felt proprietary. One effect of the civil rights movement had been to condition a generation of white children to seeing evidence on television of qualities in Negroes that seemed heroic. Another was the interlude of public optimism they associated with the ending of what struck many—indoctrinated by their schools and entertainments to believe that fair play was a defining American virtue—as a living pageant of injustice righted. Consequently, more than a few white adolescents were already inclined toward sympathy for the Negro, even before Motown records entered millions of their interior lives.

These black voices spoke to them of feelings evoked in situations they could imagine were like their own and thus began to engender an abstracted empathy. But there was a slickness about Motown that was too reminiscent of their fathers' show business to seem authentic, once the self-preoccupation of sixteen-year-olds turned into the self-seriousness of nineteen-year-olds considering themselves the vanguard of a "counterculture."

Yet the way they conceived of Otis Redding was only a variation on the way their parents thought about Mahalia Jackson. They were prone to idealize in him qualities they'd admired in the television composite of the southern Negro they'd seen growing up. In his voice they heard a singer of country blues, familiar from when it was fashionable as folk music and advertised as an authentic expression of the Negro's true self.

Onstage, even while his act was climaxing in a controlled frenzy, Redding's presence exuded the dignity of his labor. He was an open-hearted performer, a sprayer of honest sweat, eager to please. As he drew his bulk up spasmodically in a crook-legged, two-footed hop and contorted himself in bending hard into his work, he seemed to a young white audience to be as "anointed" as Brownlee and Cheeks had seemed to congregants in black churches.

To the Monterey crowd, and to millions who wished they were in it, Otis Redding personified "soul," a property Negroes had, as if in compensation for their unequal share of more materially useful gifts. If applied in curative doses, they hoped, this mystical quality they'd heard Negroes proclaim in themselves could have redemptive effects on a society of white Americans that had mortgaged its humanity in order to purchase comfort, wealth, and power.

Exactly three years after the death of Sam Cooke, who had been his idol, a small aircraft that was transporting Otis Redding crashed into a frozen lake near Madison, Wisconsin. He was on his way to perform on the campus of a state university on the edge of the farm belt because six months earlier he'd appeared at the Monterey Pop Festival. Fifty-five thousand young white people, among them the arbiters of a newly self-conscious youth culture, had embraced him as though they were high school kids and he was the football hero they hoped might let them be his friends.

"They were mobbing the stage just wanting to touch Otis," the keyboardist that night, Booker T. Jones, recalled. "We had never had acceptance from [a white] audience in the United States. . . . There was a new feeling. . . . History was changing at that moment and we knew it."[11]

Otis Redding was a Negro admired for the superiority of his character by all the southern white men who knew him. He reminded them that Negroes were their oldest familiars. However blunt and heartless the means employed for keeping them apart, black and white people of the South were reared among one another, albeit in separate pews of the same church. Generations of all their kindred acquired a place-centeredness on common ground.

Redding's manager was an enterprising schoolboy of the madras-pants, tasseled-loafer-wearing type both common and specific to his age and class in the deep South of the late 1950s. Phil Walden was booking local acts for fraternity parties around Macon, Georgia, when he was introduced to "Rockhouse" Redding, a late-teenage imitator of Little Richard in Johnny Jenkins's Pinetoppers band.

Before he died at twenty-six, Otis Redding would make it possible for Phil Walden to become the booking agent for many stars of black popular music. By the early 1970s he'd parlayed this lucrative stake into owning a franchise in the record business. Within a decade of Redding's passing Walden was a mover in industrial circles lofty enough to make him useful in presidential politics, as a key backstage money-gatherer for Jimmy Carter's winning campaign.

Walden and Redding would become business partners and were by all accounts a devoted couple. Neither's parents approved of their association; it was like an improbable high school friendship made tighter by the shared perverse pleasure its principals took in being considered a bad influence on each other. "They ate together, slept together," Redding's widow once remarked dryly, "and fortunately they made money together."[12] Middle-class white boys like Phil Walden were brought up in Georgia to believe Negroes wouldn't harm them.

While Otis Redding was dreamily ambitious enough to dare to think of the advantage that Walden could be to him, he was just a mannish boy himself when they met and still living where he was raised in the custom of avoiding unnecessary contact with white people. That he would have been as accessible to such a relationship is surprising, but Redding's apparent ease at openness was a gift.

It disarmed and attracted white people of reasonable good will. Phil Walden must have felt at times like Huck Finn traveling down the river with a Jim of such noble character and bearing that white men were proud to think themselves his friend.

In 1967 Redding seemed to embody the rising potency of Stax Records of Memphis, the "little company that could," whose white proprietors, black stars, and integrated supporting cast had accidently become engaged in joint enterprise during a time of flagrant racial animus in the divided heart of the South and now prospered together. Redding was the face of another New South, an idea reconstructed in the debris of the lately broken apparatus of long-standing social tyrannies. As northern cities roiled and backlash set in, Walden was selling a symbol of racial reconciliation under the same label that other regional boosters had used, near the last turn of a century, when they were pitching the economic benefits of cheap black labor.

If he'd lived longer, Otis Redding might have become a symbol of transracial possibility as iconographic for young whites as Sam Cooke had been for black Americans. If that had happened, Redding would have been, for as long as it lasted, a black pop star of a magnitude beyond Cooke's imagining, back when he and Blackwell were wondering how brightly white kids could make him shine if they were his strongest source of illumination.

Somewhat later a journalist caught up with Johnny Jenkins, the used-to-be guitar star of the southern-white-boy fraternity circuit who'd given Redding his first singing job. Jenkins was a man for whom things hadn't much worked out. In 1962 his best chance at a recording career went so badly, it became the accidental opportunity from which Otis Redding's was launched.

By the time Jenkins was asked by Peter Guralnick about the impact of Redding's death, he had reached a conclusion shared by many others who still experienced residual benumbment from the concussive aftershock of the half-decade in the 1960s when serial killings snatched away the heroic public presences of Evers, Cooke, Malcolm, Redding, and King. "That's what happens," Johnny Jenkins said sourly, "to n[egroes] with ideas."[13]

A month after Otis Redding died, Atlantic Records was bought by Warner Brothers for $17 million. This, of course, gave Stewart the option of vacating their agreement. He didn't want to run the risks of independence, but after trying to sell Stax to Atlantic and being offered too little, he fidgeted for six months, then swallowed hard and cut the cord. Once he did, the contract he'd signed blindly five years before came crashing down around him.

Jerry Wexler claimed he never knew until then that his company's lawyers had slipped in a clause that assigned to Atlantic ownership of all the Stax records it had distributed.[14] The dollar Stewart thought was sealing a distribution deal, when he'd taken it from Wexler's hand, had actually transferred his and Axton's property rights.

Wexler disavowed any intention of taking advantage of Stewart, but never failed to press any he was ever given. Having expropriated everything of value in the Stax catalog by means of their prenuptial agreement, Wexler walked away after the divorce with Sam and Dave and the deed to a trove of unreleased Otis Redding material. This Atlantic converted into four albums and six single releases, thereby squeezing another two and half years out of a dead man's career.

Thus was Stewart instructed on the limits of fellowship in the business he had chosen and the consequences it exacted for naive assumptions about the kindness of strangers. Dispossessed of its history, stripped of its most valuable commercial assets, Stax was faced with starting over bereft of any capital but its wits.

Stewart came from people who didn't trust prosperity. By 1968 he had already done more than he set out to do in the record business. He knew now from painful experience how exorbitant was the cost of putting a foot wrong on this treacherous terrain. He thought it prudent to cash out his insecure holdings in a commodities market and convert them into more tangible wealth than he ever expected to possess.

Jim Stewart's wondrous ride was never as much fun for him as it would have been for a lot of other people. Ensnarled as it lately was in the perplexities of commerce in the world beyond his mom-and-pop store, the scope of his business had gotten too big for his vision. Its everyday was more complicated than Stewart's straightforward nature could bear without abrasion.

Although the urgency of his discomfort gave him some incentive to surmount an ingrained disbelief, Stewart's decision to accept the evidence of Al Bell's merit and entrust the stewardship of his estate to a Negro gotten out of his place was still an act of bravery. The defining irony of Jim Stewart's existence was expressed in his reliance henceforth on Al Bell to pursue his interests, while at the same time thinking to safeguard them by making himself both the valued client and a familiar of bankers at United Planters, in the line of others who'd built from cotton-patch bounty the region's premier financial institution.

His encounters with the society of propertied white men persuaded Stewart that for as long as it took him to get his money out of Stax, protecting it would require his vigilance at appearing to be in charge of the company. He already accounted himself lucky to have gotten this far without official Memphis taking more notice of his unorthodoxies.

Acting for Stewart, Bell engaged an acquaintance in New York to find a buyer. Less than a month after its contract with Atlantic expired, Stax was sold to Gulf and Western. The purchase price of $4.3 million was accepted entirely in Gulf and Western stock. Stewart and Axton got $1.3 worth of it immediately; the rest would be forthcoming in annual increments based on a percentage of however much money Stax made that year and converted into stock at a rate based on its valuation at the time of the sale.[15]

This was the enticement for Stewart, because if the value of shares in Gulf and Western rose half as much over the life of this deal as its executives assured him was likely, he and Axton would recoup nearly twice the original purchase price. But it was true, as Stewart's lawyer pointed out, that "in essence," Stax was bought with "their own money."[16]

Belonging to Gulf and Western at least had the advantage of affording Stax the means of hiring more staff to "work" records. The reconstituted company had three hit singles the summer after it was sold, thereby reassuring its haphazardly diversifying, formerly oil business–minded proprietors that they owned a renewable resource. Stewart rewarded Bell with a 10 percent interest in Stax.

Bell remembered being promised a third when he agreed to come aboard,[17] but in his experience no white man's good faith could ever be taken for granted, and even partially fulfilling a commitment made to a Negro exempted one from being an object of wholehearted complaint. Upon receipt of this bestowal he thought compensated him too little for the increased value of Stewart and Axton's property since he'd begun tending to it, Al Bell took on the role of the firm's managing partner. Having been given the keys to Stewart's vehicle, Bell would steer Stax onto the street where all his dreams resided.

These were of a scale matched to Berry Gordy's example. Bell was toiling in black radio, a part of the audience nearest the ground on the outskirts of the music business, watching the Motown wave billow higher and higher as its rolling in gathered phenomenal force. He was awed as its flood tide washed over the embankment that had kept people like him out of the traffic in the mainstream conducting goods to the big marketplace. Bell was a smart, ambitious, preacherly country boy slickened by a decade's close contact with the street-greasy side of the record game. Now he felt able to dare what Gordy had done.

Bell believed he had ways and an opportune means of becoming the first international Negro since Booker T. Washington to come straight out of an old-country backwater like North Little Rock, Arkansas. His gift for conviction endowed Bell's constitutional optimism with the resilience of faith, making it as unbreakable as a great salesman's or an inveterate missionary's. He cast his business ambitions in an ideological light, having been an espouser of economic development as the liberating path back when he was encamped with SCLC.

Bell's mental pitch was attuned to his era's vibrant consciousness that it was making history. If this inclined him to be self-dramatizing, it also disposed him toward a perspective with which he saw clearly to the core of what was at issue: music "was our natural resource, it was our gold, our magnesium, it was our oil, with [it] we would be able to build our economic base."

Where Jim Stewart had seen himself as an exporter of regional crafts, Al Bell envisioned himself at the heart of a complex modern enterprise that manufactured and sold black American popular culture all over the world. He began by dressing Stax up to look the part of an established record company. He signed up six small labels to distribute. He opened a New York office. He spun off a gospel imprint. He sold licenses to distribute Stax records in Canada, England, and France. He hired a woman to do public relations.

By 1968 Al Bell, alert to the shifting rhythms of his times, understood the moment of the urban Negro to be at hand and recognized the implications for a music enterprise that depended for its basic livelihood on the patronage of Aframerican consumers. "The problem we had then," he has said, "was that Stax was viewed as [making] 'Bama music."[18]

Accordingly, Bell undertook to revamp both the company's product and the process by which it was made. He bought better equipment. He retired Jim Stewart as supervisor of production and chief engineer. He assigned the creative staff to work with artists in prescribed pairings. He refined away some of the rawness in the Stax production style, chiefly by making copious use of strings.

Bell thought of crossing the Memphis strain of music with Detroit's to produce a hybrid that the children and grandchildren of upsouth migrants would want to claim. He recruited Don Davis from the community of skilled practitioners in Detroit who comprised its alternative Motown.

Davis was among the record-makers assembled most often under the flag of Ed Wingate, a numbers don and nightclub owner who doggedly competed with Motown for several years by using its moonlighting musicians and the city's overflow singing talent, until Gordy paid him about a million dollars to go away. Lacking either Motown's global ambitions or resources, these receivers of its style could afford neither its pretensions nor its awareness of an audience at far remove.

In its preparation the native cuisine that Wingate served didn't filter out as much as Motown did the flavorings used in kitchens on the side of Detroit where Wilson Pickett and Aretha Franklin learned to cook. This cadre of Gordy's unchosen produced an unadorned version, from which the church had not been expunged, and so the Golden World, Ric Tic, and Revilot imprints were borne by many successful records. One of them was Davis's own in the summer of 1967, a Top Ten hit called "Baby Please Come Back Home," sung by J. J. Barnes, the alternative Motown's Marvin Gaye. Thinking of Davis as the right synergist for the job was a mark of Bell's discernment.

When Don Davis beheld Stax, his reaction was much the same as Jerry Wexler's had been: "The records in Detroit were too polished and did not have enough of the real earthy gospel simplicity to them. . . . [In Memphis] the music . . . filled me with so much feeling and it vibrated me in such a way that it just overpowered all my emotions. I knew that it was a sound I had been missing all through my life." In the fall of 1968 Davis produced for Stax a record by Johnnie Taylor called "Who's Making Love" that sold two million copies.

Bell made Davis a vice-president in charge of artists and repetoire. This further disaffected the so-called Big Six—comprised of Jones, Cropper, the drummer Al Jackson, the bassist Donald Dunn, Hayes, and Porter—who were Stax's creative mainstays.

They had been chagrined by Jim Stewart's singular indulgence of Steve Cropper, giving him a 10 percent share in the value of all their published songs. They seethed at Davis's predilection for recording horn tracks in Detroit while noisily professing his love and admiration for the inimitable Memphis way with horns. The most sophisticated and versatile craftsman among them, Booker T. Jones, felt the most aggrieved and would become the first to leave.

In the Christmas week of 1968 Stax staged a gala show at the Mid-South Coliseum, the biggest indoor venue in Memphis. "The Stax/Volt Yuletide Thing" featured eleven of the company's acts and an appearance by Janis Joplin. Bell regarded her presence as a promotional coup, since it would draw toward Johnnie Taylor, Eddie Floyd, the Staple Singers, Carla Thomas, and Booker T. and the M.G.'s the attention being lavished on her by the youth-market fashion arbiters of the newly coined rock press. Joplin was the latest proof that white people liked black music best when they weren't asked to identify with a black person singing it.

She was a cartoon of black style, an unmusical screamer, and a brutalizer of songs originated by her betters. She was given a costar's place on the evening's bill of fare, right below Johnnie Taylor, who had the Number 1 record in the country and was closing the show. When she left the stage after the third of the five songs she'd planned to sing, Joplin was dismissed by the crowd. It didn't ask her back for the encore that she hadn't expected to have to earn. She slunk off with her entourage into the midnight striking for the I-think-it's-so-groovy-now-that-people-are-finally-getting-together era, leaving behind a trail of cigarette burns on Estelle Axton's carpets.[19]

Six months after it bought Stax, Gulf and Western dispatched the superintendents of its record division to inspect the property in Memphis that it oversaw dimly from Los Angeles. Finding neither of the principals of Stax on its premises, these visitors tracked down the all-purpose lawyer who served as Bell and Stewart's part-time corporate counsel. When they arrived at his office, the unforewarned Mr. Rosenberg mistook the president and vice-president of Paramount Records for prospective criminal clients. This misperception by so practiced a hand in local human affairs suggests the breadth of the cultural chasm across which the inflamed modernist Al Bell hastened to leap.

Bell had become Jim Stewart's partner. Estelle was shunted aside in 1969, bought out bitterly in a deal to which her brother brought the actual wherewithal and Bell only a promissory note backed by G&W.[20] Bell had converted his personal resources into a currency hard enough to purchase 45 percent of Stax Records. While Stewart kept a larger stake, Bell ran the company. He proved a leader to whom self-doubt was unnatural. This deprived him of an adult's normal quotient of caution.

If Al Bell was a tactician too often made reckless by an impatience hot enough to boil prudence away, he was also an astute judge of larger possibilities and mostly sound in his commercial thought processes. But as zealous in a righteous cause as he was in his self-conviction, Bell was in too much of a hurry to move and shake for someone whose only bona fide capital was human.

He first moved boldly to replace the backlist that Stax had lost to Atlantic. To comprise an "instant" catalog, he mobilized every act on the company's roster to mass-produce albums. Twenty-seven were released, along with thirty singles, during the last two weeks of May 1969. Bell thus consigned to the market in one lot more than half as many albums as Stax ever made before. Conventional wisdom was thereby flouted; so small a company straining to produce more goods than it could possibly sell at the same time offended common sense.

In New York Jerry Wexler snorted: "Think of the costs . . . the assets they used up . . . sit[ting] around the office isolated from the world and play[ing] 'record industry.'" He thought Bell's audacious tactic a symptom of "parochial insanity."[21] The established music business held the strong prejudice that a place like Memphis could not be the seat of a consequential enterprise.

But the dauntless Bell was convinced he was a player of consequence in history's own arena. If Berry Gordy had built his business selling singles, Bell understood that these days only album sales certified a record label's credibility. If Gordy had prospered by modulating the releases of relatively few well-made and -chosen products, Bell would flood the market to make a splash.

He was willing to overspend for sudden credibility, as television executives have often been in buying broadcast rights to sports events. But when it is taken by a thinly financed seeker of profit that leaves no margin for error, "loss leadership" is a tactical approach.

Stax was spared having to pay a crippling tab for Bell's production spree through the accidental intervention of Isaac Hayes. Among the profusion of hothouse blooms that Bell had forced that spring was an album by Hayes called *Hot Buttered Soul*. The writer and producer of "Soul Man" was casting about for a singing career of his own. Another black country ragamuffin who'd early subsisted on a radio diet of hill-billy music, Hayes had been, whenever he had to be, a workaday lounge singer around Memphis. The effects of both sorts of exposure were evident in *Hot Buttered Soul,* which featured eighteen minutes of "By the Time I Get to Phoenix," wherein a stage-setting monologue spoken in Hayes's deep-ply baritone was the startling first manifestation of "Ike the Rapper."

Hot Buttered Soul sold more than a million copies and changed the black record business. Every song on the album was too long for Top Forty radio. It was out and already beginning to sell before Stax pared down "By the Time I Get to Phoenix" to a length that fit the standard form of airplay.

The single served to entice sales of the album and was owned only by those consumers who couldn't afford to spend six dollars. For eight months *Hot Buttered Soul* was at or near the top of *Billboard's* charts in four categories—jazz, pop, R&B, and easy listening—an unprece-dented swath of penetrated markets. He was sold broadly, as white acts increasingly were, on commercial FM radio. Belying the industry's long-standing presumption that its black customers were disposed by small means and short attention spans to serial purchases of single records, Hayes became an "album artist," the first ever in boogaloo.

The aggrandizement of Isaac Hayes further rent the formerly tight-knit group at Stax's core. Booker T. Jones, the company's most valuable player, barely outlasted Estelle Axton. He left as the composer of a well-noticed movie score, from which a Top Ten single had recently been extracted, a rare and precious occurrence in popular music's modern times for such instrumentalists as the M.G.'s.

Nominally a vice president at Stax, Jones had chafed at being treated like an employee. He resented Jim Stewart's favor to Steve Cropper of a 10 percent stake in the publisher's royalties from all their songs. Moreover, Jones disapproved of Bell's design for the company's ideal future. As small as Stax was, he would later lament, "things had become quite corporate."

When Jones removed himself to California, Bell didn't mind much. Within a year of Jones's departure, however, Cropper also broke ranks, complaining that "the whole air . . . and . . . feeling had changed."[22] Others of the house band's original white boys had grown uncomfortable with the atmosphere—"chain link fence in the parking lot, guards on the front door"—and had already moved away.

Stax made a $2 million profit in 1969, on $8 million in sales. Bell used the windfallen cash from *Hot Buttered Soul* to kick his business into higher gear. He hired more promotion staff. He signed more deals to distribute smaller labels. He rented more office space. He brought in as a vice-president the young advertising executive who'd made "beautiful people, use Afro-Sheen" the "ring around the collar" of late-1960s Aframerican life.

Bell wanted to establish the "sound of Memphis" as an international brand as respectable as Motown's. For that to happen, he was convinced, Stax had to be disassociated from the taint of its "'Bama" origins. In any self-made man from the black bottom of small-town Arkansas, a lurking consciousness of perceived insufficiencies in background would be expectable.

Bell was determined that Stax should quickly gain the appearance of sophistication in its form and function. Bell aimed to make and sell an image of "new" southern Negritude that was as embraceable by city-bred black Americans, and as tolerable to as many white Americans, as Gordy's "new" Negroes. Stax's public face was made over at the hands of the Chicagoan Larry Shaw—which most lately had wrested from Kool an advantage for Newport among black tobacco smokers—and was presented to subscribers of *Ebony* magazine for their certifying approval.

For Bell, making necessary refinements would partly entail the deposal of one white man's influence in favor of some others'. Beginning in 1967, Jim Stewart was retired from the recording studio. When he returned after four years, his sense of displacement was profound. To a collegial advisory that he should take more account of the mass audience that Stax was courting, Stewart retorted: "I don't give a good God damn if we never sell another record to a white person." By then Bell had moved a lot of music production away from Memphis, to a deep-country outpost where the most commercially fashionable musicians in the black music trade at that moment were white boys collected in Florence, Alabama. These so-called Dixie Flyers were the house band at Fame Studios.

Bell would apply his own hand there to making records, prompted by Stax recording artist Jessie Jackson, who counted the great Mavis Staples a special friend. The "Country Preacher" had suggested to him that because he understood Mississippi and had once been a church-man, Bell should produce the Staple Singers. Under Bell's auspices these veterans of gospel's golden age achieved six Top Ten popular records in three years. Every hour days between fall 1971 and the fall of 1973, somewhere in America one of three hits by the Staple Singers was playing on the radio. In Bell's mind, the Staples' improbably wide-spread appeal was reverberant confirmation of his acuity as a record man.

Bell meant to assure that Stax merchandise recurrently bore modernity's latest imprint. He hired as boss of production an engineer from Los Angeles who'd been recommended by Mickey Stevenson. Tom Nixon was a beat-counter who analysized each crop of Top Ten records to calibrate their tempo ranges, on the theory that beats-per-minute was the key specification in the design and manufacture of a best-selling song. His "system" impressed Al Bell as innovative and sci-entific. So did the idea of statistical market analysis, for which he employed a cousin who taught high school science and history in Lonoke, Arkansas.

10. It's What's in the Grooves
That Counts

Berry Gordy himself wrote and published more than four hundred songs, some well known and probably even loved, but none as good as many of Smokey's, or as Holland, Dozier, and Holland's best, or perhaps a hundred others made by the toilers on his workshop floors. All these and about ten thousand more became inventory in the catalog of Jobete Publishing. As an exploited songwriter, he knew the value of copyrights as well as Dorsey had when the record business was still new. Once he became an exploiter of songwriters, Gordy developed the most lucrative source of new copyrights ever before assembled under one roof. His publishing house has been the repository of Gordy's treasure.

While he never stole a credit from the writer of any song, as a condition of their employment Gordy extracted from them the right to publish whatever they wrote. The lien he held on their intellectual property entitled him to receive, in perpetuity, most of the income their songs produced. The publisher gets paid whenever a song is performed or its sheet music sold. He makes money each time any recording ever made of that song is bought, or played on the radio, or on television, or in a movie.

There are two trade associations that define and protect the interests of property-holders in the music-publishing business, calculate and collect the "mechanical" royalties accruing from broadcasts and live performances, and distribute these revenues among their members. The elder American Society of Composers, Authors and Publishers (ASCAP) had been formed by the Tin Pan Alley establishment. Commercial disputes in the era of network radio's sway in the mid-1930s spawned the rival Broadcast Music Incorporated (BMI), to which belonged overwhelmingly publishers of the music, sold by upstart record companies after the war, that took hold of America's youth in the 1950s and by the 1960s constituted nearly all of what was popular.

In 1965 Motown was the industry's biggest seller of single records, with fourteen Top Ten pop charted hits.[1] Jobete had for three years running been named by BMI as its top publishing house. Gordy told a reporter, "[W]e're signing people with talent to do songs we've already got on hand." From this perspective, the ulterior purpose of creating pop stars was to fatten the Jobete catalog.

For most of a decade, until Marvin Gaye and Stevie Wonder broke his stranglehold, next to nothing was recorded by a contractee of Gordy's that he didn't publish. By then Jobete was the largest music publisher in America, had a staff of more than twenty writers, and made its proprietor about $10 million a year.[2]

In the mid-1960s there were twenty million American teenagers with $10 billion to spend. Their money enlarged the market for records, and their buying power changed the economics of music publishing. In the previous decade the dollar volume of record sales had nearly tripled.

The scale of worldwide commerce in the Beatles—sellers by then of about 180 million records—drove the value of their copyrights high enough to start a tide running that lifted all boats. In 1965 a company without appreciable assets but fifty-six copyrights to Beatles songs, and a contract for sixty more as yet unwritten, sold out a public stock offering of 1.2 million shares.[3]

An adjustment in the tax code in 1960 had already made music publishing more profitable; now the pay-for-play rates on radio were about to be raised by 12.5 percent.[4] Copyrights and catalogs had begun to be traded as if they were commodities futures. But Gordy was rooted in his old-country grandfather's faith in real estate as the only commodity with permanent value. So into a future that lasted four decades he amassed and closely held property claims of steadily enhancing worth. Fifteen years after he left Gordy, Eddie Holland said he was then earning more from the songs he wrote for Motown than he did while he was there.

At stage shows in the big theaters, once the telltale opening chords of "Ooo Baby Baby" were struck, anyone unseated near the front, upstairs or down, risked being trampled by an onrush of girls who were determined to get close enough to look Smokey Robinson in his pretty green eyes. His peak as an inflamer of teenage passions coincided with the two most fertile years of his songwriting career, which began at the end of 1964. In this span Robinson produced, among others, five hit records for the Temptations, four for himself and the Miracles, three for the Marvelettes, and three for Marvin Gaye. These encompassed a monument ("My Girl"), a landmark ("The Tracks of My Tears"), and a masterpiece ("The Hunter Gets Captured by the Game"). Bob Dylan touted him as "America's greatest living poet."

Smokey's gifts flowed so effusively that their blessings fell upon the lesser known of the company's acts—Carolyn Crawford, Brenda Holloway, the Contours—as well as its famous ones, and so expansively that for amusement's sake he put them to odd and antic uses, as in his sly celebrations of the player's code ("I don't care if she wobble like a duck, or talk with a lisp / I'll still think I'm in luck if the dollar bills are crisp") and street slang ("All That's Good"). But he reserved for his own voice the most beautiful and delicate songs of this period, from the haunting "Ooo Baby Baby," as dumb-striking in its first effects on a young black audience in the early springtime of 1965 as a sudden clap of loud thunder, through "Choosey Beggar" ("If beg you I must, then I'll never give up, cause you are the only one to fill this beggar's cup"), to "I'm just like a fallen leaf on a windy day, and you like the breeze that blows leaves away / You're like a broom, I'm like dust in the room . . . cause you know that I'm swept for you baby, way down deep in my soul."

Smokey Robinson was the embodiment of Gordy's highest aspirations as a songwriter, an alter ego who was the artist Gordy would have wanted to be if he could have been more than a technician and teacher. But as a teacher Gordy was an artist, and his most enduring accomplishment may have been the making of a popular songwriter who, if the genre prejudices that are likely to be permanent inhibitors of his reputation were ever overcome, would be considered the equal of Cole Porter. No less impressive than the evidence already accumulated of his star pupil's prowess was the level of general achievement in Gordy's crowded classroom.

The talent there was stacked so deep that George Clinton was overlooked, and Nick Ashford and Valerie Simpson would leave because, even as proven songwriters of the highest rank, they couldn't get enough work of their own. But useful people kept turning up, as Norman Whitfield had in 1961, when he was a pool-hustling sixteen-year-old hired to help around the office and baby-sit a kid Gordy had just signed and rechristened Little Stevie Wonder. Whitfield quickly became an apprentice writer/producer of precocious mastery. He would be on hand and primed to step in years later when the departure of the company's most reliable breadwinners, Holland-Dozier-Holland, could have damaged Gordy beyond repair.

For six of Motown's sunniest years—1963 to 1968—HDH were the company's mainstays and America's most robust challengers to Lennon and McCartney's primacy in the pop music marketplace. After tuning up on Martha and the Vandellas, they engineered the Supremes' and Four Tops' astonishing career flights in the mid-1960s. More than any others, records made by Holland-Dozier-Holland drew white teenagers into Motown's tent.

They emerged as a unit in 1963, when eleven million young girls spent more than half of the $650 million the record business took in. Though not widely credited with being especially gifted at either words or music, no men better evoked the wistful ache of adolescent girlhood longings or the poignancies of defiantly heartbroken young women. At their best—straightforward and stringless—HDH were capable of the effect produced in "Take Me in Your Arms" by mounting a Kim

Weston vocal performance of heart-tearing pathos atop an unremitting orchestral power surge that throbs with crosscurrents of melancholy and abandon.

Above all else they were master builders of danceable rhythms, another pillar of Gordy's faith. Dance music was Motown's leading export, and HDH could manufacture it in various colors and shades. They mostly addressed females, but when they took their manly ease with gutbucket singers like Junior Walker and Shorty Long, they comfortably exercised seldom-used muscles in striking such iconic male street poses as the loner ("I'm a road runner, baby, match up to me and I'll be gone . . . cause I'm gonna live the life I love, and I'm gonna love the life I live") and the libertine ("there'll be breathtaking, hip-shaking cuties, talking 'bout some fascinating, devastating beauties, now, They'll all be gathering here, from far and near, for the function at the junction").

Once HDH got rolling in 1964, they became production engineers of the assembly line that Motown was often said to be. They were able to keep pace with the company's relentless release schedule by writing as many as two or three songs a day. A complicated production like "Reach Out I'll Be There" in 1966—the Four Tops' greatest hit—might have taken them two hours to record.

They assembled such songs from warehoused parts: one of these from their inventory of verses, one of those from their stockpile of hooks, bringing to bear classical influences they picked up, like the pipes they smoked as part of the college-boy poses they adopted when they got successful, and the gimcrackeries of the earliest generation of electronic musical devices.

They had learned to work fast in meeting regular contingencies, like one late in the spring of 1965 when a record of theirs by the Four Tops called "I Can't Help Myself" grew at an unbridled rate to popularity on an unforeseen scale. The urgency of this chance at a windfall of profit required that a "follow-up" be hastily made and marketed. Ideally the new song would be distinguishable from its predecessor yet sound similar enough to appropriate some of the authority of "I Can't Help Myself"'s claim on the public. With intended irony Holland-

Dozier-Holland entitled the Four Tops' next release "It's the Same Old Song" and, when it proved almost as popular as the prototype, had their joke and cashed it, too.

Before they knew anything, HDH relied on the resourcefulness of the company's gifted studio musicians, who at first held them in the amiable contempt that seasoned practitioners in any workplace reserve for superiors whose authority can't indemnify them against inexperience. One who was being upbraided by Eddie Holland for not playing something exactly right, retorted that it didn't matter much since "all y'all's shit sounds the same anyway."[5] But HDH nevertheless became stewards of a shop that was innovative as only the aggressively self-taught can be when they are working under the pressures of time, budget, equipment constraints, and fierce internal competition and are being buoyed by serial successes:

> After [the Supremes'] "Baby Love" became a hit, somebody wrote about the genius of handclapping on the backbeat. Said it was a new sound, revolutionized pop music. Hell, it wasn't even handclapping. Ain't no way we gonna pay twelve people session fees to clap hands. It was two by fours, man, two by fours hooked together with springs and some guy stompin' on them to make a backbeat. We knocked that song off in two takes.[6]

Holding rock-steady against the comings and goings of artists and producers were the musicians Gordy assembled in his house band, known around the company as the Funk Brothers, though never in public, because Gordy didn't regard *funk* as a word fit for polite company. He plucked many of them out of Detroit's underemployed jazz players and suckered them into signing on for low wages with the promise of being able to record the music they really loved on Motown's short-lived jazz label. But it was regular work and allowed them to condescend to the greenhorn talent and unlettered bosses whose bumbles they salvaged and designs they improved.

Sometimes a producer needed only to hum a tune for the musicians to invent its orchestration. The piano player and organist Earl Van Dyke and another Funk Brother improvised a conflation of two Tin Pan Alley melodies into the introduction to "My Guy," noodling while Smokey took too long to work the thing out. "We were doing anything to get the hell out of that studio," he recalled. "We knew the producer didn't know nothin' about no 'Canadian Sunset' or 'Begin the Beguine.' We figured that song would wind up in the trash can anyway."[7]

These musicians were instrumental in defining the sound that sold 250 million records, and Gordy kept some fully employed for longer than a decade, transforming them in the process from the unknown and idle to the uncredited and underpaid. Whenever they could, most snuck across town to make money on the side working undercover for Detroit's other record company. Gordy dispatched Mickey Stevenson to sit in a car across the street from Golden World's studio at three o'clock in the morning and record the names of comers and goers. He hired detectives to surveil the moonlighters. When caught, offenders were bludgeoned with confiscatory fines into submitting to Gordy's exclusive claim on their services.[8]

Some, like Earl Van Dyke, were shrewd enough negotiators to end up making more for a while than many singers did. But inasmuch as a couple who didn't—bassist James Jamerson and drummer Benny Benjamin—were among the most influential of their time, musicians were still the company's most exploited class. On tour they took to calling their designated section at the back of the bus "Harlem" and referred to the front, where the singers rode, as "Broadway."[9]

Feeling left out of the strenuous social climbing going on around them, their dispositions toward what they could see of Gordy's ambitions turned gently ironic. For him, no place was warmer than the shadow of Ed Sullivan's smile. And like others of their tribe's unassimilable many, they would have known that when he got there, they wouldn't be anywhere around.

In the summer of 1966 a visitor to Motown's annual outing on Belle Isle entered a festive circle of several hundred employees, family, and friends spread over the picnic grounds at tables mostly groaning under copious food and drink and the weight of bulky portable record players "that took a dozen batteries and were so heavy you had to stagger to [carry] them." In moving around, a browser of tables would encounter the blare of their aggregated emissions as an aural mélange of song samples from the company's current inventory, the equivalent of a movie trailer for Motown's summer soundtrack.

Many who gathered were giddy with mutual exhilaration at being actors in one another's dream scenarios. "These," the observer reflected, "were the days of milk and honey, of new houses, new cars, expensive furs and jewelry. Most of these kids were coming very quickly from a whole lot of nothing into a whole lot of everything, and they all wanted to be picked to record the next sure-to-be-a-hit song so they could buy more."

Accordingly, those assembled vied hard for Gordy's attention. They competed in teams at softball and other games. Though they had come expecting to be at lavish ease and so were dressed as Milanese golfers or models of *Ebony* Fashion Fair cruisewear, the singers were spurred by Gordy like fighting cocks into "cutting contests," wherein cruel sport was made of mocking one another in derisive impersonations.[10] At BG's court even the play arranged for his subjects was rehearsal for work.

In June, with race at the forefront of America's public concerns, Motown had released Stevie Wonder's rendering of Bob Dylan's "Blowin' in the Wind," which before summer's end became a Top Ten record on the white charts. This was Gordy's only stab at figuring out the social comment most commercially appropriate to the political temper of his times. "Blowin' in the Wind" would have seemed to him a market-tested folk song that, if pitched in the right emotional key by a freshly changed adolescent voice, could be purged of angry undertones unbefitting a pop version of "We Shall Overcome."

While Motown's message filled the air, official Detroit was basking in the approbation of the national press. The simmering discontents of black urbanites flared chain-reactively across the country, but Detroit— an image-conscious plutocracy with a telegenic mayor and a thriving one-crop economy—was touted as a model among cities for having so far avoided racial tumult.

Since the early 1960s the mayor had been Jerome Cavanaugh, a young, smooth New Frontiersman chosen by the the city's industrial elite to prepare the New Detroit and elected with overwhelming black support. For half a century, the "old" Detroit had been rubbed raw by its citizenry's acute consciousness of tribe. The coarseness in its everyday life was so ingrained that residents called one another's neighborhoods Jewtown, Poletown, Germantown, Hunkytown, Corktown, Greektown, and Black Bottom. Now the balance of tribal heft, if not power, was tipping.

The city by then was about a third black and darkening steadily. The Negro presence in Detroit was more than twice as substantial as it had been fifteen years earlier. Its resident class of black strivers sensed that their turn at being important in the city's public affairs was nearly at hand. Living in the suburbs had already been an official American ideal for twenty years, during which time more than a quarter of the city's white population had moved into outlying towns. Increasingly, the white element Detroit's black citizens considered unfit to live among— the sort who'd viciously asserted their racial animus twice in living memory—were retreating behind Eight Mile Road into towns known now as "bubba suburbs," safely beyond the advances of a perceived "Negro invasion."

In July 1966 a panel of commissioned citizens issued a report on how things stood in Detroit between the races. While hopeful in the main, it warned of combustibility in the interactions between Negroes and police. Local newspaper talk that summer was buzzing with speculation about whether the conditions for an outbreak of racial unrest were as yet fully present. In August an encounter between police and seven black men accused of loitering provoked a flurry of rock- and bottle-throwing that injured ten cops and eleven civilians before it subsided. The mayor and police were praised for their restraint and decisiveness. By dousing sparks that had ignited in so many other places, they enhanced Detroit's lately made reputation for relative temperance in its racial climate.

This perception of Detroit was no doubt encouraged by the ongoing phenomenon of a notably black enterprise turning a contraction of the city's nickname into a popular brand. During the mid-1960s Motown sold more single records than anybody else, which meant that subliminal advertisements for Detroit were always on the radio.

No one in Berry Gordy's business had ever produced quality in such quantity; of the 537 singles issued by Motown between 1960 and 1970, 357—two-thirds—were hits. The industrial average of hits to misses was less than 20 percent; more than three-quarters of all the records on the market failed to recoup what they cost to make. "After a while it was like Dial-A-Hit," recalled one of the Motown songwriters. "Just like dialing the fire department."[11] Motown was entitled to acclaim itself "the sound of young America."

In 1967 white kids bought 70 percent of the $21 million worth of Motown records sold. In three years the dollar volume of the company's annual take increased fivefold. Motown was doing as much business as Atlantic Records, which by then had diversified into white rock and roll but was still reaping its biggest harvest from southern soul music; Aretha Franklin and Wilson Pickett were in their fertile primes, and—same as the Delta cotton barons—Atlantic took nine-tenths of the bountiful yield from the crops sowed in its Memphis colony.

But neither the pop market's embrace nor the hard squeeze of its competitors loosened Motown's grip on the purse strings of black record-buyers. In most Aframerican young an overindulged compulsion to want to "dance to the music [and] make romance to the music" had turned into an uncurbed habit.

In those days Motown had plenty of what the pop culture business these days calls "street credibility." It suggested the possibility that blacks could become acceptable to whites without compromising anything essential of themselves, which was what the street still felt it ought to aspire to. According to *Billboard* magazine's weekly index of black audience appeal, the Temptations were in the middle then of a three-year unbroken sequence of fifteen records that all were among the five most popular in Aframerica.

The Temptations were as definitively the establishers of young urban black style as rap stars are today. Schoolboys went to their shows to see what they had on. When they began wearing single silver bangles on their wrists in 1965, they started a fashion trend among Aframerican males that lasted two decades. A dance called the "Temptation Walk," adapted from the group's stage choreography, had a spring season in 1966 among black teenagers coast to coast.

About a year later Black Panthers marched in California chanting, "No more water in the well (Off the pig!), the pigs are gonna catch hell." To express their defiance, the protesters had appropriated from a recent Temptations album the hook that Smokey had implanted in a song of his about consequences payable for taking too much for granted too long.

It wasn't until Gordy grew obsessed with remaking Diana Ross from Brewster Homes into "the black Barbra Streisand" that he let his finger slip off his people's pulse. Between the late summer of 1966 and the end of the next winter, the Supremes had three consecutive Number 1 records. Every three months of the nine between the fall of 1966 and the spring of 1967, the Four Tops had out a new record that was fast becoming one of the three most listened-to in Aframerica.

In the early summer of 1967 the Miracles were off on their streak of seven Top Ten records in a row. That spring was the latest of seven seasons on end in which a Vandellas record had been at or near the top of the soul music charts.

In the spring of 1967 "Hey Love" set off Stevie Wonder's run of six Top Ten records in eighteen months, of which two hit Number 1 and two others narrowly missed it. That summer Marvin Gaye entered into a two-year lease on the Top Ten, the last six months of which were never without a record of his on the radio that either wasn't, or wasn't going to be, or hadn't just been, the most popular in black America.

"It flipped Berry out," Gaye recalled, "like he was playing the machines in Vegas and three cherries came up ten times in a row."[12] Like Harry Cohn and most other Hollywood moguls, Gordy was a compulsive gambler: no other exhilaration could compare with the feeling he got when he was taking the house's money.

An associate reported that Berry Gordy never finished a book until he read *The Godfather* when he was almost forty. He got so swept up in Puzo's gangster epic that he read passages aloud to secretaries and other minions. He read with difficulty and was embarrassed to have never completed high school. Even while he was conquering clouds, an internal voice speaking in echoes of the childhood catechisms of his mother's faith would nag him.

It would remind him that he was insufficiently self-improved for the company he aspired to keep. He asked one of his college-educated hirelings to put together an autodidact's short survey course on the great books of history. Gordy was so readily bored and defeated by the first of these he attempted that he never bothered with any of the rest. His capacity for attention to the written word was no greater than that of most of the kids to whom he taught his writers to tell "three minute stories."

The output of Motown's lyricists partly comprised a body of literature addressed to a young black audience largely indifferent to print. Smokey Robinson and Curtis Mayfield bestrode their literary world like twin colossi. But many other writers, so long disregarded they are now thought anonymous, were notably present.

Most were contributors of brilliant fragments, memorable for the occasional sparkling of an amateur gift: a resonant line or artful phrase; an intact metaphor standing starkly amid narrative rubble; a precisely realized emotive intention; a flash of poetic insight. Among the street literati who created the black popular music of this era, one-scene scenarists and rhyming couplet–makers who ran out of gas before they finished a compound thought were much more plentiful than coherent tellers of three-minute tales.

Ever accountable to the dictates of fashion, Gordy's song shops were also disciplined by ideals of form; even run-of-the-mill Motown goods were of a higher literary grade than any but the best that others regularly produced. "Truly Yours," a song written in 1966 and recorded by the Spinners, provides an example:

As I read the words written in your letter, my tears began to rise
I could read between the lines, though you thought it was

better,
Not to use the words "good bye"
As I struggled to hold my pride, finally I broke down and I
cried
Your letter ended "Truly yours,"
Though you know that you were never truly mine. . . .
Although you're gone and I'm left alone, and we are far apart
The shell of a man that you discarded behind you, still love
you with all his heart,
But the one thing I'll never understand,
Is how you found the nerve to take a pen in your hand,
And sign your letter, "Truly yours"
When you know that you were never truly mine.

"Truly Yours" was written and produced by the piano player Ivy Hunter and Mickey Stevenson, by then far into the wane of his influence within Motown's creative hierarchy and about to be fully eclipsed by Brian Holland. Stevenson's close seven-year association with Gordy was curdled by anger at his wife's suppressed career and by his conclusion that a long-harbored expectation of just recompense for the contributions he'd made had floated on empty promises. In the late spring of 1966 a project of Stevenson's would have been a minor priority of the company's marketeers.

Though dwarfed by the scale of a half-dozen other contemporaneous Motown hits, this one still managed to become a moderate commercial success. However clear its distinctions, "Truly Yours" was ordinary goods by company standards, a potboiler. At a time when most records were bought by girls, it had the commercial disadvantage of being the testimony of a male complainant who was justified in thinking badly of the story's only female character.

For their part the Spinners, were top-notch professionals, trained exactingly by Harvey Fuqua to the Moonglows' polished style. Under his auspices at Tri-Phi Records, in 1961 the group hit freakishly big with a retrograde ballad. Expressed in doo-wop's last gasp, "That's What Girls Are Made For" was for one summer week the fifth most popular record in Aframerica. Nevertheless, when Fuqua delivered to Hitsville the human assets of his and Gwen Gordy's small music enterprise, the recipients of this cargo thought the Spinners an incidental item among others on the bill of lading to which they attached greater value.

Word was that Motown producers thought the lead singer's voice unsuitably light. When the Spinners weren't on the road, opening for the company's first-string acts, they sometimes worked in the mail room, or as drivers, to earn their weekly stipends. Although they had a Top Ten record on the black charts in the summer of 1965, their next release, "Truly Yours," didn't follow for nearly a year.

Even Motown's corporate afterthoughts circulated widely then. "Truly Yours" would have gotten regular airplay on every black radio station in America in the summer of 1966. In an aural mélange comprised of many vivid elements, only the most salient qualities of a few records would leave a residual impression on most listeners. The ironic tone in "Truly Yours" of dignified indignation, and a plaintiveness even its stoical narrator couldn't repress in his story's telling, were ingrained that summer in the texture of the emotional fabric of everyday black adolescent life.

In Aframerica's insular urban enclaves the young were abuzz with stimulations from without. They were a generation awakened in the morning of American popular culture's industrial age. Not much on television or in movies then correlated with any heartfelt experiences of teenagers devoted to cartoons, commercials, *I Spy*, the *Untouchables*, and James Bond. Songsters of the black teen market naturalized a citizen of the movie world to employ as "Agent Double-O Soul" and later recast him as the action hero of a bawdy short subject called *Sock It to 'Em J.B.* In 1967 George Clinton, even then attuned keenly to the place of television in children's lives, bent the punch line from a Hertz commercial into "let hurt put you in the loser's seat."

"Truly Yours" was a lesson to boys about how a gentleman loses at love. The Motown writers were empathetic elders addressing the young, sentimental educators with a danceable curriculum. The Jobete catalog contains few of the "he's so fine, wish he were mine" schoolgirl-crush songs that were, until the 1960s ripened, a staple of hack writers for the teen market. Even then, for every "He Was Really Saying Something" in its inventory, there were five sassy advisories like "(finding a good man, girls, is like finding a) Needle in a Haystack" and five more wistful fables like "Ask the Lonely" or "What Becomes of the Brokenhearted," about the consequences to young men of manly vanities.

In those days writers of black popular songs were subject to business assumptions that determined that their principal targets were young women whose attention was best captured and held by stories of the human heart. In a literary context shaped in part by such considerations, men were often beggars for love or forgiveness, self-castigators left sadder but wiser by the high cost of a bad choice, and deceivers scorned in their unmasking, or sentenced by one woman to the certain punishment for current crimes. Males in emotional disarray featured prominently on the soundtrack of black adolescent lives. This had a tenderizing effect on a generation of man-children as conversant as today's is with the players' code that affirms as its cardinal precept that "all bitches" are whores.

Motown's transracial currency in the mid-1960s provided the industry's first true measure of how large the payoff could be when black music that was as appealing to many whites as it was to most blacks was made as available to whites as it had been to blacks. The prospect of selling more than twice as many copies of the same record to whites as blacks is why "crossing over" has always been the holy grail for makers and sellers of boogaloo.

When Gordy succeeded at it, black music's value on the commodity exchange skyrocketed. He was a revelation, as stirring to his generation's major holders of music-business property as Bessie Smith had been to hers. Within a decade black popular music would account for about two-thirds of the industry's $3.5 billion take.

From the first Motown was kept closely and privately held. A week after he and Raynoma, as partners, legally incorporated Tamla Records and Jobete Publishing, Gordy induced her to remove her name from the papers they'd jointly signed and filed. Her signature was also redacted from the promissory note they'd cosigned for the eight-hundred-dollar start-up loan from his family.

By the mid-1960s there were a thousand shares of stock in Gordy's corporation, and he owned them all. In 1968 he paid himself a dividend of $3,100 a share. By such means, in the last three years of the 1960s, he took more than $5 million out of his company.[13] He used some of it to stake his introduction into Los Angeles show-business society. He opened an office on Sunset Boulevard. He quietly bought a house in Beverly Hills from the fallen television star Tommy Smothers, at about the same time he moved into his lavish Italianate pile in the estate district of Detroit, nestled among others built by the planter aristocracy of that one-crop town.

Buying the mansion on Boston Boulevard, which had cost a million dollars to build and appoint fifty years before Gordy lived in it, certified him as the richest local Negro of all time. This distinction was commemorated in an oil-painted portrait presented to him by his older sister—the keeper of family accounts—that superimposed his face on Napolean's torso against the backdrop of an enlarged section of a Detroit street map.

It hung over the cavernous marble fireplace in Gordy Manor, beneath the frescoed ceilings in the gold-leafed living room. For Esther Gordy Edwards, a local politician's wife, it represented what her brother and his company had come to mean to black Detroit.

The automobile industry's steady growth had produced a sizable, home-owning black and blue-collar middle class that was beginning to assert itself in the city's official civic life. "Pops" and Bertha's thirty-five years of doggedness at putting one foot in front of the other had given the Gordy clan a potpourri of small businesses and a local reputation as assiduous strivers. Now in a single bound one of them had leapfrogged over respectable "n[egro] rich" ghetto entrepreneurs like the undertaking Diggs family (which had produced a congressman) and the scornful progeny of old-settler professionals (who fancied themselves a branch of Negro high society) into a category of wealth that applied only to white people.

As this fairy tale of attainment vividly unfolded in plain view, the Gordys began to look as glamorous as Kennedys to ordinary black citizens of Detroit. At the very moment when the city was changing its public face to make it more comely to the social aesthetes of the Great Society era, the worldwide awareness of Gordy's brand gave Detroit an identity that was distinct from automobiles. Motown, the term of convenience for all of Gordy's enterprises, now served as the quasi-official trademark for the whole city, and nothing could have better expressed the sense Detroit's emergent black establishment had that it was settling into influence, even permanence.

In the mid-1960s when Negroes were more on the minds of white Americans than ever, the sudden transcendence of one local family of black bootstrappers seemed a harbinger. The son of Bertha Gordy and the brother-in-law of George Edwards was now America's best-known black businessman. He'd become such by developing a resource that he had discovered in natural abundance among the city's "jitterbug . . . conk-wearing . . . [black] lower class," whose only value had previously been thought measurable as a census number or by the price of its physical labor. Now goods owned and made by the hands of black Detroiters were being sold as widely as automobiles made by Ford and General Motors.

When the governor of Michigan visited England in early 1966, he was pressed wherever he went by teenagers wanting to know if he'd met the Supremes. They, it seemed, were as popular there as the Beatles were in America. Ten years removed from living in his sister's house, Gordy's life had gotten too big for Detroit to contain.

While her brother was ensconcing himself in California, Esther reassured home folks that he could never really leave. "People try to get us to move away," she told the local press, "to take on New York or Hollywood or one of those places. But Berry is crazy about this town."[14]

Earlier that year Gordy had moved the company's headquarters into a sold-off municipal office building downtown. It was never intended as anything more than a way station. One former executive called it "the shittiest building you ever saw . . . Offices with shades hanging on the windows, that sort of thing."[15] Ten stories of gray brick, painted "an institutional olive green" on the inside, the Donovan Building had been a warehouse for bureaucrats. It was emblematic of the new Motown, Inc.

Having amassed substantial property, Gordy hired white men to manage and secure it. This inevitably changed the sense of being family, which had been so much a part of self-consciousness in its early days and the basis of its morale. Once Gordy was no longer served by the illusion of a Motown "family," few of those he'd kept faithful to it could ever again count on communicating directly with the head of the house.

Gordy never outgrew certain of his received cultural assumptions; he wanted Italians to collect his money and Jews to keep his books, handle his finances, and do his lawyering. He had been partial to Jews since befriending the ragpickers he encountered in back alleys around Hastings Street in his Black Bottom boyhood. These "little guys with long beards" reminded him of his father.

They were unashamed of an occupation others thought undignified because their true vocation was making a dollar out of fifteen cents. After he recognized a pair of his own discarded shoes in a neighborhood pawnshop—now restored and on sale for half their original price—Berry was sure these men were alchemists who knew how to turn found objects into money. Unlike his father they didn't even have to buy the raw materials of their trade.

Upon learning that these junkmen he knew were called Jews, and that the shop and most of the other properties around belonged to Jews, the thirteen-year-old Berry was filled with admiration and wonder. It appeared to him that Jews must have a way of converting other people's throwaways into stores and buildings. He never forgot the advice they gave him not to buy anything he couldn't afford to pay for in cash. He held on to that as though it were a necromancer's trade secret.[16]

Gordy subsequently learned, from bruisings he took breaking into the music business, that to contend in an unruly arena dominated by Italians and Jews, he needed contentious Italians and Jews of his own.

He preferred them fast-talking, dutiful, and snappish as Rottweilers in the pursuit and protection of his interests. He didn't mind at all if they were abrasive to others, since their job was mainly to say no to requests to spend his money.

From the first Gordy saw the necessity of having a white boy around to deal with others for him. Alan Abrams, who was affable and loyal, scuffled alongside Gordy through Motown's predawn. But Gordy knew he needed someone who could induce big distributors to place his records on retailers' shelves within white kids' easy reach.

As a former employee of his noted, "after you give the records to a distributor, you always have trouble [getting paid] . . . unless you have . . . a guy who goes around and collects."[17] For Gordy, such a man was Barney Ales. Gordy had lately reduced his business to a piece of paper on which he had written, "CREATE, SELL and COLLECT," and he taped it to the wall above his desk so that his eyes would stay on the prize.

Ales seemed to appear mysteriously at Gordy's shoulder in time to navigate the spectacular crossing over of "Shop Around" in 1961. Raynoma remembers being told by her husband, as he introduced her to Ales, that Ales would replace Abrams as head of promotion and make four times as much as the company's highest-paid employee, her sister-in-law Loucye, who had been heroically staving off bankruptcy by squeezing accounts receivable for every dollar to be had.

At first sight of him, Raynoma saw her own disadvantage reflected darkly in Ales's "attractive Italian features": an Italian in the wholesale record business with a name camouflaged to make it mistakable for Jewish. She knew her husband's affinity for larcenous hearts and recognized in Barney Ales the makings of a potent rival. She expressed misgivings about paying an unproven stranger so much money. Gordy's rebuff was snarly and blunt: "the guy is hired, and if you don't like it you can kiss my ass." Much as she distrusted him, Raynoma conceded that Ales's work was "phenomenal": "Barney orchestrated the participation of all the major white distributors nationwide, and in so doing set up the machinery to repeat [the] success [of "Shop Around"] in the future."[18]

Ales would parlay his skill at collecting Gordy's money into a vice-presidency of marketing, distribution, and sales. Eventually he would become president of the record division of Motown, Inc. Because of their closeness many presumed that Ales was Gordy's silent partner or the agent of others who were. Gordy was unfazed by such perceptions, supposing them, on the whole, good for his business. Their relationship was different from any others Gordy had, for Ales usually got his way.

Of all Gordy's associates, Ales was the most critical to his cash flow. Gordy let him stock his offices with cronies and tolerated their petty thieving.[19] This was part of the cost attachable to the only employee Gordy felt he couldn't afford to lose. Perhaps he thought Ales smart enough to fear. At all times Gordy took careful measure of Ales's position—"I knew the more excited I got the more it would cost me"—but never could he outmaneuver him in the cat-and-mouse play of their personal business dealings: "The pro [Ales] had regained his footing. . . . I had said yes too fast the last time and Barney thought he hadn't asked for enough."[20] Gordy respected no one more.

In 1967 fewer than 10 percent of Motown's two hundred or so employees were white, but nearly all who were held positions in senior management. Ales was a conduit for others who followed, like Ralph Seltzer, a lawyer who started as Gordy's special assistant, and the Noveck brothers, a lawyer and an accountant, who were his fiscal watchdogs and made sure his books could always stand inspection. Another vice-president named Michael Roshkind ran the New York office. Ales, Seltzer, and Harry Balk, the "creative director," oversaw things in Detroit when Gordy was in Los Angeles. Although there was still plenty of family on his payroll—Gordys comprised a third of the company's phone directory—only Esther was near the inner circle.

"Negroes just don't understand the kind of general-market business I'm trying to run," Gordy once groused,[21] even though some of his longest associates clearly did, having laid every brick in the edifice he was building. This disdainful response to criticisms that he hired too many white boys bristled with his presumption that the complainants were jealous Negroes.

Once Gordy came into the bounty he never meant to share, he trusted the conditional loyalty he bought from white people would outlast the allegiances of his oldest associates, which had been formed by the expectation he'd encouraged that those who had labored beside him would profit commensurately. The only long-standing loyalties Gordy rewarded were Esther's and Smokey Robinson's. Later, after he split the stock in his company into five times as many shares, he gave them each two hundred.[22]

Otherwise he was relentlessly proprietary about his holdings. He forswore the tax-abating structural conventions then standard in the contemporary designs of music businesses, because any such elaborations in the architecture of his own would have come between him and direct control of his money. Besides, Gordy preferred giving the government too much to having to endure its scrutiny.

The riot season of 1967 began in the middle of June, and within a month it had already been commemorated in Tampa, Boston, Chicago, Cincinnati, Atlanta, Buffalo, Milwaukee, Minneapolis, and Plainfield, New Jersey. Twenty-six people died in Newark in mid-July. Most of these outbreaks were incited by friction between white constabulary in black neighborhoods and the subjects of their policing.

Even though Detroit law enforcers hadn't changed much in complexion or temperament in the thirty elapsed years since it was a Klan klavern, the city's veneer looked so much shinier after its recent hard polishing that its leading citizens were taken by surprise when an arrest at an after-hours club erupted into a week of rioting in which forty-three died, all but ten of them black. It took the National Guard several days to restore order. Thirty-eight hundred people were arrested. About $50 million worth of property was damaged, stolen, or destroyed. Five thousand residents were made homeless.

"Many of the places we knew, stores we'd patronized over the years, places we'd hung out at were gone," recalled Otis Williams. "Afterward lots of people talked about bringing Detroit back, but no matter how much money they threw at it, [the] city wasn't ever going to be the same."[23] Whites fled town as if from a house afire. Even the better off among them, merely discomfited before by the unsightly buildup of Negroes in their backyards, now feared infection from the spreading taint of the city's despoilment and were certain their property values would never recover.

For the first time Negroes could buy houses where they had previously been excluded. White people were in such a hurry to get out that the restrictive covenants they'd erected and protected to barricade their residential enclaves no longer had practical effect. Since it wasn't possible to find willing white hands into which properties could pass, houses were being sold to whoever could buy. Many of those being run from were inclined to see other opportunities in abandonment.

Detroit's black establishment, though still several years away from electing a mayor, figured that as dire as the human consequences of the riots had been, they also afforded a means of political ascent. If white people were going to leave Detroit to them, some believed it could be reconstructed as a shining Black Metropolis. In these optimists' view, the riots had been, as *Ebony* magazine put it, the "birth pangs of a new city."[24]

Detroit's officialdom and its corporate masters scrambled to certify Negroes as spokespeople for other Negroes in civic colloquies to promote racial understanding, and serve as conduits for the money flowing into the streets as jobs and programs. They became models of powerful white men conspicuously trying to do the right thing. But their city nevertheless became the backlash capital of America, a national model of the inexorable workings of white flight from anyplace Negroes became too concentrated. And what a week of burning and bloodletting had unhinged in Detroit, the contraction of the American car industry subsequently made irreparable.

By the late 1960s the bulk of the region's employment base had already shifted out of the city into the suburbs. By the early 1970s, half the jobs associated with making American cars were overseas, and most of the rest had migrated to states with right-to-work laws. After he'd concluded that Detroit was unsalvageable, Henry Ford Jr., who worked and lived in the suburbs along with the rest of his industry's managerial class, left behind a monument to their abdication: the Renaissance Center, a colonial-fortress pied-à-terre for people who lived somewhere else and occasionally needed to use the city at night.

By the early 1980s a city whose population had been 70 percent white twenty years before was more than 70 percent black. Aframericans had inherited Detroit when it was already assured of becoming what it is now—the poorest, blackest big city in the country.

After the summer smoke cleared in 1967, Detroit stank of failure, an aroma guaranteed to clear any room Gordy wanted to frequent. During the riots, Marvin Gaye recalled, "we could . . . hear the gunfire [from Motown's offices] on West Grand. Berry freaked."[25] He had already decided to move Motown out of Detroit, although it would take four years to become official.

He had chosen and begun to train Suzanne DePasse as "bottom woman"-in-waiting to replace Esther in California. The city never knew he was leaving until it could count the days he was gone. It preceded by a year the election of Coleman Young, Detroit's first black mayor, and coincided with the department store magnate J. L. Hudson's timely observation that "the black man has the feeling he is about to take power in the city . . . he is going to be left with an empty bag."[26]

While his hometown's old social order still teetered on the verge of its undoing, Gordy began disestablishing his Motown "family." Some of the first to go were the senior black men who had helped him first, when their help was the best he could hope to have. They had taught school at Hitsville, imparting the traditions and disciplines of Negro show business to Gordy's raw recruits.

One was Jack Gibson, who handled Motown's relationships with the black radio and record worlds and was of the pioneer generation of black disk jockeys. Gibson was let go in 1967 because he didn't "fit with the company's image."[27] In truth, by then Gordy no longer cared "if a black disc jockey never played another one of [his] records."

He early understood the effects that television had on selling records to white people and on certifying his acts for bookers of performances on college campuses, at the Hollywood Bowl, and in the showrooms of Las Vegas hotels. The Supremes were being sold on network television, where they appeared twenty times in 1965 and 1966, when six of their nine records made Number 1 on the pop charts.

Another casualty was Thomas "Beans" Bowles, a former horn player in the house band at the Flame Show Bar. He'd recruited other musicians to work for Gordy and taught scoring to musically unlettered youngsters who later became company mainstays as writers and producers. Bowles also road-managed the Motortown Revues and the early European tours.

In the studio he contributed the toneless saxophonic bleats and honks of which instrumental bridges were constructed that became an identifying characteristic of Motown records. But Bowles had given offense by running for a minor local office over the objection of Esther Gordy's husband. Twenty years later he spoke for all the others left holding on too long to a misplaced faith: "Up until the moment we found ourselves outside, we believed Berry would come through with some kind of profit sharing."[28]

By 1967 it was clear to Motown's longest-serving hands that their loyalty would be unrewarded. Harvey Fuqua divorced Gwen and moved on. Mickey Stevenson left and took his wife, the singer Kim Weston, whose career he felt had been flattened to clear Diana Ross's path. Before the year was out, Ralph Seltzer would be running the Creative Division. Gordy, a sucker for much that was conventional in America's official wisdom, regarded it as axiomatic that a good manager could manage any kind of enterprise.

Upon being given his new assignment, Seltzer began charging producers 25 percent of the costs of the recording sessions they supervised, even though these were being reimbursed from artists' royalties. This practice allowed the company to recoup 125 percent of its outlay. "The old feeling," Raynoma Gordy wrote, "was of having our own piece of ground . . . now it was turning into a plantation."

"Berry was a deal-cutter," Ralph Seltzer has said. "Administration wasn't his strength. BG always suffered with organizational problems."[29] Seltzer brought in management consultants to suggest possible efficiencies. As a result, the Artists Development department was eliminated; Maurice King and Cholly Atkins and Maxine Powell were cast aside without any parting recompense but the cold satisfaction they must have felt, a decade and a half into their unpensioned retirements, at seeing their old school's last graduate, Michael Jackson, become the most popular entertainer in the world.

This step served official notice that Motown was no longer gearing to develop new assets but rather to extract every dollar of value left in those it already had. As layers of strangers and corporate policy were interposed between Gordy and the creative talent, Motown's artists and producers began to defend themselves against the sudden chill in the air by stiffening their own attitudes about business. Others besides Raynoma had noticed that "the administration of company finance seemed to result in only Berry's accumulation of wealth and no one else's."[30]

Many got outside lawyers, asked to see the books, took another look at the substandard deals they'd signed, and resolved to leave. "[W]hen BG stopped giving anyone any real money," Bowles noted, ". . . a lot of folk fell away from him."[31]

Despite his daily checkings-in from Los Angeles with Barney Ales and Ralph Seltzer in Detroit, Gordy didn't know the Holland brothers and Lamont Dozier hadn't been at work in months. "We had a lack of material and I was unhappy about it," Gordy later avowed. "I would call Brian's office and he was not there."[32]

Brian Holland had entered the "family" circle as a member of a group called the Satintones, one of a small constellation of young aspirants orbiting Gordy before he even had means to record them. He had slept on Gordy couches, attended the birth of the Rayber Music Writing Company in 1957, and been a background voice on the demo tapes that Berry and Raynoma used to make in a local disk jockey's basement.

Gordy's frustration with the Holland brothers waxed as 1967 waned. Whenever he found Brian unreachable, Gordy "would call Eddie's office about the same thing and he was not there."

Eddie Holland had been part of the Hitsville community for ten years. He was at first paid two dollars a week to do odd jobs while Gordy groomed him to be a singer as closely approximated to Jackie

Wilson as anyone could hope to make from ordinary human material. He even had a hit record in 1962 bigger than any others in the company's early life but "Shop Around" and "Please Mr. Postman." But after 1964 his own career as a singer was displaced by the volume of splashier successes that he helped author for others. For more than five years the Holland brothers had worked together as producers and songwriters with Lamont Dozier, a twice-recorded singer who came to Motown as small change in Harvey Fuqua's pocket.

Perhaps his sense of having sacrificed a dream made Eddie Holland the threesome's most "money-minded." As their self-appointed business agent, for several years he had pressed Gordy for a better deal collectively than each was afforded in the ungenerous individual contracts they'd signed. Gordy's habitual indifference to any interests but his own could well enough make sullen an advocate of others', particularly ones whose position didn't compel a response. Holland's old resentment at the scuttling of his recording career, so that his inconvenient personal ambitions could not distract him from serving purposes more important to Gordy, would make him a more rancorous negotiator for having been doubly thwarted.

Although their lawyers would later maintain that HDH had never actually seen it, they knew their contract was due to expire at the end of 1967. Inflamed by a three-year hot streak that lit up the pop charts like nobody black ever had, and disgruntled at being such minor stakeholders in the evident wealth they'd created, HDH decided to sit out the last six months of their obligation to Motown.

That fall, when "informed that [HDH] hadn't recorded [anything] in [a] couple of months," Gordy "became . . . alarmed."[33] Convinced that Gordy had reneged on a promise to give them stock or its cash equivalent, they now had the idea of going into business for themselves. Once Gordy understood their self-absention was not a ploy but a declaration of intent, he brought suit to bring them to heel.

Holland-Dozier-Holland were justified in thinking Gordy couldn't abide their loss. Since 1964 they had stood eye to eye with the Beatles as makers of commercial music. The Supremes were already the best-selling female group in history. Marvin Gaye once complained that in the mid-1960s Gordy considered the Supremes and Four Tops his "only real pop acts."[34] Both were written for and produced exclusively by the Holland brothers and Lamont Dozier.

They felt entitled to think themselves responsible for Berry Gordy having all of a sudden gotten filthy rich. One measure of how well their songs sold between 1965 and 1967 was the $2.2 million in royalties they were paid by Jobete Publishing. From the size of their own, they could extrapolate the dimensions of Gordy's unseen pile and rankle at the disproportion.

Holland, Dozier, and Holland countersued Motown for $22 million (and thus began years of acrimonious litigation that ended in a quiet settlement midway through the next decade). As soon as these hostilities were formally declared, they were enjoined from working for anyone but Gordy for two years. Once their enforced hiatus was over, they started their own company.

Though Invictus/Hot Wax Records did well for several years using the generation of young talent whose growth Gordy had stimulated in Detroit and then left behind, HDH alleged that Motown had campaigned against them, intimidating people whom they might have done business with and blacklisting many who had. In the meantime Gordy was left with a hole agape near the center of his grand design.

Before they stopped work, Holland, Dozier, and Holland had warehoused enough finished product to keep Supremes and Four Tops releases arriving on schedule into early 1968. But the quality of these goods was lackluster, and the Supremes didn't have a bona fide hit for nearly a year.

Gordy's plans then were centered on Diana Ross. One of the hoariest truisms in the black music business is that a white girl who sounds black, in the right hands, can make millions. Gordy instead took a black girl and made her into an honorary white girl—and made many millions. He aimed to introduce her into the realm of celebrity inhabited by immediate presences who had no pasts worth mentioning or futures worth caring about.

The Supremes were the platform from which Ross was meant to ascend into the major leagues of show business. That the group's popularity should falter just as he was preparing her solo launch—"betting the bank on Diana"—created a fearsome circumstance for Gordy. He mobilized hastily to patch this leak in his flagship's hull.

He commissioned an emergency detail of Motown's able second-string songwriters to come up with a hit song. They went to ground in a Detroit hotel room and emerged three days later with "Love Child." Gordy himself attended to every aspect of its production. It was a triumphant moment—reaffirming of the grace still present in the master's touch—made legendary by seeming to be an act of will.

The record rocketed to Number 1 on the pop charts. Ross's luster was restored; within a year she was sprung from the Supremes and out of Detroit, her identity purged of Brewster Homes and her awkward professional beginnings as a demitalent with a small, nasal voice who had apprenticed in lovecraft on tour buses so that she might apply it more persuasively to men who were able and willing to abet her climb.[35]

From now on Gordy intended her for a well-heeled white clientele. By 1970 she was performing at the Coconut Grove in Los Angeles, the Waldorf-Astoria in New York, and the Theater in the Round in Chicago. He knew he had in Ross a potential white man's money magnet.

She was what the players on John R Street called star material, primed to do whatever she was told to do to go out and get Daddy his cash. But they might well have advised him that "a pretty n[egro] bitch will get in a stable to wreck it. . . . You gotta make 'em hump hard and fast. Stick 'em for the long scratch quick."[36]

Gordy "worked those girls to death" at making him rich. When the Supremes caught fire in the summer of 1964, they were an overnight conflagration that blazed ravishingly for two years. Ross was so hard-ridden she broke down, collapsing onstage in Boston from overuse.

That night Gordy slipped into her hospital room, and for the first time they made love.[37] "Be as sweet as the scratch," the pimp's adage goes. "Always stick a whore for a bundle before you sex her."[38]

Another Supreme, Mary Wilson, later claimed that during this period her "funds were withheld over long periods while she received only $200 to $300 per week."[39] ("The real glue that holds any bitch to a pimp is the long scratch she [knows] she's stuck for.")[40] They were into their twenties and generating millions, but all their large purchases required Gordy's written approval.

In 1965—during nine months of which one or another of three Supremes records was the most popular in America—the cash they received and their houses, cars, and clothing allowances amounted to an annual stipend of about $250,000 each, for all their hard humping. Wilson says, "[W]e stuck to him so close, all three of us, that if he stopped in his tracks, we'd all pile up behind him. . . . People would die to be around him. All the artists [wanted] to be his favorite."[41]

The effects of Gordy's favor apparently made her too giddy to notice that he had already chosen among them, although it was clear enough to others: "Flo and I could hang out . . . with the other girls and be comfortable. But it was very difficult for the other[s] . . . to like Diane."[42] By the middle of 1966 the company was already planting rumors that Ross was going to leave the Supremes. "He was now her man only," Martha Reeves recalled thinking, her jealousy and hurt still palpable after all those years.[43]

Once Gordy saw the indications of her stunning trick appeal, Diana became his preoccupation. "Berry had made her his from the very word go," said Thomas Bowles.[44] He sent her for a five-month course in grooming at the John Powers School for Social Grace, where she was given a practical education in acting like a white girl: how to sit, stand, talk, eat, and laugh, whether she was in public or in polite company. They had to break Ross of her tendency to giggle. ("A pimp is happy when his whores giggle. He knows they are still asleep.")[45]

Gordy attended personally to her making, both as a performer and a public image. He coached her unsparingly through her recorded vocals, monitored every performance, even wrote her stage patter. "She meant everything to him," according to Gaye. "Vegas, Broadway shows, movies. . . . He worked like a demon."[46]

The fullest extent of Gordy's investment in Artists Development coincided with the urgency he'd begun to feel by early 1965 about preparing the Supremes for legitimate show business. That was when he brought in the choreographer Cholly Atkins and music director Maurice King full time, along with a couple of arrangers who worked on nightclub acts. It is said that Mary Wells was pushed over the edge by her resentment of Gordy using the money she'd made him on "My Guy" to hang Diana Ross's star.[47]

He "personally produced [Ross and the Supremes'] nightclub act, spent unbelievable sums . . . on costumes and scenery and lighting,"[48] Martha Reeves recalled. In England in the spring of 1965 Gordy bought the Supremes "new red dresses" for their appearance on a television show that she had expected would feature her.

After interceding in the production to reapportion camera time in Diana's favor, Reeves recalled, "Berry took me aside to explain . . . that the Supremes—'his girls'—were on the top rung of the ladder and that my group was on the lower one. . . . Ron White of the Miracles saw me backstage . . . and said . . . , 'We all get a turn at the top. You had your turn.'"[49] Martha Reeves never recovered from Gordy's cruel delineations of the limits of his interest in her.

Mary Wilson, still proud, twenty years later, of having pleased him, spoke for more of Gordy's "girls" than were Supremes or even female: "We really became what Berry had imagined."[50] As Marvin Gaye observed, for Diana Ross that entailed becoming Gordy's "living, breathing brainchild."[51] She would pledge allegiance to Gordy by saying, "What you can think, I can do."

"I always wanted a Cinderella," Berry once said, in a rare recorded moment of reflection. He was speaking to Raynoma of why he'd forsaken her long before for Margaret Norton, the beautiful but unstrung adolescent he was briefly weak for, before casting her into lifelong chilly exile—like a spurned queen kept out of the way in a modest palace on the edge of the kingdom—wherein he dabbled with her until finally she went mad.

He later accounted Margaret "the most selfish person in the world." She would have to be, since she was "the only woman he'd ever been involved with who had never done anything for him."[52] But in Diana Ross he saw the real prospect of fulfilling a longing even older than his ambition.

On the other hand, it would be hard to discern any longing more native to Diana Ross than her ambition to be Cinderella. When she was a high school girl busing tables at Hudson's Department Store, on her way to and from work she would gather her coat around her, so nobody could see the uniform underneath, and daydream about being one of those rich ladies from Grosse Point who stepped out of limousines and were swept into the store grandly by brass-buttoned doormen.[53] ("You have wanted since you were a little girl to live an exciting, glamorous life. . . . I'm gonna make your life with me out-shine your flashiest daydreams. . . . I'm gonna be your mother, your father, your brother, your friend, and your lover. The most important thing I'm gonna be to you is your man. The manager of the scratch you make.")[54]

"People said she was Berry's puppet," Marvin Gaye observed, "[but] I knew it was only a matter of time before Diana would get what she wanted."[55] She got to be Gordy's consort and lord it over the rest of his stable. This she did with such relish that Kim Weston, one of the women who thought her career suppressed by Gordy to Ross's advantage, said, "Diana is lucky someone didn't kick her ass."[56]

However many would have welcomed the chance, "the girls were too scared of Berry" to have risked his sanction. ("[T]his family is like a small army. We got rules and regulations we never break. I am really two [people]. One of them is sweet and kind to his [whores] when they don't break the rules. The other comes out insane and dangerous when the rules are broken.")[57] While you were his, he could punish you unmercifully (as he did Florence Ballard) or lock your career in a closet until it wasted away (as he did Martha Reeves's) and if you left him, he could ruin you (as he did Mary Wells).

In 1964, when Mary Wells turned twenty-one, the contract she had signed with Motown four years earlier became invalid and had to be renewed. She was the biggest-selling pop female vocalist in the world that year. Wells was the first to make the company open its books to her, and whatever she saw, she liked so little that she signed with another label. As a circulating unverifiable rumor had it, Gordy paid disk jockeys all over the country not to play her records. Wells's career was permanently blighted. ("I celebrate . . . when a whore leaves me. It gives some worthy bitch a chance to take her place and be a star.")[58]

Diana Ross was hungry enough to stick. Marvin Gaye thought she and Gordy were bound together by "fear and money." But he admired her: "Any woman who gets involved with Berry Gordy—and hangs in like Diana did—must be made of steel."[59]

11. Crackers and Flies

In March 1970 Jim Stewart convened a staff meeting to introduce Stax's newly appointed controller, Ed Pollack, a lawyer who for six and a half years had been part of Berry Gordy's auxiliary of white middle managers. The old proprietor read a five-page speech that extolled the past year's progress but decried its heavy toll on company stores of comity and trust. "AND ALL THE WHILE THE RUMORS ROLL ON," he thundered. ". . . the Blacks are taking over; the Whites are taking over; Al Bell is getting rid of Jim Stewart; Jim Stewart is taking power away from Al Bell . . ."

He inveighed against "STAX-ITIS," an invidious malaise "resulting in underdeveloped minds and overdeveloped egos." His jeremiad concluded: "There is no Black Power. There is no White Power. There is only GREEN POWER. There is no White House or Black House. There is a STAX HOUSE, and I say to you neither Jim Stewart or Al Bell is 'taking over.'"[1] Either Stewart was like the ghost captain Benito Cereno exercising his hollow command on the deck of a slave ship commandeered by its cargo, or a cracker ahead of his time.

Even as he spoke, Stewart and Bell were scrambling to buy Stax back from Gulf and Western. The assets of their partnership were mostly embodied in G&W stock. In less than two years the value of these holdings had been halved. They were also convinced that G&W's maladroit handling of product distribution impaired Stax's growth.

Reacquiring his own company for a million more dollars than he'd sold it for took Stewart many times to New York and Los Angeles and nearly a year to accomplish. His forays into foreign capitals of finance resulted in Bell becoming partner to a mortgage held by Gulf and Western and a heavy cash indebtedness to the Deutsche Grammophon company.

At the moment of Jim Stewart's cri de coeur, Isaac Hayes's next album was starting to circulate. After nearly a year its predecessor was still among the five most popular in Aframerica. By the middle of that May and for three months thereafter, *The Isaac Hayes Movement* was Number 1 on the black album charts; it registered on the white side for half a year, partly in the Top Ten. Hayes was now officially crossed-over. Those discordancies in "Stax house," which hadn't been provoked by Al Bell's assumption of command, were festering around Hayes, who had swollen overnight into a figure large enough to carry an entourage.

Prominent in his was the gangsterish Johnny Baylor, who first appeared in Memphis at Bell's behest after the King assassination, when local ragtag hoodlums were emboldened to try to extort money from people at Stax. Bell and Baylor had encountered each other scrummaging in the rough-and-tumble of black radio, which is to say they had met on a ghetto street corner of the music business.

Baylor was a strong arm inside a silk-and-mohaired sleeve, hailing from New York by way of Alabama and the Korean War. There had always been work for such men on properties owned by whites and labored upon by blacks. Some, like Nate McCalla, started as enforcers for the likes of Morris Levy, then went into business for themselves.

At the top of this class was Joe Robinson of All-Platinum Records, who broke the leg of Frankie Crocker when the reigning king of black radio took money for a record he neglected to play. Johnny Baylor drew a gun on a disk jockey nearly as powerful, in calling the question of how much cash in the suitcase that contained the proceeds of E. Rodney Jones's "benefit" concert in Chicago was Isaac Hayes's proper share.

That night Baylor's thuggery was enlisted in the performance of his regular duties as Hayes's fee-collector. On another, in his capacity as

Hayes's sergeant at arms, he put a gun to David Porter's head. Occasionally he pistol-whipped someone to make a point with emphasis. In the pulp-fictive filings of contemporary writers of FBI reports, Johnny Baylor was characterized as a "Black Mafi[oso]."[2]

In partial exchange for his services, Baylor's one-horse stable, Luther Ingram, was given the well-paid job of opening Hayes's show. This exposure so heightened demand for Ingram's records that Baylor was induced onto the road in the prospect of "breaking" his only act. While making his rounds, Baylor also looked out for Stax's interests with local distributors who, as a rule, were prone to the crookedness of snakes.

He was soon reporting to Bell evidence seen of Stax "product . . . being bootlegged to distributors" out of its own back door.[3] After uncovering nested thieves and grafters in the company's sales and marketing departments, Baylor became a sort of consultant to Bell for expediting corporate affairs with unsavories in the shady business circles nearest the street, wherein Stax's cash flow streamed dollar by dollar through untrustworthy alien hands.

By early 1971 Isaac Hayes's fourth and latest album was doing about as much business as the one before. Though it was self-realized, his sustained success confirmed the rightness of Bell's fix on the middle of the road as the location from which a gentrified Stax "sound" could most profitably be sold. Even as Hayes was writing and producing brilliant, churchy gutbucket for the Soul Children, his star rose as a crooner of songs by Burt Bacharach and Jimmy Webb, in a variation of a style that had once served Billy Eckstine.

At their best, his thickly orchestrated interpretations of recycled hits achieved the balance of panache and languidity to which Luther Vandross has since aspired. In Hayes Stax had a star that gleamed more brightly than Otis Redding, over a marketplace grown bigger and busier by several years. And so a scant decade after Dr. King's campaign in the South had staggered out of a Georgia yet unreconstructed, southern "new" Negritude's first celebrity now dared to expect the same portion of excess that any white boy would receive who was the peer of a "Black Moses."

Uplifted on the shaven head and chain-mantled shoulders of Isaac Hayes, Stax reached its commercial zenith in 1971, when $17 million worth of its records and tapes were sold. The trajectory of Hayes's ascent was steepened by marketeer Larry Shaw, and his rate of climb quickened by the movie-consciousness of Al Bell.

Hayes had already created for himself a larger-than-life-size persona as a black Spartacus, the rampant slave-set-free: powerful, brooding, aglitter with gold and beaded sweat. Packaging him as Black Moses in a Judaic prophet's cowl and sandals was as right for its day in Aframerican times as "wantu wazori" had been in 1967 for selling Afro-Sheen.

Bell was a premature synergist who recognized the cross-marketing potential of a movie and its soundtrack. He negotiated the arrangement with MGM by which Isaac Hayes scored and Stax sold the soundtrack of official Hollywood's first black-faced action film. *Shaft* spawned a genre of movies for which a contemporary black disparager coined the descriptor "blaxploitation." Its wild success in 1971 located for film producers and their backers an untapped vein of hard-spending customers.

If they hadn't fallen on bad times, makers of movies would never have stumbled on the submerged riches that the first phonograph-record industrialists had similarly discovered four decades earlier. In 1960 Hollywood stood about where the music business had in the 1920s: it was being undercut by a pervasive new medium that gave consumers free use of entertainment products they'd previously had to pay for. Americans in 1960 were buying fewer than a fifth as many movie tickets every week as they had in the 1940s.

After the decrepit studio patriarchy relaxed its grip, and before its holdings were consolidated into corporate oligarchs' far-flung domains, the hard-pressed film industry of the 1960s splintered into a confederacy of makers and marketers of movies who formed temporary alliances in foraging for fresh customers. This situation proved opportune for independent producers adept at making movies that appealed to the young and others theretofore uncatered-to.

Near the end of the 1960s the public attention commanded by rebukers of America and back-to-Africa psychological absconders who'd made themselves conspicuous in the discourse of tribe and nation, suggested to culture-mongers that "black identity" could have a selling season. Al Bell dipped his toe alongside other early testers of the depth and temperature of the pool of ticket-buyers for movies with black faces.

A couple of years before Melvin Van Peebles became the picture industry's Mamie Smith, Booker T. Jones had done the music for Jules Dassin's remake of *The Informer.* The French filmmaker transposed the original Irish context of John Ford's movie into an American ghetto setting with a mostly black cast, a conceit meant to exoticize an old story for white audiences.

By middecade Melvin Van Peebles had arrived in San Francisco with the cachet of having been a directorial award-winner on the European film-festival circuit. An actor and writer as well as a moviemaker, Van Peebles landed a contract with Herb Alpert's A&M Records, a major independent label with high standing in the pop music establishment. His albums of spoken rhyme and rhythm acquired a small following among black America's more-numerous-than-ever college-goers.

These progressivists knew Van Peebles as a jazzily accompanied dramatic monologist, the author and performer of "Lily do the zampoo-oogie, every time I pull her coat tail." After a lackluster turn at "helming" a one-note situation comedy for Columbia Pictures, Van Peebles wrote, directed, starred in, barely financed, and shot in nineteen days a movie of his own.

In the spring of 1971 *Sweet Sweetback's Baadasssss Song* opened in Detroit and Atlanta. It was trumpeted by *Ebony* magazine as "the first American film in the black idiom made entirely outside the white power structure's control." The industry was stunned by its quick amassing of $14 million in box-office receipts, nearly all from the pockets of black Americans.[4]

This haul made *Sweetback* one of the biggest commercial successes in the elapsed history of motion pictures. Al Bell bought the sound-track, and Larry Shaw put hawkers of the album in lobbies of movie theaters. Stax had become associated with a cultural event.

Selling the *Sweetback* soundtrack was a warm-up for the company's concentrated effort at selling *Shaft*. In anticipation of the movie's release, Shaw organized his network of black advertising and public relations hands into a consortium to market Isaac Hayes's companion album. The single, "Theme from *Shaft*," sold a million copies. The album became America's most popular and was listed among the best-selling for more than a year.

Hayes won Grammys and an Academy Award. The latter was received in a fur-trimmed tuxedo. Once the poorest of Stax's original cadre, Hayes would now brook no less than a rock star's portion of wages and benefits. Behind his demands for a gold-plated Cadillac out-fitted with a television set, refrigerated bar, and gold windshield wipers, and a house with staff in Beverly Hills, glimmered boyhood daydreams about what he would do if he ever got "n[egro] rich."

Stewart and Bell bought out Deutsche Grammophon with $2.5 million borrowed from the Union Planters National Bank of Memphis. Flush with cash, they were able to pay off this loan in seven months. They were doing so well that even spending twice as much to reacquire what they'd sold the year before hadn't obviated the need for tax shel-tering. They used an $800,000 loan from the same bank to set up a divi-sion of cattle ranching.[5]

Six months after becoming entirely theirs, Stewart and Bell's "little company that could" employed nearly two hundred people. So many were new that some who'd been around awhile complained of being treated like strangers. For most of them, Al Bell was more in evidence as an image on office walls, or in his signatory flourish at the bottom of memoranda from the "chief executive," than as an actual presence. He was often abroad, campaigning to get Stax's goods onto the floor space of mass-merchandisers like Sears and E. J. Korvette, opening an office in Los Angeles, backing a Broadway production, or launching gospel- and country-music subsidiaries.

While Bell was making himself worthy of the Department of Commerce's bestowal of a National Pacesetter Award, management consultants were streaming through Memphis at his behest, prescribing cures for Stax's organizational lassitudes. After these visits Bell would often hold "big meetings . . . pontificating like Jesse Jackson up and down the stage" and post quotations from *The Prophet* on bulletin boards.[6] Though Jim Stewart was willingly a captive of Al Bell's imagination, the hurly-burly it created wasn't his style, and he receded from Stax's day-to-day.

Stax had become freestanding when smart money in the record business was looking to conglomerate. For the midsize ambitious to get bigger, going it alone wasn't practical. In its best year Stax had less than a twentieth of the income of CBS or Warner. The revenue from four-fifths of the top-selling records passed through the counting houses of six multinational corporations. As raw materials—the performing talent—got pricier, the infrastructure that had made it possible for twenty-five years to distribute goods independently of major companies was crumbling.

Navigating an uncharted course at a reckless pace on unsteady terrain would require close attention to the path underfoot, but Bell seemed indifferent to the workings of his business at ground level. So it was left to Johnny Baylor from afar to alert Bell to the corruptions under his nose: men who ran the sales department at Stax were running a side business in under-the-table sales.

It was hard for someone in Bell's position to find help who could keep outsiders from stealing his money and weren't also practicing thieves. Around this time Berry Gordy promoted Michael Roshkind to chief operating officer while he was under indictment for neglecting to pay taxes for kickbacks he'd taken from the purchaser of rights to repackage a consignment of old Motown hits.[7] Roshkind was rehired as soon as as he got out of jail. For Gordy, knowing about and tolerating the petty self-dealings of key employees made them easier to control. As long as his money stayed correct, he was prepared to overlook the underhandedness of Barney Ales.

Gordy had the hustler's expectation that men who handled and sold his product would "juggle" with it when they could, to make a little for themselves of what they made so abundantly for him. But Al Bell was caught unaware, like a preacher whose secretary had been stealing from the building fund. A preacher's son, Bell looked after Stax's money as if it weren't his own.

By early in 1972 the music business tasted sour to Jim Stewart, and he told Al Bell to find a way to cash him out of it. RCA offered $16 million worth of its stock for 80 percent of the company and would have paid both partners handsomely to stay on.[8] But the once-burned Stewart was shy of another stock deal. He had reached the limit of his capacity to suspend a country boy's ingrained belief in the sovereignty of cash. This requirement of Stewart's consigned Bell to spending most of that year hunting a buyer at suitable terms.

Even thus preoccupied, Bell continued to practice visionary leadership at his usual manic clip: pursuing trade agreements with store chains; becoming a regular name in boldfaced type on the pages of *Jet* magazine; overseeing the development of a feature film project; or—having seen the future at a demonstration of new video technology in Spain—producing two Staple Singers promotional videos to be shown in movie theaters. He would make *Ebony*'s list that year of America's "100 Most Influential Blacks."

He had as well a thriving business to attend to, whose lifeblood flowed through one-stops, radio stations, and mom-and-pop record stores in cities and towns across Aframerica. Midway through 1972 Bell contracted out Stax's promotion and sales functions to Johnny Baylor, who six months earlier had walked into the company's offices, dismissed the secretaries, cornered Isaac Hayes with a drawn pearl-handled pistol, and threatened to shoot him.[9]

Bell later said he hadn't thought it appropriate to make any key hires while Stax was about to be sold and so had turned to Baylor, a proven hand and trusted "friend of the family," to plug the hole in his operation. Baylor brought along a handpicked team of "field representatives": his sidekick, Dino Woodard; a childhood friend from Birmingham with a felonious past; Jamo Thomas, the maker of two records of modest reknown turned proprietor of a one-horse label and freelance hustler-for-hire, who signed on in talking his way out of the retaliatory beating Baylor's crew had been commissioned to inflict on behalf of a roughed-up disk jockey in Washington, D.C.; and Hy Weiss, a grizzled remnant of the postwar class of Jewish owners of small urban record plantations.[10]

Weiss grew up in the Bronx alongside Morris Levy. "Given where we came from," he once reflected, "we were capable of a lot of things." He had dangled a man from a window in settling a dispute, punished bootleggers with baseball bats, and substituted Cadillacs for royalties owed to the luckiest of "these bums off the street" who should have paid him for their chances to make a record. Weiss branched out from his brother's wholesale record business in the mid-1950s. In serving himself and others he became known as the "payola king of New York."[11]

For a couple of years Weiss flew into Memphis three or four days a week to take command of Stax's sales desk, while the rest of Baylor's crew "would go into a marketplace and hit everything that needed to be hit . . . like the Green Berets." As payment for Weiss's services, all the business of manufacturing Stax's goods was steered to a company that shaved him off a sliver of what it made on every record and tape. The others would be taken care of out of Baylor's end, which Bell had promised him as soon as Stax was sold.

To tide Baylor over, Bell favored him with all the sales revenue and half the publishing income from the records on his Koko label, distributed by Stax. In the ensuing instance of Luther Ingram's million-selling "(If Loving You Is Wrong) I Don't Want to Be Right," Stax flexed its well-conditioned marketing arm to line Baylor's pockets. Bell rented an apartment for Baylor on Manhattan's Upper East Side and paid his sister-in-law more than $100,000 to line the back wall of its remodeled dining area with mirrors and adorn its living spaces with African art and craftwork, gazelle-skin throw rugs, and pillows covered in the hides of leopards, giraffes, and zebras.[12]

Bell had invoked "the sky [as] limit" on the cost of furnishing Baylor's lair, for whom a hotel suite was also rented as a Memphis pied-à-terre. Bell remains unapologetic about any of his arrangements with Baylor, if regretful for having been too little mindful of their improper appearance. Bell still thinks him worth every penny, even if Baylor occasionally shot bullets into ceilings to relieve tension. His posse rode hard on distributors, radio stations, and retailers; by hook and crook, Stax got paid, its records were played, and merchandise moved smoothly in and out of stores.

Bell the "race man" was capable in those days of mystifying Johnny Baylor into a "field marshal" in Stax's campaign of economic self-assertion. As a country boy prone to high-mindedness, Bell was a sucker for urban outlaw mystique. As an embattled crusader, he appreciated the sheer instrumentality of a competent thug. Larry Shaw believes Baylor was at heart a "race man," too, tender for the cause, "who loved Al and loved the effort." Neither Bell nor Shaw had known the associate whom Baylor once told that, prepared as he was to kill in her defense, "for the right amount of money he would kill [her] too."[13]

Early in the fall of 1972 Bell struck a deal with Clive Davis, then president of Columbia Records and the biggest man in the record industry. The empire of sound and air declined an outright purchase of Stax at Bell's asking price of $15 million. Instead, CBS agreed to lend Bell $6 million to buy Stewart out, in return for ten years' exclusive license to supply the marketplace with Stax's best-selling product lines.

Stewart exited with a theoretical $7.6 million: a third in cash, another half forthcoming in monthly installments over five years, and the last fifth or so due on the first business day of 1978. To avoid spooking the arbiters of commercial respectability in Memphis and beyond, all parties to this deal, including Stax's bankers, agreed to conceal Stewart's departure. Stewart consented to maintain the appearance of being Bell's partner for five more years.[14]

For Al Bell, to have ended up in business with CBS as Stax's sole proprietor after Stewart stepped aside was certification of destiny's blessing. A master of cash-bearing property turned his over to its croppers, whom Bell was commissioned to lead. A prince of the imperial realm had engaged him not as a subject but as a trading partner. By means of this bold, statesmanly stroke, Bell seemed to have made Stax's place in the widening world of culture commerce.

Like heads of state, once Davis and Bell had agreed on the basic terms, the ministers and bureaucrats were left to work out the business protocols. And while he had only Johnny Baylor's reserves to throw against the giant's heft, Bell still expected to have his way with CBS as the cat does with a human whose lap it uses for convenience in bounding from floor to tabletop. A trade alliance with this "larger than life white company" meant that Bell had been spared the figuring out of how to get his wares displayed where white customers were sure to see them.

To Davis, the same transaction seemed minor enough to have announced offhandedly at a regular meeting of staff to whom even its possibility had never been suggested. He'd lately struck a couple of other deals in the same vein: Columbia was paying the Isley Brothers and Gamble and Huff $5,000 for every single and $25,000 an album to produce records for CBS to manufacture and distribute.[15]

Davis's legend was made and augmented by such demonstrations of prophetic trend- and talent-spotting; in 1972 four of Columbia's nine biggest-selling single records were "custom"-labeled in Philadelphia by Kenny Gamble and Leon Huff. Ten years later a third of the nearly four hundred acts Columbia Records would have under contract were black.[16]

In 1972 "The Stax Organization" was the cornerstone of Memphis's third-largest industry; the music business accounted for $185 million of the local commerce. The city had become the world's fourth-busiest hub of record production. Colonizing underdeveloped territories rich in exploitable resources was an age-old imperial response to times of flat revenues and rising expenses.

Though only about 10 percent of all records sold were made by and for Aframericans, "soul music" was now a third of what was played on Top Forty radio. This was predictive of a darkening pop music universe. After bringing Stax into its orbit, CBS controlled 15 percent of the boogaloo trade. In less than two years Clive Davis bought three-quarters as much of it as Berry Gordy had spent more than a decade acquiring from scratch.

For his part, Al Bell now owned and operated a company without any means, besides income from record sales, to repay $8 million of

debt, expand promiscuously, and finance films. Bell banked on Columbia's clout to double such revenue within five years, and as well on having use of generous portions of the slush funds CBS allocated to purchase influence with radio stations, wholesalers, and store owners. He
thought Davis, in agreeing that Stax's goods would be distributed
through rather than by CBS, had promised as much. Bell expected that
Stax would retain autonomy in promotion, marketing, and sales.

Since Stax lived by cash-cropping, its sales managers' job was to
influence Columbia to lean on rack jobbers to take heavy consignments
of goods. Johnny Baylor telephoned Larry Tyrell, a vice-president of
marketing, to persuade him of the certainty of his need for a helicopter
to get safely back and forth to work if CBS didn't meet Stax's expectations.[17]

Tyrell brushed off Baylor's threat. A business agent whose principal
had about $484 million in yearly income to expend in defraying costs,
meeting obligations, protecting interests, and achieving goals would feel
a licensed immunity from fear of snatch-and-grab thuggery. Baylor's
gorilla-suited street dramatics couldn't make the hands of men who
were paid to tend Columbia's profits quaky enough to release their grip
on the throat of Al Bell's cash flow.

Within weeks of closing his deal with CBS, Bell made good his
word by authorizing payment of a first installment of what he figured
Johnny Baylor was owed: a million dollars in "promotion fees" and $1.6
million in royalties from sales of records on the Koko label, accrued at
a rate twice as high as Isaac Hayes's. On the last day of November 1972
airport security in Memphis fingered Baylor as the suspect bearer of a
satchel containing $130,000 in cash. Upon disembarking in Birming-
ham, he was detained by FBI agents, who also found him in possession
of a half-million-dollar check drawn on a Stax corporate account at the
Union Planters National Bank.[18]

This incident immediately triggered a federal investigation spear-
headed by the IRS, which impounded Baylor's holdings and started
poring over Stax's books. Not even a grand jury's mulling of tax-fraud
charges deterred Bell from disbursing another $1.85 million to Baylor
over the next nine months.

However offensive to probity his disdain for written contracts and bookkeepers' orthodoxies appeared to be, Bell was serene in his self-assurance of rectitude. Because he felt them legitimately due, Bell sent five more payments to Baylor, even as the government hovered, waiting to sieze each one in turn. Perhaps in the blush of such approving notice as would warm the subject of a feature article in the *Hollywood Reporter*, Bell was oblivious to the foreboding chill of the tax man's attentions.[19]

Bell was consumed by preparations for his coming-out party: the release of *Wattstax*, a concert film and record album featuring Stax's whole roster of acts in live performance at the Watts Summer Festival attended by a hundred thousand people in the Los Angeles Coliseum. It was conceived as a self-advertisement of global scale.

Larry Shaw marshaled a full-bore assault on the "young white market of middle America." He sowed advertising dollars across America's Top Forty and FM stations, big-city newspapers, and college campuses. He postered buses and billboard space throughout the country's metropolitan regions.

To influence the 80 percent of Aframericans who lived in twenty cities, Shaw flew a couple hundred of black radio's elite word-of-mouth spreaders into New York, Atlanta, and Los Angeles for advance screenings. Other screenings were held for representative welfare mothers, community outreach workers, and Model Cities–funded program participants, who were broadcasters of news and opinion on the grapevine networks.

Wattstax got a lavishly self-promoted Hollywood send-off and was shown to acclaim during the opening week of the Cannes Film Festival. It went on to sell a million dollars worth of tickets in the movie houses of Europe. Bell managed to stage his celebratory pageant of Southern American Negritude in half the world. Clamor for *Wattstax* in Nigeria caused ticket prices in Lagos to rise.

Those days the outlook from Memphis was expansive. Stax was now a licensed brand in seventeen African countries and well established in the strategic diasporan outpost of Jamaica, from which Bell planned to build a bridge to Brazil. Bell now professed himself a Pan-Africanist, though he objected to public characterizations of Stax as a "black" enterprise.

Larry Shaw, the consummately professional servant to Bell's righteous cause, recalls the company's *Wattstax* venture as "profitable."[20] But Bell had ceded the first $400,000 that the movie took in to his partner in producing it, David Wolper Pictures, as well as half of any American profits to the summer festival's organizers. What was left of these twice-trimmed revenues subsidized Bell's flourishes of impressive spending. He chartered a Learjet to drop off to far-flung disk jockeys advance copies of the two-year-old studio-made Staple Singers single he'd slipped into the first volume of ostensibly live concert cullings about to be released as the *Wattstax* album.

Even as his wildest dreams were raging, an article of Bell's true faith abided with him through the storms: "the bread and butter of all Stax records was black radio."[21] The Staple Singers record he'd airlifted around was two months on the soul charts, peaking at Number 4. But for all Larry Shaw's woo-pitching at the general market and CBS's presumed sway, the *Wattstax* album sold no better than respectably: 225,000 copies, about half the volume of Isaac Hayes's two most recent.

No doubt Bell had persuaded Clive Davis that there was plenty more where Hayes came from. In its capacity as distributor, CBS ordered too much of Stax's product and paid promptly for it besides. Awash in Columbia's cash, Bell was able to retire Stax's $1.7 million bank loan by early 1973 and within two more months to repay another of $888,725 that had been taken less than a year before.[22]

These loans were replaced by a $3 million line of credit at the Union Planters National Bank, routed through East Memphis Music, since Stax was already mortgaged to CBS. As soon as Bell's fresh credit was approved, he dispatched a million dollars to Johnny Baylor.[23]

On the first working day of 1973 the trade papers received notice that "The Stax Organization is moving heavily into the television musical variety field." A couple weeks earlier the first of six planned hour-long segments of *Isaac Hayes and The Stax Organization Present the Sound of Memphis* was taped before an audience of two thousand at Caesar's Palace in Las Vegas. This event stimulated discussions between Larry Shaw and Merv Griffin Productions, the show's coproducer, about a prospective movie project.

Aside from *Wattstax*, Stax's stabs at the movie business all landed low. Such misbegotten orphans of commerce as *The Klansman*, *Darktown*

Strutter's Ball, and *Truck Turner*—which featured Isaac Hayes in the title role—were among the shoddiest of goods being foisted on the ghetto market.

As hard as movies and television were for black upstarts to crack, Shaw and Bell had in common the relentless optimism of men governed by their sense of mission. "We knew the film world was against us," Shaw recalled, "and we were just going . . . to push [it] on through."[24] He believed Stax had the wherewithal to back its bold play: "and we had more money than most of the other pushers." Shaw clearly had faith in the appearances that likewise lured John Burton to Stax.

A lawyer, Burton had been for many years consigliere to the Chess brothers of Chicago. He was as canny in the street-level politics of the record business as Shaw was practiced in marketers' wiles. He was recruited to ride shotgun on Bell's wagonload of designs for glory. Burton thought the cargo's promise would make the ride worth taking when he signed on as chief operating officer of a company that was growing so fast its payroll had gotten bigger by a third in the previous year.

Bell thought Burton "one of the finest entertainment minds [he'd] ever encountered in the business. . . . Every word that came out of his mouth was wisdom and jewels." Apparently none were meant to discourage Bell from proceeding not by sight but by his faith in the espousals of Memphis bankers who steered their own business by the maxim "Pursue growth at all costs, and profits ultimately will follow."

Burton soon found himself plowing back the harvest of Bell's enterprise into the salaries of $600,000 worth of fresh hires. Within the year Stax's annual payroll had swollen to $2.26 million. "It was a status thing for a black guy to be at Stax with a silk suit and a briefcase [with] nothing in it," a fallen-away white charter Memphis Horn once groused. "There were street hustlers over there with a desk and a secretary."[25]

In the spring of 1973 Clive Davis was abruptly deposed at CBS, toppled in a chain reaction from a payola scandal. Federal prosecutors in Newark, who were career-climbing in hot pursuit of juicy cases to bring against organized criminality in the record business, found handiest as first pickings the habits of mutual support that CBS-sponsored Gamble and Huff had fallen into with black radio's people-to-see.

The stain of these public misdemeanors had spread into Davis's office, where its taint proved sufficient to afford his enemies at court the means to accomplish his undoing. After Davis fell, the old guard was reinstated at CBS. To its sterner eye, the terms of the commercial relationship that Davis had established with Stax seemed unduly sentimental.

His successors didn't see how Stax had escaped the yoke of a standard production and distribution contract that would have yielded Columbia a dollar more of every album sold. They pressured Bell to recast the deal he'd struck with Davis to conform better to their preferred specifications. But he persisted in the idea of relationship he thought Davis had consented to share, wherein Stax was a stand-alone company paying CBS a tariff of 15 percent of the wholesale price of every record sold in exchange for passenger space on the imperial juggernaut. Bell was unwilling to let Stax become Goddard Lieberson's colony as once it had been Jerry Wexler's plantation.

Nor would Bell yield to the temptation of a fat-salaried vice-presidency with emoluments on the side that CBS put up as bounty for delivering Stax into its fold. "They would have paid the artists," he has claimed and others confirmed, "paid the producer, and given me an override." To the excitable mind of Al Bell, declining to become Columbia's lawn jockey meant forswearing appointment as "the biggest n[egro] in America."[26] But by any reckoning Bell was bold to be rebuffing men who were not just his creditors but also regulators of the only means of repayment he had.

From the beginning most of Stax's people never believed CBS meant them well. They were soon frustrated by its indifference to placing enough of Stax's goods where demand for them was highest. Stax's customer base previously had been beneath the attention of product-handlers at CBS, who couldn't see why they were now being asked to trouble themselves over whether too few copies of Little Milton's latest forty-five were available in the neighborhood record shops of Shreveport, Louisiana. Columbia's capacity to manufacture goods and have them on retailers' shelves a week later was geared to keeping minimal amounts of stock idling in warehouses. Its bureaucrats scoffed at Stax's ignorance of modern methods of inventory control.

The record game familiar to Memphis was played by hustlers' rules, wherein an advantage was gained by inducing wholesalers to accept overloaded consignments of goods. Since independent distributors were as cash-dependent as small record companies, tying up their money in Stax's inventory assured it of getting a harder sell.

At first Columbia indulged Stax by putting more of its product into the marketplace than wholesale traffic would truly bear. The empire of sound and air could afford to allow retailers to return all the goods they couldn't sell without penalty or even reproach; moreover, it could stand to outlay money to Stax and then wait months to settle its accounts. CBS's cash proved highly addictive; in the throes of Al Bell's manic bingeing, Stax was like a dope fiend running up a tab between paydays.

Before too long, CBS was returning between 50 and 80 percent of the records Stax shipped. Bell's employees complained of being toyed with, lured into pressing too many records by telephone orders from Columbia that turned out to be much smaller as invoices. At the same time shopkeepers from all over were howling about their inability to get Stax product through CBS branches. The money CBS had advanced Stax for merchandise that came back unsold was deducted from its payments for subsequent consignments. The effect on Stax's cash supply was slow strangulation.[27]

In little time its arrangement with CBS came between Stax and its steadiest customers. Stax still made its daily bread in many small pockets of black-belt America; CBS was too grand to think that the sale of another ten thousand Soul Children singles in greater Atlanta was worth the required kneading. The company had no winners that summer at the Soul and Blues Awards, an occasion lately invented by the radio and record world's leading ghetto citizens to celebrate themselves. The year before Stax had been "Record Company of the Year," and its acts had won in a third of the categories.

"I can't say CBS is totally blameless," Jim Stewart later reflected. "If we'd had blockbuster records, then we would have been sitting in the driver's seat. . . . Nineteen seventy-two was the last year we had [quality] product . . . all our creative people were gone."[28] In 1973 Stax was supplanted at the top of its class by other Memphians in the workshop of Willie Mitchell, whose sparer designs were the architecture of Al Green's stardom. The house band at Hi Records was the equal of any ever recorded in Memphis. At its bottom was the drummer Al Jackson, a metronomic timekeeper who'd been a cornerstone in Stax's foundation.

While a money-broker in Memphis was foraging for a fresh $12 million to buy Bell's freedom from CBS with enough left over to fund his expansion plans, Stax executives were subpoenaed by a federal grand jury in Newark. Prosecutors there were following the trail of 400,000 kicked-back dollars taken by the schemers Johnny Baylor had exposed in the sales department two years before.

Within several months another grand jury convened in Memphis to weigh apparent improprieties in Bell's dealings with a branch manager at Union Planters National Bank. Ed Pollack—the Stax comptroller who had been too self-professedly upright to tolerate Motown's loose practices—was immunized from federal prosecution so that he might detail for IRS investigators the undercover cash dispersals the company routinely made to disk jockeys and radio stations.[29]

While Bell was borrowing another half-million to buy an outgrown Memphis church building to renovate into new offices, Burton looked to acquire radio stations in St. Louis and Detroit. Three months after chronic shortages of cash had depleted Stax's $3 million credit reserve at Union Planters, Bell and Burton bought a half-interest in America's last black-owned wholesale record distributor. They were envisioning a national chain of two hundred retail stores.

In the fall of 1973, though he needed to borrow nearly $3 million more to stay afloat, Bell spoke confidently of crisis abating as soon as the $12 million deal with Polydor for European licensing rights was closed, or the *New York Times*'s down payment on an imminent purchase of the East Memphis song catalog came through, or CBS released some embargoed funds.

Al Bell's conviction of his own innocence of bad intention was a shield against consciousness of behavioral risk. Even the simmering heat from two federal investigations couldn't make him sweat. But broadly experienced men around him became infected with Bell's blindness of assurance. It was a time in Aframerica of widespread susceptibility to contagions of certitude.

Al Bell's bleak Christmas season of 1973 was brightened faintly by Isaac Hayes's first hit record in nearly a year. Hayes had been distracted and diminished by movie hackwork; his latest two soundtrack albums sold tepidly. But Bell had no choice about negotiating a new three-and-a-half-year contract with Hayes that contained thirty-five pages of terms befitting someone irreplaceable.

In February 1974 Stax executives had their salaries halved. A month later Hayes was given $1.9 million as a signing bonus. His contract provided him with sinecures worth $300,000 a year, company-subsized recording costs, insurances, a Cadillac with gold appointments, a house with staff in Beverly Hills, and very generous royalty rates pegged to retail rather than wholesale prices.[30]

In effect, Hayes would get about half the gross profit from every record of his that was sold. But at that point even a minority interest in Isaac Hayes was more than Bell could afford to lose. Who could have known that Hayes wouldn't have another hit record for fourteen years?

Nine days after Hayes was sent the first of his signing bonus's six monthly installments of $270,000, Stax couldn't make its loan payments to the Union Planters National Bank. Its $3 million credit line was overdrawn by half. A fat portfolio of bad real estate loans and a million dollars of recent bond-trading losses had brought the bank near the brink of ruin. Federal regulators were poised to certify that Union Planters was "out of control";[31] the comptroller's office was threatening to shutter it.

The bank's hired salvage team cast stony eyes at Stax's mounting debt. Once they learned that CBS had frozen $1.3 million of Stax's revenue stream, Bell's bankers threatened to call in his loans. Jim Stewart put up his house and the $4.3 million he was still owed for his half of the company as stopgap collateral. "I reacted with my heart instead of my head," Stewart would later lament. He compounded this offense to prudence by replenishing Stax's capital with $400,000 of his own cash.

Stax had fallen so far behind in its reimbursements to CBS for returned merchandise that 40 percent of what it was owed for each new shipment of goods was being garnisheed. Squeezed for money, Stax started leaking records into the marketplace through other outlets. Once CBS became aware of outlaw "inventory on the street," it refused, on grounds of uncertain provenance, to accept retailers' returns of any Stax merchandise.

Within a year of Clive Davis's ouster, CBS pronounced Stax "over-advanced beyond [the] sales potential of recent releases" and alto-gether ceased payments. It occurred to John Burton then to tell Al Bell that "people are trying to put you out of business and you just don't see it." Bell was taken aback: "I'm from Arkansas and Tennessee. I hadn't been in that big business world. . . . I didn't know how you took over corporations."[32]

Slapped into consciousness of the dire immediacy of his peril, Bell was frantic to belatedly counterpunch. Claiming to have been violated by antitrust abusers, Stax sued for disengagement from CBS. In need of whatever shelter nearby white boys of good standing might be able to afford him against the combined assaults of government and corpora-tion, Bell and John Burton campaigned for the favorable opinion of established Memphis.

With inflow of cash at a bare trickle, they flirted in public with buy-ing the down-at-heel Memphis franchise of the American Basketball Association. They hoped thereby to create an impression of Stax as a corporate citizen prosperous enough to afford such an indulgence and public-spirited enough to want to preserve an endangered civic amenity.

Of course, Stax was too broke to acquire even the cheapest item at a bankrupt sports league's going-out-of-business sale. And it was already too far past the pale of respectable society in Memphis to improve its reputation even by an association with Johnny Neuman, the city's first and only homegrown white basketball star. Once Stax's dis-pute with CBS became grist for the mills of Shelby County justice, Bell was exposed as its true proprietor. This made moot for official Memphis any question regarding Stax but that of the local IRS agent, who asked Bell "how . . . a nigra boy like [him]" got ahold of "this kind of money."[33]

But Al Bell yet believed that history's tides could turn on an individual's tour de force. During the summer of 1974 he enlisted Larry Shaw's help on a speech entitled "Who Will Own America?" for expected broadcast on Memphis television. With Stax's fate hanging on its beleaguered captain's capacity for last-ditch heroism, Bell prepared as if for his moment at the Lincoln Memorial.[34]

A long discipleship had versed Bell in King's rhetorical style and had inspired awe at its effects. Though Bell's rallying cry began on a preacherly grace note—a Job-like embrace of his unearned persecution as a "mystical blessing" in disguise—it was mainly pitched in the strident keys of complaint, defiance, and righteous indignation that had been adopted by the chorus of black public voices raised since King's fell silent. If Bell thought to sway white Memphis with argument, he was sure of an appearance before a hostile court.

By hosting the era's most notorious race crime, the city had forfeited its citizenship in the New South. The temper of civic life on King's killing ground was made surlier by the repressive impulses of its jittery public servants: in 1969 police cracked down fiercely on native black militants; between 1970 and 1975 an average of seven black citizens a year were shot and killed by police; in 1971 the city council closed public swimming pools rather than comply with a court order to integrate them.[35] At middecade some judges in Memphis still refused to marry mixed-race couples, and white resistance to school desegregation was turning brutish.

Though plans for its telecast fell through, the text of Bell's ungiven speech was issued to Stax employees as an in-house manifesto. Thus a record survives of Bell's indignance at local supermarkets' refusals to cash any more of the company's payroll checks. After all, he suggested, Stax was "one of the largest customers of South Central Bell," a "direct" spender of "over $750,000 per year with the telephone company." In the course of his argument the very client Bell had represented to the court of opinion as a quarter-billion-dollar rippler of economic effects in Memphis was reduced to establishing its bona fides in the way of applicants for public assistance who have to show a utility bill as proof of address.[36]

In indicting official Memphis for nonsupport, Bell pointedly excluded his bankers at Union Planters. Bell still believed he had an ally in the bank's new president, who spoke appreciatively of the music business's value to the local economy and of wanting to be its financier. At first Union Planters tried to stay the foreclosing hand at Stax's throat.

The bank proposed to CBS a partnership of lien-holders that would converge their respective interests in the record and publishing companies. With Stax already in its clutches, CBS declined an invitation to lend Bell another $3 million, of which the bank would have extracted enough to pare his debt down to an allowable size and thereby placate the federal regulators nosing over its books. But in cold fact Stax had already seen its last of Columbia's money.

CBS's rebuff encouraged the bank to consider Stax a $10 million deadbeat without any plausible means to repay. To the Union Planters president, Bell's circumstances made him subject to sharecropper's rules. In a conversation that he says ended with Bill Matthews snarling at him, "N[egro], I didn't ask you to do it, I told you to do it,"[37] Bell claimed to have been importuned to launder money into the bank through the accounts of a nonprofit music foundation. After Bell refused, Matthews joined the circle of wolves panting to take Stax down.

From then on the bank's only concern would be for its place in the pecking order of carcass-strippers. Matthews imported specialists in laying bare the choicest parts of crippled enterprises to the scavenging tooth and claw of holders of bad corporate debt. In the late summer of 1974, after a month of on-site inspection, the team from Crisis Management Incorporated concluded that Stax was, for all practical purposes, "bankrupt."

Stalked by the Office of the Comptroller to the brink of certified insolvency, Union Planters' survival depended on recouping assets from defaulted borrowers like Stax. The bank's failure would expose to ruinous personal liabilities a board of directors comprised of the city's most solid citizens. Official Memphis resolved that Union Planters had to be saved.

The handiest recourse was the bank's bonding company, from which losses to theft, defalcation, or fraud were recoverable. Over the next year Union Planters provided the evidence federal prosecutors used to bring fourteen criminal charges against Al Bell and one of its former branch managers.

In the summer of 1974 Stax was touted in *Black Enterprise* magazine as America's fifth-largest black business, but was unable to pay Richard Pryor $200,000 of royalties owed on his Grammy Award–winning comedy album and thus forfeited the property rights to a gold record. Even quarterly payments to such earners of small royalties as Little Milton were suspended. The company bounced the second of the $270,000 checks that Isaac Hayes had coming and was sued for breach of contract and $5.3 million in damages.[38]

Union Planters strong-armed Bell into releasing Hayes to quickly sign a $7.5 million deal with another record company. The bankers expected to take from Hayes more than five million of these dollars in exchange for retiring his debts and assigning him their claim on the assets Stax had pledged as loan collateral. Hayes's habitual indulgence in easy credit kept him working for the bank. And when squeezed into bankruptcy three years later, he lost to Union Planters all the royalties he ever would have gotten from any material he wrote, produced, or performed at Stax.

As desertions of Stax's veteran campaigners mounted, the stakes of its embattled survival increasingly seemed to Al Bell as consequential as any imagined by combatants of religious wars. But there were no voluntary diehards among the ranks of careerists for whom Stax had made careers to manage. He received a "Dear Al" mailgram from Pops Staples, by then a minor pop star, advising that "under present circumstances we have determined that Stax Records, Inc. is unable to serve the Staple Singers as agreed to."[39]

Long years of scrappy breadwinning on the gospel highway had taught this famous abjurer of the "downward road" that it was paved with promoters whose good intentions included paying him from the proceeds of walk-up ticket sales. Staples promised "more details to follow in a letter by counsel" but thought to "ma[k]e this request personally to avoid litigation."

Bell had no recourse beyond the bitter expression of hurt feelings; his fired-off response to Staples ended "(I SEE YOU)," an accusing finger pointed at the revealed canker on a betrayer's accidently bared soul.[40] Within six months of losing Pryor and Hayes, Stax defaulted on the contracts of its other marquee acts. By the following summer all were lodged with major labels, three of them at CBS.

After a half-year siege, early in 1975 Bell sued for peace. Columbia agreed to vacate its distribution rights, provided that the $6-million-plus-interest that Stax owed was repaid within eighteen months. After their parting more than $4 million worth of Stax inventory stayed in CBS's hands. The room to wiggle that Bell had bought was only space enough to squirm.

Now beyond any likelihood of financial redemption by agency of a business partner, Bell searched far and wide for a benefactor's saving grace. Improbably, John Burton seemed to snare one in King Faisal of Saudi Arabia, who was reportedly poised to make many millions available. But even as Burton laid over in Beirut en route to Riyadh to close the deal, Faisal was undone in a nephew's palace coup.

This hope of rescue evaporated into the mists of other notional cash-raising schemes: dumping product in South Africa and Australia; selling directly to retail record stores at wholesale prices; telemarketing "best of" album packages; raising $25 million through the private sale of corporate junk bonds; Stewart's fanciful proposal of a $50-million loan collaterized by $41 million in Treasury bonds that the lender would purchase and hold for ten years, while their value appreciated enough to pay off Stax's debt.[41]

Flat broke but unbroken at the bottom of his $16 million hole, Bell scrambled to regroup with leftover talent of a class that CBS had previously derided as "cotton patch artists."[42] The Stax organization's dwindling corps was down to fewer than a hundred employees. From his bunker Bell issued an exhortatory screed. Aimed at stoking causist fervor in the faithful remnant, its three pages of rant in turn braced the dispirited, chastised uncheerful givers, and indicted backbiters for nameless treacheries: "I tried to make it . . . plain that these days would come. . . . Not one time did I promise . . . a Cadillac in every garage. . . . I explained that 'the battle is over but the war has just begun.'"

"WE SHALL AND WILL WIN—ONLY THE STRONG SURVIVES . . . You can make the overall job easier by giving more . . . and doing what weak, lazy, careless and selfish people call the impossible . . . we will WIN THE WAR . . . There has to be UNQUESTIONED LOYALTY . . . however, ONE BAD APPLE CAN SPOIL the whole barrel . . . the will to live brings out the BEST and WORST in a person. Check yourself out—your REAL character may be beginning to show. . . . STAX WILL PREVAIL . . . WILL YOU??" Bell added the postscript, "Recommended reading for understanding: PSALMS 23."[43]

On a vessel in such straits that its captain commended this prayer to his crew, even Shirley Brown's Number 1 record meant no more than a "drop" in Jim Stewart's bailing bucket. Though he'd known Stax was sinking, Stewart clambered back aboard. However appalled he long had been by Bell's tolerance for "overhead, waste, excess baggage," the seduced accountant abandoned his last good money to love gone bad. "I could not be objective," Stewart said, "because I was fighting for my life, my baby's life, even though it wasn't mine anymore."[44]

While Stax made payroll spottily in the latter half of 1975, it kept making records. In the two weeks before its offices were padlocked in mid-December, 144,000 pieces were manufactured and shipped. The loyalists who achieved this feat of dogged resistance to the hopelessness of their cause ended as bygone others had begun: as an artisanal cadre making records with old-fashioned equipment in a converted movie theater. But a year's effects of their guerrilla ingenuity amounted to but $1.3 million in revenues, only $300,000 of which had eked in over the last six of the company's months.

One diehard later suggested that the spirit of Otis Redding hovered over East McClemore Avenue in Stax's twilight, when such sacrifices as cars and houses were common among those who had devoted fourteen weeks of unpaid service. Money from Al Bell's father subsidized his son's month in Switzerland with Stewart, Burton, and a "personal secretary to Anwar Sadat," who was pressing his "international connections . . . to raise moneys for us at that time."[45]

The rest of Reverend Bell's life savings prolonged by several weeks Stax's hand-to-mouth existence. Four years past one in which $17 million worth of its records and tapes had been sold, Stax folded with $305 left in the bank.[46]

To the last, Stax produced goods of genuine quality. Strains of the company's valediction, "It's Worth a Whippin'," sung by Shirley Brown—neck and neck with Mavis Staples as the best female voice Stax ever recorded—were faintly heard in Atlanta, Baltimore, and Chicago at the time of its demise. Five weeks after Stax was closed, Johnnie Taylor's latest Columbia release appeared on the record charts. Produced by Don Davis in the very style and manner that he'd employed as a Stax vice-president, "Disco Lady" sold more than three million copies in becoming America's most popular song.

Once the Union Planters Bank held the whip handle, Al Bell fell under an overseer's lash. "It was [more] prudent . . . and profitable to prosecute him," Jim Stewart observed, "than to let [Stax] try to work its way out."[47] The bank's plan of escape from ruin depended on its being a proven victim of fraud. The $10 million bond claim, which already counted as an asset on its financial statements, was crucial to the bank's appearance of solvency. No doubt Union Planters colluded with the Justice Department in Bell's prosecution. The language of its insurance filing mirrored the government's bill of particulars against Bell and his codefendant, the former bank branch manager Joseph Harwell.

In the go-go years before Union Planters crashed, Harwell had been its conduit for pushing loaned money to Stax. He rose in the bank's hierarchy as Stax's value as a customer increased. But Harwell turned embezzler and eventually used an unwitting Bell to further a fraudulent loan scheme.

A thief with character, Harwell never implicated Bell in his crimes, refusing an early release from prison in exchange for testimony that he wouldn't stoop to give. Nevertheless, Bell's exoneration would require the high-toned advocacy of James Neal—the Tennessean who'd recently been Haldeman and Ehrlichman's special prosecutor—and nine hours of jury deliberation.

Nearly a year before Bell's acquittal, Ralph Abernathy and fifty others had protested his arraignment on the steps of a Memphis court-house. King's successor said he'd come "to prevent another assassination of a famous black leader." Bell had fertilized many grassroots causes with Stax's money and was due some show of support.

Within a month of his indictment, he was honored in St. Louis at the National Conference on Minority Development as an "outstanding entrepreneur and humanitarian." A legal defense fund was set up for him by E. Rodney Jones at the Nation of Islam's bank in Chicago. Its self-proclaiming press release decried Al Bell's persecution for "borrowing from the rich and giving to the poor" and attributed the cause of Stax's impending death to "sophisticated corporate economic strangulation, the new legal lynching in the south."[48]

The fund-raising for Al Bell's defense fell $92,500 short of its announced goal of a hundred thousand dollars. Jesse Jackson called for an international effort to rally money and support, without evident effect. A Chicago firm was hired to run a "Save Stax" public relations campaign, which elicited an offer from a consortium of black business-men to underwrite the company's relocation to Gary, Indiana.

In Memphis, "even [among] the black community," Jim Stewart noted, ". . . everybody ran for cover that ever had an affiliation with Stax."[49] The local branch of Jackson's Operation PUSH tried to organize a boycott of Union Planters Bank. For some days a few picketers milled outside the bank's main office, handing out mimeographed broadsheets to passersby.

While Bell was awaiting his criminal trial, Union Planters pressed a civil court to declare Stax an involuntary bankrupt and affirm the bank's primacy among creditors-in-waiting. The matter was decided in the bank's favor by a judge who was also a stockholder. Bell stayed away from those proceedings, so as not to provide more fodder for the state's lurking cross-examiners.

This abstention left his reputation defenseless against the assaultive scorn of lawyers for a bank scurrying to dodge the severest of federal penalties after the previous year's loss of $16 million had exposed its buried chicaneries. In court, the kettle-caller on hire to these rogue bankers blackened Bell as the "inept, gullible, and corrupt" operator of "a dishelveled . . . defunct business."

After Al Bell's trials were over, Union Planters collected $4.5 million on its bond claim. Its share of Stax's liquidated remains came to another half-million. The bank sold the publishing company for $1.6 million, of which $200,000 was cash in hand, the rest made payable over five years. By then East Memphis Music had been resold for four times as much. This was about $3.5 million more than Union Planters was ever able to clear from the rubble created of Stax.[50]

The bank's posse rode Johnny Baylor down a couple of years later in federal court. At trial its lawyer characterized him as "a laundry service . . . a bag man for Al Bell . . . caught with bag in hand at the Birmingham airport." Baylor was adjudged to have been paid $2.5 million "with the actual intent to hinder, delay or defraud the creditors of Stax" and was required to remit to the bank's stooge—the court-appointed divider of the bankruptcy spoils—as much of it as he still possessed.[51]

Bell maintains this grab-back "was wrong." He has never equivocated about the deal that began his undoing or the man he made it with: "That was Johnny Baylor's money." Of this and all else its creditors recovered, Stax's payless staff and stiffed artists were apportioned $100,000 to divide with the IRS.[52]

After a quarter-decade of separate reflection in the ruins of their joint enterprise, Bell and Stewart shared a blessed assurance that Stax's way out of no-way could have been found, if only the bank hadn't contrived to make the company more valuable dead than alive. "We were operating and could have done well," Jim Stewart insisted. "I just don't understand."[53]

No matter that a court's official estimate of their indebtedness fell between $25 and $30 million, or that Stax's income from record sales was about $50,000 a month toward the end. Or that IRS investigators claimed evidence of 159 "overt acts" of tax fraud, insurance policies had been canceled, barter had become a regular means of doing business, employees were depending on the neighborhood's charity, and the company was surrendering master tapes to artists and producers in lieu of unpaid royalties. In Bell's view, the bank had interceded when he'd "finally gotten Stax to the point where I could go on and build it."

Even now, after many reconsiderations of a disaster too predictable not to have been foreseen and avoided, Bell's self-confidence remains untroubled. "I believed I could have prevailed in bankruptcy court," he mused, "but I had to make a decision between saving Stax and saving my life."[54] Then thirty-six, Al Bell had already lived long enough to see the righteous forsaken.

As 1977 was dawning, he forsook Memphis for Washington, D.C. Working out of a telephone booth and a friend's car, he started another record label there, the bravely named Independence Corporation of America. Bell, his wife, and two spider-bitten children were reduced to living for several years in the relative squalor of an unfinished basement.

Bell sued Union Planters for malicious prosecution. Its president had boasted of "getting all the n[egroes] out of Stax." At trial the bank's lawyer maligned Bell as a tax felon and associate of drug dealers. A Memphis jury found Union Planters faultless.

Bell kept his case in court for five more years, vainly seeking redress for damages to his purse and reputation. During this time he managed to put out more than thirty records on his shoestring label, aimed at the market of adult black southerners he'd by then rejoined: Bell was back in Little Rock, having abandoned D.C. as unaffordable.

Jim Stewart's signature had been as evident on Jim Harwell's fraudulent paperwork as Al Bell's, but he was untouched by prosecutors. Official Memphis adopted the theory that Stewart must have been bamboozled into signing over his property and reserved its malice for Stax's "head n[egro]."[55] If Stewart's ruiners thought him an eccentric who had been dangerously misguided in his associations, they were satisfied to let his ruin be an example to prove the rule that no good deed goes unpunished.

One of them later allowed that Stewart's problems had resulted from his being "more of an artist" than businessman. In fact, Stewart never bothered to put his name on records he produced or that other people wrote. Consequently, the old proprietor was left empty-handed, bereft even of future entitlements to income from royalties.

His sister Estelle made out better for having been pushed out of Stax while it was still moving at high speed. She converted into apartment buildings some of the cash that had bought her out too cheaply. She dabbled in the record business, starting another small label of her own, mostly to provide an occupation for a ne'er-do-well son. The bricks-and-mortar once containing the Satellite Record Shop that Mrs. Axton established to support her brother's record-making operation in the back, was given by Union Planters National Bank to the Southside Church of God in Christ.

The congregation had no lasting use for this famously unconsecrated corner of Pentecostalism's first official seat. They would see the old movie theater torn down rather than allow its preservation as a memorial to Stax. In 1988 the place that Otis Redding had stepped into out of Johnny Jenkins's band was a vacant lot.

12. The Further You Look the Less You See

There is a photograph of Berry Gordy taken in 1967 at the Roostertail, black Detroit's place to be seen in at night. He is visiting the work site of the Four Tops. He leans forward, fiercely concentrated, mouth ajar with chewing his tongue, as is his custom when excited or absorbed. Gordy's intentness appears menacing, as though his sharp critical faculties were bristling at the Tops' stolid, graceless movings about the stage.

He would have been seeing their act in its best light, since the voice of Levi Stubbs could command a nightclub as it couldn't the cavernous theaters, but the Tops never impressed any audience with their half-stepped routines. Respected cabaret jazz singers of the Hi-Los' sort before they got to Motown, they were already old for the teenage circuit they burst upon in 1964.

Gordy's mien suggests that of a trainer watching his fighter's sloppy workout. Across the table Diana Ross—with oversize, square-framed sunglasses parked atop her head—looks insolent and bored. Next to Gordy his sister Gwen strikes the perfect pose of spectator, eyeing the stage with a demure half-smile.

Having caught in the corner of her eye a photographer poised to snap, Miss Powell's star pupil is ready for her close-up. Esther sits beside Gwen and stares off in another direction, wishing she were someplace else. But at the end of the table the elderly man sitting upright in sporty business attire is transfixed by the view beyond his son's slumped head. Behind his glasses and trim white goatee Pops's expression is as rapt as a young child's at a puppet show.[1]

For as long as Berry Gordy's father lived in Georgia, Booker T. Washington was the "Wizard of Tuskegee," the most effective public black man in America, and an authentic international celebrity. Forty years before Gordy started to amass his fortune, his father stole away from Georgia with what seemed like a fortune to him. He was a practical man who understood that the white people he lived among were authorized to take whatever he had whenever they wanted it.

His son inherited the assumption that a theoretical limit existed on how high white people would allow him to rise, and that his hold on wherever he perched once he got there would be tenuous. But he reckoned the distance between ground and ceiling altogether differently. Berry Gordy Jr. dared to imagine he could have what the rich and powerful white boys had. That dream was no less audacious in its time for having found its most meaningful fulfillment in a standing invitation to Hugh Hefner's parties and a credit line in Las Vegas as big as Sinatra's.

Not disposed toward humility, Gordy made himself discretion's servant. He removed himself from broad public view in the mid-1960s, when he stopped giving press interviews. Once he began beating his industry's establishment at its own game, he comported himself, while in its sight lines, as delicately as if he were integrating the University of Alabama.

He gave his white trading partners white faces to deal with and receded into the shadow and safety of his company's meeting rooms and shop floors to apply his monomaniacal focus and incalcuable shrewdness to conquering by stealth. In this respect he was as much a Washingtonian as the real estate and insurance tycoons A. G. Gaston in Birmingham and Alonzo F. Herndon in Atlanta, who both made money under the noses of hostile and capricious white overlords and kept it out of their hands by working longer, being smarter, and knowing how to maneuver in the briar patch.

And so, even after his dream came true, on late Friday afternoons

Gordy still prowled the offices of what had become the most successful organization in the history of the music business, admonishing any within whose pace had slackened to keep working. "Haven't you heard?" he would growl. "Money's not on strike."[2]

Its 2 percent of the billion-dollar record business sufficed to make Motown Aframerica's biggest enterprise in 1968. In the larger scheme, however, it was but one of a hundred medium-fry sharers of 35 percent of a market dominated by five companies. This industrial elite's 55 percent of record-business revenues was secured by album sales, and hit singles were necessary to lure customers. But radio played only thirty at a time of the eleven thousand single records the industry put out in a year. Three-quarters of them, and two-fifths of albums, didn't even sell enough copies to recoup costs.[3]

In 1967 only twenty-three singles and fifty-seven albums broke through this marketing logjam with force enough to move a million "units." The profit margins of big companies—and the fortunes of those Gordy's size—swung in the balance of a relatively few records in any year that would generate such large-scale commerce.

Creating more of these to go around meant either spurring growth in a customer base that was steadily enlarging itself by 10 percent a year or selling the same customers more records and tapes. The latter strategy required exposing those customers to a more various inventory. In 1967 the commercial advent of FM radio in San Francisco cut a broad new channel in the advertising stream for music.

FM's relaxed format accommodated longer-running songs and thus favored album play. The big companies backed the supersession of FM radio, which made the marketplace more conducive to selling albums. At Motown albums were still packaged as three-hit singles encased in filler from the Jobete catalog. A holder of the two most recently made forty-fives by any Gordy contractee but the Temptations rarely had incentive to buy the album that would contain their next single release.

The Christmas 1968 edition of *Billboard*'s pop charts listed five Motown records among its Top Ten singles. Of that moment Gordy later wrote, "The not-quite-grown-up kid who had once depended on lucky rolls of the dice and who had watched and studied the numbers guys on the streets computing the odds in their heads, had 50 percent of all the ten top-selling records in the country. . . . And, we'd done it without HDH."[4]

In the blush of this triumph Gordy sent his staff a memo announcing—as if he were the CEO of some regular business routinely setting a target for the next quarter's earnings—that henceforth the company would release nothing it could not confidently predict would become a Top Ten record, and none would issue under color of its flagship, the Supremes, that wasn't a prospective Number 1. Of course, nothing like that would ever be possible in any business that depends upon anticipating the fashion cycles of the mercurial young, but then no other man who was ever in such a business was more entitled to so arrogant a presumption.

Anyone else who felt indicted for most of thirty years by the implications of his family's "if you're so smart why ain't you rich" brand of bootstrap Calvinism might have been as susceptible as Gordy was to the warping effect a rapid transformation from a factory hand into a $10-million-a-year tycoon had on his self-esteem. Later, "I earned $387 million in sixteen years" would become his one-size-fits-all rejoinder to almost any challenge. "That's your problem" was his customary reply to subordinates' complaints, as well as to most queries about the how of the doing of whatever he asked of them.

Gordy had weathered the defections of chief lieutenants and mutinous rumblings among his crew, and sailed on. The transition of Diana Ross to solo stardom was accomplished by turn of the decade. Fittingly, in her last appearance with the Supremes, she sang "Someday We'll Be Together" from a Las Vegas stage. Five years after Sam Cooke was finally about to get a permit to work there, Gordy had the keys to the city. Its hotel casinos had become his playgrounds. For amusement he gambled and golfed—"the leisure game we'd won the right to play," it seemed to Marvin Gaye, who along with Smokey was once his brother-in-law's regular companion in sport.[5]

Norman Whitfield, who sulked for years about being kept out of Gordy's favor by Smokey's cabal of insiders, emerged over the next sev-

eral as the most commercially successful black producer in the music
business. His rise through the late 1960s coincided with Robinson's
decline; popular music had turned against sweetness.

When he took over, Whitfield contemporized the company's output
with the quickly changing times by infusing it with some of their raw
spirit. As never before, boogaloo (black popular music) was permeable
to the influences of the music white kids made for themselves. Whitfield
flavored his productions with rock-and-roll techniques brought into the
black mainstream by Sly Stone, and served many in a coarsened style
that acknowledged the pop market's newly formed perception of Memphis as the authentic brand of soul music.

But even through the long, dispiriting endgame of Motown's
slow-motion abandonment of Detroit, in the late 1960s such other
writer/producers as Ashford and Simpson, Pam Sawyer, Johnny Bris-
tol, and Clarence Paul were fruitful enough to keep standards high
and business booming. In 1969, so flush with young creative talent that
he could stock it in two locations, Gordy put together a project team
in California to design a vehicle for the Jackson 5's entry that would
guarantee that his latest "discovery" made a splash in the marketplace.

He worked with three young writers to produce "I Want You
Back," one of Motown's best-ever records. Gordy registered the song
and production in the name of "the Corporation," as if to send a message that the company still made the stars.

Even in an expanding market music was a profit-lean business for
the grinders-out of corporate livings. At the end of the 1960s the big
record companies' deepening dependency on selling many millions of
a few items made more and more valuable the small number of artists
who could consistently produce such sought-after merchandise. The
price and prerogatives of talent were on the rise.

Nevertheless, both Stevie Wonder and Marvin Gaye, who would
carry Motown into the mid-1970s, had to hardball Gordy into giving
them the creative freedom—they exercised ingeniously enough in the
cause of his enrichment—to buy him into the bigger game of producing motion pictures. Gordy may have thought that if he had to start

paying singers as if they were movie stars, he might as well make movies.

Many who worked at Stax believe that its end began when Berry Gordy went into the movie business. "Al Bell was out to emulate . . . Gordy," said Don Davis, who'd made fine dining in Detroit of Gordy's leftovers. "We spent a lot of money . . . making movies that we weren't prepared to make."[6] Gordy spent most of 1971 preparing to make *Lady Sings the Blues,* the vehicle he'd chosen to launch Diana Ross's movie career.

Marvin Gaye had spent much of that year fighting for the release of an album of self-authored material his brother-in-law thought too unorthodox to sell. As start-up neared on the film production that Gordy already had $2 million sunk into, his storehouse was being copiously replenished by the harvest of Gaye's insolence. Three singles from *What's Going On* were simultaneously in the pop Top Ten. Gordy's begrudged concession to Marvin's obduracy had panned out golden: he was well reimbursed for the liberties taken.

By prevailing in their test of wills, Gaye broke Gordy's upper hand on his stabled talent; within four years Stevie Wonder would extract from Motown the industry's richest recording contract. Once the talent got access to outside lawyering, fewer seemed worth Gordy's trouble. Lately, any who thought they had began leverage to challenge him for the publishing rights to their songs.

The high price of rock stars had driven up the value of pop music's top black guest attractions, who were all Gordy now cared to employ. Losing its stranglehold on artists' management meant that Motown squeezed less profit from every act and had less incentive to capitalize the development of new ones. By 1973 its talent roster was half the size of seven years before.[7]

From the Hollywood Hills the focus of Gordy's lively business concerns had narrowed to a cock-of-the-walk producer, a diva, one sister's valuable performing husband, a boy genius, and a last project—the Jackson 5, whose blaze of popularity among younger kids in the early

1970s illuminated a career path taken onto Saturday-morning television as cartoon heroes of their own show. Gordy molted in California, and anything of Detroit no longer essential to him was shed like a snake's outgrown skin.

Most of those divested were stable hands and musicians, but included performers whom he considered of unsteady appeal to the white market. Martha Reeves's career just stopped. "Free-floating without a direction or a safety net, I felt lost in the shuffle," she remembered. "... I had ... million-selling records ... headlines [at] the Copa, and became an international star, [but] Motown treated me like a poor stepchild. ... Berry zeroed in on the one act that was likely to personify his dreams."[8]

Five years after Sam Cooke died still trying to get to Las Vegas, Diana Ross made her farewell appearance as a Supreme at the Frontier Hotel there. Tended closely and driven hard by the shepherding Gordy, Ross circuited America's lushest watering holes—the Coconut Grove in Los Angeles, the Theater in the Round in Chicago, the Waldorf-Astoria in New York—singing in Bob Mackie gowns for Streisandesque wages, as much as a hundred thousand a week. No expense of Gordy's effort or Motown's know-how was stinted in engineering the biggest of all black female singing careers.

The tooth-and-claw striver from Brewster Homes threw herself into acting the part of a star—Joan Crawford, perhaps, as imagined by Maxine Powell—insisting even then that she be called "Miss Ross" in public by the oldest of her acquaintances on Gordy's payroll, dismissing a grade school class of blind autograph-seekers in an icy fit of backstage pique. Less than four months after Florence Ballard—the Supreme cast out on the eve of their Las Vegas debut—sued her lawyers in Detroit for having colluded with Motown to fix at $160,000 the price of all her once and future claims, Diana Ross—carrying Gordy's child and the sting of his turndown—married a convenient "public relations executive" named Silberstein at the Silver Bells Chapel in Las Vegas, by then Gordy's playground and thus the "family's" official business and resort destination of choice.

Gordy once confided that Ross's wedding was the "happiest day of his life." "I can't marry this woman," he told Raynoma. "[She's] as selfish as I am."[9]

In April 1971 the hour-long special *Diana* was broadcast on network television. Ross sang and pattered, did sketch comedy with Danny Thomas and Bill Cosby, and mimed impersonations of Charlie Chaplin, W. C. Fields, and Harpo Marx. Gordy thought these "brilliant," a persuasive advertisement of her acting promise. Soon afterward the William Morris Agency brought Gordy a proposed movie about Billie Holiday that was in need of financial backing. The director attached to the project was willing to give Diana Ross the starring role.

Gordy agreed to put up half the budget—a million dollars—and to assume any cost overruns. He disdained the original script as wanting in "blackness." Assigned to rewrite it was Suzanne DePasse, the latest right-hand female and brunt-bearer of his frequent barbed needlings about her "high-sidity" provenance. Gordy had a consort, the white singer Chris Clark, spice the dialogue with authentic Negro flavor.[10] The resultant screenplay got an Academy Award nomination and earned DePasse promotion to chief of Motown's product development.

Gordy applied his method of making records to the making of his Diana Ross movie. He treated its director like a Motown staff producer. Gordy was on the set every morning at seven-thirty. He coached his star on the delivery of her every line. He regularly invited office staff and hangers-around to view rough-cut work in progress and tell him what they didn't like.

Undaunted by ignorance of craft, Gordy commandeered the editing room after filming was over. "He kept saying things like 'let's try the first two words of Take 15 with the last two words of Take 22,'" recalled an attending minion. Gordy finally backed off in frustration and permitted Sidney Furie to edit the picture.

Gordy's idea of *Lady Sings the Blues* was rooted in biopics of the 1950s about hard-knocked torch singers like Helen Morgan and Lillian

Roth. Doris Day made one of these in 1955, *Love Me or Leave Me*, in which she portrayed Ruth Etting. Gordy was freshly in mind of a more modern elaboration of this tried formula—the movie musical *Funny Girl*, a commercial triumph for Barbra Streisand in the role of Fanny Brice.

Lady's weather-beaten plot structure was refurbished with ethnic specificities that were employed as decorative effects meant to titillate the tourist's imagination without troubling his eyes or expectations: soft-lit slum grit, darktown exotica after dark, tormented dope fiends, sharply suffered racial indignities. To fashion packages that white Americans would buy, Gordy had learned to wrap articles of authentic Aframericana in reassuring banalities.

Having determined that $2 million wasn't enough to make his movie properly, Gordy bought out Paramount's interest in the production. His control thus unencumbered, he anted up another million and a half to complete the project to his specifications. Gordy's compulsive gamble paid off. *Lady Sings the Blues* would draw customers on a scale that was impressive to movie industrialists who hadn't expected to much notice its existence.

Ross's performance was of a competence that inspires overpraise because its source is surprising. She became the first black woman ever to receive an Academy Award nomination as best actress. Her singing evoked Holiday's well enough that the movie's score was also nominated. Fifteen million dollars worth of tickets were sold to see *Lady Sings the Blues*, of which two-thirds were divided between Motown and Paramount, which retained distribution rights.

Once it ceased to be his singular passion, Gordy's record business sputtered as an engine of profit. The pace of record sales was growing slack. Motown tried to expand its market by diversifying its product line but lacked aptitude for country, rock, or adult-contemporary music. Over the previous half-decade Gordy had taken many millions out of the company to finance large living and broad ambitions.

Feeling pinched, Gordy had lawyers and accountants prepare the paperwork for a public stock offering in 1972. But at the point of decision even the pressure of depleted cash reserves couldn't induce Gordy

to sacrifice control for capital. Certain of his dispositions were permanent. Fifteen years before he'd needed less than a thousand dollars to
get started in the record business and spurned his sister's offer of it
because he didn't want partners.

After the Detroit record works shut down for good near the end of
1972, Gordy made himself chairman of Motown Industries and
installed Ewart Abner as president of its Music Division. A dean of the
old-school black record hustlers, this former architect and despoiler of
Vee-Jay Records had ripened into elder statesmanhood as a vice-
president at Motown. As Gordy concentrated on Ross, Abner became
a surrogate paterfamilias to the other high-yield talent. When he
appointed Abner his stand-in at Motown Records, Gordy felt freer to
pursue his heart's superseding desires.

In a photograph of Gordy taken between takes on the set of *Lady Sings
the Blues,* while two Hollywood white boys looking anxious to oblige
hang on to his words, Diana Ross—seated before them with folded
arms—stares off in another direction, staying resolutely in character
while technicians ready the next shot. Gordy's valet had dressed him
that day in the manner of a baronial numbers racketeer showing himself to the neighborhood on a Saturday afternoon: the sealskin car coat
is opened to expose a prosperous paunch swathed in Italian knitted
wool; the broad-brimmed fedora is broken precisely down in front with
the proper hustler's élan.[11]

At home in Bel-Air Gordy was catered to by a French chef and
served by an English butler. Such refinements in his style of living made
the house he'd bought from Red Skelton a sumptuous arena for the psychological blood sports Gordy still played with the purposeful cold-
bloodedness of a pimp disciplining whores.

While meeting there with staff, he once directed Suzanne DePasse
to "get up and show 'em how fat you are . . . pretend you're an ape—
be a gorilla for everybody." By one witness's account: "Suzanne didn't
hesitate nor . . . look around. She stood up and began to do this gorilla
routine," snorting and "scratching her armpits" as twenty onlookers

"roared with laughter."[12] DePasse would become president of Motown in a few years, having passed every test.

Gordy holed up for long stretches inside his pile of dark polished wood, damask napkins, crystal goblets, fresh-cut flowers, French antique furniture, and remote-controlled electronic devices, attended by retainers, business callers, and consorts-in-residence. Dispersed about him in Los Angeles were his relocated "family": parents, four siblings, seven children, two ex-wives, his "bottom woman," star money-makers, and high-level retainers.

He married his daughter to the choicest of eligible Jackson brothers in a lavish display costing $200,000, highlighted by the release of 175 white doves into a ballroom at the Beverly Hills Hotel festooned with seven thousand white camelias. Watched on closed-circuit television by overflowing invitees, Hazel Joy wed her family's first second-generation celebrity husband in a white pearl-beaded dress with a train of mink.[13]

Sufficient youth-market currency now bought its bearers' way into highly respectable circles in an industrial society that was respectful of its newly rich because they were presumed to have recent knowledge of the whereabouts of fresh money. Motown could be of only small account in the multibillion-dollar record trade, but by force of the movie's stunning success Gordy became the Jackie Robinson of big-league culture commerce. At the turn of the decade the convergence of music- and movie-business elites was happening fast, and Gordy was quickly in the mix of Hollywood's upper crust.

Though he appeared in satin dinner jackets at the charity galas and awards ceremonies required of good-standing members of the show-business chamber of commerce, he kept shy of cameras and the press. Apart from squiring Ross in public, Gordy gathered with his clan or caroused in the private salons of town gentry accustomed to sequestering their guilty pleasures. His were taken often at Hugh Hefner's backgammon table, whereupon he laid down with relish tens of thousands of dollars.

Hefner's was the model of a working life that Gordy considered appropriate to a struck-it-rich player with a free-flowing stream of legitimate income: conducted mostly from home or hotel rooms at gambling resorts, where business and pleasures could keep close company. Whenever he swept "down from the hills" to review the troops barracked in Hollywood, the staff at Motown's headquarters snapped to attention. But more than ever he was prone to snap "That's your problem" at querying aides and dismiss pled causes by shrugging "My hands are tied."

In Gordy's near abdication of Motown's daily affairs, Barney Ales—capo of its cash-flow division—found an opportunity to accelerate past tolerable limits the pace of his self-dealing. Ales had refused to move to Los Angeles. "He was all over the place," Gordy complained, "busy in Europe, in Detroit and in Florida where he had bought a house, hoping to get me to move the business there."

While Gordy had been off making *Lady Sings the Blues*, Ales disdained to answer to anyone at Motown but its inaccessible chairman. "Ours had always been a complex relationship," Gordy later mused. "The situation was not unlike me being president of a small nation . . . and him being the big general who controls the army."

When Gordy came back to check on his record company between Diana Ross movies, Ales dodged phone calls and stonewalled queries about sales and collections. "I thought perhaps he wanted to go his own way," Gordy recalled, with delicacy that bespoke respect for an old tenderness. "I made it easy. I told him he was fired."

Ales's banishment plunged Gordy from the exhilaration of masterminding movies into the odium of such workaday mercantile chores as telephoning recalcitrant record wholesalers to dun them for millions in uncollected receivables: "Barney was one of the few executives at Motown whose job I could not do." Because of the imminent release of a Stevie Wonder album, midsummer 1973 glistened with the instant prospect of recouping large amounts of long-overdue cash. As Wonder's last album had been the first ever by an American to debut at Number 1 on *Billboard*'s pop chart, the marketplace was frothing in expectation of his next.

In its early California years the "new" Motown's estate was upheld by stalwarts from Detroit's old guard. Marvin Gaye got rock-star big, and Norman Whitfield was blazing away. Stevie Wonder went on tour with the Rolling Stones in the twilight of his boyhood career and came back a full-size profit center. The Jackson 5 were established as the prototype of Gordy's next-generation product line: geared to an emerging class of preteen consumers, designed and crafted to Motown's customary standards. In 1973 sales revenues approached $50 million.[14]

A pitchman sold Gordy the idea for the next Diana Ross movie with the visual aid of "a bunch of pictures that looked like a comic book . . . some easels and other props":

> Quickly flipping the pages, he told the story of a young woman from the inner-city ghettos of Chicago who dreams of being a big fashion designer and who eventually makes it to the top. At the height of her career in Europe, she realizes that the happiness she really seeks in life has always been back home in her own neighborhood.[15]

Gordy—who burned rubber on Detroit and hadn't looked back—accounted this scenario an immediate chord-striker, resonant with his "own feelings that happiness is within you; and the real fun and real love are usually in the valley where we start out rather than the mountaintop where we hope to end up."[16] In Gordy's legend of himself his ascent was a journey on a quest "to be loved."

But his success as a culture-monger owed in part to his long habit of bearing in mind that well-dressed cheap sentiment never goes out of style with the American public. He hadn't watched a television network promote *The Wizard of Oz* into an annual cultural event without appreciating the instrumentality of "there's no place like home" in getting it elected America's national bedtime story. Gordy had the tunesmith's wolfish instinct for spotting a juicy hook, if not always the knack of catching one. The next Diana Ross movie's hook—"success is nothing without someone you love to share it with"—would be of his own devising.

Gordy engaged three white scenarists to write a fable of black life that contained a love story in which again to pair Diana Ross with Billy Dee Williams, to further establish a "franchise" that he hoped could become as lucrative as the movies of Rock Hudson and Doris Day. The profitability of *Lady Sings the Blues* meant that Gordy had to put up only half the money to control the making of *Mahogany.*

He hired the eminent British director Tony Richardson. He approved location shooting in Rome. He slotted Anthony Perkins into the villianous role of a star-making fashion photographer who ensnares the heroine in a web of continental decadences and despoils her innocent lust for acclaim with his unconsummatable lust for her. In this movie Diana Ross would make doubly true her own shopgirl's dream of becoming a fashion designer by playing the part in fashions she designed.

Three weeks into production of *Mahogany,* while screening dailies, Gordy began to rail that Richardson was "ruining [my] movie." On the set, in the midst of shooting a scene, a squabble provoked an icy confrontation between them that ended in Richardson's abrupt recusal. It may have been, as Gordy supposed, that Richardson had appraised his situation and contrived to get himself fired. Gordy paid off Richardson in full to keep his crew from leaving, too.[17]

Then he had no choice, Gordy says, but to pick up the director's discarded mantle of command. Entirely untrained and innocent of experience, his heart pumping adrenalized presumption, Gordy stepped into a $4 million movie in the middle of its making, and just started to direct. "I will never forget my first take," he wrote, evoking the sense of a twenty-year-old wonderment. ". . . I called 'Action!' From stillness to movement, everything swung into gear: Extras started walking. . . . The whole street had come to life. . . . What a thrill!"[18]

After a performance at the Hollywood Bowl Aretha Franklin was driven "up a narrow road that wound around the side of a mountain," past "a checkpoint with security men in dark glasses," then another half a Bel-Air mile to Berry Gordy's "mansion." To a shy upsouth migrant's daughter raised in Rust Belt cities, this was a ride as glamorous as any taken by Hearst's guests at Xanadu. She and Gordy were acquainted, though not from back home, having moved in different circles of black Detroit. The Motown "family" was unchurched and thus outside the Reverend Franklin's sphere.

Aretha was under contract to Columbia when Motown was on the rise and mostly in New York. A decade and a half later she'd recently joined the residential colony of black music celebrities in Los Angeles. She was flattered to be received by Gordy at home and excited for a tourist's glimpse at so private a lifestyle of the rich and famous.

He walked Aretha over landscape graced by an "exquisite aviary," "manicured gardens," and "peacocks on parade," before leading her through the house. When the tour reached his "private quarters," Gordy pointed out a portrait of Diana Ross, "done on black velvet." Franklin sensed in her host that night a sentiment for "the old and early days, when we all were just starting out to realize our dreams."[19]

Mahogany opened nationwide in the fall of 1975 to a torrent of reproach from film critics. "Berry panicked after reading the first line of the *Time* magazine critique," said Rob Cohen, the junior executive at 20th Century Fox whom Gordy had recruited to run Motown Productions. "He was crazed. He wanted to re-edit the film," as if it were the first pressing of "Shop Around" he'd pulled back after hearing on the radio, took into the studio, and doctored into Motown's breakthrough hit. Though *Mahogany* made face-saving money for Gordy, it was a commercial disappointment, a falling off from *Lady Sings the Blues.*

Aimed by Gordy at America's masses, *Mahogany* missed its mark, snaring ticket-buyers mainly among extended families of *Ebony*'s target audience for Fashion Fairs. Most white moviegoers of all ages avoided an entertainment whose life-affirming lesson was taught by the suicide of its only major white character, played by Perkins as a cartoonish embodiment of qualities that black males stereotypically ascribed to white boys of the master class: insipid, mean, and sexually deficient. *Mahogany* not only failed to broaden Diana Ross's box-office appeal, it defined her limits as actor and movie star.

Gordy had delivered to a marketplace bristling with youth a "woman's picture" he labored heavy-handedly for a year to fashion after the style of the late Lana Turner era. Having come of age early in the 1950s, Gordy had no more affinity than is typical in midlife for the particular sensibilities of subsequent generations of the coming-of-aged. He prospered in the record business by his acuity at hearing what his young market would buy, not from an ability to articulate it himself.

He'd last written a hit song in 1962. While Smokey, and HDH, and Norman Whitfield produced the "Sound of Young America," Gordy was harboring at Motown such legitimate citizens of Ed Sullivan's show business as Sammy Davis Jr., Leslie Uggams, Billy Eckstine, Tony Martin, Bobby Breen, and Hop-Sing, the Cartwrights' coolie on *Bonanza*.

Gordy's idea of American popular culture formed on the wrong side of the 1960s to have reliably informed his speculations in the cultural-commodities market of the mid-1970s. The total authority he'd impulsively seized to govern every jot of *Mahogany*'s creation was his license to follow this idea to its logical conclusion.

Once gone too far down this slippery path, he was likely to end up another of its routine casualties. "I'm not the boss," Gordy was known to tell subordinates in dismissing an unpersuasive appeal. "Logic is."[20] A man ruled by his idea of logic is subject to being taken over by the logic of his idea.

Though in his entry in the 1976 edition of *Who's Who in America* he accounts himself firstly a film industrialist, Gordy—chilled from getting caught in a shower of opprobrium hard upon the strenuous completion of an undertaking he'd experienced as a "personal disaster"—never again directed after *Mahogany*. He did exert a final push to put over Diana Ross, partnering with Universal to mount a movie version of *The Wiz*, the black-cast Broadway musical adapted from *The Wizard of Oz*.

This time, when he fired the future director of *Saturday Night Fever* for being disagreeable, Gordy paid Sidney Lumet a million dollars to step in to the dirty work of making Ross—fifteen years older than Judy Garland had been when she played a Dorothy five years younger—seem a plausible wonder-struck ingenue in a Las Vegas–style revue so grandiose that one scene staged in New York, on the plaza of the World Trade Center, required four hundred synchronized dancers to change in and out of twelve hundred costumes.

The Wiz cost $23 million to make, more than three times the expense of the two previous Diana Ross movies combined. Only a third as much as that was spent at ticket windows by the *Wiz*'s aggregated patrons, an amount little more than twice the size of its promotion budget. Diana Ross's career in movies was over.

But for Gordy's last-ditch effort to hang his Galatea's star on silver screens in shopping centers across America, Motown pitched its cinematic products at the high end of the downscale youth and Negro markets. After *The Wiz* five years would elapse before the company's next and last movie—a kung-fu epic branded with Gordy's name—issued into the commerce of a youth culture that was tumescent with first-generation hip-hop kids. Motown was often more successful at producing for television, a bastion of congenial, old-fashioned show-business values.

In attending to these fancier properties, Gordy became his record company's "absentee landlord." While he had been in Rome making *Mahogany*, Ewart Abner queered contract renegotiations with the Jackson 5. Gordy was told too late to intercede in the process of Joe Jackson discovering that his sons were worth three times as much to CBS as he'd asked for from Motown.

Gordy knew that by being neither here nor there in actual presence but ever-presently in effect at Motown Records, he'd left his placeholder "without a lot of authority."[21] But even while he was admittedly a proprietor gone slack in his attentions to upkeep, Gordy expected no lapses in the steadiness of his property's yield. "Productivity was down and I held him responsible," so Abner was jettisoned.

Gordy then hired a fresh team of bureaucrats picked from among the welter of management consultants engaged in helping him puzzle through the late period of "financial difficulties." He'd installed his bottom woman, Suzanne DePasse, on top of the Creative Division. Having banked his own hustler's gut-fire, Gordy needed someone to focus on "sell" and "collect" who could stomach the nasty churn of street-level record commerce: "a scheming . . . demanding . . . czar-like character" not unlike—but not—himself, to restore an organizational sense of churlish urgency about getting the Chairman's scratch.[22]

He was pining for Barney Ales, his secret sharer. When asked back into the fold, Ales eagerly abandoned his unlucrative entrepreneuring in Detroit. He returned on time to orchestrate the unprecedented opening of a Stevie Wonder double album at Number 1 on the pop charts. Enough were sold to recoup more than half Motown's $13 million investment in his new contract at the beginning of its seven-year life.

Still, Gordy found the price of Wonder off-puttingly high. He objected on principle to the fairer apportionment of any whore's earnings, no matter how gilded a Thoroughbred the mud-kicker in question: "to me it became values versus value." He also had a constitutional aversion to being force-played: "I had a problem anteing up more every time an artist we had developed got a better offer."

"[S]tubbornly," he admitted later, ". . . I would not always pay what it would take to get them to stay."[23] Albeit softened on Gordy's public tongue, the attitude underlying such personnel decisions was expressed once by Iceberg Slim as "I have never had a whore I couldn't do without."

By the late 1970s, "holding whores was like trying to cinch-grip quicksilver,"[24] since syndicated white boys had inflated the wages of talent and ruined the game. "In these changing times," Gordy noted ruefully, "the value of a proven artist was skyrocketing into the multimillions."

He "had to laugh [thinking] back to 1968 and how we were gloating over having five records out of the Top 10 in one week. We had no idea at the time that the seeds of our undoing were being planted."[25] Less than a decade later, by the lay of the board Gordy reckoned his record business was in the beginning of its endgame.

As the world's demand for American popular culture intensified during the 1960s, none of its exporters had outdone Motown at becoming an international brand. By the mid-1970s overseas customers accounted for 40 percent of Motown's revenue from product sales. In 1975 7.5 million of its records were shipped abroad. But no matter how successful, independent operators in the music business faced insurmountable problems of scale.

In 1978 the British conglomerate EMI—already music publishing's largest property-holder—manufactured and distributed a quarter of all the records sold in thirty-two countries, more than a billion dollars worth. When $4 billion and change were exchanged worldwide for records and tapes that year, Polygram—a Dutch multinational—also grossed more than a billion in retail "music and entertainment sales." Within another year CBS also topped a billion dollars in sales.[26]

In 1977, when all black-owned businesses in America combined to sell $836 million of goods and services, black popular music was a $2.3 billion resource of which Gordy—the largest black stakeholder in its exploitation—controlled 2.5 percent.[27] In ratcheting up its mass appeal, Gordy had raised boogaloo's value on the cultural-commodity exchange enough to make worthwhile the weighings-in of global commercialists. By 1972 the opportunity to grab meaty shares of the black music market in ready-sliced chunks had been obvious to MBA students at Harvard whose professor was paid by CBS to assign his class as consultants-in-training to analyze the boogaloo trade and to propose to a hypothetical corporate client a strategy for summarily acquiring a substantial position in it.

By the late mid-1970s—after Clive Davis showed them how—the six so-called major labels were regulating fourth-fifths of the traffic in black music and had appropriated most of its high-yielding human assets. Muscling into the wholesale distribution business, large manufacturers rapidly squeezed out all but the hardiest smaller competitors, then used this leverage to strong-arm their open palms into the cash flow of independent record companies. The industrial oligarchs exacted tribute by means of trade agreements that effectively granted access to rack jobbers, subdistributors, and retailers who were the gateway to the mass market and that required as toll payment about one-seventh of a grantee's income from product sales.

Whether, by mortgaging their sovereignty, they hoped to prosper or only to survive, most of the voluntarily colonized were bled into prostration, as Stax had been by Columbia. The shrewdest handful of free-standers put themselves on the best possible terms with the inevitable and succumbed agreeably to great advantage, as Atlantic did to Warner. Motown and another holdout of like size threw in with each other to assure their own means of bringing goods to market. This partnership of stout resisters couldn't long withstand history's implacable currents, breaking apart in 1979 when A&M Records signed a distribution deal with RCA.

In the modern scheme of music commerce even a robust independent had too little ballast to buck a swallowing tide. Since the mid-1970s Gordy had been resigned to bulk having its way in the marketplace and knew that as an unavoidable consequence living space for lighter-weight classes would be reserved to the cramped margins. But "Pops" Gordy's son inherited an unshakable ancestral wariness of letting white men get a foothold on his property. He would soldier on for four more years against that foregone conclusion.

Motown was no longer the hard-driven Detroit enterprise run on the model of an old-fashioned movie factory. Upon its arrival in Los Angeles, it began reforming along the lines of a California-contemporary "record and filmworks," becoming a contractor rather than a proprietary developer of the talent it merchandised. The company's overhead was lightened by paring its herd of all but the healthiest producers and lopping off stable hands who were no longer needed for care and feeding of the culls.

Casualties among the wayside-befallen quickly mounted in the East. Martha Reeves went haywire, ex-Temptation Paul Williams blew his brains out, and Florence Ballard, the banished Supreme, died on welfare. These notable sufferers among the homeless veterans of Gordy's victorious campaigns were early conscripts into the rank and file of a displaced legion of once-familiars who were unticketed, as he later put it, "to make the long trip with me."[28]

Motown West was further shorn of old-school ties by corporate raiders who carried off the Four Tops, Norman Whitfield, and the Temptations. Smokey seemed to have dry up into semiretirement in Los Angeles, and Diana Ross was on the wrong side of her record-selling prime. Marvin Gaye had infected Stevie Wonder with the virus of self-determinism and planted the seditious idea of an artist's rightful claim to exemption from clockwork. Now Gordy's two highest earners were working for him at the languid pace of rock-star aristocracy to produce flurries of fresh commerce every other year or so.

To offset such fallings-off in formerly reliable income, throughout the 1970s Motown had only the Commodores and Rick James to mature into compensatory breadwinners. Over those years Motown diminished into a famous brand that peddled its progressive identity confusion in product lines with a few dependably popular items but otherwise comprised bric-a-brac: goods of nonstandard style and quality, designed to possibly strike a public's fancy but certain to fatten the Jobete catalog.

By redeploying Suzanne DePasse from her post atop the Creative Division at Motown Records to oversee movie and television productions, Gordy suggested he'd picked up his stake from a cooled-off table and removed it to another game of livelier prospect. He already had begun to replace his disestablished human stable with a string of equine Thoroughbreds. By decade's end he was a buyer of million-dollar racehorses.

Berry Gordy turned fifty while bunkered in a Las Vegas hotel room at the dawn of the hip-hop age. Even as the Sugar Hill Gang's harbingering "Rapper's Delight" careered noisily up the record charts, it would have seemed merely novel from the vantage point of a Jacuzzi at Caesar's Palace, wherein Gordy mulled overhead and crimped revenues while meaning to soak away a darkly reflective mood that even last night's ritual $10,000 bloodletting on the baccarat tables hadn't dispelled. He would be visited in Los Angeles the next day by his money-minders from Detroit. The Noveck brothers brought news of his insolvency.[29]

He was advised that selling off Jobete for $27 million would be the quickest way to square himself. He later said he thought hard about doing it, a process of weighing the faith of his forefathers that real estate was the only unassailable currency against their admonitions to stay clear of indebtedness to white men. Gordy chose to mortgage a business to preserve property. For once he rose above his native abhorrence of bank debt and—having assumed a large one—hoped, like any farmer of collaterized land, for a rich harvest duly reaped.

As if the crisis stalking Gordy had tripped the wired trigger of a buried reflex, Smokey Robinson kicked in just then with a trans-categorical hit, a career-capping ballad sweetly reminiscent of his best days. By next Christmas Stevie Wonder's album was *Hotter Than July*, which sold in abundance until the middle of spring. Gordy, flush once more with cash, retired his debt within a year. Though restored to solvency in 1980, Motown never regained enough command of the marketplace to impose discipline on its disorderly network of independent distributors.

Wearied of ransoming cash held hostage by recalcitrant wholesalers, Gordy bowed to the pensioner's logic of tolerating less return on investment for the convenience of getting a regular payout in one check from a single timely source. In 1983, by standard means of a distribution deal, Motown became a client of MCA. Gordy's submission to the inevitable came in the embrace of someone known as the "Poison Dwarf" among certain of the well-positioned in their mutual trade.[30]

Irving Azoff of MCA was a newly made record mogul of a breed recently evolved from managers of rock stars. Once the market value of highly prized talent became equivalent to those of thriving small record companies, its agents and handlers could use their effective control of these assets as a form of capital to parlay into proprietorships and corporate presidencies. David Geffen, an original of this modern species, was a kid working in the mail room at the William Morris Agency when six years of Gordy's bootstrapping—and the feverish creativity of the most productive artisanal community in the history of popular music—culminated in "Where Did Our Love Go."

Over the next decade, as Gordy superintended Motown's peak years, Geffen—a maker of nothing but deals—turned his half of the $4.5 million he got for the publishing rights to a client's songs into a boutique record label, which he quickly sold to Warner Communications for $7 million and a place of favor in the court of its powerful chairman, Steve Ross. While Gordy was sweating out *Mahogany*, the thirty-three-year-old Geffen was made vice-chairman of Warner Brothers Pictures. He abandoned this post to a cancer scare and spent the next four years collecting Tiffany lamps, teaching part-time, and expecting the worst.

In 1980, as Gordy staved off Motown's ruin, Geffen—recovered from only a botched diagnosis and unemployed—was reinstated in the record business with backing from Warners sufficient to support the expensive contracts of such celebrity signees as Elton John and John Lennon. The new Geffen label's establishing stroke of luck came by the hand of Mark David Chapman; Lennon's murder promoted the sale of three million copies of his current release, a big-ticket double album otherwise unlikely to have sold a third as many.

At the time of *The Wiz*'s crash, Geffen was launching himself as an independent producer of films subsidized by Warner Brothers. If Gordy's mountainous climb came up the rough side of the culture business, Geffen had maneuvered as high an ascent in half the time, through a succession of airlifts and soft landings.

Geffen had set off his former protégé Irving Azoff's rapid rise to become the world's leading manager of rock-star talent. By the early 1970s the amassed value of the assets he controlled made Azoff among the several most powerful men in music commerce. Increasingly, the conglomerators were turning to such brokers of youth-market commodities as Azoff to run their record divisions. His breed of label boss organized business on the model of a talent brokerage: revenues would mainly stream from direct commercial relationships with a handful of heavily marketed brand-name acts, and the steady dividends of profit participation in the entrepreneurial ventures of other commodifiers of talent.

While Gordy supped with Lew Wasserman, the lion of MCA, when evening fell Motown was bedded down with Azoff, the old don's running dog. Once Gordy had locked up and barricaded the raw materials of a manufacturing fortune against Irving Azoff's predacious ilk. Since the days of "Shop Around," Gordy expected that sooner or later a horde of Allen Klein's marauding spawn would arrive to storm his gates. He'd held them off for twenty years, enough time to have extracted nearly all his patch would yield.

In that vein Gordy took his parting shot of whore money off Teena Marie, the proverbial white girl with a black voice, who was indentured to him in 1976 on the very terms of the standard Motown contract that

Sister Loucye had pulled out of her desk drawer in 1960 for Mary Wells to sign. Five years later, under the management of a Gordy brother's common-law wife, Teena Marie was salaried at about a hundred dollars a week while two of her albums were making millions.[31] Such a display of by-the-book pimping was as old-fashioned by then in Gordy's business as it was on the street.

Five years after that its president Irving Azoff sold MCA his talent brokerage for $15.7 million. His brazeness ruffled the industry. "For MCA to be in the management business—it's shocking," David Geffen sniped.[32] "They'll be dealing out of self-interest." Azoff characterized such opinion as "small-minded," having just stretched his own far enough to find the operating principle by which for most of thirty years Gordy steered his assets clear of threat until he'd milked them almost dry.

But Gordy's deal with Azoff turned out to have bought his record company barely two years' grace. And as the Chairman had been heard to say, "Every form of shelter has its price." Gordy knew the truth of these desperate alliances: "They really want to sell their records, not your records. And the only way to make your records their records is to buy you out."

He'd gotten old in the business of selling to the young. "It was not [just] that we were losing money," Gordy attested. "I had lost interest."

When Billy Davis was dying, he cautioned Gordy against taking on "one fight too many," lest his lifelong friend and employer end up like Sugar Ray Robinson, "just another n[egro] who made it to the top and died broke."[33] In his mid-fifties Gordy thought to give up adventuring in business and settle into living well on his property. It had already occurred to him to make a museum of "Hitsville, U.S.A.," Motown's homely original quarters on the west side of "the forgotten city that never forgot," where Esther, the local politician's wife, kept the Gordy flag flying.

An evergreen publishing catalog was a form of permanent wealth, and Gordy planned the last third of life as a gentleman cultivator of

Jobete's asset value. In a culture that preserves everything it can sell for as long as it can be sold, Gordy's storehouse of such antiquities as the fifty-four Motown songs that made the pop charts in 1971 might hold a rich deposit of renewable resources.

In 1984 the celebratory television special *Motown 25: Yesterday, Today and Forever* kicked off Gordy's second career as an appropriator of the past for present uses. The show was made an event by the appearance of Michael Jackson while he was still a fresh craze. It is remembered for his moonwalk, and Diana Ross shoving Mary Wilson out of a spotlight. A year later came *Motown Returns to the Apollo*, which featured Rod Stewart, Joe Cocker, George Michael, and Boy George, a demographically balanced slate of pop stars.

Gordy was using prime-time network television—the heartland medium—to establish the Motown franchise among middle-aged middle Americans, whose junior ranks its original customers now comprised. This was the surest first step toward attaining the status of permanent cultural institution, at which point Gordy would have put himself into an annuity business that was as stable as owning parking lots.

No marketer's "branding" strategy was ever better executed. Within six years former Temptations would be performing a whirlwind medley of old hits at an occasion of state: the Gulf War Super Bowl, a jingoistic pageant over which war planes in tight formation were brandished in a dusky Florida sky. This event seemed a fitting national celebration of the way of life Americans were then at war to preserve, since under the star-spangled canopy that night, Berry Gordy was still getting paid.

For almost half of the previous decade Gordy had dickered over the price of selling out. In the months before he finally disembarked he sent for an experienced captain of a doomed ship. In 1988 Al Bell was tapped to be the face of Gordy's ghost at the helm of Motown Records.

As that spring reached its peak, Gordy was in the halting last throes of his divestiture of Motown. He fretted about whether he could get his price, between occasional spasms of remorse provoked by phone calls from such of the people's emissaries as Jesse Jackson and Jim Brown, protesting the sale on grounds of tribal honor.[34]

Gordy was raised when "race men"—conscientious agents of group pride and progress—were a cultural ideal of the serious-minded. He knew he was obliged to make himself available to the importunings of his social conscience, but felt most deeply about getting paid. At this stage Gordy was unlikely to betray a dearly held conviction that had served him so long to now make so lush the prospect of cashing in.

A month later he'd sold out to MCA, the only one-sixth of the industry's ruling cartel willing to part with as much as $61 million to own little else but Motown's "brand equity"—the value of its name and history—and the deed to its last trophy property, Stevie Wonder. Though Motown Records had passed from its founder's hands, Jobete's proprietor retained a perpetual right to compensation for any commercial use of his former property.

Gordy had kept the kernel of his franchise and gotten paid a small fortune for the husk. He awarded Rolls-Royces to Smokey Robinson and Suzanne DePasse—like prizes to marathon winners—then set his sights on sitting with his sisters in an owner's box at Churchill Downs on Derby Day.

On the first June day of 1991 David Ruffin died smoking crack in Philadelphia, where he'd just returned from touring Europe with the other notable Temptations-in-exile, Eddie Kendricks and Dennis Edwards. Almost a quarter-century before, Ruffin had stuck his head out of a dressing-room door backstage of a high school auditorium in Cambridge, Massachusetts, and admitted a caller he instantly recognized from an airport encounter the previous spring. Shown into the presence of Temptations in bathrobes and head rags getting ready to go to work, the visitor might imagine he'd stepped into the very half hour before a photographer had recorded the last-minute primping depicted on his favorite of their album covers.

But the real Melvin Franklin was sitting between racks of stage attire, swaddled in terrycloth, shivering in a feverish sweat forty-five minutes from the onset of an hour's hard labor under hot lights. Smokey's perennial rival for the "Motown Spirit Award" was girding himself to meet the

Maurice King Professional Academy quality-control standard of never failing to rise to such a duty as loomed on this night to incite female crowd eruptions when his famously pure basso profundo would be called upon for its required star turn on "Old Man River."

Almost from the point of this sighting, David Ruffin had been adrift, cut loose from the Temptations in 1968 at the storming height of his fame and vainglory. "Gordy was trying to break my spirit," the broken Ruffin seethed, "because I refused to kiss his little short ass."[35] Across the next two decades he existed as a man would without a country, sustaining a marginal recording career that made no more than a couple of small claims on public notice into the mid-1980s, then as a citizen of oldies road shows, sitting in hotel rooms at dawn with Motown expatriates in forlorn ports of call like Tulsa, drunkenly excoriating Gordy for having pimped them all.

Perhaps the most gifted of male vocalists in the Motown stable, Ruffin was no doubt the churchiest—having sojourned in Memphis as a Dixie Nightingale—and the hardest-scraped. As a motherless boy run away from his Mississippi home, he was picked up in New Orleans and taken on the road by a Faginesque character named "Father" Eddie Bush. This itinerant country scamster put his young ward to work singing for his keep in backwater barrooms and revivalists' tents. By the time he turned fourteen, Ruffin had already been eight years in the business of entertaining.

Twice recorded elsewhere before he came lately to the Temptations in 1963, Ruffin was an ace drawn into two uneasily allied pairs of childhood friends after an original outsider was discarded. He was further set apart by the country wildness of his gift. In Paul Williams the Temptations already had a subtler singer in Ruffin's vein who was arguably as good. But Ruffin was of the breed of gospel highwaymen and enough in the "anointed" line of Brownlee to have also risen from a hospital bed to tear a house down near the drug- and drink-ravaged end of a shortened life.

His emergence in 1965 was Smokey Robinson's doing. Among four luminous soloists in the group, Ruffin's light burned at the highest wattage. When the Temptations had four consecutive Number 1 records the following year, the last three were his. During the three years Ruffin sang on their records, the Temptations had fifteen of them reach the Top Five of the soul music charts. These became the standard curriculum for boogaloo's modern school of contrapuntal rough- and sweet-voiced group vocalizing in the classic manner of gospel's quartet masters.

A quarter-century later David Ruffin awoke on the day of his death no less a historical artifact for still being alive. Nobody involved with burying him expected public feeling to still be fresh for a figure so briefly grand that long ago. But crowds of sufficient size and constancy to draw rotating details of police gathered outside the Philadelphia funeral parlor wherein Ruffin's body was embalmed and lockered four days, while Dr. King's casket-maker in Atlanta customized a donated steel coffin and shipped it to Detroit.

There, over four more days, in a roped-off alcove at Swanson's Funeral Home, David Ruffin's remains were garnished with Berry Gordy's flowers and displayed to "maybe twenty thousand or so" passersby. His former valet thought Ruffin looked as though moments before showtime he'd lain down in his tuxedo to catnap on "an expen- sive quilted sofa" without bothering to remove his glasses or rhine- stoned patent-leather shoes.[36]

On the Monday morning of his funeral mounted police and barri- cades kept ten blocks full of onlookers from altogether claiming the streets around Aretha's daddy's church, but failed to impede the onrush of an uninvited throng trying to force its way inside. A man lost part of his thumb in a stampeded door. To avoid worse, successive small groups of these frenzied sightseers were allowed to visit seats in the balcony for twenty minutes at a time. Outside, hawkers were selling David Ruffin funeral programs to shut-out British pilgrims for ten dollars each.

Stricken half blind by the glare of camera lighting, mourners with reserved seats had to clamber over "miles" of television cable in getting down a center aisle clogged with curiosity-shoppers straining to get a look at the corpse. Many in this congregation had come to mourn in the raucous dress of early June: "halter tops and bustiers, backless and sleeveless dresses . . . bright red and vibrant oranges, greens, pur- ple . . . Mariah Carey wannabes in . . . microminis . . . Diana Ross clones in sequins, bugle beads, and hair."[37] As much as possible of black Detroit's grassroots was there to see and be seen.

The crowd inside the New Bethel Baptist Church was hard-packed and stewing in the compressed midday body heat, when Fruits of Islam brought the unruly house enough to order for the service to begin. Before Esther Gordy recounted the official legendary past—in which members of her family had twice favored David Ruffin with opportunities to make his dreams come true—police arrived to arrest Eddie Kendricks as a child-support scofflaw. But for the priestly intercession of Louis Farrakhan, he would have been taken out of the church in handcuffs.

After Stevie Wonder performed a song from his new album, the audience leaped to its feet in exuberant applause. Once this incitement had passed, the service reportedly settled into four and a half hours of "every few minutes . . . another outburst, another standing ovation . . . a song, everybody rising to their feet . . . a prayer followed by another song, then someone reading, somebody falling out, somebody being rushed out of the church . . . photographers . . . crowding to snap pictures, TV cameras rolling into a shot, another prayer, another song."[38]

It fell to Aretha to restore proper perspective. When her time came to close this show, she "got up slowly and walked down past the now closed casket. As she reached the steps leading up to the podium, she stumbled slightly, and everybody gasped. . . . Visibly shaken, she said a few soft words about love and sadness."[39] The hymn Aretha sang for all her buried dead reduced even the coarsest despoilers of C. L. Franklin's temple to speechless awe and shame. When she'd finished, Minister Farrakhan chased away the chastened with a blistering lecture about their improper dress and conduct.

While Ruffin's coffin was hauled to the cemetery, Eddie Kendricks was being hauled off to jail. He would have been locked up longer for want of his $10,000 bail but for Martha Reeves, who reached Berry Gordy in Bel-Air. Recently, after two decades in stony exile, Gordy had telephoned Reeves to suggest they resolve a dead-letter lawsuit about money that she claimed she was owed since 1963. This mere glance in her direction had brought "Crazy Martha" trotting back to heel.

She'd come breathlessly when beckoned to a teatime meeting at the

"Gordy mansion." Seeing him again transported Reeves back to "days when he and I would sit in the front seat of his car parked outside my parents' house in Detroit." She was aglow with his attention; he seemed "engrossed" in her. These moments of deeply sensed "rapport" immediately superseded half a lifetime of her bitterness. "He still had that sparkling gleam in his eyes,"[40] and she was once again a tender bud opening by its light. Her weakness for Gordy was as incurable as Ruffin's for cocaine.

Even when most stuck on the pipe, Ruffin never got unstuck of Gordy. For the last half of his life Ruffin ranted about Gordy ruining it. Whenever he binge-smoked, all his demons wore one face. "So shut the fuck up," he snapped at a would-be rescuer from being held prisoner by cocaine for three days in a Tampa hotel room, "and if I feel like talking about Berry Gordy for eight hours straight, you're going to listen."[41] In the drug-induced throes of paranoid dementia he was often sure Gordy planned to have him killed.

In his own mind Ruffin never stopped being Gordy's subject. Gordy was the giver, keeper, and taker-away of Ruffin's only meaningful identity. Those three years at Motown of youthful bingeing on the strong stimulant of a fabulously reinvented self had addicted Ruffin for life.

When told who'd posted bail—and with how much dispatch—Eddie Kendricks denied his bad day's redeemer any portion of gratitude. "It's nothing but some of my money back he stole from me," Kendricks snorted. "He stole more than that from all of us in a day."[42] While he would naturally curse Gordy—author of all miseries—on such an occasion of sharply felt loss crowned by humiliation, Kendricks's true despair was in having been robbed of one of boogaloo's definitive voices.

His instrument was beyond repair, and now he had no choice but to try making a dollar out of every fifteen cents worth of use left in it. Kendricks would barely survive another year living as best he could as a currently unlicensed former Temptation. He dwindled into a stand-in for offstage voices singing his parts from the wings, then faded away.

As a desolated Detroit went on entombing artifacts on the premises of his vacated kingdom, the Thoroughbred horseflesh in Gordy's new stables broke out onto the national racing charts. When his first equine investment had won a race, quadrupled in value, and not "com[e] back to renegotiate his deal," Gordy's nose for racing stock opened wide. Years later a Gordy stallion would carry the family silks on a respectable ride in the Kentucky Derby.

Sister Gwen was set out to ripen past middle age on a California ranch, where Maxine Powell's prize pupil could inhabit the role of society horse breeder she'd been taught to imagine as a character played by Claudette Colbert. Her brother, Raynoma's arch "thief of dreams," slipped into the gentlemanly cover of the "sport of kings," as smooth as Cary Grant.

After he sold Motown, Gordy arranged to make a pilgrimage of the heart. He wanted to present Doris Day with a framed copy of the sheet music of the first song he'd written more than forty years ago, and sent off to her at no known address but "Hollywood, California." His fantasied object of youthful desire lived up to expectations.

"Doris was as enchanting, pretty and sweet as she had seemed to [him] back then," when he'd known her only on the screen. She asked to hear his song, and as Gordy shyly crooned, "You are you— And only you can be the one I love and yearn for, the one my heart burns for," "America's girl next door" melted into tears.[43]

PART III

Negribusiness (Sharecropping in Wonderland):
George Clinton and Hip-Hop

13. Urban Legends

In the last days of 1992, from his headquarters in Wildwood—not far from Bel-Air—the CEO of Death Row Records was proclaiming himself the next Berry Gordy and his enterprise the new Motown. He was poised to release into an expectant marketplace an album by his partner, the Holland-Dozier-Holland of the hip-hop business. Given the American youth market's current scale—and escalating demand for similar goods—even if the commercial impact of this new product proved unexpectedly less than monumental, he rested assured of soon laying hands on a windfall of cash. On such an eve of likely triumph, he'd earned a satisfied moment's pause-taking from half a decade of sharp-elbowed upward maneuvering through a nasty squeeze of thick traffic in and around an open portal from the street onto an outskirt of global commerce where quick pickings were now lusher than ever in the fatter-than-ever boogaloo trade.

Gordy's self-professed emulator was born in Mississippi while "My Guy" was Number 1 on the pop charts. His parents moved to Los Angeles four years later, during the high season of Marvin Gaye and Tammi Terrell. There they settled into factory and custodial jobs and bought a house in Compton. Their son, Marion Knight Jr., was a mama's boy tagged "Sugar Bear" by his childhood peers, in accordance with his size and assessed temperament.

He belonged to a generation that had grown up watching *Soul Train* in households whose elders listened to Al Green and Johnnie Taylor, Aretha and Gladys, the Dells, Dramatics, and Chi-Lites. They were P-Funked before puberty and graduated from high school on the morning of the hip-hop epoch. Of bearish build, "Suge" played college football in Las Vegas, then gravitated back home into steady work as a nightclub bouncer, security-for-hire, and celebrity bodyguard. A connection made while employed at watching the widely exposed back of black teen idol-du-jour Bobby Brown put Knight into the music business.

At twenty-eight the current Suge's outlook—from offices painted red to signify an unforsworn tribal allegiance to Compton's Piru Street Bloods—was unclouded by an overhanging charge of criminal assault, the result of his sixth arrest for gunplay or mayhem in two years since he became notorious as the extorter of Vanilla Ice's ill-gotten stake of publishing rights to seven songs on an album that sold eighteen million copies.[1]

As this tale grew taller in his putative victim's public retellings, Suge's name soon rang out across the hip-hop nation like Robin Hood's in Sherwood Forest. For all its citizenry's everyday theatrical bluster about "jackin'" a white exploiter, Knight was certified by the *Wall Street Journal* to have actually done so. To young actors playing gangsters as undercover cops would—by appropriating as their own the experiences of others and melding them with true elements of self to concoct a plausible fictive identity—Knight's minor hoodlum exploits bespoke John Gotti. Since Suge's tactical approach to bogarting a juicy slice of music business was to hijack bankable assets while recruiting a sweatshop labor force of aspirant talent, a documented reputation for thuggery was his best advertisement.

In July 1992 two brothers trying to break into show business were beaten, stripped, and broken down at gunpoint for using a public telephone in the lunchroom at Death Row Records when its proprietor was expecting a call. Before he let them go—acting out Robert De Niro's part as the outlaw Jimmy Burke in a scene from *Goodfellas*—Knight fished their pants pockets for a wallet from which to snatch a driver's license to hold hostage against the threat of victim outcry.[2]

Such jailhouse sport was an ordinary entertainment of the old-head gangbangers in Death Row's entourage who formed Suge's paid brigade of militant ex-offenders. As a commodifier of thug art, their employer traded on the imparted cachet of street authenticities. While it served him in the push-and-shove along the fast track by which he'd arrived at the brink of commercial legitimacy, Knight's blatant embrace of the criminal also aroused the interest of federal prosecutors sniffing after the scent of such career-accelerants as a made-for-tabloid-television RICO case.

When Death Row released its eagerly awaited album by Dr. Dre, public response was even warmer than hoped for. *The Chronic*—California thug-speak for marijuana—sold three million copies and stayed on the pop album charts for two-thirds of 1993. It set off an industrial earthquake, exposing a market among white youth of uncharted breadth for a "hardcore" strain of hip-hop known as "gangster rap," a term of art and commerce that had been coined several years before by the founder of its West Coast school, currently author of *The Chronic*, and Suge Knight's partner.

When *The Chronic* hit, Andre Young already owned a property in Calabasas that he'd "paid a mil-plus for" the last time he struck it rich, but he lived with his mother since being evicted from an apartment he was forced into after half-incinerating his own house as host of a "drunken barbeque." The label that Dre abandoned for Death Row had blockaded his earnings until agreeable terms of disengagement were struck. His previous year's royalties of $690,000 by then no more than a spotty paper trail, "the most successful rap producer in the industry" had subsisted on "chicken wings and McDonald's" while waiting most of a year for the weather to break.[3]

Andre Young was old enough to have taken the honorific "Dr." as a teenager in Compton when Julius Erving still had cultural currency with the young. He was sixteen when "it's like a jungle sometimes" was the street's beating pulse. Grandmaster Flash's was the earliest voice of true-life existential reality that was heard by the hip-hop nation's original citizens, and it jolted into many like Dre their first conscious idea of music as an authentic expression of collective identity.

The democratization of sound and recording technology had been the age of disco's enfranchising gift to kids growing up like Dre. In the mid-1970s technology began to migrate from the exclusive province of audio engineers through the dance clubs into the underdeveloped country of the street, which—out of want and necessity—took such of those formerly arcane tools as they could acquire and converted them to their own ingenious and unorthodox uses.

What began as a way of using turntable techniques associated with radio production—like segueing—to make dance records last longer in the discotheque, evolved quickly into a new métier, whose practitioners used the output of what the music industry had always considered its "talent"—singers, musicians, songwriters, arrangers, producers— merely as raw material for their own craft. Records were pried open, pulled apart, and pieces of others inserted; the effect was patchwork without seams or evident stitchery, a new and different whole fabricated from entirely independent parts.

At sixteen Dre enrolled in his neighborhood's apprentice class of mobile deejays (street vendors of the disco trade) who spun records into dance mixes on the homeliest occasions (block parties, cabaret nights, house parties, school events) in the nooks and crannies (parks, school-yards, rec centers, small clubs) of ghetto social life. New York's hip-hop pioneers had been young men like these, who might have been on the radio if their dreams had come true, or spinning records in joints if any would have had them. Instead they patched together their own equipment and outfitted trucks and vans.

"The hip-hop itself started in the Bronx," according to Afrika Bambaataa, one of its acknowledged founding fathers:

> comin' from Kool DJ Herc. Now, you had DJs before him that used to come out, but they was playin' like disco music. He the one that brought the whole concept of playin' beats, and playin' that little certain part of the record, and doin' some talk over it.[4]

In the late mid-1970s the pulse running through America's young and black throbbed in the cadence of "we need the funk, gotta have that funk." Even the throwaway noise that attends "cueing up" a record to prepare it to be played was made useful as a source of rhythm—the process called "scratching." Even spoken words were enlisted into the service of percussion. The street broke down what the technicians made, stripping records to the "beats" at their naked cores, these to reclaim for use as the building material of reconstructed rhythms.

Its methods eventually allowed for the creation of soundtracks assembled from such components as rhythm-box burble, snippets of stolen riff or purloined hook, and four-second fragments of appropriated bass lines, chopped up so small as to be no more than a blip of an echo of something remembered, then laid end to end in sequences programmed by computers: a process called "sampling." Mechanical samplers capture and record sounds as pieces of digital information. Arrayed and recorded, they are then manipulated by other machines called sequencers, which arrange them in any way wanted. Many such previously advanced capacities had devolved into the inventories of mass-marketers of consumer electronics.

This made it possible to deconstruct all of recorded boogaloo history into scraps of sound for everyday use in the making of some new thing from something else no longer identifiable as what it used to be. Just as elements of many newspapers are conjoined to become a shopping bag, the music of James Brown—not often in a recording studio in those days—was still integral to records selling in the millions, and nobody would know but the plunderers of his work and a few copyright lawyers.

By the mid-1980s Andre Young had gotten good enough at this trade to join the World Class Kru, a loose alliance of vinyl-slingers who were proficient at making the "high-tempo techo-pop" dance mixes favored by Los Angeles club-goers. In back of the rising crest of rap's first popular wave, corporate trawlers were casting wide nets for approximators of the on-screen attractions drawing teenage droves to *Beat Street* and *Krush Groove*. Even the World Class Wreckin' Cru had a production deal with CBS. But Dre was an uneasy traveler on the path leading in the direction of Will Smith and MC Hammer, and he turned away.

Rap requires its best performers to be able to do at least one of two things—"kick game" or "drop knowledge"; the most skilled can both entertain and inform, and a few original talents can do both at the same time. Within a decade of its advent hip-hop had become boogaloo's predominant form. By then its extollers were proclaiming it a youth movement, as enthusiasts in another era had of rock and roll.

They believed that rap music was bringing the races together and would teach black children about their culture and history. Indeed, more than a third of several dozen black children interviewed in 1990 by the *Boston Globe* had never heard of Malcolm X before they listened to Public Enemy. Hip-hop, some would say, was "young black America's television screen."

But for those who could remember what black radio sounded like before its proprietors dared even to hope that enough white people might be induced to listen to allow them to raise their advertising rates, rap music seemed less like television than alternative radio: a mutated medium, subscription-programmed for a nation of the young and the black, broadcast on spools of cassette tape, where everything on the air was meant to be danced to and the commercials were people advertising themselves.

The hip-hop nation's first heartbeat emanated from New York. For much of the decade after rap became an article of cultural commerce, most of its personalities, commodifiers, and compelling voices were located there. While most hip-hop music was—is—not about much else but "the pussy, the money, and the mic[rophone]," the most respected of the New York school of rap performers tended to be more cerebral and high-minded and think of themselves as messengers and "righteous teachers." One of them—in authoring an entertainment intended as mordant social commentary—had pioneered gangster rap.

In 1986 Boogie Down Productions released an album called *Criminal Minded* that featured an iconic representation by Chris (KRS-One) Parker of a murderous street-corner drug-dealer, in a slice-of-life drama called "My 9-mm Goes Bang." His character was fabulized from the observed world of young laborers in the Bronx's booming cocaine economy, a caste of adolescents so inured to being denied the substance of what they have been told to want that they consume their lives chasing after its shadows.

Early in the same decade that hip-hop sprang from New York's streets, children became a retail sales force in the city's dope trade, as an unintended effect of the so-called Rockefeller drug laws. These required adults convicted of selling narcotics be given mandatory sentences of a severity meant to be daunting. Because children are generally more focused, callous, less considerate of risk, and more congenial to discipline than grown-ups, they are well adapted to working the dope stroll, a name for all places there is street traffic in heroin and cocaine. Within a couple of years stories began to surface, beyond the neighborhoods in which they lived and worked, about black and Hispanic boys buying German cars with cash clotted up so thick, they had to bend over to take it out, and playing ball in the park for hundreds of dollars a game.

The Nixon administration's campaign to stop the importation of Mexican marijuana was the only interdiction policy in recent history to work, at least enough to make dearer the staple commodity of America's drug culture. At about the same time cocaine, which had been a specialty drug, regularly used by the well-to-do underground but for most others an indulgence for special occasions, crossed over onto college campuses and spread from there into the American mainstream.

Once that happened, its price immediately doubled. The basic equation of dope economics changed; cocaine was easier to smuggle than marijuana and became more profitable. A huge American market developed for cocaine, exclusively controlled by a cartel whose proprietors in Colombia had figured out how to bypass the industry's traditional networks when they moved and sold their goods. By the mid-1970s a major transshipment artery ran through the Caribbean.

Miami had become a flourishing Latin outpost on the mainland of North America. Ironically, immigration reforms that had been enacted to scant public notice during the Great Society's tumultuous heyday did more to shape the evolving nature of urban Aframerica than all of that era's ballyhooed social legislation. In cities throughout the Northeast first Cubans, then Dominicans, moved into and around black neighborhoods, to become foot soldiers and shopkeepers for the oligarchy of Colombians who held the monopoly on the runaway American cocaine commerce, worth by 1986, according to a presidential commission's best guess, more than $50 billion a year.[5]

During the 1970s Jamaicans brought their model of criminal enterprise to urban Aframerica: posses—organized, violent, and centered on guns and drugs. They spilled over from the slum districts of Kingston called Trenchtown, Concrete Jungle, and the Gully. Street gangs were armed by politicos contesting the island's vicious electoral wars of the early 1970s, and were used as instruments of state-sanctioned crime during the regime of Edward Seaga, the antidote to socialism prescribed and administered by America's attending cold warriors.

Jamaican outlaw culture was steeped in American movies; musicians and badmen often chose public identification as namesakes of such as Clint Eastwood and Jim Brown. The introduction of cocaine and automatic weapons updated the theatrical style of Kingston's murderous gunplay from cowboy to "Scarface" and Rambo. Commonplace carnage rose to the level of butchery in the political season of 1980, the so-called "reign of [Seaga's] wall-eyed gunmen."

In the 1980s a tenth of Jamaica's population migrated to America. Brooklyn became home to more Jamaicans than Kingston, including its transplanted gangster tribes, who were soon occupied in moving drugs and guns up from Miami into cities along the East Coast. They trafficked so heavily along Interstate 95 that a composite image of Jamaican smugglers was stamped into the original mold for the racial profile that became a staple of highway policing in fourteen states. Their arrival as a presence in urban Aframerica converged with the explosive growth of its street trade in smokable cocaine.

Toward the middle of the decade, after almost fifteen years of unabated growth, cocaine prices responded to a glutted market by declining sharply and suddenly. This circumstance had been forestalled for a while by the introduction of a process for smoking cocaine called freebasing, which involved distilling away by homely chemistry the adulterants in powdered cocaine and smoking what was left—a paste rendered nearly pure—once it dried. The effects of freebasing are intense, short-lived, and for many, relentlessly compelling. Its practice requires consumers to buy much more cocaine and to use it up more quickly.

Still the cartel overproduced, and—to expand the market to fit the supply—needed a way to get its product into the hands of customers whose pockets held only five or ten dollars at a time. This was crack, which from a merchandising standpoint was nothing more than "new and improved" freebase: already processed, ready to smoke, packaged, marketed as never before, and made as available to its consumers as a two-pound box of sugar at the corner store.

According to the Drug Enforcement Administration, the price of a kilogram of pure cocaine in New York City fell from $100,000 in 1980 to $16,000 by 1988. This price deflation made it easier, in communities where drugs were economically important, for local entrepreneurs to become major employers of neighborhood youth. When CBS News reported in June 1990 that 48 percent of young black males in New York were unemployed, it didn't know to point out that many who were without jobs were not without work.

Running a street-drug franchise has much in common with owning a small supermarket; proprietors share in maintaining an orderly, stable environment in which to do business. Outlaws have to do their own policing, either by violence or by the threat of it regularly applied to poachers, to associates who are persistently irresponsible, and every so often to ordinary citizens who don't get out of the way.

Armaments are a natural accoutrement to the dope stroll, where patches of concrete on which to sell are as valuable and as jostled-for as department-store floor space. Its young sales clerks—being creatures of fashion—made the 9-millimeter pistol's identity as the "drug dealer's favorite weapon" a law enforcement cliché in the mid-1980s, and—since only athletes had as much regard from peers—established the gun as a high-status lifestyle accessory among the trendy adolescent herd.

In 1986 enough young men died to depress the average life expectancy of the Aframerican population as a whole. Homicide had become the leading cause of death for black males between the ages of fifteen and twenty-four. Their rate of dying had increased by 67 percent in four years and now was six times greater than for other Americans the same age. Ninety-five percent of all the killings that accumulated into this statistic were attributable to guns. Youngboys said that in cities in those days it was just live and let die.

Bootleg small-arms distributorships flourished in such an environment. In October 1987 the Bureau of Alcohol, Firearms and Tobacco aimed "Operation Rum Punch" at Jamaican posses, fanning out to lock up 124 in their putative ranks who were linked variously to 625 drug-related killings in New York, Miami, Boston, Philadelphia, Washington, D.C., Cleveland, Detroit, Kansas City, Dallas, Denver, and Los Angeles.[6] But apart from making more deadly the ways and means of local criminal enterprise, wherever Jamaicans were concentrated—and particularly in New York—they impressed themselves into the fabric of Aframerican street life and style.

The imagistic vividry, epithetical bombast, and syncopated flow of the Jamaican tongue seeped into hip-hop's New York roots system. If KRS-One's tale was textured by contemporaneous Bronx street legends embroidered from crimes attributable to the Shower—a drug-slinging posse so-called because it "rained" bullets on enemies—the very form and method of its telling had originated with young men often caught in aural drenches of Jamaican rhythm-talking over bare-bones instrumental dance music whenever they passed through the permeable walls of sound attaching to their neighborhood record shops twelve hours of every day.

Criminal Minded engendered a hip-hop genre of true-crime pulp fiction, and the industrialization of street chic was on. Quickly, next out the box came Schoolly D's apocryphal tales of the gang of Philadelphia "corner boys" called Parkside Killers. "I grew up around gang wars," the ex–shoe salesman said, reacting to criticism of his piece's luridness. "If Rambo can tell a story . . . and Dirty Harry . . . why can't I tell [mine]?"[7]

No city had a more highly elaborated culture of violent criminality among its young than Los Angeles. From there the rapper Ice-T soon emerged with a back-storied identity as a gang warrior graduated into player, who'd traded in the "bang and hustle" of street enterprise for the "big game," by transposing his "crime posse" into a "rhyme posse." He was a skilled miniaturist of action scenarios—three-minute "automatic Uzi motherfucking bloodbaths"—that seemed both to update and to recall the gangster film and radio melodramas of the 1930s and 1940s: "I grabbed my AK[-47], my 16[-mm], my baby Mac [10], threw a 9[-mm] in the small of my back; Twelve o'clock midnight, posse was airtight, twenty-five cars under the street light. . . . cars hit the corner like a long black snake, just looking for a life to take . . . then we spot him, Evil E shot him, dead in the face to make sure we got him."

If many young in Ice-T's wide audience of young black males were settled in their conviction that they were society's permanent outsiders, more than a few determined to become the most American outsiders they knew of: gangsters, our national urban outlaw archetype. Newly pointed in this direction, Dr. Dre teamed up with a neighbor, Eric (Eazy-E) Wright, to form a group called N.W.A., an acronym for Niggaz With Attitude. In 1988 Dre produced an album of theirs called *Straight Outta Compton*, which evoked its locality as a war zone peppered with nightly sprays of automatic-rifle fire, background scenery for characters who were dangerous enough to cow women and taunt police whenever they went prowling.

In particular, a "song" entitled "F___ Tha Police" not only brought Dre into the fawning embrace of elements in Compton he'd slunk out of the way of in high school corridors, but pricked up young white ears that were instinctively drawn by the sounds of raging at authority into the headier pleasures of a theme-park ride through a pop-up gallery of larger-than-life representations of fierce ghetto wildlife. Once again, as they had for Little Richard and Alan Freed, denunciatory law enforcers provided the best kind of advertising. Overnight N.W.A. got famous for being objectionable, and *Straight Outta Compton* sold two million copies.

Its vocal star was O'Shea Jackson, son of a landscaper and library clerk. In "Ice Cube" Jackson conceived a hoodlum-poet persona of such authority that his voicings of experiences, perceptions, attitudes, and violent fantasies common to those of the dark, feral figures in over-size clothes seen on television striking poses for news cameras at murder scenes in attitudes meant to suggest they wanted to enter the popular imagination as militant thugs who expected nothing more from American society than what they could take:

> Word, yo, but who the fuck is heard
> It's time to take a trip to the suburbs
> Let 'em see a nigga invasion
> Point blank on a Caucasian
> Cock the hammer and crack a smile
> "Take me to your house, pal."[8]

A quarter-century after less incendiary rhetoric had gotten H. Rap Brown indicted in Maryland for inciting to riot, Ice Cube's merely befitted a celebrity endorser of St. Ives Malt Liquor. The makers of this brand of fortified beer found a lucrative niche in the underground consumer market comprising the latest and noisiest descendants of that original class of "masterless men" whose presence in cities of the Reconstructed South had outraged white and unnerved Negro society.

And so, to persuade present-day city-dwelling young black males to abandon the fashion of Olde English 800, they employed hucksters paid to know of Ice Cube's value as an authenticator of the "lifestyle choices" of self-identified "niggaz." A greater stake in this micro-economy was worth contesting a dominant rival for, inasmuch as dope-stroll commerce kept more discretionary income churning in the streets of Aframerica than Lyndon Johnson ever had.

The narcotics trade's young retail sales force learns about the power of commodities over people. For the right stuff their adult customers will mutter and suck teeth but will still obey when told to stand here, wait over there, "come correct or get the fuck on." The dope stroll's junior enterprisers disdain equally the use of their own product and anyone who cannot. But then they are scarcely unique in selling what has power over other people to buy what has power over them: clothes, cars, gold, Hennessy cognac, or "hydro" weed—whatever is supposed to be "dope" at the time.

There is little they can see of a culture disclosed to them through their small window on the world that doesn't suggest that the value of a human being is measured by the value of what he can consume. This descendant class of the old-country's first "masterless men" has bound itself over into a volunteer slavery to brand names.

Ice Cube left N.W.A. in the wake of *Straight Outta Compton,* crying foul over money. On his own, Cube did so well at seeming an authentic embodiment of the caste consciousness of those young black males whom George Will said were "rebarbarizing" America's cities that O'Shea Jackson's would soon become the human face of *gang-related* on shopping-mall America's movie screens. By then the country was starting to keep twice as many citizens in jail as it had before 1985, and blacks were six times more likely than whites to be among them.

In 1990 Ice Cube's album *AmeriKKKa's Most Wanted* contained a short monologue spoken in the voice of a white female newscaster bearing down on the close of her nightly broadcast:

> At the bottom of our news tonight, there's been a new animal aimed in the direction of falling off the face of the earth. Yes, young black teenagers are reported to be the oldest and newest creatures added to the endangered species list. As of now, the government has not taken steps to protect the young blacks. When asked why, a top law official replied, "Because they make good game."[9]

The ensuing decade saw the rise of law-enforcement television—documentary cops-on-patrol and criminals-brought-to-justice shows—as mass entertainment. Dark, grainy videotapes of black and brown perpetrators scampering out of stolen cars or being handcuffed face-down on concrete, and "perp walks" writ large—lurid crime reenactments, full-screen mugshots of glowering thugs, leg-ironed predicate felons in Day-Glo jail garb shuffling into court—became a habit of millions of Americans' leisure. The widest-spread of the "reality" cop shows rolled its closing credits over a jumpy montage of faceless ghetto youth in stages of capture, while a Jamaican-sung reggae tune called "Bad Boys" played in the background.

In the 1990s almost a third of the prime-of-life black male population was imprisoned, paroled, or on probation. Of locked-up Americans who were younger than nineteen, blacks—15 percent of that age group as a whole—comprised nearly half. As the 1990s were a boom time for commodifiers of black youth culture, by end of decade "jailhouse chic" was being marketed by an "urbanwear" subsidiary of Perry Ellis, and chain stores on the West Coast were retailing the Oregon Department of Corrections' line of convict-made apparel, brand-named Prison Blues.[10]

If public exclamations of official America's disapproval paved the studio gangsters' way into the earphones of white children, then steadily piping street dramaturgy into suburban family rooms on MTV had the effect of a subliminal advertising campaign for the prison-industrial complex. In the last century's latter two decades, the number of state prisons doubled, and their inmate populations increased by 75 percent. While the overall prison population has quadrupled since 1980, the number of jailed drug offenders—mostly nonwhite—has increased twelvefold.[11]

Currently, more than $40 billion a year is spent to keep people in state and federal penitentiaries. Incarceration has become rural America's only growth industry. Texas and Virginia built so many jail cells that they became landlords, renting excess capacity at a profit to other states that had more prisoners than they could house. The value of a typical body in government custody—$23,000 a year in the average state, more in the federal system—exceeds his worth on the labor market.[12]

When Ice Cube left N.W.A. crying foul over money, his defection left Eazy-E no shortage of available materials for Dre to fashion into salable goods. In common with Art Rupe and the Bihari Brothers of Los Angeles forty years past, they were knee-deep in found objects to package. The price of admission to the rap game is cheaper for those who aspire to play in it than for any other performing art, payable in coin more common than discipline or talent. For most, the entrance requirements are a modicum of verbal facility and the will to self-proclaim. Moreover, by the industry's conventional standards, producing rap records was relatively free of overhead. High-enough-quality demonstration tapes could be made in poor kids' basements. No form of commercial music ever cost as little to make. Local hip-hop cottage industries mushroomed across the American cityscape.

A layer-down of "beats" with Dre's deftness of touch and a record label hookup would draw around him like bees to honey a swarm of aspirants with stories ready to set to music. One such was Tracy Curry—stage-named the D.O.C.—who'd followed Dre home from Dallas after meeting and impressing him when N.W.A. came through town. Curry slept on Dre's living-room floor until his debut album sold half a million copies within a month of its release.[13] As an overnight ghetto celebrity with a falsely advertised thug résumé, the teenaged D.O.C.—for whom stardom without display was unthinkable—found himself in need of the bodyguarding services of Marion Knight.

This toehold inside Dre's circle would provide traction enough for Suge to get the necessary footing to wedge himself between Eric Wright and a black youth-market franchise as golden as McDonald's arches. Dre may have been like Midas in the studio, but Eazy held title to the consequent bounty. Their professional association had begun with Dre working off a nine-hundred-dollar debt, and even though he was the impetus for starting Eazy's label, he remained its hired hand, as much a contract producer at Ruthless Records as any ever were at Motown.

Hip-hop had reopened music commerce to street entrepreneurs, and grassroots record production cropped up more abundantly than it had for twenty years. But unlike start-ups of the past, these "independents" had umbilical corporate ties. Not since the 1950s had music come directly from the streets into such widespread popularity among white teenagers. This time, with an exponentially richer youth market at stake, the industrial oligarchs were hawkish in overseeing their claims on profits from the boogaloo trade.

Because hip-hop money had a disreputable taint, a pillar of international trade like Sony (CBS) would subcontract with an Eric Wright to supply it with a line of coarse but profitable goods to market under cover of a "custom" label. A Death Row associate once observed of its corporate overlord that "Time Warner [came] around to collect their money and check on their prostitutes in the darkness of night." To the lawyerly Gerald Levin—an executor of the aggregated industrial legacies of Henry Luce, Jack Warner, Ted Turner, and Steve Ross—his business partner once-removed, Suge Knight, would seem almost as unsavory as a distributor of pornography or an owner of strip clubs.

For the hip-hop entrepreneur, control of a talent source, the means to exploit it, and some rudimentary lawyering were enough for licensure to operate a stall in a multibillion-dollar marketplace. This gave him much in common with other species of hustlers trying to become players in the dope and sex trades.

According to the classification system applied by street taxonomers of an older school, Suge Knight's markings and traits identified him as a "gorilla pimp"—defined by Iceberg Slim as "all muscle, no brains." His method of break-and-entry into the music business would be aggressive and unsubtle: hijacking assets while dubiously camouflaged in as much legitimacy-by-association as he could appropriate from a succession of more respectable partners of convenience.

Knight wormed himself through Dre's ear into his confidence and thereby gained sway within the hit-maker's circle of protégés, whose debut albums all had sold at least half a million copies. Like a jailhouse predator, Suge's game was sharpest at convincing tender recruits that he was their true friend and protector in an institutional jungle. Appointing himself Dre's cudgel, Knight started to batter on Ruthless Records with the intent to break contracts. Eazy's money man Jerry Heller was terrified.[14]

The intercourse between global entertainment conglomerates and street entrepreneurs was accomplished through a prophylactic layer of lawyers and accountants. They were attached to "talent" and its commodifiers as agents and business managers, composing the white face their cleintele presented as a necessary reassurance to corporate bureaucrats, civil authorities, and bankers.

Heller, the business manager of Ruthless Records, was an agent who'd gotten fat handling upper-middle-class rock stars before hooking into Eric Wright, an unschooled gherri-curled kid from Compton in possession of a cash machine who needed to set up and carry on a legitimate business. A few theatrical displays of threat by Knight's Piru Street Players drove Heller scampering to ground in his suburban tract mansion guarded around the clock by a private security force. Suge responded to this show of softness by increasing his demand of Ruthless Records from mere royalty payments to the full surrender of contractual rights to Dre and four of his acts.

Knight had enlisted a third conspirator in the plot to free Andre Young, a party who had sufficient property to afford a record company-in-waiting an entire floor of space in his own office tower. Dick Griffey was a hustler of Suge's parental generation who'd parlayed clubs, concert promotion, and Don Cornelius's *Soul Train* franchise into Solar Records, black Los Angeles's biggest-ever homegrown music enterprise. His experience only deepened Griffey's appreciation of the value of the asset that Knight was trying to steal.

With the brand of boogaloo long defunct that once had made his small fortune, Griffey saw in Dre a basis for Solar's renewal. He had the same deal with Sony as Eazy did, and a longer relationship. If Suge's grip on Dre held fast through this unfolding grab-and-snatch, Griffey expected to step into Eazy's vacated seat on the backroom trading floor where money and hip-hop commodities passed between the street and international corporations. He was sure Sony would as soon traffic with one procurer of Dre's services as another.

Sony's lawyers drafted the papers releasing Dre and several others from their obligations to Ruthless Records. Suge is said to have extorted Eazy's signature at the head of a phalanx of henchmen brandishing lead pipes. Sony was indifferent to untidy particulars. Eric Wright could no longer deliver Dre, and apparently Knight and Griffey could. The moment after faxes of those signed releases came over the wire, Sony began arranging to underwrite a new Dre franchise—named Futureshock Records for a favorite P-Funk song—that would be run by Suge Knight and marketed through Dick Griffey. The agents of empire who attended these negotiations reported that Mr. Knight seemed throughout as amiable as a "teddy bear."[15]

Ruthless sued with a vengeance, its court filings sharp and raw as a street-crime victim's public wail. A complicitous bystander, Sony ducked away from the scene, slipping the accused racketeers half a million dollars of please-keep-us-in-mind by the speculative purchase of an uncharted parcel of Dre's intellectual property. With Dre enjoined from working and prospective corporate financing in abeyance, without wherewithal to make records or pay the starry-eyed novices who labored over demonstration tapes and subsisted on charitable donations of cannabis and Popeye's chicken, Knight nevertheless kept production humming at his shadow company on the third floor of the Solar Building.

He had a stable of recording talent on layaway, bound up in the Gordyan double knot of moonspun "family" ties and management contracts as hard to break as steel wire. He had as his partner the hottest young product designer in the boogaloo industry. But without the resources to convert his holdings of raw material into finished consumer goods, he was stymied.

Knight's faith in Dick Griffey's enabling capacity had about soured when a white man presented himself who was versed in the connivances by which dirty cash became seed money and operating capital for clean ventures. The attorney David Kenner had a criminal client named Michael Harris who had, in the course of becoming an imprisoned don of the black Los Angeles underworld, diverted ill-gotten gains into several legitimate businesses. Among them was a small record company called Death Row, which he ran through his wife from a pay phone in the Metropolitan Detention Center. Kenner brokered a deal that Harris believed had made him Knight's equal partner in Godfather Entertainment—the parent of Death Row, which Suge was to operate with $1.5 million of the cocaine merchant's laundered profits.[16]

After Kenner finished playing three-card monte with shell corporations, Death Row ended up the subsidiary of a tiny firm of which he was chairman, Knight the CEO, and Michael Harris unaware. In late February 1992 Death Row Records was expensively launch-partied at

Chasen's, the landmark of old Hollywood in Beverly Hills. By arrangement of a rented publicist, its advent was heralded in the trade press. But for most of the year that followed, Death Row never got up and running. Only big money from one of a handful of sources could buy Dre's way clear of his contractual tangle, and none was forthcoming.

At the time the industrial oligarchs were in recoil from another flurry of backlashings that cultural antimiscegenists had whipped up against gangster rap. Once again a virulent new strain of "jungle music" had spread to a large unintended audience of young white males and bestirred antibodies in the official culture into defensive attack.

Not since N.W.A. had politicians howled as they lately did over "Cop Killer," the Ice-T production some deemed an affront to public order more egregious even than the recent offenses to public decency committed by 2 Live Crew. The corporate parent of Ice-T's company professed shock and dismay that even an arm's-length business associate would traffic in such sordid goods, then called a press conference to announce that its lowlife step-relation had been kicked out of the house.

The conglomerators were scurrying to appease license approvers, corporate taxers, regulators of cable franchises, and potential disturbers of future mergers and acquisitions, with public sacrifices of unclean profits from their ghetto trading outposts. In such a penitent season Dre's open embrace of disreputability hadn't helped his cause. He'd strutted with shotguns in music videos and fondled a pistol on the cover of a magazine. He got locked up in New Orleans for brawling at a trade convention. He'd been subject to house arrest in California. He consorted with hoodlums.

While this heat wave of official scrutiny lasted, a flagrant propensity for lawlessness would make even so surefire a commercial prospect as the recent producer of seven million-selling albums too hot for the publicly held to handle. So while demand soared for the hip-hop variety of which his was the leading brand, Dr. Dre was forced to spend 1992 as Andre Young, like a penny waiting for change.

For his part, Dre's notorious company-keeper Suge Knight was acting the boulevardier on the street of dreams. Unsupported but by guile, bluster, and his contested claim on Dre's future, Knight was conspicuously romancing already-spoken-for desirable talent. While he pitched superior designs for wish fulfillment to the impatient and insufficiently gratified, Knight was also determining to clear his own thwarted path of Dick Griffey, who—once Sony slid out of grasp—had ceased being a convenient partner.

Toward the end of 1992 Dre and Suge finally found a backer to break their disabling legal impasse. Interscope Records was the $30-million joint venture of Time Warner and Ted Fields, the gone-Hollywood heir to a mercantile fortune. The accommodation they struck would allow Death Row to release Dre's output without disturbing existing property rights. In effect, Interscope rented Dre from Ruthless Records, which received as payment a percentage of the sales of anything he produced. If Dre were ever to stop making goods that Interscope distributed, claim on his services would revert to Ruthless. Income from the Dr. Dre franchise would be split six ways.[17] Plenty to go around was more than enough to fight over.

Within weeks of Interscope's catalytic agency, a *Chronic* boom had lifted the unsanitary cloud over Death Row. The rehabilitating effects of a triple-platinum album improved a menace to society into a cultural phenomenon. On the day of its release David Kenner filed incorporation papers for Death Row Records that designated Andre Young and Marion Knight as sole directors and excluded Dick Griffey and Michael Harris from mention.[18]

By the end of *The Chronic*'s eight-month selling season, Dre was restored to ersatz French colonial domestic splendor in the San Fernando Valley. In the immediate glow of his nouveau n[egro] richesse, Knight's exuberant self-regard had him imagining he was a young Gordy for modern times. At his new offices on Wilshire Boulevard Suge was the engaged record executive, "choosing artwork and promotional materials, picking out singles and B sides, casting directors and female extras for videos, deciding where parties would be held, composing guest lists, and telling artists what to wear."[19]

But nothing so emboldens a reckless public man as having been the object of an official censure that was nullified in effect by the popular will. Once he was shown that demand for the product he sold was stronger than the government's capacity to suppress it, Suge comported himself with the swagger of a vice lord marking every corner of newly claimed territory with showy sprays of violence.

He throttled a nightclub bouncer who gave offense and an Interscope promotion man who'd given too little satisfaction. His attendant squad of jailhouse irregulars administered savage discipline to exemplary unfortunates who happened to cross a Knight mood or purpose. Knight's testosterone surged apace with hip-hop's fast-rising gangster tide. "All these n[egroes] in the record business is bitches," he sneered. "We fittin' a blow up and all these other little punk-ass n[egroes]ain't shit."[20]

Though they were partners, Suge and Dre kept separate company and quarters. Dre abandoned Wilshire Boulevard to Knight's crowd, setting up shop in a succession of rented recording studios with his coterie of talent and its hangers-on. Owing to the relentless, surly churn kicked up by Dre's boistrous crew, this series of abridged tenancies would number as many as nine. Near the last of 1993 the real estate of Death Row Records was in Tarzana, where Dre was closeted with "thirty-five or thirty-six reels" of tape, putting the shine in his next star. "[T]he tracks that I'm doing . . . right now," he proclaimed, "are the future of the funk."[21]

Billed as Snoop Doggy Dogg, sleepy-eyed, ferret-faced Calvin Broadus had debuted triumphantly on *The Chronic,* and Dre was preparing his grand coming-out. Studio gangsterism was now in high season, and by the rap industry's prevailing standards Snoop's purported two-year hitch in a Long Beach chapter of the Rolling 20 Crips and year in jail made him the equivalent of young John Dillinger. Snoop was a hand-to-hand salesman of crack cocaine, an occupation that was congenial to someone more natively inclined toward duck-and-dodge than cut-and-shoot.

To protect himself from shank and fist, a prison inmate like Snoop would sharpen his bardic skills rather than metal. In the street's taxonomy he was properly classified not as a thug but as a hustler, albeit of the commonest species whose treadmill existence in the outlaw trades makes an unintended irony of their self-identifying use of the term. But in a visual age Snoop had the street-greasy look of feral youth so prized in the fast-growing export market for exotic ghetto fauna.

After televised radio took hold in the early 1980s, records were promoted to young customers as soundtracks of short films meant to illustrate a song's theme, mood, attitude, or story line and to display its renderers in alluring poses, roles and settings. Music videos were the hybrid cross of television commercials and movies, and enabled recording artists to simultaneously perform as actors, fashion models, and product endorsers. Once the efficacy of video radio as a marketing tool became evident, more was spent on bigger, glossier productions. MTV quickly superseded Top Forty radio as the music industry's preferred medium for advertising pop merchandise.

A video in "heavy rotation" on MTV would make the faces of its featured players as familiar to suburban teenagers for several weeks as those of characters on situation-comedy shows in syndicated reruns. In their first such exposure to Snoop, white kids saw danger's smooth and cunning face digitally transmogrified into a cartoon Doberman's, ahead of a pack of marauding dogs that overruns a quiet group of picnickers in a public park. This allusion to real-life "wilding" that ghetto "boyz" made in the visual idiom of child's play tempered its evocative chill into a shiver of titillation. "[W]e made a million dollars off that . . . video," Suge Knight would later chortle to one of its makers.

These barbarians at suburbia's gates were cartoon sidekicks of an action hero who struck sinister poses and dark attitudes but identified himself with another cartoon character whose iconic benignity was a universal element of American childhoods, a sinew of basic human connection. Menace disarmed was as much Snoop Doggy Dogg's stock-in-trade as it had been Muhammad Ali's or must be for any black and affirmatively male transracial star of American popular culture.

Sam Cooke had once relied on his radiant public likability to reassure skittish middle Americans of the wholesomeness of his attentions to their daughters. Nearly forty years later Snoop's subtler manifestations of the same attribute reassured their grandsons that vicarious thrill-seekers were welcome to visit his Dogg Pound pavilion inside the theme park of unwholesomeness called Thug World.

On native ground Snoop's inviting public qualities were subject to other interpretations. Wherever the studio gangster must regularly be seen lest he appear inauthentic, a self-proclaiming bad man's life and art are prone to conflate. The custom-outfitted Lincoln Navigators, diamond-encrusted Rolex watches, and golden-roped neckware that are the flaunted wages of his falsely advertised badness collect particles of resentment and static in the street as inevitably as a velvet pant leg picks up dust and lint from its brushes with carpet and couch.

Late in the summer of 1993 Snoop's bodyguard killed a young hanger-about in the Palms section of Los Angeles, who—aspiring to a breakthrough performance in the major motion picture of his own life—had opened fire on their Jeep Cherokee, pursuant to a point of honor left dangling from an earlier confrontation he'd provoked with another of the vehicle's passengers. Though he darted for cover at the first sound of a gun's report, as Snoop Doggy Dogg prepared for his scheduled grand opening right before Thanksgiving, Calvin Broadus faced a murder trial.[22]

The attendant notoriety was good for business. Within a week of its release *Doggystyle* sold 800,000 copies. Snoop's introductory "What's My Name" video with the eye-catching cartoon hook was a sensation on the nation's basic-cable stations, an indisputable factor in the album's sales spiraling upward of four million. But then, *Doggystyle* was just the latest and loudest confirming evidence of Dre's salience in black music commerce. He'd already proven to be as ingenious a fabricator of raw boogaloo into the stuff of popular fashion as any ever were.

Film directors often have said that the trick of their trade is casting, and the producer of Death Row's first pop star was astute in his matching of performer to vehicle. Dre's approach to refining uncut funk into consumer goods with mass appeal was to mellowize without compromise. Snoop's basal groove was top-down convertible, not like Ice Cube's drive-by-shooting-styled rat-a-tat-tat. His sinuous flow emitted in a cadenced stream of vestigial old-country drawl that would soften a lyric's nasty edge. Snoop Doggy Dogg bespoke southern California as plainly as the Beach Boys had.

The facet of Snoop's persona that caught and reflected glint from the street's sunny side accented Dre's designs. Although Andre Young was the seminal stylist of hip-hop's hardcore school, he also had a tune-smith's fine attunement to the sweet sound of a cash-registering hook and, at his fingertips, a universal catalog of the previously created, from which to cut out brilliant snippets to paste into aural collages.

"[Dre]'s a good orchestral conductor," said the manager of one of his artists. "He's best at taking different people's thoughts and putting them together to form something extraordinary."[23] Dre was an assembler of the work of many hands. As many as twenty-six indentured hands—including David Ruffin's namesake son—were tied to Death Row, supplying beats, bass lines, song lyrics, and vocal work for which most never got justly compensated.

Over the years Dre would be accused of taking credits from collaborators as remorselessly as such compulsive looters of intellectual property as Leonard Chess and Morris Levy. But then Death Row was a sweatshop operated according to old-fashioned industrial principles; Suge routinely euchred indigent performers out of royalties and publishing rights and bought others off with jewelry and cars for pennies on the dollar.

After *Doggystyle* hit, a staffer recalled, it was "raining Xmas" on Death Row. The company's share of the shank of the $60 million worth of Death Row products sold during its first two years began pouring in on top of residue from *The Chronic* and millions more of Interscope and Sony's start-up cash. Suge bought houses, cars, boats, jewelry, and a nightclub in Las Vegas before he ever had use of a credit card. On the road he kept a fleet of hired limousines in around-the-clock attendance of his entourage. He was often in those days out prowling on foreign preserves, a bold poacher openly stalking big-name New York talent in plain sight of its lawful claimants.

Suge was looking to expand the scope of Death Row's focus to encompass "R&B," a term the young now applied categorically to boogaloo that was not hip-hop. Though derided as retrograde and soft by the culturally ascendant party of the street, a lively market for harmonizing balladeers persisted among young females, including preteen white girls. The pervasive youngboy singing style was pallid, mannered, and small—a second-generation echo of Donny Hathaway. Two decades after the tormented Hathaway—underlit in life—flung himself out a fifteenth-floor window of the Essex House Hotel in New York, he'd turned out to be the seminal influencer of male vocalizing in boogaloo's modern times.

Since his death twenty years of industrial striving to make perfect records had rounded off edges, blunted emotion, flattened styles, reduced variation, and processed out the shout. Youth's hegemony over the black music marketplace pushed the previous generation's graying classicists off the airwaves into commercial obsolescence, their places partly taken by a downsized junior class of squeal-inducing male crooners and group vocalizers like Jodeci and sultry urban chanteuses like Mary J. Blige, both of whom Suge Knight had eyes for.

Suge's template of seduction called first for establishing position as a broad-shouldered friend in need to the discontented, otherwise-engaged talents he targeted. Jodeci and Blige were obligated to Andre Harrell, a successful young entrepreneur of new-breed boogaloo from New York, and his apprentice-cum-usurper, Sean "Puffy" Combs. Having lately become top-selling brands, both acts felt underpaid. Shortly after announcing that Knight would represent them, both received liberally upgraded contracts.

This was said to have been accomplished by the making of offers that Harrell and Combs couldn't refuse. *Newsweek* reported as rumor-presumed-true that Knight had paid Harrell an "unfriendly visit," and as fact that the CEO of Uptown Records had since been protected day and night by rented Fruits of Islam.[24] The appreciative Blige compared Suge to "that guy in the movies who goes around getting the bad people: Charles Bronson, right?"

Because it was performed on the New York stage, Suge's feat of drop-in godfathering was the talk of the rialto in the world's media capital and the music industry's home office. Within months Knight would be the subject of profiles in *The New Yorker* and *New York Times Magazine*.

Subsequently, his exploits were chronicled in the *Wall Street Journal, Fortune*, and both major newsweeklies, featured on the prime-time magazine shows of two television networks, and breathlessly retailed week by week in the glossy pages of three competing rap music fanzines.

Though he took from it only modest spoils—a management contract with Jodeci—Knight's "terrorizing" of Andre Harrell was a publicity coup. His sphere of commerce was the land of the simulated gangster, wherein every officially circulated rumor of Suge's behavioral authenticity exalted his kingly reputation. Seeking the same effect on other labels' contractees that a pimp means to have on other men's whores when he sweeps into an after-hours spot with one of his lavishly appointed own, Knight bestowed a quarter-million-dollar Lamborghini sports car on Jodeci's producer. By then an accountant-to-the-stars had been brought in from Coopers and Lybrand to mind Death Row's finances, but no institutional barrier erected against Suge's "cop-and-blow" mentality could insulate its accounts from overdrafts.

As hard as Knight was "macking" in the city of industry's native quarters, he was uniformly genial and respectful in his relations with the white men he had to see to get paid. For their part, while Suge's corporate patrons clucked disapprovingly at his profligacy, and blanched at his reputation, so long as the unsightliest of his profitable practices were confined to the hip-hop demimonde, they went unreproached in the pertinent boardrooms of New York and Los Angeles. In those circles Knight was thought of the way Sonny Liston and Don King once were by mobsters in St. Louis and Cleveland: as a strong-arm Negro who kept unruly street Negroes from disrupting white folks' business with the street.

And Death Row was making its silent partners truckloads of money. The combined retail sales of *The Chronic* and *Doggystyle* amounted to $113 million. Within four years Time Warner had realized a $50-million profit on its original $40 million investment in Interscope Records, whose annual sales revenues by then approached $100 million.[25]

14. Ready to Spread

In 1996 the *Washington Post* reported on the talk of an overflow crowd that was waiting hours on line to buy tickets in advance of the local reappearance of George Clinton and the P-Funk All-Stars after more than a decade's leave. A nest of Aframerican cultural sophistication in the late 1960s, D.C. had been a hotbed of Funkadelic cultists even before Parliament's "Chocolate City" became its civic anthem in 1975. Clinton was nowhere more ingrained.

As the *Post*'s correspondent passed among the knots of well-heeled middle-aged black men huddling against midwinter's nocturnal chill, he eavesdropped as an air force colonel heatedly reaffirmed to his scoffing companions—an assistant deputy undersecretary and a trader in municipal bonds—that he had too seen the roof of the Capitol Center open up to admit the Mothership that night twenty years ago when the P-Funk Earth Tour came to town.

When asked once where his idea of "spread[ing] all over the world for the Funk" had come from, Clinton replied, "Ever read *Mumbo Jumbo?*"[1] It fits that Clinton should be a secret sharer of Ishmael Reed's, whose comic masterpiece is a serious novel dressed as cartoon. Just as its hero, the New Orleans hoodooist PaPa LaBas, would have expected, after a series of outbreaks of the chaotic Earth Tour in major American cities, P-Funk "jes' grew."

The Parliaments are remembered dimly from their appearance in

August 1967 at the Apollo Theater as looking like a usual Detroit vocal group in Motown's high season: hair done smartly; one-button "continental" suits that shimmered burnt orange under the spotlights; white shoes, perhaps to match the white-on-white shirt-and-tie ensembles. Onstage they reminded one of the Contours, their "routine" rough and clownish.

The Parliaments were there to perform one song then among black radio's most heard. "(I Wanna) Testify" was a gripping and grunting Detroit dance record, set apart from others by a cheekiness attributable to lyrics that subverted the Motown literary style ("Once I was a hollow man in which a lonely heart did dwell") and bawdrified a church allusion by means of a salacious hook, the testifier's thrice-moaned, "oooh, ooooooh luscious . . . you sure been delicious to me."

The song's writer was George Clinton, a twenty-six-year-old ex-barber from Plainfield, New Jersey, who'd been ten years trying to break into the music business. He'd held the Parliaments together since teenage doo-wop days. When Raynoma Gordy briefly ran a branch office of Jobete Publishing in New York, she'd employed Clinton as a staff writer. A couple of years later he took the Parliaments out to Detroit, boogaloo's Emerald City. They didn't meet Motown's standards but were sufficient to those of the city's able second string.

In the year after "Testify," Revilot Records released several more songs by the Parliaments. They were too scant of melody and too off-beat to be quite commercial, but they bore evidence of the handiwork of a dark and nimble wit. In "All Your Goodies Are Gone" Clinton twisted the hook from a famous contemporary television commercial into "let hurt put you in the loser's seat." In "The Goose That Laid the Golden Egg" he skirted bald lewdness: "I'm as happy as a monkey with a peanut machine . . . but I don't need no nut machine because I'm right now holding you." To the observant, Clinton's was noticeably an uncommon sensibility at work on the edge of boogaloo's classic age.

In the entrepreneurial churn at the street level of the music business, thin-monied pursuers of minor riches in overlooked niches tried catching black teenagers' fancy with dance records cheaply made by enlivening an instrumental track with exhortatory chatter. Most of these records were premised on the idea that dancing was copulation's public stand-in.

A standard dance-record scenario positioned its audience at the shoulder of a voyeur peeping at sex through a keyhole and providing bystanders with descriptive commentary laced with salacious double entendres. These coarse goods were fabricated expressly for sale to black kids. The particularity of their intended appeal made dance records a membrane through which black radio patter and street argot leaked into popular music.

Localized dance cultures flourished in cities, where fashions and outlooks could still be parochial. In 1968, when asked by a television interviewer why, given his evident relish for deadly combat, he didn't enlist in the military and go to Vietnam, a Philadelphia gang warrior replied: "I'd rather die for my corner than die for my country."

Where he was from, a stranger's neighborhood of origin, was discernible from the way he danced. In jitterbug society dancing was required of males, who practiced it as competitive sport. It was as much a "representation" of affiliational pride as flashing gang signs would be twenty years later for the "thug life" generation.

In 1965 a comedic banter-and-dance act from Chicago paused in their habitual scuffle along the local club circuit to make a record called "Boogaloo." In it Tom and Jerrio introduced two phrases—"sock it to me" and "let it all hang out"—that, laundered of their off-color stain in Goldie Hawn's mouth and mongered for a couple of years on America's favorite television show, would become common household items in the early 1970s.

"Boogaloo" was the rare dance record that caught a wave exactly right. When it came out, the boogaloo had already begun spreading like new slang across the nation of black young.

Without music television to expose a standard practice simultaneously to black kids across the country, sometimes Philadelphia "crossfired" instead of "monkeyed," and Chicago "twined" rather than "jerked." Dances done at the same time in essentially the same way all over the jitterbug nation were unusual. Any sifters through the commercial detritus of black music in the mid-1960s would commonly find vinyl artifacts of dances that never caught on or were particular to one place.

The boogaloo moved from city to city as if propagated by ghetto Johnny Appleseeds. Its season lasted most of a year. Tom and Jerrio's record sold close to a million copies, though they profited little from it. Motown, it seemed, had staked the production, and as soon as "Booga- loo" became popular, Gordy claimed the copyright. He sued Tom and Jerrio out of most of the proceeds.

Like Dorsey and Whitaker when they were Famous Hokum Boys, Tom and Jerrio made "Boogaloo" knockoffs for the next three years. The boogaloo was a dance craze of long-felt effects. A year and a half after it began, another record out of Chicago called "Alvin's Boogaloo" got cross-country airplay; a year after that Thomas East of the Fabu- lous Playboys, a band of other locals in a protofunk groove, exulted in the sight of his beloved "doing the African boogaloo."

The boogaloo was called on the roll of dances that James Brown memorialized in "There Was a Time," a major supplier of party fuel during the winter of '68. Nuyoricans of the period who were mixing into local salsa ingredients of soul music named their style of fusion cooking Latin Bugalu.

Some who witnessed have recalled the latter mid-1960s as "days of the boogaloo and shing-a-ling."

If Detroit was a center of refinement then and Philadelphia the dance academy of the jitterbug world, Chicago was its dance-record capital. With a vibrant and specific youth culture and a higher concen- tration of wildcatting black record enterprisers than anyplace else, the city was a portal through which the street could squeeze into the music commerce of a wider world.

In 1965 three kids who sang without polish in a South Side park recorded a self-composed ditty for a Chicago label started by two men who'd driven by one night and happened to hear them. Exuberant and raw, "Michael the Lover" was the jitterbug national anthem of early 1966, a Top Five record on the soul music charts. Black schoolboys walked around with the tune on their breaths, substituting their own names.

The C.O.D.s were a recreation-center edition of the Impressions. Their homely song's stunning appeal for black teenagers lay in its celebratory embrace of street vernacular: "for his rap is strong, with lots of fame / When the girls see him coming they tighten up their game." The record seemed to its audience expressive of an attitude they could authenticate as one of their own.

"Michael the Lover" was adolescent male self-proclaiming masked in the third person, an ancestral form of hip-hop's favorite conceit. It was background music to scenes performed in front of mirrors by mannish boys starring in movies of their own lives, and a processional that their minds played to accompany entrances made into spaces occupied by eligible females.

"Michael" was a jitterbug hero of the first aural cartoon made for black kids, the dashing star of a "perp walk" through a cluster of hard-eyed peers so moved by this "loveliest boy" 's manifesting graces that exclamatory praise broke out as he passed. No one before his creators had used the word *rap* in commercial song lyrics. A slang coinage, *rap* meant "talk" when used as a verb. As a noun it meant "conversation," as in "I got some rap for you." Once it implicitly pertained to transactions between the sexes. Males didn't rap to one another; if anything, they "conversated."

Before the late-1960s fashion in poets of the black vernacular and before the name H. Rap Brown began appearing in print, the word was unwritten except in folios wherein some schoolgirls transcribed meaningful song lyrics, recorded the latest slang expressions, and memorialized the couplings—real or fancied—among members of their social sets. In these casual jottings it was likely spelled *wrap*. Such a rendering accorded with the image of a pursuer "streaming his lines" to envelop and ensnare an intended quarry, a metaphor for courtship.

In a cover story on Brown in 1968 *Time* magazine fingered *rapport* as *rap*'s putative etymological father. This unlikely attribution would seem plausible to middle-aged white men who'd learned of the word from their college-age progeny, who got it third-hand from race-mingling hippies and counterculture politicos, who were promiscuous construers of language they picked up from the street and adapted for secondhand uses.

From the progressive edge and rejectionist fringes of white youth culture, *rap* made its way into the discourse of legitimate society. By the early 1970s it was a coinage in wide circulation. In the heavy hand-to-hand trafficking of any common currency, denotations once sharply drawn are flattened by use into near indistinction.

People aired grievances at "rap sessions," "rapped" about big ideas, or dropped by friends' places to "rap." By then its uses were also broader on native tongues; *rap* became interchangeable with *speak*, as in "rap to the core!" the street equivalent of a church deacon's affirming cry of "preach" or "teach" at flourishes of pastorial eloquence.

As a noun *rap* was applied as freely to formal speech as to conversation. It could deliver three freight-loads of meaning in the single conveyance of a spoken syllable. "His rap is strong" was at once an appraisal of a performance, a faculty, and a body of work.

Two years after "Michael" street spirit was running high; ghetto had by then replaced plantation as the central metaphor in Aframerican life. The attention of the news media focused on cities. The public face of black America by now bore the pockmarking effects of its regular exposure to the street's stormy distempers.

Instead of redemptive country preachers, television's picture shows now starred Negroes costumed as guerrilla soldiers and exotic aliens espousing dark and dangerous creeds. Words these actors spoke were suitable as voice-overs for scenes set in blighted cityscapes beset by felonious rabbles running amok. Thereafter in the minds of most citizens the image of violent crime in America would be embodied in the young, black, and male.

As American society looked askance at the fresh revelation of yet another unsightly aspect of its despised caste, the objects of this disregard became more self-regarding. Among the young the street was now the certifying institution of the authentically black. Ghetto romanticizers held artistic sway in the new tribal homelands. "C'mon down . . . take a look around," sang the Major IV, as though beckoning "snowbirds" to Florida, ". . . in the ghetto, there is love." Unfiltered voices of the male young reverberated in cities throughout Aframerica.

From Newark ("the walk is long, but the girls are there / you know, the buildings are high somewhere"), to Cleveland ("standing around telling jokes / can't go nowhere because we're broke . . . just me and the fellas, under the street lamp"), to Los Angeles ("young people shouting, drowning out fear and doubting / a bit of gladness, out of so much sadness"), songs expressive of the sensibilities of homegrown mannish boys were airing on local black radio and beyond.

While cameras stalked Black Panthers and conspicuous others of militant stripe, black popular music was reticent of overt politics until early 1968, when the Impressions released "We're a Winner." Even the smattering of songs about Vietnam were sentimental ballads of the type written during World War II for women left behind on the homefront, save for one by the Mighty Hannibal that spoke of "laying in a foxhole covered in blood." After James Brown's "Say It Loud— I'm Black and I'm Proud" came out near the end of that turbulent summer, it seemed monumental merely for being a direct political statement.

The previous fall, three months before Curtis Mayfield sensed that the time had come again for uplifting social comment, an unknown singer from the West Coast named Jesse James made a startling record called "Believe in Me Baby." Set in a simulated nightclub, it starts out as a workmanlike appeal for a woman's help and forbearance. At about the point in a live performance where a singer ordinarily breaks a song down and ad-libs awhile with one of its parts, James wheels into another story line, introduced with a sharply drawn contrast between the honest toiler's debilitating fatigue and "the man who doesn't do no work, who rides around in a Cadillac all day long . . . he's able, you women say he's able . . . to do it."

James addresses his audience in the studio as intimately as any other he might have been playing to in black neighborhood joints around Oakland: "People say, Jesse why you always talk about the fast life." "I don't knock the game," he continues, to the noisy approval of a very small crowd, "it's a good game if you play it right." But he then takes a quick preacherly turn, professing heartsickness over "the women out there [who] won't take care of their children" as a prelude to telling the story of a child who wakes up in an empty house at three in the morning and searches for his mother.

James sings the little boy's entreaties in a voice as sweet as Smokey Robinson's, until finally his anxious bleatings dissolve into scared and angry squalls. By now the background sounds of affectedly high female spirits have long gone silent. Though aiming more to prick than reproach, "Believe in Me Baby" discomfited women who were its natural audience and spooked the teenage girls.

It was played on radio more heavily than it sold. But if it barely made the record charts, "Believe in Me Baby" was heard, listened to, and thought about on the street, where Jesse James would be seen as a kind of documentarian, holding up a mirror to one face of Aframerica's private self.

Though Detroit was still the hub of the black record business, the market was beginning to favor music with rougher edges that bespoke, as Perry Bradford had put it, "that part of ourselves . . . we have sacrificed to civilization." From Valentine's Day of 1967 through Thanksgiving, one or the other versions of a song called "Funky Broadway" was played on black radio.

The original, by Dyke and the Blazers, was a low steady rumble in the land for six months, long enough to create new meanings and an era of steady employment for *nasty, filthy,* and *funky* in the mouths of black kids from coast to coast. Dyke was the stage name of Arlester Christian from Buffalo, who reworked James Brown's premise into an urban style of modern gutbucket. The dance music of Dyke and the Blazers sweated like Brown's and was as greasy as one of his head rags. The Blazers packed a hard punch, and the suggestion of dope-slur in Christian's vocals imparted a kind of loopy menace to their aggression.

Funk was a word from the old country, invented to improve on the combined efforts of *must* and *musk* at signifying the malodor particular to unwashed human crotches and armpits and of rooms and clothing that too long have contained either. Once it was used to characterize behavior, *funky* came to mean not only "bad-smelling" but also "lowdown" and "dirty," as in "ain't that a funky way to treat somebody." Musicians appropriated it to refer to the same survivals of aboriginal tribal style Dorsey's time called gutbucket. In the year after "Funky Broadway" the word's use was promoted among the young only on records from the South.

White kids took it up, and by 1969 *funky* could as well suggest "natural" as "unclean," as in "everything I do gonna be funky from now on." The fad black children made of the funky chicken—a cartoonish dance created by minstrelsy's last remnant, a grizzled Memphian named Rufus Thomas—prepared the youth market for "Funky Man." As conceived by Kool and the Gang, this apocryphal character was a ghetto Loki, who manifested "funk" as a comic-book hero would a supernatural power.

This introduced the idea of *funk* as both a force and a property. When "Funky Man" appeared in the fall of 1970, the fashion of Negritude was so prevalent in Aframerica that project girls idling on stoops amused themselves by making their toddlers say "black power" before obtaining a withheld toy, or a can of soda, or a dangled morsel of food. The stage was set for the 1970s, when *funk* would acquire mystique. It would be thought of then as a proprietary attribute of Aframericans, like *soul*.

At the beginning of 1968 the San Francisco disk jockey Sylvester Stewart, formerly the producer of Bobby Freeman's "C'mon and Swim," became a pioneer of cultural miscegenation. "Dance to the Music," his first record with the Family Stone, embraced the hurly-burly in white rock and roll that black kids had theretofore disdained as corny.

Before long a few would be turning up the radio volume when "Come Together" by the Beatles came on; records by Pacific Gas and Electric and Three Dog Night were appearing on the soul music charts. But in the late 1960s, while the skills of singers were more coveted on the street than those even of ballplayers, its resident poets still wrote songs of love and heartbreak. One of these that came and went near decade's end was mainly authored by members of the Icemen, obscure singers from Chicago:

How can I get over
A fox like you
How can I get over
A stone fox like you

When we first met, pretty baby, you treated me so sweet,
Couldn't nobody tell me, foxy, I didn't sweep you off
your feet
I guess I pushed you a little too hard
You dropped an axe on my heart . . .

How can I get over
A fox like you
How can I get over
A stone fox like you

Standing on the corner, sugar baby, from eight to five
Lip-popping to the fellas, rizzapping a little jizzive,
But they can see through my game, like looking through
that window-pane
I feel, didn't I feel . . .
(Coming on strong)
Loneliness . . .
(Coming on strong)
Pain . . .
(Coming on strong)
Unhhh . . .

Only in the street's aural literature were such feelings inside mannish boys engaged that otherwise would have been little examined and
never discussed. The social protocols of adolescent fellowships of
mostly fatherless sons discouraged public disclosures of their private
selves.

In May 1969 records by the Parliaments and Funkadelic scraped into
the lower tier of boogaloo's Top Fifty. Funkadelic was the Parliaments'
band, comprised of younger North Jerseyans in Clinton's Plainfield

orbit. As the name suggested, they were fusionists of boogaloo and white rock—steppers through Sly's door, with an ear cocked in James Brown's direction and the other toward Jimi Hendrix, who sounded then like "headache music" to mostly unattuned black ears.

Later that year "I'll Bet You"—made in the manner of the Family Stone but of coarser grain—was played all over black radio and left an impression. While the Parliaments maintained a separate recording career, the personnel from both groups commingled. In 1970 albums on different labels by the same players under two names sold slightly but caught the notice of tastemakers in the vanguard of the equal-opportunity generation, Aframerica's first broad wave of college-goers.

In the era of Motown and Memphis, Clinton's was a counter-cultural strain of boogaloo. The iconoclastic exuberance evident in "Mommy, What's a Funkadelic?" and "I Call My Baby Pussycat" accorded with the spirit moving in the quarters where the movie *Putney Swope*, Ishmael Reed's novel *Yellow Back Radio Broke-Down*, a Richard Pryor album called *Craps (After Hours)*, and Gil Scott-Heron's *The Revolution Will Not Be Televised* came into cultish fashion. This small pocket of young black culture-consumers bore promise of becoming a market niche; collegiate buzz promoted the sale of 300,000 copies of a record by the Last Poets that was released on a minor jazz label and never aired on commercial radio.

Mainly billed as the Parliaments, Clinton's crew took to the stages of clubs and campuses from Boston to Atlanta, looking like Sun Ra's troupe dressed for Halloween: Clinton in a bedsheet, others in long johns, wizard-hatted, or wearing a diaper. On some lightning bolts and crescent moons were cut into Afroed heads, twenty years ahead of the style. As overamplified as any rock band, they were just as disposed to throttle an audience into submission.

In those days of Wine Psi Phi–led factions imposing their wills on student activities committees, the Parliaments often got booked into black colleges on homecoming weekends. They were known to make some parents and alumni draw back and exclaim, "Oh my God," when from the stage they would incite a rapt crowd of young degree candidates to chant in full-throated unison, "Shit! Goddamn! Get off your ass and jam!"

One night in 1970 James Brown fired his band because they threatened to strike over low wages. These musicians had been the instrument of his rise from "hardest-working man in show business" to "Soul Brother Number One": together, more or less, since the sea-changing "Papa's Got a Brand New Bag," through "Cold Sweat" and "There Was a Time," to "Say It Loud—I'm Black and I'm Proud" and lately "Mother Popcorn."

For a half-decade they'd expressed the serial burst of rhythmic inventions by which Brown was forming the basis of modern boogaloo. Muscular and tight, coiled like a panther ready to spring on his command, they were the best show band in the business.

Discontent was rifest in the Parker brothers: drummer Melvin and Maceo, the featured saxophonist Brown made famous exhorting by name on record and stage to "play [his] lickin' stick," so to "make 'em stay, while I do the Funky Broadway." Fifteen years case-hardened at keeping road companies punctual and alert by iron-fisted means, their employer also had the classic Napoleonic little man's disposition to take any subordinate's challenge as a towering affront.

So having Learjetted replacements in from Cincinnati and readied them in the wings, Brown ran his incumbent grumblers off the stage of a municipal auditorium in Columbus, Georgia. Called the Pacesetters, Brown's strikebreakers—known to him from recording sessions—were anchored by guitarist Phelps "Catfish" Collins and his seventeen-year-old brother Bootsy.

"When I met [Bootsy]," Brown's memory served, "he was playing a lot of bass—the ifs, the ands, and the buts. I got him to see the importance of the 'one' in funk—the downbeat at the beginning of every bar."[2] The Pacesetters stuck with Brown about a year—through *Sex Machine* and *Super Bad*—and he credits himself with schooling their kid bassist in the higher essentials of his craft: "I got him to key in on the dynamic parts of the one instead of playing all around it. Then he could do all his other stuff in the right places—after the one."

"The one" was a term of art coined by Brown that, over a decade and a half of widening usage, acquired literal, metaphorical, and symbolic meanings. By the late 1970s "on the one" was a descriptor as well—applied to a good meal a favorable outcome, a beat, a timely insight, an admired performance, or life in a balanced state. From that decade's start and for eight of its years spent in becoming a briefly neon-lit star, Bootsy Collins was a proselytizer of Brown's doctrine of "the one" to Aframerica's children.

However often Brown takes credit for the young, he never had much patience with youth. He said Bootsy was looked after like a son who "wasn't bad or anything, just determined to be wrong."[3] When he tired of the bumptious company of youngsters, Brown invited his prodigals to return from the wilderness where they'd been wandering as Maceo and the All King's Men. The old guard was mostly restored for the successive triumphs of "Hot Pants" and "Make It Funky." The Collins brothers were restored to Ohio, playing as the Houseguests in small midwestern clubs.

At the height of this latest of James Brown's hot seasons—the summer and early fall of 1971—records by Parliament and Funkadelic nosed into the bottom half of *Billboard*'s soul music charts. Once again the same group appeared under two names on different labels, being more listened to than bought. The Funkadelic single "Can You Get to That" was written and produced to get airplay on radio, a song baited with juicy hook, as catchy as "Testify," as dark and sardonic as "All Your Goodies Are Gone." But as good as it sounded, black kids couldn't dance to it, and white kids couldn't hear it.

"Can You Get to That" was on an album, *Free Your Mind and Your Ass Will Follow,* that featured liner notes from the Process Church of Final Judgement, and Clinton's spoken-word introduction to a tortured nine-minute solo called "Maggot Brain" by a guitarist told to "play like [his] mother died," about "tast[ing] the Maggots in the mind of the Universe," and "Mother Earth [being] pregnant for the third time." If Clinton's artistic nature was divided into roughly equal parts of commercial sense and experimental sensibility, his young musicians—being mostly from black neighborhoods in white suburbs—bent sharply toward playing "black rock," a lonely road then over unbroken ground and a less-traveled path since.

They soon were joined by important others from hometown circles. The keyboardist Bernie Worrell was a conservatory student who would become black music's first virtuoso of the Moog synthesizer. He was to be George Clinton's Booker T. Jones. Gary Shider brought guitar skills, a strong voice, and a personality large enough for a star turn in Clinton's upcoming aural videos.

About the time Clinton and Bootsy Collins met each other in Detroit, James Brown (now in the employ of a German conglomerate) and his reconstituted band (now known as the J.B.s) gathered themselves for another of the Maestro's great leaps forward. "Get on the Good Foot" was advanced enough to inspire premature break-dancing in the summer of 1972, and it cut so deep into the quick of tribal culture that "the good foot" became a workaday metaphor in the permanent lexicon of the idiomatic Aframerican spoken word.

In the obscurity of Motown's deserted capital, Clinton and Bootsy by then had formed a mutual intent to form the creative partnership of which it later was proclaimed, "My name is the One, but some people call me the funk."

George Clinton went into business with Neil Bogart of Casablanca Records in 1973. An old boys' fair-haired new boy, Bogart was a crack promotion man who had been tapped six years earlier to run a start-up major independent record label at the age of twenty-four. Although he became known at Buddah Records as the original marketer of "bubble-gum rock" to prepubescent white girls, the company's steadiest money came from boogaloo. Bogart had profitable commercial relationships with Curtis Mayfield and the Isley Brothers, oversaw Gladys Knight's glory years, and was a leading buyer and seller of the stylish output of Philadelphia's boutique production houses.

By 1973, when Bogart talked Warner Brothers into financing Casablanca Records, Philadelphia was coming into a high fashion that would last for several years. Local boogaloo had been recorded there since the early 1950s, but the city became a hothouse in the mid-1960s and stayed one for a decade. Gamble and Huff—trademarkers of the "sound of Philadelphia"—had outstripped Motown and Detroit's post-Gordy remnants in the design and production of orchestral dance music.

They were the most prominent outgrowth of a highly particular indigenous music culture, wherein doo-wop stayed current until 1965, and the strength of white kids' affinity for black song and dance held off the "British invasion." The essential flavor in Philadelphia boogaloo was sweet-and-sour: the effect produced by Barbara Mason's flat-noted voicings of sweet, girlish melodies; Sam "Little Sonny" Brown's off-key crooning on the Intruders' lushly strung ballads; or William Hart of the Delfonics trilling "If you ever make me cry, I hope your momma die" over a flight of Thom Bell's sunny violins.

In the absence of fresh pop music of sufficient commercial appeal, boogaloo filled the merchandisers' void. By 1974 Gamble and Huff's house band had ushered in the disco era, wherein a form of black dance music was mass-marketed, then for several years continuously improved by product engineers striving to make it ever more broadly consumable.

With the control of goods from Philadelphia's brand-name suppliers in other hands, Bogart aimed at cracking open underserved teen markets. Two early Casablanca signings were of an unrecorded rock band called KISS, whose theatricality Bogart figured he could make promotable to junior high school kids, and Parliament. Clinton used Bogart's money to entice Bootsy into the studio, and in the summer of 1974 "Up for the Downstroke" became his first record in boogaloo's Top Ten since "Testify."

This earliest and least elaborate of the Parliafunkadelicment Thang's greatest hits was elaborated "street funk," black dance music that white people couldn't dance to, as proprietary in that regard to born citizens of the boogaloo nation as James Brown. Its branch off Brown's trunk had been extending for seven years: from Dyke and the

Blazers, the Meters, Charles Wright and the Watts 103rd Street Rhythm Band, early Kool & the Gang, to the Ohio Players, Funkadelic's label-mates on a last-ditch Detroit independent, Westbound Records.

The song's hook embedded itself so deeply in the recipient genera-tion of black young—and migrated so far across those succeeding—that a quarter-century later suburban-bred scriptwriters of ESPN sports highlight shows still routinely enliven their copy with references to basketball players "getting up for the downstroke." Still, under-pinning the decorative sophistication of "Downstroke"'s surface con-struction—the jazzy time changes and horn figures, pitch-perfect jin-gles, and tone-deaf atmospherics—was the basic architecture of "Sex Machine." "I love [Brown's] music," Clinton once professed. "It's like a dirty word. It makes your dick hard."[4]

Three successive Number 1 singles made 1974 James Brown's best-ever and last good year in a middle-aged lifetime of recording. The first of these, "The Payback," was commissioned for the soundtrack of a cheap black-cast action movie and was rejected by its white producer and director as "not funky enough." Brown proclaimed the second—"My Thang"—"a brand new funk," even while bridling at the felt con-straints of corporate masters. As if to ward off the sensed coming of a bad turn of affairs, Brown changed his official self-designations from "Godfather of Soul" to "The Minister of New New Super Heavy Funk" and imprinted this new honorific on every label of subsequent releases. Within a scant year of "Papa Don't Take No Mess," he'd dwindled into commercial irrelevance.

"The Payback" would prove to be the sudden end of James Brown's memorable output. "By the middle of 1975 disco had broken big," he later reflected. ". . . It hurt me in a lot of ways. . . . Disco is a very small part of funk . . . the end of the song, the repetitious part, like a vamp. . . . I was trying to make good hard funk records that Polydor was trying to soften up, while the people were buying records that had no substance."[5]

Soon after drought set in on James Brown, his featured horn players—Maceo Parker and band director Fred Wesley—set out for George Clinton's greener pastures. Clinton's "mob" now sported the next and last electric bassist in the transformational line of James Jamerson and Larry Graham, the auteur of "Doing It to Death" and a trailblazer in applied instrumental technology, the original master of the synthesizer bass.

For most of September 1975 these players and Clinton's others—three guitarists, three drummers, a second bass, and the third émigré from Brown's brass section—encamped in Detroit at United Sound Studio, recording the stuff of five albums released over the next year by Parliament, Funkadelic, and Bootsy's Rubber Band. In effect, the goods made that month in Clinton's workshop established the P-Funk brand, no doubt *Mothership Connection* most of all.

Two years before *Star Wars* Clinton found a concept one night while motoring with Bootsy on the road from Toronto, when suddenly lights started "bouncing from one side of the street to the other." By his account, a flash of "light hit the car . . . [and] all the street lights went out," just as he'd finished speculating out loud that "the Mothership was angry with us for giving up the funk without permission."[6]

This occurrence served to put him in mind of a band of space-voyaging "Afronauts" from Funkadelica, returned to Earth to reclaim the "secret of true funk" from its long sequestration in the Pyramids, therewith to free humankind from mental slavery. He imagined a saga of conflict between the agents of forces as primal as life and death, a story line with heroes and villains, secondary characters and subplots, sequels and spin-offs. Neil Bogart, who'd succeeded at putting KISS over with "high-concept" gimmickry and a hard sell, backed Clinton's idea with the enabling production money.

A half-decade before MTV Clinton had conceived of aural videos. What he immediately wrought was a record album like a danceable sci-fi radio cartoon, made imaginable to listeners by evocative sound effects, vivid narrative patter, and comic-book cover art. By any reading of seismic effects measured in units of influence not commerce, *Mothership Connection* was among its decade's most important works of boogaloo.

Though Clinton's biggest-selling album yet, *Mothership*'s unorthodoxies were a drag on its commercial buoyancy. It never would rise above the thirteenth position on the black record charts, lower than expectable of a vessel propelled by such robust fuel as "Tear the Roof off the Sucker," a radio hit and party anthem in the spring of 1976.

While the anarchic rip-roar of its chanted punch lines—"we need the funk, give up the funk" and "turn this mother out"—was catnip to kids, the rest of *Mothership Connection* seemed as much a cartoon for adults as *Rocky and Bullwinkle,* never a particular favorite of child televiewers in Clinton's target demographic. The buyers' pulse that beat to "Roller-coaster . . . of love, say what?" faltered over "the desired effect is what you get when you improve your interplanetary funksmanship."

Eleven years later hooks extracted from "(Make My Funk the) P-Funk" and "Starchild"—never better on the black singles charts of their day than Numbers 33 and 26—were the selling points of a rap album purchased by three million young customers. But however much it was to prove a trove of recyclable treasures for hip-hop's heaviest pocketers of the black-teen dollar, in 1976 Clinton's show and its intended audience hadn't yet entirely found each other.

"(Make My Funk the) P-Funk" was his calling card, like a promotional flier for the Pied Piper handed out on ghetto street corners. It was ironic sketch comedy lovingly drawn from old-school black radio, whose "personalities" talked all over the records they played and evangelists directed healing vibrations via rented airwaves expressly into afflicted body parts of prospective buyers of five-dollar "prayer cloths."

"P-Funk"'s lyrics were chattered not sung, but for a punch line remindful of the "make mine Maypo" commercials of television yore: "Make my funk the P-Funk / I like my funk uncut / Make my funk the P-Funk / I wants to get funked up / I want the Bomb, I want the P-Funk / Don't want my funk stepped on / Make my funk the P-Funk, before I take it home."

This anthemic chorus discloses the terms of Clinton's cultural exchange with the street; for the metaphors appropriated from dope-game parlance, he repaid in like currency. *P-Funk* quickly came into use as the street's all-purpose signifier of the best available grade of its trafficked-in drug commodities. Even now the marching song of many a dope fiend's "mission" is that snatch of Parliament's twenty-five-year-old refrain rippling in his head.

Tom Vickers, for five years Clinton's press attaché, explained to one reporter that what was said on the record was "the way they talked on the bus between shows." For example, he noted, "having a three on it" ("I went down south and heard some funk . . . sounded like it had a three on it to me") was a reference to a drug that had been cut three times, "but ultimately mean[t] anything watered down."[7] These "part[yers] on the Mothership" were both coiners and spenders of the people's language.

The mid-1970s were awash in disco. The tidal pull of mass-merchandising black dance music on a global scale had crossover currents running fast and deep in the boogaloo mainstream, enough to push it out away from the ghetto's shoreline. To Clinton, the unobliged cultural preferences of young millions living there represented a large parcel of abandoned commercial beachfront property.

"Give Up the Funk (Tear the Roof off the Sucker)" and Bootsy's "Stretchin' Out (in a Rubber Band)" had affirmed his know-how of the teenage party groove, but Clinton determined that to put his "package" across, he needed to recalibrate its cultural reference points. It had to get bigger, bolder, louder, and faster and take into account the Saturday-morning television ouevre of the Krofft brothers.

It was time for serious child's play. This would impose no hardship on the artistic temperament of a thirty-five-year-old matriculated cross-registrant in the homefront-Africanist "burn down the ghettos in your mind" and Yippie "trespass inside your own head" schools of liberated late-1960s thought.

P-Funk's concept "got so freaky," Clinton once said, "because the world got so scary."[8] He recognized the youthful audience he was after as inhabitors of the edge of chaos and mostly ungiven to thinking beyond the next few hours of existence. Unprotected by the insulating

framework of bourgeois life, they were laid bare to the relentless psychological assault-and-battery of television's permanent campaign to
induce want.

It was long known, as the Last Poets had put it, that "n[egroes]
love[d] commercials." Clinton knew as early as *Sesame Street*'s originators
that the urban-bred black juvenile attention span was form-fitted to the
thirty-second TV spot. Since ghetto children's playthings were the detritus of American popular culture, they were prone to catch its diseases
earliest and most severely, like canaries in a mine shaft.

Since they'd been conditioned to require visual stimulation for full
engagement, Clinton thought to animate his musical cartoons on the
stage of a road-show pageant—a Chocolate City Ice Capades for a
young urban class of "sneaker people." Parliament's record commerce
hadn't prospered more that year than Johnnie Taylor's (who never
worked above the Mason-Dixon Line) or the Brothers Johnsons' (who
couldn't carry a show on the road), or even the last-gasping James
Brown's, yet Clinton envisioned a production that was sized to indoor
sports arenas, on the technological scale of Rolling Stones extravagan-
zas in outdoor stadiums.

Clinton's audacity found an accomplice in Neil Bogart, whom
Morris Levy, an admiring mentor, likened to Florenz Ziegfeld.[9] Bogart
had a promoter's spend-money-to-make-money mentality that disposed him to invest heavily in "tour support" for acts that held promise
of a higher-yield return in record sales. The black youth market mattered to Bogart, because from it the independent distributors of
Casablanca's products squeezed sustaining lifeblood. So he bankrolled
the quarter-million-dollar mounting of Clinton's P-Funk Earth Tour.

Bogart was backing the grandest spectacle that had yet been staged
in the elapsed history of boogaloo. A "mothership" was designed and
rigged to descend thunderously from the eaves of cavernous public
spaces by the best set-makers and theatrical technicians rock-star
money could buy. Clinton knew that keeping levels of visual engagement high in young audiences would require heavy doses of industrial-
strength smoke and mirrors.

Wires were strung from arena rafters so that characters could apparently soar on high of the modern keyboard master, state-of-art bassist, precocious teenage guitar wizard, trio of ex-J.B.s, brace of Sly Stone's former backup singers, and covey of North Jersey black rockers who were furiously amplifying James Brown's famous question, "building is you ready, cause we gonna tear you down."

Stages writhed with the moving parts of props and persons outfitted as the cast of a circus of the studiously bizarre. Clinton, the ringmaster who wore long "fright" wigs, tall boots, and outlandish sci-fi raiment, would make his entrances riding in a "polyester pimpmobile."

Not long after *Star Wars*, late in the first month of 1977, the Earth Tour opened on the Los Angeles Lakers' home court. To coincide, Casablanca rolled out the P-Funk repertory's next cartoon musical, *The Clones of Dr. Funkenstein*, introducing Clinton's new stage alter ego in the title role.

"Bop Gun," the single released to be the album's commercial propellant, brought Bernie Worrell to the fore. It pulsated with densely layered rhythms and electronic effects, but was hookless and too squirrelish afoot to be a hit dance record. Clinton's idea of one step ahead of the kids in the street still went a half step too far.

Clinton's road show stayed out for about half of 1977, breaking ground and bleeding cash. A veteran of this campaign has said that for most of it his job was "to tell the musicians why they weren't getting paid."[10] However raggedy a business, the Earth Tour was a glorious marketing invention—"like a neon sign for everything else."[11]

But as much as the show spiked consumer awareness of the P-Funk brand, its backers at Casablanca still rankled at having bought the exposure for Bootsy that sprang another label's Top Ten record, while "Bop Gun" peaked too low. Parliament's want of a hit right then was so keenly felt that Clinton said for once he set out to write and produce one, although others recalled him commandeering a piece of material intended for Bootsy.

Honed by his months of direct communion with audiences, Clinton's commercial stroke this time struck dead on its mark. No matter how frantic the electronic traffic got on "Flashlight" 's surface arteries, its heartbeat held steady at a snarlish, dance-friendly tempo.

It opened with a line quoted from a nursery-rhyme prayer and ended with the smiley-faced coda, "Everybody's got a little light under the sun." In between a catchy one-word punch line throbbed like neon on the blink. Comic-book balloons filled with helium-voiced jabber were flash-carded at intervals timed to short attention spans. Young senses were kept pleasurably overstimulated throughout.

"Flashlight" was a high-powered electro kid-magnet. It became the first Number 1 single of Clinton's twenty-year recording life. When "Bootzilla" immediately succeeded "Flashlight" atop the charts, March 1978 was undeclared National P-Funk Month in Aframerica.

Clinton had suddenly stepped into a patch of tall cotton about two years wide, from which the P-Funk organization was to harvest six Number 1 singles, two Number 1 albums, and two others barely short of that mark. Over the same period the yield from Berry Gordy's holdings amounted to three Number 1 singles and two Number 1 albums. Back in the Plainfield barbershop days of 1960 Clinton had "wanted to build our own Motown." Eighteen years later he was presiding over a "virtual" record company.

In 1978 the more than thirty players in P-Funk's cast configured themselves eight ways to put out records on five labels. Guerrilla tactics devised in the late 1960s, when the dispossessed Parliaments had to shift for survival, now served a decade later in achieving some backhanded regulatory control of the flow of their goods into the marketplace. Clinton learned early that splitting his franchise among competitive lease-holders was bound sooner or later to pit corporations against one another, trying to sell more of different products made by the same hands.

Clinton divided the whole of these many parts into hemispheres: Parliament was commerce, Funkadelic self-expression. He spoke of Funkadelic as a "movement," apportioning to it most of his monologue flights of "slam" poetics, the darkest of Pedro Bell's cover art, such songs as "No Head, No Backstage Pass," such album titles as *America Eats Its Young*, and such publicity stunts as the press party he hosted nude at the Americana Hotel in New York.

"We need hits and craziness," he said at the time. "The craziness gives more staying power. We have to play both against each other to stay in front of the pack."[12] The shape-shifting properties of P-Funk's identity made Clinton the more artful dodger of commercial droughts, killing frosts, and other perils of the industrial briar patch: "having four, five groups in the same organization makes us hard to predict . . . if we do get one group overexposed we'll send them underground and concentrate on another."[13]

Between Parliament's theatrical seasons, Funkadelic went on "anti-tours," playing as they pleased in "little halls," open-endedly and without accoutrements. They inspired a core following as hard as Deadheads, of self-designated "maggots," "clones," and "funkateers." Twenty-five years later they still put out newsletters.

By spring of 1978 the output of this artists' collective had been consigned for more than a year to the marketing and sales departments of Warner Brothers without a commercial result worth even a junior-grade corporate product manager's time and trouble. Of the P-Funk organization's three leading brands, only the one Warner was licensed to sell had yet to put a dent in mass-merchandisers' shelf space.

At risk of falling from an oligarch's grace, Clinton reached into his "libraries of skeleton tapes" for an instrumental track he'd once thought of dismissively as "too pop." So his corps of black rockers-at-heart trooped into the studio to record their vocal parts singing, "Corny or not, here we come."[14] From their derisive lips to Casey Kasem's syndicated mouth: in mere months these brand-name counterculturalists had a record in America's Top Ten.

In 1978 "One Nation Under a Groove" was boogaloo's biggest seller, the *Jet* magazine "song of the year." "It's corny but it's clever," Clinton allowed, "and the time is right . . . it was only when this disco thing got so big"—and his need for a hit so pressing—"that we felt we could use [it]."[15]

Clinton regarded disco as "a concept of musak," and "One Nation"—its gentle, sonorous groove made to be embraceable by the market that embraced Donna Summer—was P-Funk "for passives." The uncut stuff was still an ethnic taste. Nine months previously

"Bootzilla" had been Number 1 on the black charts, but never at any point in its given time was it among the hundred most popular pop records.

If Bootsy had emerged as the star personality of P-Funk's human cast, the population of its soundscapes was exploding with vibrant fictive personae. During the last half of 1978 Clinton's production line cranked in high gear to turn out *Funkentelechy vs. the Placebo Syndrome*, then *Motor Booty Affair*. Bundled with the former was a pink poster of the archvillain Sir Nose D'Voidoffunk—Dr. Funkenstein's new foil—and a twelve-page comic book by house illustrator Pedro Bell.

In keeping with the latter album's underwater theme, its cover opened into a pop-up cartoon representation of Atlantis. The buyer was invited to place against this backdrop such characters as Rumpofsteelskin, Queen Freekoleen, and Moby Dicked, whose cardboard figures he'd cut out of their perforated outlines on the record jacket's inside.

Motor Booty Affair gave Clinton top-selling albums for two companies at the same time, and from it came "Aqua Boogie," his fourth Number 1 single on three different labels in the past year. From before Christmas 1978 until the next Easter, Aframerican airwaves rang with the jabberwocky chant "Alphapsychodiscobetabioacquadooloop." But whenever their attentions weren't drawn to this raucous billboard calculated to jar and amuse, a ten-second infomercial about the metaphysics of tribal existence—"with the rhythm it takes to dance to / what we have to live through / you can dance underwater and not get wet"—was playing repeatedly on the mindsets of "Aqua Boogie"'s young consumers.

The whole of Clinton's package was contained in this nutshell: a cartoon scenario enacted by squawking, cackling, cawing voices in a densely packed soundscape riotous with writhing layers of aural effects and stop-and-go rhythm bustle. Unlike "Flashlight," the unruly "Aqua Boogie" was not a well-made dance record. That it did about as well in spite of this deficit signaled that Clinton's conceptual theme park of the air had caught hold of a market. The Mattel toy company thought so and opened negotiations for the licensures to sell a line of Bootsy, Starchild, and Dr. Funkenstein dolls.

Motor Booty Affair occasioned another grand tour, but Clinton's mind raced past the technical complexities of staging plausible deep-sea illusions to equal the Mothership's monumental splash. Casablanca Records now had a Filmworks. "It's going to be a movie," he told a British interviewer on eve of the show's launch. "Like *Star Wars* under-water." A step ahead of MTV's time to come, he planned a feature-length mix of animated storytelling—a cartoon opera with a P-Funk score—and live performance footage.

When he spoke of his plans early in 1979, Clinton seemed to be standing on the verge of the imagined "empire . . . we tried to build back in Plainfield."[16] From this pinnacle just attained he looked out over a fruited plain ripening with the promise of his rich pickings and observed: "See, as soon as you make it, in most people's minds they're finished with you . . . they are programmed to get rid of you, like a car."[17]

On the steam of its chart-topping album, Parliament's *Motor Booty* tour set out in the spring of 1979 across an Aframerican heartland that had lately been consuming more of George Clinton's brand of boogaloo than any other. Several months later a disarrayed company limped off the road into a precipitous dip in the record business that its historians refer to as the "crash of '79."

Even fifty grand a night wasn't enough to go around for a cast of more than thirty, its attending flock of setter-uppers and gear-handlers, and the expense of getting from place to place. Along the way players had come and gone, been irregularly paid, and sometimes gotten stranded.

The previous tour had served the loss leader's classic function of bringing more customers into the store. Two years later few of those who hadn't come in already were ever likely to. Mounting a production bigger than most pop stars' for an audience the size of Clinton's affronted the economic rules of the road. At the time the boogaloo pro-fession's working reality was that "disco had killed off live music and a lot of middle-level venues with it." And Clinton could no longer rely on cash tidings from Neil Bogart.

Casablanca was managing to lose millions on gross revenues of more than fifty. Bogart was a notorious profligate, bingeing on a Moroccan-styled Hollywood office compound, nepotistic payroll bloat, and ornamental deadwood for Casablanca's "talent" stockpile. He was also a wanton industrial grafter, lavishing "drugola" on the nation's programmers of Top Forty radio.

Bogart floated his deficit spending the same way Al Bell had: Casablanca shipped wholesalers—and booked payment for—hundreds of thousands more copies of the KISS, Donna Summer, and Village People albums than the millions that were actually sold. Months later, when this excess merchandise was returned to the company, money came off its books; but as long as a sufficient volume of Casablanca's product kept moving, Bogart's juggle kept up. All the while the costs of excessive manufacture ground away at operating capital. If sales ever faltered badly, pressure from the gush of cash outflow would bring playhouse walls tumbling down.

When CBS gripped Al Bell's accounts receivable in just such a vise as Bogart was putting Casablanca's into, Stax got squeezed lifeless. But then Bell's ruinous business practice was Bogart's industrial standard. In 1979 CBS and the other oligarchs would find themselves in the same circumstances that beggared Stax, as a consequence of the same behaviors that paupered Bell.

Like Bogart, the whole industry was caught holding an outsize investment in disco futures the year of disco's overnight death. In the absence of forthcoming new strains of music with mass appeal to white youth, the pop market shrank, like a stomach accustomed to getting less food. As James Brown put it, "[E]xcept for a few blockbusters every now and then, you couldn't give records away."[18]

An industry whose waistline had been expanding every year for a decade went right on oversupplying goods to buyers who weren't there. The music business was pitched into a downspin that lasted until its oligarchs colluded to force the obsolesence of the phonograph record.

Compact discs were introduced that year, and in less than half a decade vinyl was eradicated. Consumers were thereby obliged to pay more for the same products and to repurchase any old inventory they already had and wanted continuing use of. In the middle of the 1980s industry revenues were higher than ever.

Late in 1979 Bogart's wastrelcy so alarmed his Dutch and German partners that Polygram bought him out of Casablanca for close to $15 million.[19] With Bogart packed off into a lush exile, Clinton lost his highest-placed industrial ally at the inopportune moment of needing a friend in the oligarchs' court. The soldier of fortune now sought a land grant from some obliging corporate liege: Clinton was after a "label deal."

With the P-Funk wave cresting, he would never be in better position to command the conglomerator's chartering stake that would put him into the record business for himself. By disposition he "would prefer to spread the acts out because it means less work for me." But in this case opportunity was unavoidable, and he had no choice but to face it. The logical imperative of converting ephemeral commercial clout into tangible property overbore Clinton's basic indifference to proprietorship.

His dealings with corporate masters pursuant to a deal were fraught with mutual suscipions. The oligarchs were leery of Clinton's intentions—"always afraid . . . that I would take all of the big name acts over . . . once their contracts were up"—as he was wary of their retributive potential. He expected companies then harboring the P-Funk talent diaspora to "depopularize the groups [if] they think they are going to lose them."

Relations with Warner Brothers had never been good, and now Bogart no longer stood between him and the burgermeisters' men at Polygram whom James Brown accused of "destroying my sound . . . and cost[ing] me my audience."[20] It would take four years for Clinton to get the deal from CBS that begat Uncle Jam Records, and by then all his goodies would be gone.

When he was flush with 1979's early promise, George Clinton declared, "all our monies have been invested in building the organization, and the label deal will prove it was all worthwhile." But the "organization" Clinton spoke of was the figment of a man with disorderly gifts and a talent for uproar. He'd then likened the corporate personality of the Parliafunkadelicment Thang to "a form of controlled schizophrenia," in which he functioned as "referee."[21]

Its core had begun to unravel as early as 1978, when a dissident faction broke off and recorded an album called *Mutiny on the Mothership* that made barbed reference to Clinton's egotism. Like most whose egos dominate a collaborative enterprise, Clinton thought of his as under control. "I know when to tell it to sit down and be quiet," he said.[22] But the egotistical force behind Clinton's insistence on self-indulging in the excesses of his own nature would split P-Funk, Inc., along seams wearied from the stress of strains endured over two years of spurting growth.

The first prerogative that performers who have risen to commercial consequence by means of their own productions typically feel owed is relief from the taxing road. "[P]eople don't know which one is George Clinton anyway," he said, rehearsing his brief for recusal. ". . . Anyone could put on a wig and boots and be me." A lover of cocaine since before he had money who became a fiend once he did, Clinton began taking license to miss performances.

"As far as I am concerned, Bernie Worrell is more me than I am," he pronounced, giving his convenience the appearance of a plan. "I have protected myself and the group so that people won't feel let down if I am not there."[23] A year later Clinton's company was sundered by his surprise "retirement" on the eve of their weeklong engagement at the Apollo Theater, from which he absented himself except for occasional droppings-in to walk about onstage.

"I guess that basically I am a lazy motherfucker," he allowed once, when things were going well. "I have found that by having that attitude, I've caught less hell than if I tried to take it seriously." Of Clinton's habitual indulgences, acquiescing to the rule of his temperament did him more damage than cocaine. "Nothing is that serious," he declared, with the glib assurance of a practiced self-justifier of business undone. "Funk it and it will go away."[24] By the middle of 1981 it mostly had.

This didn't owe to creative failure but to a center that would not hold. As Clinton's business-mindedness wandered, stars-in-residence began falling away. Momentum carried as far as the spring of 1980, when both Parliament and Funkadelic had overlapping albums that skimmed the top of the boogaloo charts.

While there were further adventures in Funkadelica with a proliferating gallery of characters, other themed road shows, and a couple more Top Ten singles, in retrospect these seemed elements of an attenuated anticlimax a year and a half long. When the end of Clinton's enterprise came, quiet and abrupt as a curtain drawn shut, what had appeared no worse than irregular breathing proved to be its last gasps.

In 1981 three of the original Plainfield cadre members decamped for California and, under the name of Funkadelic, released an album of songs deriding their erstwhile "mob" boss. "I told them point blank, it's gonna get rough and it would be hard to stay together," Clinton would say of his crew to an interviewer from *Billboard.* "They said they wouldn't leave, but when things did get tight, many did." Coincidently, Warners was spurning much of the proposed content of Clinton's new Funkadelic album, even though the last two had sold back-to-back millions.

Electric Spanking of War Babies was cut back from two records to one, its cover art censored, and its promotion neglected. He stopped speaking to his corporate handlers and wouldn't again for more than two years. "In fact," Clinton snorted, "they change presidents [at Polygram/Casablanca] so often that I don't even know who I need to talk to."

These confluent rancors set off a chain of lawsuits that within a year would result in Clinton's being cut off from further commercial use of the brand names Parliament and Funkadelic. "Lawyers and wives make it a bitch to keep any band together," he shrugged.

While he was in litigant's exile from the P-Funk business, Clinton supported himself as a producer-for-hire. He'd always kept one foot firmly planted in the boogaloo old school. Even while P-Funk was raging in 1978 and 1979, Clinton produced records in Detroit with the Dells, David Ruffin, and revamped upsouth soul singer Laura Lee, for Don Davis—an associate since the Revilot days and hub of local post-Motown recording commerce.

Clinton was a committed Detroit loyalist. "We'll be there until we get our own studios," he said early in 1979, when this prospect seemed inevitable. "And even then I would cut my bass and drums in Detroit."[25] His original plans for Uncle Jam Records contemplated tapping the city's storehouse of such "ready and waiting" producers as Ron Dunbar, other left-behind Motown graduates, and young veterans of the five-year rise and fall of HDH's successor enterprise.

With P-Funk shut down, Clinton produced James Brown and Sly Stone to no avail. He launched another protégé and lost him to Warner Brothers in a contract dispute. "Right now," he complained, "I must have twenty different albums complete and ready to release. But there are simply not enough outlets."[26] Nor would there ever be, since Clinton had already acquired a permanent reputation for visiting "legalistic and financial chaos [on] his projects."[27]

Blocked from recording as Parliament or Funkadelic, unable to distribute anything he might release under cover of the P-Funk All-Stars, Clinton signed on to Capitol Records as himself: "I had to have an outlet and a name nobody could cause trouble over. . . . And I had to eat."

Backed by Worrell, Hazel, Shider, Morrison, Wesley, and other old familiars, he put out an album called *Computer Games* near the end of 1982. Invoking continuity with the truncated glories of P-Funk's recent past, Clinton touted his merchandise as the "funkentelechy of the '80s." Five months later, "Atomic Dog," the second single released from that album, replaced Michael Jackson's "Billie Jean" atop the black record charts.

Fresh off a drug arrest that was the most notable product of his collaboration with Sly Stone, Clinton had "walked into the studio [to record "Atomic Dog"] blind as a bat and out of my head, and didn't realize the track was backwards, so I just started singing. . . . [T]hen suddenly the hook ["Why must I chase the cat? It's nothin but the dog in me"] hit me like 'Whoft.'"[28]

Although in 1983 "Atomic Dog" didn't even register as one of the hundred songs most popular among white people, the last commercial noise George Clinton made has reverberated in widening circles of American culture ever since. Nearly twenty years after "bow wow wow yippie yo yippie yay" would come a season when suburbanites by the millions in major-league ballparks across America woofed on cue whenever a song by three obscure Bahamians called "Who Let the

Dogs Out" blared over the loudspeakers between innings. For a moment at the beginning of this new century, official America had adopted an echo of George Clinton as its universal athletic fight song.

A year before Ronald Reagan proclaimed the dawn of "morning in America," George Clinton warned of nightfall's imminent arrival. By 1984, he foretold, "the system will really start to suppress us. They won't wait any longer . . . to start to genetically deal with us." This would be the moment, Clinton said, of the nation's "Uncentennial," when ". . . there will be things like illegal expressions" and "[t]hey will no longer suffer people like me . . . [o]r a president that the people like. No characters, no personalities. If by [then], they haven't got what they want they'll just do it by computers, technically."[29]

Actually, in 1984 the agents of Clinton's suppression were the DEA and the market forces subject to the cyclical tyrannies of youth fashion. Hip-hop—the new boogaloo—claimed his young audience. And after years of absorbing disco's industrial wastes, the turbid mainstream of boogaloo ran toward the toned-down and broadly acceptable.

Under these circumstances Clinton was neither here nor there. Partially regrouped and intermittently active as the P-Funk All-Stars, Clinton and crew became displaced from the music commerce. The P-Funk movement returned underground, where it was taken up and adapted for the lucrative uses of a class of young recyclers who in early adolescence had been previous Funkateers.

Back in the fall of 1979, just as "Knee Deep" became Clinton's last Number 1 record, "Rapper's Delight" debuted on the charts. Not long after Tom Vickers—P-Funk's "minister of information"—auditioned a tape of the rapper Grandmaster Flash for members of the band. "This shit will never happen," they reportedly scoffed.[30] Disdain for the craftlessness of rhymed-over beat boxes would be natural in these crafters of the most sophisticated popular music of the twentieth century's last quarter. It was easy for them to underestimate the crude power that authentic simplicity could bring to bear. "George saw rap coming," Vickers observed, "and tried to deny it."

He'd gotten past denial by the time he made *Computer Games* three years later. In "Loopzilla," the album's first cull, he cited "Planet Rock"—a declaration of kinship with hip-hop's establishing text and its author, Afrika Bambaataa. Washed up near decade's end, Clinton was restored at the start of the next and was publicly avowing that "hip hop saved the Funk."

It had certainly preserved the value of his estate. Classic P-Funk was a standard reference in the hip-hop of the early 1990s, as James Brown had been several years before. In the market Clinton's recyclables were fetching more than they had as original goods. "(Make My Funk the) P-Funk" would be transposed into the stuff of three million albums sold, and a famous gangster rapper–cum–movie star overlaid the soundtrack of "One Nation" with a patchwork of rhymes appropriatiated from Clinton's collected wit and wisdom.

15. Two Tears in a Bucket

As Morris Levy once would have turned to Nate McCalla, in late 1993 Jimmy Iovine of Interscope asked Suge Knight to take a troublesome asset in hand: a budding movie star whose latest rap album sold more than half a million copies but who'd gotten too disreputable for even Time Warner's bagman to be seen with in public while the hounds of culture war were loose on his employer's patch, looking to sink their teeth into exposed corporate flanks.[1]

Tupac Shakur was born in dramatic times of such innocence that the most farsighted of Aframerican progressivists reckoned confidently, by the *Battle of Algier*'s guiding light, that a foreseeable revolution in the nation's near future would arise from the streets with a convulsive force sufficient to disrupt Americans' regularly scheduled television viewing. A mere half-decade after the black South's ascendant moment, the supreme article of Aframerica's current nativist faith upheld Ghetto as the seat of authentic Negritude. In tribal politics and the arts it was springtime for street theater.

Alice Williams, Tupac's mother, traded her enrollment in New York's Performing Arts High School for a ragtag local troupe of Black Panthers. As Afeni Shakur, she became one of those arrested in 1969 and tried for conspiring to dynamite police stations, school houses, department stores, railroad yards, and the Bronx Botanical Gardens. Tupac (née Parrish) was conceived near the middle of his mother's seven-month trial and was born about a month after the acquittals on ten criminal counts that her jury took twenty minutes to reach.

Tupac's arrival coincided with the first bloom of street literati. The summer before he was born his mother had been among thousands gathered at Temple University in Philadelphia for the Black Panther Party's national convention. Down the street at the Uptown Theater the Last Poets—a minor fashion among the college-aged and consciousness-raised—were appearing on a bill with the O'Jays and the Spinners.

The declaimings of these trenchant rhymers were accompanied in 1970 by spare rhythm sections of Harlem Africanesque percussion. Their album on an art-house jazz label sold 300,000 copies. They were precursors of Public Enemy as surely as the penis folklorist Rudy Ray Moore, who told heirloom tales of sexual apocrypha in rhythmically intoned rhyming couplets, begat 2 Live Crew.

At trial, when the matter of Afeni Shakur's pregnancy became pertinent to an issue before the court, one observer noted that "she spoke as if she were bearing a prince." But the early life she provided her son was grim and unsettled. He grew up fatherless and shuffled-around, "crying all the time," not fitting in: a lonely mama's boy of artistic bent and temperament who wrote poetry, felt "unmanly," and dreamed of being a famous actor.

When Tupac was fifteen, Afeni Shakur drifted into Baltimore. He became a student there of acting and ballet at the city's High School of the Arts, where he thrived under the cultivation of white adults and in the society of white peers. After Tupac's junior year, his mother—fearing for her sensitive boy's safety on Baltimore's violent streets—sent him to summer in California. In a forlorn suburban ghetto outpost in Marin County, the reinventive Tupac cast himself in the part of MC New York, a young urban sophisticate of superior East Coast style and breeding. He wanted to play with the local hoodlums, who only tolerated him, "as you [would] a dog or a neighborhood crack fiend."

At seventeen Tupac flirted with a white woman sitting on a park bench who was so immediately smitten with the potential of this bright, glib, dark-skinned pretty boy that she took him home and got him work dancing in the stage show of a high-riding rap group called Digital

Underground. Tupac's particular job was to feign copulation with a life-size blow-up doll while demonstrating the "Humpty Dance" to audiences of Digital Underground's live performances. Within weeks of completing this tour of duty, Tupac had a contract with Interscope Records and a meaty role in a motion picture of a type that was at the vanguard of blaxploitation's artier second coming—a boyz-in-the-hood crime melodrama directed by Spike Lee's cinematographer.

In 1991 the release of the movie *Juice*—marked by Tupac's eye-catching portrayal of a high school role-player-at-criminality's descent through delusional gangsterhood into cold-blooded sociopathy—coincided with the popularity of his first album, from which "Brenda's Got a Baby" emerged as an anthem du jour of Aframerica's street-struck young. Never before had such a combination punch landed as heavily on the black youth market at the very start of a performer's career. At twenty Tupac was an image torn from the pages of fan magazines and taped inside the locker doors of black schoolgirls across America.

Late in the election season of 1992, after *2Pacalypse Now* was recovered from the cassette player of a car in Texas whose youthful occupant had slain a state trooper, Vice-President Dan Quayle denounced Shakur's work, and its like, as having "no place in our society." The opprobrium of Quayle and his ilk assured that before long pictures of Tupac—costumed as a California gang warrior with "Thug Life" tattooed above his heart—would hang on the bedroom walls of teenage boys.

For twenty years by then the proportion of Aframerican men in cities living within what society considered its social and economic mainstream had grown progressively smaller. During the late 1960s and early 1970s millions were stricken—many in their late adolescence and early manhood—by the heroin epidemic that scholars of urban social phenomena have suggested took nearly a decade to subside. Tupac Shakur was born to this time.

Never before or since has heroin been fashionable among Aframerican youth. But in the urban black belt's hardest-hit locales, it seemed in 1968 like an entire peer cohort of males between the ages of fifteen and twenty-one was passing in lockstep through sequential stages of

opiate contagion: from sniffing, to skin-popping, to intravaneous injec-
tion. Of those beguiled then by the "tragic magic," some died; many of
the rest never fully recovered and by the late 1980s were in their forties
dying from AIDS or had succumbed along the way to one or another of
the predictable consequences of long-term addiction: jail, disease,
social isolation, financial marginality.

Members of this winnowed generation were meant to be governors
of the boys they spawned but weren't around much to look after them,
a generation raised to abandon women by women abandoned by men.
While heroin primarily scourged males, the crack epidemic of the mid-
1980s ravaged child-rearing females, Tupac's mother among them.
Many sons of the ghetto grew into lives mostly disassociated from older
people for whom they had much respect. They learned in the places
where they grew up that the best parts of men's lives were lived outside
families.

In 1990 the sociologist Terry Williams, a student for several years of
a crew of teenage dope-stroll laborers in the Washington Heights section of Manhattan, wrote of walking through that neighborhood and
seeing in its streets the next "generation of Cocaine Kids in faded jeans
and unlaced sneakers, draped with gold chains, their arrow-pointed
haircuts topping fresh faces and hard-edged frowns . . . grown before
their time, wise before they leave home, smart before they go to
school . . . rule-breakers before they know the rules and law-breakers
after they know the law."[2] Across America such youngsters as these
would make Tupac Shakur a star and Suge Knight a man of consequence.

Once he was given his career-making role, Tupac lived like an actor
researching a part. "He could be with this poet, this pimp, this thug,"
Shakur's road manager once observed, "he could suck everything from
each of them, and that would be part of him." He moved to Los Angeles and ran with Crips and Bloods, making their war stories his own.
His second album came out in the spring of 1993 and established his
position among hip-hop's upper classes.

He started misbehaving in public with guns and baseball bats and regularly scraping against the law. Relocated to Atlanta, he shot two drunken white off-duty policemen, after one had pulled a gun on him in a dispute arising from an argument among passengers in cars stopped for a red light at a downtown intersection. If this incident elevated Tupac's standing with his customer base, it also made him an editorial target of the nation's mainstream press.

That fall Tupac went to New York for a movie job and fell in with a Haitian "promoter" who introduced him around Brooklyn's black underworld. He caught a rape case involving a woman who'd come to his hotel room expecting a private audience and been made sport by several men. Back in Los Angeles he was sentenced to fifteen days in county jail for assaulting a film director he'd quarreled with on the set of a music video.

As both his fame and his notoriety mounted apace, Tupac's cry of "only God can judge me," became the self-advertising slogan of one of the black youth-culture industry's hottest consumer brands. The notes of plaintiveness and defiance in his claim of exemption from authority's censure struck a dominant chord in the international anthem of the adolescent heart. In Tupac Shakur a presence existed with the potential to create mass appeal for the most dangerous image of a black male ever to be admired by white teenagers of both genders.

From the point of Jimmy Iovine's first entreaty, Suge openly courted Tupac hard. Three times over the next couple of years he would ask for the hand of Interscope's unruly young star, and Tupac thrice demurred. Where Knight had once thought him soft and fake, Tupac's manic flights of transgression now certified him as fit for Death Row service. By late in 1993 its CEO was likewise a target of prosecution. Suge's own propensity for scenery-chewing street dramatics had concentrated the mind of the district attorney's office in Los Angeles County on sending him to prison.

In the past six years Knight had pleaded guilty in two states to seven separate offenses—all but one an assault or gun charge—at the cost of only five days in a county lockup. Now he faced charges of having assaulted with a deadly weapon a pair of unfortunates who'd ignored a prohibition against using the pay phone on Death Row's premises when the proprietor was expecting a call.

Suge's prosecutor huffed to the press that the quarry in his sights was a "thug" who "gets [the] charges pushed back because he has money."[3] To the governors of a city grown infamous as a rutting ground for murderous factions of ghetto youths, such a preening criminal scofflaw as Suge Knight—at once a legitimately successful rogue profiteer in a respectable commerce of highest local importance and an insistent standard-bearer of the Piru Street Bloods—had become a municipal affront.

Quietly, a federal task force in Los Angeles had already begun spreading prosecutorial flypaper around Suge's feet, expecting the inevitable misstep that would snag him in a RICO case. He was by then an established national figure of official ill repute.

Early in 1994 the U.S. Senate held committee hearings to publicize the social evils attributable to gangster rap. They were engineered by C. DeLores Tucker, an erstwhile Philadelphia politico with a checkered career in public service, who'd seized a ready opportunity in the early 1990s to capitalize on the confluent generational dismay of middle-aged Aframericans over the state of their young, and rising rabidity of antimiscegenational sentiment among official America's cultural rear guard.

Schooled in the wily arts of professional civil rights activism by Cecil Moore—a longtime Philadelphia NAACP boss of legendary slickness—then attentive to Jesse Jackson's modern refinements of technique in the craft of corporate shakedown, Tucker took up a lucrative late-in-life career as a public crusader against the demoralizing effects on black youths of black youth culture. For going on twenty years a path veering rightward had been the fast track for Aframerican careerists willing to go that way. Mrs. Tucker cheerfully encamped with official America's official conservative culturalist, William Bennett, a known reviler of the class whose souls she'd appointed herself to rescue as a horde of barbarian despoilers at Babbittry's gates.

Tucker set up shop in Washington, D.C., as the National Political Congress of Black Women and deftly began using the platform she'd been given by a titillated media corps to get in position to play her mark. Angling for Time Warner's wallet, she trumpeted the perfidies of Tupac Shakur, Snoop Doggy Dogg, Dr. Dre, and Death Row Records to create diversionary commotion.

Tucker's campaign was sure to catch the natural sympathies of a sizable caucus of tribal elders who were able to lend her their institutional letterheads for use in creating illusions of political heft. Her rebuke of hip-hop music evoked a long line of maternal authority represented in the mind's image by the face of Mary McLeod Bethune but embodied in so many others. Such women chastised their strayed young by reminding them of indignities their grandfathers endured in silence and the acres of white folks' dirty laundry their grandmothers labored over so that they could stand now at the threshold of opportunities that worthier forebears could only imagine. Tucker spoke to the deep disquiet of an outgoing generation fearful that the transmission of the essentially conservative social traditions they inherited had been permanently broken, and that their own progeny were something apart. She rallied to her flag many in Afro-Christendom's established ranks.

Brandishing the support of "sixty black organizations," Tucker backed Ben Chavis's desperate-for-youth-currency NAACP off the planned bestowal of its 1994 Image Award upon Tupac Shakur. She commanded the op-ed page of the *New York Times*. The reverberant effects of Tucker's campaigning began to make Time Warner quaver. Once jeremiads had rumbled down from Bob Dole and William Bennett denouncing publicly held and regulated corporate inflicters of "nightmares of depravity" on America's children,[4] Time Warner quailed. It buckled in the summer of 1994, abruptly divorcing Interscope and Death Row and pledging to set up Mrs. Tucker with a record label of her own.

Interscope's portfolio of fast-appreciating stocks of white "rage rock" and gangster rap was scooped up by MCA, now a property of the House of Bronfman, a conglomerate elaborated from a family fortune built on the sale of unwholesome commodities. Suge's enterprise was unfazed by the troubles C. DeLores Tucker meant to cause it. The two albums that Death Row next released quickly sold millions.

Its CEO passed out expensive cars to key contributors like cigars after a baby's birth, albeit in lieu of the greater entitlements that recipients of these gifts had signed away when they enlisted to fight for spoils and glory in Suge's declared culture war between "ghetto n[egroes] and phony n[egroes]." One of his young paladins—a featured vocalist in the Dogg Pound ensemble—commandeered the stage at an awards show to extend to the assembled industrial bigwigs an invitation "from the bottom of [his] heart" to "eat this dick."[5]

Tupac Shakur persisted in waging his own noisy battles of cultural identity as an army of one. Despite his rising value as a youth-market commodity, he was broke from paying lawyers to handle the scrapes that created the bad publicity that caused promoters to cancel bookings. His income from movies was exhausted in the support of an extended family. And on the last day of November 1994 he was a criminal defendant in a sex trial in the bad-publicity capital of the world.

After midnight, even as Tupac's jury slept on its decision, the accused sodomist, sexual abuser, and unlawful-weapon possessor headed into a recording studio in a Times Square office building to make a $7,000 cameo appearance on another rapper's album. He was waylaid by masked bandits in the lobby of an office building, stripped of his jewelry, and shot five times in the head and groin. Two days before being legally adjudged a mild sexual offender, Tupac was sentenced by chance to the loss of a testicle.

Although acquitted of the most serious charges against him, for unwanted fondling Shakur was given four and a half years in a state penitentary on Valentine's Day. The justice system seemed bent on administering to him with exemplary harshness. While his lawyers filed appeals, Tupac's bail was set prohibitively high: at $1.4 million, more than he could raise. With Interscope and its overlords declining to intervene, he had no choice but to wait and serve.

In jail Tupac was a twenty-three-year-old actor on hiatus who'd begun to regret having taken the role that was making him famous.

"When you do rap albums," he wearily advised, "you got to train your-self . . . to constantly be in character."[6] Scorned and harassed by inmates, demeaned by guards, Tupac wasn't weathering well "up north." He passed time doing push-ups in his cell and memorizing Machiavelli. When April Fool's Day broke over Dannemora, New York, Tupac's third album—called *Me Against the World*—had been out a week and was already Number 1 on the pop charts. From this he could extract but a small measure of cold comfort for the psychic woundings inflicted that day by heckling jailhouse reputation-seekers and the icy sneers of true-life thugs.

Chastened and reflective, Tupac told an interviewer, "If . . . that Thug Life shit . . . is real, then let somebody else represent it,"[7] even as he prepared to accept Suge Knight as his savior. By then he was ready to submit to whatever conditions freedom might impose, including matrimony and Death Row. As soon as he'd delivered himself into Knight's hands, Tupac was expensively lawyered and bonded out of jail, mostly with funds furnished by those very corporate backers who'd previously been unwilling. Suge picked up his ransomed asset in a stretch limousine and whisked him back west by private jet into a sound studio to start working off advanced legal expenses in nineteen-hour shifts.[8]

Tupac's native facility for commercial street poetics enabled him to dash off market-ready rhymes on demand, and the energy released when the lid was lifted after his months in a sealed pressure cooker pro-duced a burst of expressed creation. This rich effluence pooled into precious stockpiles in Suge's vault of master tapes. The right to exploit this natural resource, the most highly prized by traders on the black youth-culture commodity exchange, belonged exclusively to him.

For his part, taking Knight's shilling consigned Tupac to an indefi-nite term of further confinement inside the dramatic persona he'd resolved to outgrow. With no choice but to embrace this role, he gamely worked his way back into character. From under the cover of Suge's muscled wing, Tupac cawed at the magpies of the fanzine press, "there's nobody in the business strong enough to scare me"—a shrill display as empty of conviction as a televized wrestler's thumping of chest at camera and crowd.

In Tupac, Knight knew he had the right shill at the right time: a magnet for public attention and a drawer of the heat necessary to cause enough combustion to "blow up" Death Row on a global scale. Already the best-selling boogaloo was hip-hop of the West Coast–gangster style Death Row had patented. In 1994 Dr. Dre won a Grammy Award. Madonna was hounding him to produce her next album. *Newsweek* had dubbed him "the Phil Spector of rap."

Dre could now conceive the hugeness of the career advantages respectability would afford, and he had concluded that any carrier of Death Row's outlaw stigma would be lamed in its pursuit. On the other hand, Suge Knight continued to flaunt his disdain of respectable opinion by manhandling a profiler assigned by *The New Yorker* and selling wolf tickets to the readers of the *New York Times Magazine.* He wanted official America to know that any "dickster" who tried to beat him out his money would get "his drawers kicked up his behind."[9]

However brazen and foul Death Row's mouth and manner—or ill its repute—in four years $300 million worth of its products were sold, and in the culture business nothing sanitizes like sales volume. Less than two years after branding him a thug in the *Los Angeles Times,* the assistant district attorney who'd plea-bargained Suge's potential nine-and-a-half-year prison term on a felony assault conviction into five years of probation touted him in the same newspaper as "one of the few guys I . . . ever prosecuted . . . I actually believe can turn his life around and really change the community from which he came."[10] At the time Knight's business partner was brooding away for six months in a Pasadena detention center, a former partner had accused him in a lawsuit of underhanded dealings, and Death Row's biggest homegrown star was on trial for murder.

Even as federal cops were investigating his probationer's links to drug-dealers and laundered cash, hard-nosed crimestopper ADA Longo reported "never [having] seen a guy transform as much."

Within a year of this testimonial Longo's daughter had signed a Death Row recording contract and his family's Malibu beach house was tenanted by Suge Knight.

From his latest subornation of the criminal justice system Knight took license to infer that insofar as a bad character directly served the commercial interests of the powerfully placed, it could be exercised in appropriate circles without penalty. Interscope had already rewarded his badness with its fortune-assuring gift of the Tupac Shakur franchise. The prolific Shakur had produced enough material for a double album, and in early 1996 *All Eyez On Me* sold nearly 600,000 twenty-dollar copies its first week in stores. Tupac's $10 million opening coincided with Snoop beating his murder case.

Before the party ended on the night of his acquittal, Snoop was off to Tarzana to start meeting his obligations in the studio. Knight and his cronies stayed behind, toasting the "New and Untouchable Death Row." Suge was as drunk on the feeling of impregnability as a drug lord who knows he has the undead victims bought off, the witnesses scared off, and the police precinct paid off.

Though his official headquarters were near the border of Beverly Hills, in offices he owned and shared with Interscope, Suge encamped mainly on Death Row–colonized territory in Tarzana. The decorative grace note of his red-on-red-in-red bunker at Can-Am Studios was a tankful of piranhas into which he ceremoniously pitched a squirming rodent twice each day. Six television sets on his desk continually screened the monitorings of surveillance cameras, the way Tony Montana's did in *Scarface*.[11] Suge's "security" retinue included members of a small criminal cell of Blood-affiliated Los Angeles cops, who—when not on duty with the antigang unit rousting, robbing, testilying, and looting evidence lockers of large amounts of cash and cocaine—moonlighted on Death Row's casual payroll. The stink of the street was cologne to Suge's nostrils, and he liked to keep a hand in its nether parts.

Even at the highest price ever charged for a rap album, Tupac's *All Eyez On Me* sold five million copies inside of three early months of 1996. Such an influx of cash gave Suge access to life on the depicted scale of Hollywood's crime kingpins, and living in the fabulous style that rappers imagined of the boss players they portrayed in their music videos. The Death Row limousine tab started to average $40,000 a month.[12]

While prospering in a legitimate business, Knight cultivated the appearance of shady enterprise. Though he spoke of plans for movie ventures and a magazine, Death Row only ever branched out as far as Suge's custom body shop, which specialized in tricking-up cars in the latest low-rider fashions for customers of gangbanger chic. The street-minded fail to imagine the world to which they seem small.

Suge bought the house on the Las Vegas golf course that De Niro's character in *Casino* couldn't make Sharon Stone's home, if only to refurbish—even the inside of the swimming pool was painted red—for his Tree Top Piru frat brothers to throw parties in every month or so, when he would bring entourages from L.A. that sometimes required twenty-sevens rooms of the Luxor Hotel to accommodate. Suge's wasn't the Vegas of Lefty Rosenthal and Tony "the Ant" Spilatro, or Berry Gordy and Steve Wynn. His functioned at the junction of hustlers, dope merchants, whore handlers, celebrity night crawlers, "music promoters," flesh peddlers, thugged-out youths, and transient gamesters on the city's black underbelly. Suge had a sentimental attachment to his college town and planted his flag there by opening Club 622 on the former premises of a mob-owned boîte. He spent more than a year and $800,000 getting set up in the nightclub business by associates of "East Coast crime families."[13]

Marion Knight Jr., American, was a child of his culture's mystification of the Mafia and readily gulled by lowercase wiseguys whose livelihoods depended on evoking in the psyches of citizen-moviegoers mythic associations with a terrified awakening in blood-soaked sheets next to a horse's severed head. Suge felt swindled in his dealings at the margins of a declined criminal empire and had no recourse but to whine like a ripped-off shopper on a consumer hotline. "I'm the victim here," he complained, ". . . I paid a lot of money to people who made a lot of promises, and all I ended up was getting taken advantage of."[14]

The accountant who put him in the way of this fleecing was stealing from him, too. Several years before, Steven Cantrock had been posted to Death Row as propriety's consul. He'd since "gone native"—

seduced into complicity by his client's invitation to ride (and gift of a Jeep Cherokee)—then into trespass by overexposure to the heady vapors of free-flowing cash.[15] Suge forgave Cantrock's petty larceny. With the Tupac boom at its peak, money was coming and going hand over fist, and a compromised accountant with a left foot in respectable circles was too necessary to do without.

Behind the footlights of his life's brightest stage, Tupac determined to make the role he'd contracted to perform a part worthy of his playing. To deepen and enlarge it, he imbued it with symbolic resonance. "For my homeboys who are geniuses, who . . . the only thing he could see is being a drug dealer, that's why I live like this," he attested. "For my homeboys that's pimps who don't even know what a real woman is because he never met one, that's why I live like this"[16]—a self-declared surrogate voyager for the rising generation of an unassimilable caste, arcing in their common view through an emblematic American life of cinemascopic scale. At twenty-five, he'd gotten mindful of career possibilities.

"I know I signed a deal with the devil," Tupac once lamented,[17] echoing the boxer Mike Tyson's conclusion about his business relationship with Don King. He began taking steps to distance himself from Death Row. Tupac completed the last album he owed to Suge Knight and was looking to vacate his Death Row–subsidized housing. He fired Death Row's house counsel as his personal lawyer, portending a planned departure for an entertainment conglomerate that was able to mass-market the Tupac brand by cross-promoting its complementary product lines.

He settled in with a Hollywood princess, the daughter of Quincy Jones and Peggy Lipton. "Instead of going to strip clubs," she recalled, "he was cooking" and accompanying her on visits to ashrams. He had a film production company—an obligatory career accessory for a fashion-conscious young movie actor—and announced plans to sponsor good works to benefit the youth of South Central Los Angeles.

Lest his embourgeoisement come uncloseted, Tupac still made

public appearances as Suge's designated drive-by ranter and raver, spraying invective at Death Row's rivals and offenders of the realm. Shakur aimed a fusillade of vilification at Bad Boy Records, whose proprietor, "Puffy" Combs—an object of Knight's public scorn and private fury—he'd taken to denouncing as a conspirator in his semicastration by gunshot.

He boasted on record of cuckolding "Biggie" Smalls, whose character "Big Poppa"—the garrulous fatman as player supreme—had become enough endeared to America's young to serve Combs as cash cow. "Yo' Puffy, get your . . . ass in the ring and fight Tupac," Suge snorted, like the twelve-year-old boss of sixth-grade recess who amuses himself on the playground by pitting one subordinate classmate eager to impress him against another he resents for being too well liked by the girls.

When Suge undertook the turning of Death Row's stabled talent against their faith in his recessive partner, Tupac preached the revisionist gospel. Dre "was owning the company too and be chillin' in his house [while] I'm out here in the streets, whuppin' n[egroes'] asses, startin' wars and shit, droppin' albums," he railed in the adopted voice of determinative authority. ". . . I couldn't have that."[18]

Though he'd long been restive, Dre said the arrival of Tupac Shakur at Death Row was "the straw that broke the camel's back."[19] The precipitant cause of the actual fracture was heavy-handed arm-twisting, applied to make him produce an album for the woebegone MC Hammer, a recent signee whose wrecked glory Suge thought to reclaim. At the point of this affront Dre called Jimmy Iovine at Interscope and dealt himself a new hand.

Tupac issued press indictments of Andre Young as a craven betrayer. "Jumped ship?" Dre riposted. "[I] built the ship he's on right now."[20] Tupac countered with public assertions of Dre's homosexuality, the ultimate insult to the credibility of any player in the "ghetto n[egroes]" theatricals now attended regularly by audiences of millions. Death Row circulated a suggestive photograph of Dre in his Wreckin' Kru incarnation, wearing spandex, eyeliner, and too much makeup.

Suge cited the manner of Dre's parting as evidence of unmanliness: stealing away, then "hiding at home."[21] Knight brought along a complement of eight Piru Streeters when he came to Dre's house to repossess his divorcing partner's master tapes of Death Row's greatest hits. Suge's proprietary grip was steeliest when applied to recordings made under his roof. As hip-hop publishing catalogs were unlikely to be evergreen, in his business the thinking was short term, cash was king, and an inventory of master tapes a bankroll.

The police were called and arrived in force. Suge's marshals stood down. Afterward he scorned Dre for behaving like a "little bitch" in a domestic dispute. "From now on," Andre Young spat back, "Death Row don't even exist to me."[22]

Tupac was said to have been chary of the company and leery of the occasion, but on September 7, 1996, he was nevertheless on Suge's arm in attendance of a Mike Tyson fight at the MGM Grand Hotel in Las Vegas. Though well past his prime, "Mike Money" was still the undisputed heavyweight champion of the Thug World, and every professional appearance he made in Las Vegas turned out the Los Angeles street clans, the way Frank Sinatra's once drew flocks of Rust Belt mobsters. After the event, as the Death Row contingent swept through the hotel's lobby, one among them spotted a Crip who'd been a belligerent in a foregoing beef back home. Tupac sprang at the man like a terrier, instigating a confrontation. The unfortunate was then fallen upon and mauled by Suge's avenging pack of Bloods.

Later, as Suge drove Tupac to an after-fight party at Club 622, a white Cadillac pulled alongside his car while it was stopped in traffic. Two passengers jumped out and blazed away with automatic pistols. Shakur was shot four times, twice in his chest. Knight escaped with only a grazing. Six days later Tupac died from effects of the bulletholes in his "Thug Life" tattoo. His killer was never apprehended, although all of Compton thought it knew the identity of the particular South Side Crip who had retaliated for the indignity he suffered earlier that evening at the MGM Grand.

As Tupac lay dying in Las Vegas, a congregation of vigil-keepers stood fast outside the University Medical Center. Outbreaks of deadly gang skirmishing flared around Compton and persisted for weeks. Across the American cityscape, airwaves crackled and grapevines shook with reaction to the shooting of Tupac Shakur. Impromptu memorials cropped up, as ghetto muralists began filling vacant wall spaces with his image.

Death by drive-by at an early age left the impression that Tupac had lived the life he talked about in his songs. Dying certified his "realness" as living never could. He was preserved in amber as the manifestation of a twenty-five-year-old outlaw spirit, forever sealed against the corrosions of movie roles he would have played just for money and years of common handling as a commodified celebrity.

Two decades after Cooke and Redding, boogaloo's next dead young hero was expressive not of tribal aspiration but of an outcaste's rejectionist social outlook: a celebrator of "masterless men." Tupac Shakur was a black generation's James Dean; five years after he died, fan magazines devoted to him are still sold on newsstands, and his posters hang on African walls.

The way he lost it meant Tupac's life would always be in other people's keeping. Afeni Shakur, once committed to struggle against the class interests of property, now turned hard-nosed battler for her interest in a dead son's property. "Please remember that my great-grandmother was a slave, my grandmother was a sharecropper, my mother a factory worker, and I was a legal worker," she told an interviewer. ". . . [T]his represents the first time in our lives, in our memory, ever, that we have been able to enjoy the American dream."[23]

Being himself the son of unfashionably late arrivals from Mississippi, Knight was unmoved. As lawful possessor of master tapes of 152 of Shakur's unreleased songs—the stuff of twenty-two million records since sold—he had custody of Tupac's commercial life after death. The only allowance Suge ever intended to make for the welfare of any mothers not his own was the gift of a Thanksgiving turkey.

About a month after Tupac's demise, Steve Cantrock was summoned to a backyard in Calabasas to meet with Suge Knight and

David Kenner. Death Row's accounts were out of balance; millions came in, and large bank overdrafts steadily ensued. Checks had started to bounce, and American Express was barking for its million and a half overdue dollars. Suge accused Cantrock of embezzling four million and cuffed him around. Cantrock signed a confession and a promise of repayment handwritten on the spot by David Kenner, which he later said was coerced and others present characterized as a voluntary act of tearful contrition.

Under pressure of Suge's pinch, Cantrock—the used-to-be hippie gone straight then crooked—immediately sought refuge in the privileges of caste. He told his bosses that known hoodlum Suge Knight had beaten and terrorized him into bogus admissions made in mortal fear, and appealed for sanctuary. Mindful of its liabilities, Coopers and Lybrand took Cantrock and family into its protective custody, then called the feds to report a crime. For once Suge had put his hands on a citizen of official America. Someone just a half step removed from an unbroken line of black Mississippi generations should have known better.

A lapsed causist reborn into the cause of her own, Afeni Shakur would prove an implacable petitioner for Tupac's forty acres and a mule. She threatened to block the release of Death Row's posthumous Tupac Shakur album into a marketplace that was so primed for it that when *Makaveli* did come out, two-thirds of a million copies sold within a week. While Suge pointedly ignored her, Jimmy Iovine stepped in to settle on Afeni Shakur $3 million with two more to shortly follow; a 50 percent rise in the royalty rate, applied retroactively to the five million units sold of Tupac's last album; and forgiveness of Tupac's $4.9 million debt to Death Row.[24] She'd questioned how her son could still owe money to a record company that had, by then, sold $60 million worth of his records. An old Black Panther Party–schooled street dialectician never lost her knack for "heightening the contradictions."

This settlement whetted Afeni Shakur's street-sharpened instincts by suggesting to a jailhouse lawyer good enough to have won a case at trial how much the Tupac Shakur franchise must actually be worth, if Iovine and his corporate masters were willing to pay so dearly to mollify her. If *All Eyez On Me* sold five million copies, she wondered, why had Tupac made less than a million dollars from it? Thenceforth she would prosecute the cause of her dead son's rightful due as a campaign for economic justice, stalking Death Row in the courts of law and public opinion.

Having been conspicuously present at the scenes of two crimes in Las Vegas on the night Tupac was shot made Knight, a habitually lax probationer, violable by law. Even under the hot, harsh glare of the public attention and official scrutiny occasioned by Tupac's death, he eschewed mandatory drug tests and crossed borders as he pleased. In late October the court system reeled him in; Suge was locked up pending a hearing to determine whether he should serve his nine-year prison sentence. He jauntily told reporters, "It's in God's hands."[25]

A week after he was the subject of a "shocking story about violence in the music industry" that aired on prime-time network television, Suge Knight—now certified "dangerous" by ABC News[26]—appeared with his six lawyers in a Los Angeles courtroom crammed with press, television cameras, sheriff's deputies, and supporters, including, in a back row, C. DeLores Tucker. The issue would turn on whether Suge was adjudged to have been a participant in the postfight stomping in the lobby of the MGM Grand.

Hotel security cameras seemed to have caught him delivering a kick. Knight contended that he had been trying to break up the fight when the slickness of unscuffed soles on his new alligator shoes caused him to slip on the carpet and inadvertently slide into the prostrate body he meant to shield from attackers. The victimized Crip—widely presumed but never proven to be Tupac's assassin—made Suge out to be a peacemaker when he testified. But the judge said it looked on tape as though Knight was "getting a last lick in" and ruled him an "active participant."

He got word in county jail of Snoop's post-Dre album selling nearly half a million copies in its first week out—off somewhat from his last but still healthy. Death Row sold plenty records, even as its business moorings came unbattened. With Cantrock gone and unreplaced, bills hadn't been paid for months.

A couple of weeks after Suge began to await sentencing, Afeni Shakur sued Death Row for fraud. The company had sold several million dollars worth of sweatshirts, caps, and T-shirts bearing Tupac's words or image without license or royalty payments. Suge's habit of thinking he was engaged in a legitimate form of illicit business had shortened his sight to the exclusion of even so brightly lit a sidetrack of his trade as ancillary merchandising.

His idea of Tupac's exploitable possibilities was narrow as the hometown manager's of a newly hot band, who pockets the proceeds from the sale of concert souvenirs at every stop on its first national tour because he figures to lose his clients to an agency as soon as they get to Los Angeles. But if Knight lacked the long-range perspective to look beyond "flipping" product and quickly turned cash, none of the strategic nuances of modern cultural commerce eluded Afeni Shakur. Since becoming an estate manager, this former student of Maoist catechisms had been studying Russell Simmons, Gordy's late-century successor as the world's shrewdest commodifier of Aframerican popular culture.

Simmons was not just the first but the best and brightest of the original class of young black bootstrapping hip-hop entrepreneurs who began to emerge at the end of the 1970s. He parlayed stewardship of his brother's rap group into the premier hip-hop label of the 1980s, then successfully diversified into television and film production. He bundled hip-hop with hard rock. Over a decade he established Def Jam as one of the global youth market's top-shelf entertainment brands.

As the fashion industry was becoming another branch of show business, Simmons became alert to the determinative influence that street styles exerted on consumer trends in the explosive growth market for casual apparel. He learned from the sneaker companies new ways to commodify the cultural cachet attaching to urban America's young black unassimilables.

In 1990 the Houston correspondent for *The Source* reported: "It looks like the hip hop fashion for the summer . . . is not going to be that different from last year. . . . Yes, it looks like Nike has got our money again."[27] That year Nike spent $60 million on advertising, much of it dedicated to transforming athletes Michael Jordan and Bo Jackson into television stars, then into celebrities, establishing their places among the transcendent few not any longer paid for what they did but for who they were. An oft-aired Reebok commercial featured Byron Scott, then of the Los Angeles Lakers, holding up a $160 object of desire and saying to the camera, "Some people are into BMWs . . . I'm into gym shoes."

The "sneaker wars" had begun as a skirmish between two shoe companies, Adidas and Puma, over which could rent more billboard space on the most televised feet at the 1968 Olympics. They grew heated in the decade that followed, when sneakers became this country's leisure footwear of choice and exercise got fashionable.

By the late 1980s companies were fiercely engaged in a competition for huge stakes. They discovered along the way, while spinning off clothing and shoe lines to fit every market niche, that young black urban males were not only manic buyers of what they were selling, but also had a startlingly large influence in their affairs, being definers of the so-called street styles that very often anticipated general tastes in casual fashions.

In their way the sneaker companies had become more closely connected with young black males than any of this society's institutions, except maybe its courts and prisons. They came to know each other as trading partners: well enough, at least, for shoe merchants to recognize how vulnerable ghetto youths were to symbols of belonging where they thought they didn't belong. Nike showed other commodifiers of affordably overpriced deflected status how to feed an outcaste's habit of self-medicating by conspicuous consumption.

In 1990 newspaper reports from Chicago to New Haven told of sporting-goods retailers who claimed that sneaker company sales representatives had called to encourage them to organize private showings of new product lines for the shopping convenience of drug-dealers. To spread fashions, sneaker companies made sure to get their shoes onto the feet of the elite classes of young black male society: the outlaws, the athletes, and the new breed of entertainers, performers of rap music.

Russell Simmons saw past hip-hop's immediate white fan base— the teen "wiggaz" of suburban stereotype—to take the full measure of the ghetto's seepage into the mainstream of American life. From *The Jerry Springer Show*, he says, came the revelation that "white people could be n[egroes] too."[28] By the mid-1990s these raucous daily spectacles of wrong-way assimilation were being watched throughout the English-speaking world by television audiences of many millions.

They regularly featured cast members drawn from Euro-America's left-behind, performing broad-sketch ghetto street theater in whiteface: lips poked out, hand on hip, finger-jabbing, teeth-sucking, eye-rolling, crotch-pulling exhibitions by Wal-Mart clerks and fast-food servers calling each other "trifling bitches" and "stank'ho'es"; and out-of-work stock boys and drivers of delivery trucks who celebrated their serial infidelities as evidence of being "pimps" and "players."

By now many such behavioral staples of low black life were social institutions of children at all strata of American society, including those of the elite. In the spring of 2002, in accounting to a correspondent from *The New Yorker* for a scandalous website maintained by students at Manhattan's fanciest private high schools, a junior from the Upper East Side confided, "It's not that big a deal, the language. . . . We call each other 'ho's' all the time."[29]

In America's suburban ghettoes youngsters played "shooter" video games like Urban Chaos and King Pin, which invited them to "imagine . . . [being] inside a Cypress Hill video . . . racing down alleyways covered in graffiti, hearing the footsteps of a gang in pursuit. You pass a wino slumped near a cardboard box, who begs you for booze. Then you come to a street where a woman loiters under a lamp post. She advises you to 'get strapped.'"[30] The player must make his way through the game by interacting with blackface characters who speak cartoon ghettoese, canned phrases of hackneyed street slang devised by UPN television network-watchers in Silicon Valley.

Russell Simmons had a prophetic sense of hip-hop as a lifestyle business. At the height of Def Jam's fashion, he branched into the garment trade, mass-marketing an upscale line of casual wear called Phat Farm. He foresaw the time when, as the *New York Times* reported, "[f]or many urban and suburban youth, rap videos and pages of hip-hop magazines [were] the only important fashion forecasters around." Since nearly three-quarters of the rappers' goods were purchased by white kids, "cornrows and defiance [were] the new crossover."[31]

Given the commercial scale of gangster rap's cultural repercussions, had Knight been more like Simmons the Death Row franchise could have been akin in worth to a casino on an Indian reservation. For as much as Suge disparaged him as a "little bitch," whenever Death Row showed official America its behind, Simmons profited from the titillation. By last century's turn he was a merchant prince whose clothing line was bigger than his robust music enterprise: an industrial statesman, philanthropist, and major Democratic Party fund-raiser. His products were on the shelves of shopping-mall America, his brands the common knowledge of thirty-two million teenagers who in 2001 spent more than $150 billion.

Back in the day of Gordy's "Sound of Young America," the inventory of merchandise that was marketed directly to the young was pretty much limited to jeans, soft drinks, junk food, hair- and skin-care products, records, and other small-priced incidentals that kids could buy with money their parents gave them. Even as the young were becoming a demographic bulge, advertisers paid at least as much attention to influencing the disposition of their first adult purchases, like beer and cars, as to trying to sell them more than they could afford to buy. In the last thirty years or so, the kinds of businesses for which teenage labor had value—fast foods, convenience stores, services of all kinds—proliferated. In the 1970s it seemed almost as if a whole generation of kids awakened for the first time to the possibility of having regular discretionary income.

Soon more high school students were working than ever before, some nearly as many hours as they spent in school; not, as was generally supposed—particularly of the poor—to contribute to the support of their families, but to buy things they weren't supposed to be able to afford until they were grown. As people in the business of selling things caught a fresh scent, they lifted their heads and pursued it.

A market grew up around the cash that the young now had to dispose of, and the young grew prematurely into an adult taste for acquiring deflected status from commodities they had money to buy but didn't need. By the break of this century an average American teenager was spending about $5,000 a year—more than the GNP per capita of 85 percent of the world's nations.[32]

Evidence of the merchandising job Americans have done on their young these last twenty years are the outposts professional sports leagues built inside the heads of black kids in the city. Because the prevailing culture acts upon them most directly, these youngsters are its pure products. Many now resonate like tuning forks to changes of pitch in the culture of acquisiton.

By the mid-1980s street urchins had taken to naming their "crews" after sports teams, merging identities with brand names they associated with television, money, and celebrity. In 1990 a probation officer at the Dorchester District Court in Boston—one of the nation's busiest—reported that "the Greenwood Street gang wears Green Bay Packer garb, the Vamp Hill Kings wear Los Angeles Kings and Raider gear, and the Castlegate gang wears Cincinnati Reds clothes. The Intervale gang uses all Adidas stuff. . . . They even have an Adidas handshake, copying the three stripes on the product."[33] Four years earlier Simmons had fanned the ghetto's inflamed brand consciousness with Run DMC's "My Adidas" and promoted an idea of black style to the young white masses.

On February 28, 1997, Marion Knight stood in the dock of a Los Angeles courtroom facing the consequences of his violated probation. In the five months that he'd languished in the county jail, Death Row was beset with lawsuits, as creditors and such claimants as Dick Griffey and Michael Harris joined Afeni Shakur in scrambling to secure their stakes in what was salvageable from Suge's expected ruin. A spokesman for the FBI had confirmed that Death Row was being investigated "from top to bottom."[34]

Before sentencing him to serve a prison term, Suge's judge heard testimonials to his good works and redeemability, but he disdained the state's efforts to dramatize his menace. He waved off the prosecutor's motion to introduce pictures of Knight engaged in a full-Blooded ritual display of affliliation. The ten years since "F___ Tha Police" had deprived these images of the power that they once had to arouse a reflexive official response. Nowadays, this jurist said, even his own "kids throw gang signs." And less than a half-decade later, while Knight was nearing release, young people danced the "Crip Walk" coast to coast, as others had the boogaloo.

When he spoke for himself, Suge noted that even if the worst appearances were true of his behavior that night in Las Vegas, "it wasn't no nine-year kick." Garbed in jailhouse vestments, this grandson of Mississippi came into a Los Angeles courtroom to face society's reckoning as the self-conscious bearer of an ineffaceable brand of Otherness.

"Whether its's my competition or the prosecution," he told his judge, "they make me look like Frankenstein. And if I look like Frankenstein, even though Frankenstein could be the nicest creature on earth, when he failed or when he died, everybody applauded. They clapped instead of cried."

AFTERWORD

Four months after Suge Knight went to prison, Berry Gordy sold a half-interest in his publishing house to a British conglomerate for $132 million. "We're talking about more than money here," gushed the head of EMI's publishing division. "Can you put a price on a Picasso? Can you place a value on a Renoir?"[1] He was expecting to take no less a profit than MCA's, which had sold Motown to Polygram for five times Gordy's five-year-old price.

"These songs have been my life for the past forty years," Gordy mused, before adding brightly, "I'm not selling. I'm buying into the future."[2] At sixty-eight and in fat pasture he accounted himself too "tired of the business of business" for even the mild exertions required in keeping up with the rent receipts from his blue-chip income property. Jobete had passively earned him about $20 million a year.

Six months after Suge Knight was due to receive his prerelease posting to a halfway house in Oregon, Gordy was free to cash in his other half of Jobete for $250 million more. He'd reached ambition's limit. Nearly half a billion dollars harvested from the sowing of eight hundred dollars of his family's seed money abundantly certified his completed self-transformation from labor to capital into idle rich in half an Aframerican lifetime.

Fortune had followed from Gordy's early discernment of the twentieth century's late disclosure of culture as black America's most valuable natural resource. In the hundred-year struggle over exploitation rights and shares of profit yields, a black man who made boogaloo a mass-marketed cultural commodity would not only be an industrial pioneer but a caste hero. Though Gordy served no cause save his, because of what he'd dared and done, nowadays a Russell Simmons— the equal-opportunity generation's next best thing—can chortle, "I don't want the money, I want the *money*."

With 55 percent of high school seniors working at least half as many hours as they go to school, more spent cash than ever runs through American teenage hands. Hip-hop alone is a $3-billion-a-year business, having supplanted country and western as the industry's third leading "product category." Three-quarters of its patrons are white.[3]

Boogaloo was carrying the record business; even stars couldn't sell kids reliably high volumes of rock music anymore. In mid-October 1998 nine out of the top fifteen albums on *Billboard*'s weekly pop chart were by rappers. By then the *New York Times* was reporting that toy stores throughout America "had sections full of $10 plastic gadgets that [kids] can use to sample their voices, trigger sound effects or singalong to crude hip-hop beats: in arcades, along with fighting and shooting games, there is a turntable where children can play at being a rap disc jockey."[4]

A year later the female rap star Foxy Brown replaced Peter Duchin as entertainment at the Whitney Museum's Brite Nite fund-raiser. "Rap, urban city dress," explained Ron Perelman, the Revlon tycoon, ". . . today are really mainstream." As Russell Simmons noted, "Hip-hop didn't cross over from black to white. It crossed over from cool to uncool."[5]

It will be easier for the industry's largest-ever black proprietary class to make as much money as Gordy did, but harder for most to hold on to as much. Given the music these fast-rising rap millionaires sell—all self-advertisement, sexual swagger, and stylized rage, with brand names like "hardcore" and "gangster"—it seems unlikely any of them will ever own an evergreen song catalog like Gordy's.

Their long terms will likely be curtailed by short-term exposures to official America's current drug of choice: celebrity—a provisional honorary white-boy status cheaply obtainable with loads of the cover-seekers' quick legal cash. "When Puff Daddy's having white-linen parties in the Hamptons, and Ron Perelman's dressed in white linen walking through the door," Andre Harrell, an up-from-the-projects Harlem striver, marvels, "I say to myself, 'Alright, this is real.'"[6] Such men of Gordy's children's age now feel immune from the consequences of attracting too much of white people's attention.

Puffy Combs made the cover of *Forbes* Magazine's "Power Celebrity 100" issue in March of 1999, less than a year after the man who made him had advanced Bad Boy Records $55 million in the midst of an 83 percent freefall in its annual sales revenue. A half-decade earlier, Clive Davis's ten million dollars put Combs into the record business.

Upon seeing Puffy presented to the *Forbes* readership as hip-hop's public face, Davis was aghast that a functional equivalent of Kenny Gamble or Al Bell was suddenly better known around America's business roundtable than a certified industrial legend like himself. "Don't they know he works for me?" snorted the poobah of Arista Records,[7] serving grandly at the pleasure of German conglomerators.

Gordy never had the partners that successor generations of boogaloo entrepreneurs have never been without. In 1999 Russell Simmons and his partner sold to their corporate partner, Universal, the 40 percent they still owned of Def Jam Records, which he'd started with an original partner and operated for fifteen years as a highly profitable music business. Born a year before Motown into a two-government-job household in a strivers' enclave pinched by an encroaching ghetto on the outskirts of America's imperial city, Simmons plotted the course of his climb with compass fixed on a point he reckoned true: "if you want to push bigger buttons, you have to get inside the house."[8]

This meant never showing up at a door into any commercial establishment unaccompanied by someone he thought had privilege to enter. Much as Gordy appreciated the indispensability of a better-connected white boy, he let Barney Ales go rather than give him stock in Motown. Ingrained in Pops Gordy's son was an old-country grandfather's inbred conviction that a white man's foothold on a black man's property was a first sure step on the road to dispossession.

Cashed out of the music business at forty-one, Simmons had placed himself beyond the defining category that was placed upon him. By the age at which Gordy began realizing his ambition to make movies, Simmons had produced ten. Along with media companies, he had a clothing line in partnership with rag-trade financiers. "T-shirts," Simmons chuckled, "are gonna make me richer than records ever did."

"What Russell really wants to be," says Andre Harrell, "is the hip-hop Ralph Lauren."[9] In 1998, Phat Farm made licensing deals for bags, books, leather, lingerie, and underwear. So these days Simmons chose swatches of fabric and fleece as he formerly had album tracks and marketing plans for Redman and Slick Rick, as Gordy once did from staff-written songs competing to be the next Temptations record.

No longer a boogaloo merchant who'd diversified into movies and television, Simmons was now as much a commodifier of lifestyle as Martha Stewart, his wedding guest on St. Bart's, among "four supermodels, two billionaires, two princes, three movie directors, and a crackhead."[10] He has become a worldwide purveyor of Aframerican cultural cachet.

"Sean [Combs] studied Russell very carefully," an observer of both once noted.[11] Puffy's own partnership with a private-label manufacturer and a fashion designer did nearly $100 million of apparel business in 2000, even as his music enterprise faltered. But while Simmons, on appearance, would rarely be mistaken by ordinary citizens for who he is, Combs craves the camera's flash as Suge Knight does the gleam of diamonds or chrome.

On nights when he wasn't hob-knobbing with New York "bold-type names," Sean Combs went around as the rap star Puff Daddy. He promenaded the rialto stroll with models or a movie queen in tow, strutting for tabloid gossipers like an off-color Donald Trump. Inevitably, playing the mack put Combs in the way of a nightclub fracas that narrowly missed putting him in Tupac's old prison cell.

After a high-priced acquittal of gun and assault charges, a rattled Sean Combs abruptly shed the Puff Daddy persona, recomposing his public profile to present a softer aspect. To signify the disarming of his identity, Puffy renamed himself P. Diddy, which sounded proper to a suburban mama's boy who'd had a run-in with the law and learned his lesson.

"They don't send a n[egro] who's wearing shiny suits and hanging out with Martha Stewart to jail," spat Suge Knight through the bars of his cage. "Puffy is a punk . . . a fake . . . he couldn't last five minutes in [here]."[12] Fright at the sight of the penitentiary's shadow had redirected Puffy's gaze from the street to Dun and Bradstreet, for the sake of whose regard he set out to spin ill repute instantly into checkered past. Apart from the self-advertising necessary for commercial purposes, he resolved to be conspicuous only in his public charities.

A couple months after Knight emerged from four years in prison, a movie opened in America's multiplexes starring Snoop Dogg as a murdered pimp who comes back from the grave to avenge himself after twenty years. General Motors announced plans to introduce a Snoop DeVille Limited Edition Cadillac, a homage to the "diamond-in-the-back-sunroof-top-diggin'-the-scene-with-a-gangster-lean" decorative tradition: the whore-stroll aesthetic raised by a pillar of American commerce to social acceptability.

Knight was scornful. Calvin Broadus "can't walk into any ghetto," he sneered, "because everybody sees him for what he is, a fake." Snoop had deserted Death Row soon after Suge was safely locked up, and he had hired extra bodyguards soon before Suge was released. "I'll be out of this place soon," Knight reportedly had growled prior to release, "and it'll be like the Wild West all over again. . . . I got plenty of scores to settle."[13]

He was restored to a shrunken estate as a corporate pariah, sentenced to live or die at Death Row on his own. The government kept him in its crosshairs. The federal racketeering case was still open, and local homicide investigators believed they'd found the car from which "Biggie" Smalls was gunned down in the garage of a rogue Los Angeles cop who'd been on Death Row's payroll.

In the face of besetment, an unpenitent Knight blew smoke from long fat cigars. Those master tapes he possessed so fiercely still converted into working capital. A source of two platinum albums in 1999— among cash-bearing others before and since—they'd sustained Death Row when Suge went away and were now his rock in a weary land.

A publicity offensive followed upon his return, a subject of importance in the fall of 2001 to more fan magazines than ever. Suge used the exposure to renew his claim on the caste allegiance of the "have nothing" constituency for whom Russell Simmons says "rappers are spokespeople." In the street's authentic voice Knight was pitching unreconstructed Negritude to the vast, shrugged-off "them all" that Simmons—the Clintonian Democrat—had concluded, "we really can't empower."

Suge was staking out old ground beyond the pale upon which to build a new stable. To sidestep the pursuing flight of civil litigants, he reorganized his company into another called Tha Row. Late in 2001 Knight met steathily with the mayor of Las Vegas—a mob lawyer on sabbatical—about moving his operation there to anchor a civic scheme for downtown redevelopment.

When the local press caught wind, the mayor's office was "deluged with phone calls saying, don't let this guy come here." The Honorable Oscar M. Goodman was "amaze[d]" that "an awful lot of people . . . had [such] bias and prejudice" against any such paroled "genius in his field" who was also a law partner's client.[14] Forty years after official Las Vegas drew its line at Sam Cooke, Suge Knight was unwelcome where Sonny Liston had been employed, Don King embraced, and Mike Tyson countenanced in the meantime.

About a month before Bin Laden's wave of jihad broke over New York, Russell Simmons held a "summit meeting" there of selected "executives and other music industry figures" to "address various issues affecting the very survival of the . . . spirit of hip-hop." Simmons felt the president of a trade association's positive assurance of the constructive social purposes its members' business served. A committed social Democrat climbing up the party's donor list, he "absolutely believes there's a real coming-together because of this music."[15]

As hard as he was tacking into the mainstream, Simmons needed a wind that blew steady. Six months of bad news churn from Puffy's staying and Suge's getting out of jail had backwashed into boardrooms on high. These days the stakes in global negribusiness were too high for franchise-holders showing monkey-asses to befoul the game.

As the oligarchs' ex officio Deputy for the Colored, Simmons would remind those summoned that "[white] people aren't threatened by black people [like him] getting economically empowered. . . . They're threatened by rappers saying that [dumb] shit about we gonna rob you."[16] He didn't want his business "inside the house" disturbed by outbreaks of n[egro]ish behavior in the throng milling around the front door.

For this occasion Simmons—now fashionably Upper West Side eastward in his own spiritual leanings—cloaked himself in the mantle of Louis Farrakhan, the hip-hop nation's Billy Graham. When called upon for a benediction, the minister cast Simmons's agenda in a subversive light, and tinged the room with a tone of shared conspiracy.

"You're already the leaders of the world," he quietly thundered, "and it's frightening folks in power." Indeed, France had reportedly been unsettled by a tendency among children of its bourgeoisie to affect "housing-project accents," inflected after the fashion of Algerian rappers. "All over the world . . . you've taken the children of the rich," Farrakhan noted darkly, and now "those in power are asking, 'How do we get our children back?'"[17]

In the twilight of boogaloo's last age, a guerrilla band of Aframerican tribal elements disclosed to history, on the record, that "all that fuss was us." More than twenty years after the Mothership landed, perceptible noise from Clinton's boys reverberated inside a black hole in the modern world, wherein an American aid worker "recited hip-hop verses to young Afghans" wanting to know "about the African people with black skin in America" who "sing, but without music, like shouting."

One late summer evening before the war, at dinner in an outdoor restaurant three hours of bad road from Kabul, he submitted to a mild interrogation by the backcountry Talibs who'd commandeered his order of the last available fried fish in southeastern Afghanistan, and littered the ground with its bones. They asked where America was in relation to Mecca, whether any Muslims lived there, and what province he came from. "What set you claiming?" was a question as basic to organized society in south Afghanistan as it was in the streets and strip malls of South Central Los Angeles.

When informed that this alien was native to New York, one young Pashtun tribesman flicking perch crumbs off his beard said he'd heard "this is a place with many black people, from Africa, . . . right? Very dangerous." Another of the Kalashnikov-strapped peasant militiamen hauling grenade-launchers in the back of a late-model Japanese pickup truck paused in his picking at uneaten food on American plates. "The black people are very dangerous," he affirmed, gravely. He supposed them "very tall." "How tall are they?" he had to ask, confronted with the rare and opportune presence of an eyewitness to the legendary.[18]

This Talib did not know his Other's Other, nor imagine kinship with an eighteen-year-old who was descended from the Aframerican tribal homeland's ancestral outlaw caste of "masterless men," a soldier in the Tupac Shakur brigade imprisoned for shooting a policeman in the American capital. This thug-lifer's emboweled voice was delivered out of the beast's belly by film documentarians to softly make its grim pronouncement: "[his] generation died . . . when our fathers were born."[19]

NOTES

CHAPTER I

1. Harris, *The Rise of Gospel Blues,* p. 61.
2. Ibid.
3. Ibid., p. 60.
4. Ibid., p. 16.
5. Litwack, *Trouble in Mind,* p. 449.
6. Ibid.
7. Harris, p. 12.
8. Sobel, *Trabelin' On,* p. 23.
9. Harris, p. 28.
10. Ibid., p. 39.
11. White and White, *Stylin',* p. 230.
12. Harris, p. 61.
13. Ibid., p. 53.
14. Morgan and Barlow, *From Cakewalks to Concert Halls,* p. 106.

15. Ibid., p. 96.
16. Harris, p. 65.
17. Ibid., p. 69.
18. Morgan and Barlow, p. 100.
19. Harris, p. 83.
20. Morgan and Barlow, p. 102.
21. Harris, p. 86.
22. Morgan and Barlow, p. 104.
23. Harris, p. 89.
24. Ibid.
25. Ibid., p. 93.
26. Ibid.
27. Ibid., p. 96.
28. Ibid., p. 126.
29. Broughton, *Black Gospel*, p. 46.

CHAPTER 2

1.   Morgan and Barlow, p. 193.
2.   Harris, p. 148.
3.   Rowe, *Chicago Blues*, p. 20.
4.   Harris, p. 152.
5.   Ibid., p. 177–78.
6.   Ibid., p. 194.
7.   Ibid., p. 111.
8.   Ibid., p. 123.
9.   Ibid., p. 197.
10. Ibid., p. 205.
11. Ibid., p. 76.
12. Ibid., p. 237.
13. Ibid., p. 241.
14. Ibid., p. 264.
15. Ibid., p. 255.
16. Ibid., p. 257.
17. Ibid.
18. Ibid.
19. Ibid., p. 262.
20. Ibid., p. 258.

21. Ibid.

22. Ibid.

23. Ibid., p. 259.

24. Ibid., p. 299.

25. Heilbut, *The Gospel Sound*, p. 63.

26. Ibid., pp. 63–64.

27. Harris, p. 118.

28. Schwerin, *Got to Tell It*, p. 68.

29. Heilbut, p. 86.

30. Schwerin, p. 150.

31. Ibid., p. 172.

32. Heilbut, p. 152.

33. Schwerin, p. 183.

34. Heilbut, p. 305.

35. Franklin and Ritz, *Aretha*, p. 72.

36. Ibid., pp. 63–64.

37. Ibid., p. 68.

38. Ibid., p. 78.

39. Heilbut, pp. 306–7.

CHAPTER 3

1. Wolff, *You Send Me*, p. 171.

2. Ibid., p. 173.

3. Handy, *Father of the Blues*, p. 83.

4. Ibid., p. 74.

5. Lincoln and Mamiya, *The Black Church in the African American Experience*, p. 81.

6. Wolff, p. 15.

7. Rowe, p. 50.

8. Wolff, p. 39.

9. Rowe, p. 38.

10. Pruter, *Doowop*, p. 4.

11. Heilbut, p. 85.

12. Ibid., p. 80.

13. Wolff, p. 71.

14. Heilbut, p. 47.

15. Ibid., p. 125.

16. Wolff, p. 72.
17. Heilbut, p. 87.
18. Guralnick, *Sam Cooke's SAR Records Story*, p. 54.
19. Heilbut, p. 125.
20. Wolff, p. 122.
21. Ibid., p. 108.
22. Ibid., p. 126.
23. Ibid., p. 122.

CHAPTER 4

1. Wolff, p. 121.
2. Ibid., p. 135.
3. Ibid., p. 131.
4. Ibid., p. 142.
5. Ibid., p. 137.
6. Ibid., p. 147.
7. Ibid., p. 138.
8. Ibid., p. 185.
9. Sanjek and Sanjek, *American Popular Music Business in the 20th Century*, p. 131.
10. Wolff, p. 168.
11. Ibid., p. 169.
12. Sanjek and Sanjek, p. 168.
13. Wolff, p. 165.
14. Ibid., p. 204.

CHAPTER 5

1. Brown and Yule, *Miss Rhythm*, p. 329.
2. Sanjek and Sanjek, p. 137.
3. Wolff, p. 213.
4. Ibid., p. 241.
5. Sanjek and Sanjek, p. 137.
6. Gillett, *Making Tracks*, p. 48.
7. Guralnick, p. 10.
8. Groia, *They All Sang on the Corner*, p. 84.
9. Branch, *Pillar of Fire*, p. 792.

10. Ibid., p. 133.

11. Wolff, p. 269.

12. Ibid., p. 270.

13. Ibid., p. 270.

CHAPTER 6

1. Gordy, *To Be Loved*, p. 89.

2. Ritz, *Divided Soul*, p. 31.

3. Heilbut, p. xxxi.

4. Guralnick, p. 32.

5. Wolff, p. 295.

6. Ibid., p. 306.

7. Ibid., p. 278.

8. James and Ritz, *Rage to Survive*, p. 89.

CHAPTER 7

1. Shaw, *The World of Soul*, p. 193.

2. Guralnick, p. 66.

3. Printer, *Chicago Soul*, p. 301.

4. Guralnick, p. 63.

5. Wolff, p. 325.

6. Ibid., p. 322.

7. James and Ritz, p. 151.

8. Wolff, p. 329.

9. Ibid., p. 350.

10. Ibid., p. 332.

11. Ritz, p. 174.

CHAPTER 8

1. Gordy, p. 59.

2. Ibid., p. 24.

3. Singleton, *Me, Berry and Motown*, p. 20.

4. Ibid., p. 21.

5. Ibid., p. 44.

6. Ibid., p. 45.

7. Beck, *Pimp*, p. 170.

8.   Ibid., p. 215.

9.   Litwack, p. 378.

10.   Gordy, p. 10.

11.   Clegg, *An Original Man*, p. 11.

12.   Ibid., p. 15.

13.   Ibid., p. 14.

14.   Ritz, p. 64.

15.   Turner and Aria, *Deliver Us from Temptation*, p. 324.

16.   Gordy, p. 49.

17.   Singleton, p. 52.

18.   Ibid., p. 34.

19.   Gordy, p. 89.

20.   Singleton, p. 52.

21.   Hirshey, *Nowhere to Run*, p. 140.

22.   Beck, p. 270.

23.   Ritz, p. 69.

24.   Singleton, p. 56.

25.   Ibid., p. 158.

26.   Robinson and Ritz, *Smokey Inside My Life*, p. 105.

27.   Benjaminson, *The Story of Motown*, p. 280.

28.   Ibid., p. 131.

29.   Pruter, *Chicago Soul*, p. 77.

30.   George, *Where Did Our Love Go?*, p. 94.

31.   Ibid., p. 63.

32.   Beck, p. 215.

33.   Ritz, p. 87.

34.   Beck, p. 215.

35.   George, p. 185.

36.   Ibid., p. 46.

37.   Williams and Romanowski, *Temptations*, p. 98.

38.   Ritz, p. 88.

39.   Reeves and Bego, *Dancing in the Street*, p. 111.

40.   Ritz, p. 88.

41.   Ibid., p. 87.

42.   Beck, p. 197.

43.   Gordy, p. 202.

44.   Turner and Aria, p. 21.

45. Beck, p. 219.
46. Hirshey, p. 153.
47. Ritz, p. 71.
48. Turner and Aria, *Deliver Us From Temptation*, p. 18.
49. Turner and Aria, p. 21.
50. Beck, p. 219.

CHAPTER 9

1. Wexler and Ritz, *Rhythm and the Blues*, p. 94.
2. Bowman, *Soulsville, U.S.A.*, p. 12.
3. Ibid., p. 22.
4. Ibid., p. 50.
5. Ibid., p. 132.
6. Ibid., p. 61.
7. Ibid., p. 84.
8. Ibid., p. 85.
9. Ibid., p. 84.
10. Ibid., p. 115.
11. Ibid., p. 123.
12. Guralnick, *Sweet Soul Music*, p. 145.
13. Ibid., p. 329.
14. Bowman, p. 60.
15. Ibid., p. 142.
16. Ibid.
17. Ibid., p. 143.
18. Ibid., p. 152.
19. Ibid., p. 168.
20. Ibid., p. 174.
21. Ibid., p. 170.
22. Ibid., p. 191.

CHAPTER 10

1. Benjaminson, p. 66.
2. Ibid., p. 94.
3. Sanjek and Sanjek, p. 186.
4. Ibid.

5.   George, p. 115.

6.   Hirshey, p. 189.

7.   Smith, *Dancing in the Street*, pp. 160–61.

8.   George, pp. 107–8.

9.   Ibid., pp. 126–27.

10. Turner and Aria, p. 10.

11. Benjaminson, p. 66.

12. Ritz, p. 98.

13. Benjaminson, p. 96.

14. George, p. 148.

15. Benjaminson, p. 70.

16. Gordy, p. 35.

17. Benjaminson, p. 70.

18. Singleton, p. 99.

19. Ritz, *Divided Soul*, p. 128.

20. Gordy, p. 201.

21. George, p. 58.

22. Benjaminson, p. 96.

23. Williams and Romanowski, p. 124.

24. Jacoby, *Someone Else's House*, p. 239.

25. Ritz, p. 119.

26. Smith, *The Pied Pipers of Rock and Roll*, p. 244.

27. George, p. 151.

28. Ritz, p. 112.

29. Ibid., p. 128.

30. Singleton, p. 178.

31. Ritz, p. 112.

32. George, p. 150.

33. Ibid., p. 151.

34. Ritz, p. 101.

35. Turner and Aria, p. 109.

36. Beck, p. 216.

37. Singleton, p. 216.

38. Beck, p. 216.

39. Hirshey, p. 177.

40. Beck, p. 215.

41. Hirshey, p. 180.

42. Ibid.

43.   Reeves and Bego, p. 150.

44.   George, p. 143.

45.   Beck, p. 12.

46.   Ritz, p. 139.

47.   Whitall, *Women of Motown*, p. 40.

48.   Ritz, p. 139.

49.   Reeves and Bego, p. 128.

50.   Hirshey, p. 180.

51.   Ritz, p. 165.

52.   Singleton, p. 263.

53.   Hirshey, p. 162.

54.   Beck, p. 218.

55.   Ritz, p. 99.

56.   Ibid., p. 88.

57.   Beck, p. 218.

58.   Beck, p. 273.

59.   Ritz, p. 99.

CHAPTER 11

1.   Bowman, p. 204.

2.   Ibid., p. 147.

3.   Ibid., p. 227.

4.   Ibid., p. 220.

5.   Ibid., p. 207.

6.   Ibid., p. 247.

7.   Benjaminson, p. 114.

8.   Bowman, p. 250.

9.   Ibid., p. 261.

10.   Ibid., p. 262.

11.   Dannen, *Hit Men*, p. 52.

12.   Bowman, p. 264.

13.   Ibid., p. 265.

14.   Ibid., p. 278.

15.   Dannen, p. 87.

16.   Bowman, p. 283.

17.   Ibid., p. 284.

18. Ibid., p. 287.

19. Ibid., p. 288.

20. Ibid., p. 295.

21. Ibid., p. 237.

22. Ibid., p. 298.

23. Ibid.

24. Ibid., p. 255.

25. Ibid., p. 327.

26. Ibid., p. 330.

27. Ibid., p. 308.

28. Ibid., p. 326.

29. Ibid., p. 316.

30. Ibid., pp. 317–18.

31. Ibid., p. 321.

32. Ibid., p. 325.

33. Ibid., p. 359.

34. Ibid., p. 328.

35. Ibid., p. 359.

36. Ibid., p. 329.

37. Ibid., p. 331.

38. Ibid., p. 330.

39. Ibid., p. 339.

40. Ibid.

41. Ibid., p. 360.

42. Ibid., p. 326.

43. Ibid., p. 356.

44. Ibid., p. 326.

45. Ibid., p. 362.

46. Ibid., p. 370.

47. Ibid., pp. 379–80.

48. Ibid., p. 358.

49. Ibid., p. 380.

50. Ibid., p. 388.

51. Ibid., p. 385.

52. Ibid.

53. Ibid., p. 374.

54. Ibid.
55. Ibid., p. 379.

CHAPTER 12

1. Benjaminson, p. 38.
2. Ibid., p. 48.
3. Sanjek and Sanjek, p. 203.
4. Gordy, p. 277.
5. Ritz, p. 102.
6. Bowman, p. 296.
7. Benjaminson, p. 159.
8. Reeves and Bego, p. 176.
9. Singleton, p. 216.
10. Gordy, p. 312.
11. Benjaminson, p. 120.
12. Singleton, p. 233.
13. Benjaminson, p. 106.
14. Ibid., p. 132.
15. Gordy, p. 335.
16. Ibid.
17. Ibid., p. 337.
18. Ibid., p. 339.
19. Franklin and Ritz, pp. 168–69.
20. Gordy, p. 259.
21. Ibid., p. 356.
22. Ibid.
23. Ibid., p. 354.
24. Beck, p. 203.
25. Gordy, p. 354.
26. Sanjek and Sanjek, p. 234.
27. Ibid., p. 238.
28. Gordy, p. 189.
29. Ibid., p. 360.
30. Dannen, p. 135.
31. Ibid., p. 142.
32. Ibid., p. 137.

33. Gordy, p. 391.
34. Ibid., p. 305.
35. Turner and Aria, p. 190.
36. Ibid., p. 217.
37. Ibid.
38. Ibid., p. 226.
39. Ibid., p. 230.
40. Reeves and Bego, p. 250.
41. Turner and Aria, p. 189.
42. Ibid., p. 235.
43. Gordy, p. 402.

CHAPTER 13

1. Ro, *Have Gun Will Travel*, p. 36.
2. Ibid., p. 86.
3. Ibid., p. 91.
4. *The Source*, January–February 1990, p. 7.
5. Kempton, "Native Sons," *New York Review of Books*, April 1991.
6. Gunst, *Born Fi Dead*, p. 135.
7. Ro, p. 28.
8. Ice Cube, *AmeriKKKa's Most Wanted*, 1991.
9. Ice Cube, "Endangered Species."
10. *New York Times*, June 13, 2001.
11. *New York Times*, January 1, 1999.
12. *New York Times*, June 9, 2001.
13. Ro, p. 29.
14. Ibid., p. 52.
15. Ibid., p. 55.
16. Ibid., p. 78.
17. Ibid., p. 95.
18. Ibid., p. 79.
19. Ibid., p. 96.
20. Ibid., p. 115.
21. Ibid., p. 110.
22. Ibid., p. 129.
23. Ibid., p. 182.

24. Ibid., p. 157.

25. Ibid., p. 215.

CHAPTER 14

1. Vincent, *Funk*, p. 177.

2. Brown and Tucker, *James Brown*, p. 218.

3. Ibid., p. 219.

4. Clinton, interview in *Blues and Soul*, May 1979, p. 11.

5. Brown and Tucker, p. 242.

6. Vincent, p. 240.

7. White and Bronson, *Billboard Book of Number One Rhythm and Blues Hits*, p. 262.

8. Clinton, p. 7.

9. Dannen, p. 162.

10. White and Bronson, p. 250.

11. Clinton, p. 11.

12. Ibid., p. 7.

13. Ibid., p. 10.

14. Ibid., p. 6.

15. Ibid.

16. Ibid., p. 11.

17. Ibid., p. 7.

18. Brown and Tucker, p. 253.

19. Dannen, p. 178.

20. Brown and Tucker, p. 253.

21. Clinton, p. 6.

22. Ibid., p. 11.

23. Ibid.

24. Ibid., p. 8.

25. Ibid., p. 10.

26. Clinton, interview in *Black American Music Review*, Vol. 1, #3, 1987, p. 9.

27. Vincent, p. 249.

28. White and Bronson, p. 314.

29. Clinton, interview in *Blues and Soul*, p. 11.

30. White and Bronson, p. 262.

CHAPTER 15

1. Ro, p. 136.

2. Williams, *The Cocaine Kids*, p. 132.

3. Ro, p. 195.

4. Ibid., p. 216.

5. Ibid., p. 232.

6. Ibid., p. 246.

7. Ibid.

8. Ibid., p. 252.

9. Ibid., p. 238.

10. Ibid., p. 206.

11. Ibid., p. 237.

12. Ibid., p. 318.

13. Ibid., p. 316.

14. Ibid.

15. Ibid.

16. Lee and Williams, *Chosen by Fate*, p. 129.

17. Ro, p. 249.

18. Ibid., p. 274.

19. Ibid., p. 268.

20. Ibid., p. 276.

21. Ibid., p. 277.

22. Ibid., p. 278.

23. Ibid., p. 341.

24. Ibid., p. 340.

25. Ibid., p. 323.

26. Ibid., p. 330.

27. *The Source*, May 1990.

28. *New York*, May 10, 1999.

29. *The New Yorker*, May 22, 2002.

30. *New York Times*, October 21, 1999.

31. *New York Times*, June 27, 1999.

32. *New York Times*, January 26, 2001.

33. Kempton, "Native Sons," *New York Review of Books*, April 1991.

34. Ro, p. 330.

AFTERWORD

1. *Los Angeles Times,* July 2, 1997.

2. Ibid.

3. *New York Daily News,* February 4, 2001.

4. *New York Times,* October 15, 1998.

5. *New York* Magazine, May 10, 1999, p. 29.

6. Ibid. p. 24.

7. Ibid. p. 27.

8. Ibid. p. 25.

9. Ibid.

10. Ibid. p. 24.

11. Ibid. p. 27.

12. *New York Post,* December 2, 2001.

13. *New York Times,* June 2001.

14. *Village Voice,* June 2001.

15. *New York Times,* May 10, 1999.

16. *New York Post,* June 14, 2001.

17. Stilton, *New York Times Magazine,* September 30, 2001.

18. "Thug Life in D.C.," HBO broadcast, May 1999.

19. Ibid.

SELECTED BIBLIOGRAPHY

Beck, Robert (Iceberg Slim). *Pimp: The Story of My Life*. Los Angeles: Holloway House, 1969.

Benjaminson, Peter. *The Story of Motown*. New York: Grove Press, 1979.

Bowman, Rob. *Soulsville, U.S.A.: The Story of Stax Records*. New York: Schimmer Books, 1997.

Branch, Taylor. *Pillar of Fire*. New York: Simon & Schuster, 1998.

Broughton, Viv. *Black Gospel: An Illustrated History of the Gospel Sound*. Poole, Dorset: Blandford Press, 1985.

Brown, James and Bruce Tucker. *James Brown: The Godfather of Soul*. New York: MacMillan, 1986.

Brown, Ruth and Andrew Yule. *Miss Rhythm*. New York: Donald I. Fine Books, 1996.

Chilton, John. *Let the Good Times Roll*. Ann Arbor: University of Michigan Press, 1994.

Clegg, Claude Andrew III. *An Original Man: The Life and Times of Elijah Muhammad*. New York: St. Martin's Press, 1997.

Collis, John. *The Story of Chess Records*. New York: Bloomsbury Press, 1998.

Dannen, Fredric. *Hit Men: Power Brokers & Fast Money Inside the Business*. New York: Vintage, 1991.

Franklin, Aretha and David Ritz. *Aretha: From These Roots*. New York: Villard, 1999.

Futrell, Jon, Chris Gill, Roger St. Pierre, et al. *Illustrated Encyclopedia of Black Music*. New York: Harmony Books, 1982.

George, Nelson. *Where Did Our Love Go?*. New York: St. Martin's Press, 1986.

Gillett, Charlie. *Making Tracks: The Story of Atlantic Records*. St. Albans: Panther, 1993.

Gordy, Berry Jr. *To Be Loved*. New York: Warner Books, 1994.

Gribin, Anthony J. and Matthew M. Schiff. *Doo-Wop*. Iola, WI: Krause Publications, 1992.

Groia, Philip. *They All Sang On the Corner: A Second Look at New York City's Rhythm and Blues Vocals Groups*. Setanket, NY: Edmund Publishing, 1975.

Guralnick, Peter. *Sam Cooke's SAR Records Story, 1959–1965*. New York: Arco Music & Records, Inc., 1994.

———. *Sweet Soul Music*. New York: Harper & Row, 1986.

Gunst, Laurie. *Born Fi' Dead*. New York: Henry Holt & Co., 1995.

Handy, W. C. et al. *Father of the Blues: An Autobiography*. New York: DaCapo Press, 1985.

Harris, Michael W. *The Rise of Gospel Blues*. New York: Oxford University Press, 1992.

Heilbut, Anthony. *The Gospel Sound: Good News and Bad Times*. New York: Limelight Editions, 1985.

Hirshey, Gerri. *Nowhere to Run*. New York: Times Books, 1984.

Jacoby, Tamar. *Someone Else's House*. New York: Free Press, 1998.

James, Etta and David Ritz. *Rage to Survive*. New York: Villard, 1995.

Kempton, Murray. *The Briar Patch*. New York: E. P. Dutton Co., 1973.

Lee, McKinley Jr. and Frank B. Williams. *Chosen by Fate: My Life Inside Death Row Records*. West Hollywood, CA: Dove Books, 1997.

Lemann, Nicholas. *The Promised Land*. New York: Vintage, 1992.

Lincoln, C. Eric and Laurence H. Mamiya. *The Black Church in the African American Experience*. Durham, NC: Duke University Press, 1990.

Litwack, Leon F. *Trouble in Mind*. New York: Alfred A. Knopf, 1998.

Lornell, Kip. *Happy in the Service of the Lord.* Urbana: University of Illinois Press, 1988.

Morgan, Thomas L. and Jim Barlow. *From Cakewalks to Concert Halls.* Elliott & Clark, 1992.

Pruter, Robert. *Doowop: The Chicago Scene.* Urbana: University of Illinois Press, 1996.

————. *Chicago Soul.* Urbana: University of Illinois Press, 1991.

Reeves, Martha and Mark Bego. *Dancing in the Street: Confessions of a Motown Diva.* New York: Hyperion, 1994.

Ritz, David. *Divided Soul: The Life of Marvin Gaye.* New York: McGraw-Hill, 1985.

Ro, Ronin. *Have Gun Will Travel.* New York: Doubleday, 1998.

Robinson, Smokey and David Ritz. *Smokey Inside My Life.* New York: Jove Books, 1989.

Rowe, Mike. *Chicago Blues: The City and the Music.* New York: DaCapo Press, 1973.

Sanjek, Russell and David Sanjek. *American Popular Music Business in the 20th Century.* New York: Oxford University Press, 1991.

Santelli, Robert. *The Big Book of Blues.* New York: Penguin Books, 1993.

Schwerin, Jules. *Got to Tell It: Mahalia Jackson, Queen of Gospel.* New York: Oxford University Press, 1992.

Shaw, Arnold. *Honkers and Shouters.* New York: MacMillan, 1978.

————. *The World of Soul.* New York: Cowles Book Co., 1970.

Singleton, Raynoma Gordy. *Me, Berry and Motown.* Chicago: Contemporary Books, 1990.

Smith, Susan. *Dancing in the Street.* Cambridge: Harvard University Press, 1999.

Smith, Wes. *The Pied Pipers of Rock and Roll.* Marietta, GA: Longstreet Press, 1989.

Sobel, Mechal. *Trabelin' On.* Princeton: Princeton University Press, 1988.

Spencer, Jon Michael. *Black Hymnody.* Knoxville: University of Tennessee Press, 1992.

Taraborrelli, J. Randy. *Motown.* New York: Dolphin, 1986.

Taylor, Marc E. *A Touch of Classic Soul.* Jamaica, NY: Aloiv Publishing Co., 1996.

Turner, Tony and Barbara Aria. *Deliver Us from Temptation.* New York: Thunder's Mouth Press, 1992.

Vincent, Rickey. *Funk.* New York: St. Martin's Press, 1996.

Wexler, Jerry and David Ritz. *Rhythm and the Blues: A Life in American Music*. New York: St. Martin's Press, 1996.

Whitall, Susan. *Women of Motown: An Oral History*. New York: Avon Books, 1998.

Whitburn, Joel. *Top Rhythm and Blues Records 1949–71*. Menomonee Falls, WI: Record Research, 1973.

White, Adam and Fred Bronson. *The Billboard Book of Number One Rhythm and Blues Hits*. New York: Harmony Books, 1982.

White, Sloane and Graham White. *Stylin'*. Ithaca, NY: Cornell University Press, 1998.

Williams, Otis and Patricia Romanowski. *Temptations*. New York: G. P. Putnam's Sons, 1988.

Williams, Terry. *The Cocaine Kids: The Inside Story of a Teenage Drug Ring*. Cambridge, MA: Perseus Publishing, 1989.

Wolff, Daniel. *You Send Me: Life and Times of Sam Cooke*. New York: William Morrow & Co., 1995.

INDEX

PERMISSIONS ACKNOWLEDGMENTS